The Courts, Validity, and
Minimum Competency Testing

Evaluation in Education and Human Services

Editors:

George F. Madaus, Boston College, Chestnut
  Hill, Mass., U.S.A.
Daniel L. Stufflebeam, Western Michigan
  University, Kalamazoo, Mich., U.S.A.

Previously published books in the series:

Kelleghan, T., Madaus, G.F., and Airasian, P.W.;
  The Effects of Standardized Testing

The Courts, Validity, and Minimum Competency Testing

George F. Madaus
Editor

Kluwer-Nijhoff Publishing
Boston   The Hague   London

Distributors for North America:

Kluwer-Nijhoff Publishing
Kluwer Boston, Inc.
190 Old Derby Street
Hingham, Massachusetts 02043, U.S.A.

Distributors outside North America:

Kluwer Academic Publishers Group
Distribution Centre
P.O. Box 322
3300AH Dordrecht, The Netherlands

Library on Congress Cataloging in Publication Data
Main entry under title:

The Courts, validity, and minimum competency testing.

   (Evaluation in education and human services)
   Includes index.
   1. Competency based educational tests — Law and legislation —
United States — Congresses. I. Madaus, George F. II. Series
KF4156.A75C68   1982   344,73'077   82-4666
ISBN   0-89838-113-4   347.30477

Printed in the United States of America

Contents

List of Figures and Tables

List of Figures

List of Tables

PREFACE

On May 4, 1981 the United States Court of Appeals, Fifth Circuit, handed down a landmark decision in the *Debra P*. v. *Turlington* case. Plaintiffs had challenged Florida's policy requiring that students, to receive their high school diploma, pass the State Student Assessment Test, Part II (SSAT–II) — a test purporting to measure functional literacy. The Fifth Circuit ruled that the state may not deprive its high school seniors of the economic and educational benefits of a high school diploma until it demonstrated that the SSAT-II (the functional literacy test, [FLT]) was a fair test of what is taught in its classrooms. The Fifth Circuit thereupon sent the case back to the district court for a new hearing at which the state must show that the material tested was actually taught.

The ruling that a test used as a graduation requirement must measure what is actually taught in schools is one that creates immediate precedent for other litigation involving minimum competency testing (MCT) for certification and has implications in fourteen other states that presently have such programs. The ruling should affect the deliberations of those policy makers currently considering new assessment programs designed to certify or classify pupils and those charged with implementing extant programs in elementary and secondary schools. It should have an impact on the process of selecting or contracting for the development of certification tests, on the steps that a test developer must follow in order to produce a valid certification test, and on the implementation of the total program. In states or districts that mandate a certification test, the decision should affect the work of those in charge of curriculum development, implementation, and supervision and will, perforce, affect the teacher who is ultimately responsible for what is taught — and how it is taught — in the classroom.

The Fifth Circuit's finding that in the field of competency testing, an important component of content validity is curricular validity — defined as things that are currently taught — reintroduced the old concept of curricular validity to the testing community and by inference endorsed recent argument's for the need to demonstrate the instructional validity of MCTs. The court's interpretation of the meaning of content validity raises a number of important and interesting questions. What are the implications of using the adjectives *curricular* and *instructional* to modify the noun *validity*? How do these concepts relate to each other and to the prevailing concept of content validity? What are the implications of the court endorsement of two additional facets of validity at a time when the profession is abandoning a misunderstood tripartite conceptualization in favor of a unified concept of validity? How does a state go about demonstrating that its certification test measures what was taught and that the inferences made about pupils are valid? What kinds of data should advocacy groups look for in evaluating the fundamental fairness of a test used for certification in elementary or secondary schools?

In an attempt to answer these questions, the Ford Foundation sponsored a conference on the *Courts and the Content Validity of Minimum Competency Tests*, held at Boston College in Chestnut Hill, Mass. on October 13 and 14, 1981. Ten papers dealing with the issue of how one might investigate the match between the content of an MCT and a school district's curriculum and instruction were commissioned for the conference. The paper were then discussed by the thirty-six participants, After the conference, the authors revised their papers, which now constitute ten of the eleven chapters in this book. Chapter 2, written after the conference, traces the evolution of the concept of content validity. Work on this chapter was supported by the Ford Grant and by the Carnegie Corporation. The Ford Foundation also helped to underwrite the costs of editing this book; the Carnegie Corporation supported production expenses to help reduce the cost.

This book focuses entirely on what a state department of education or a local educational authority might do to evaluate the extent to which skills and knowledge measured by an MCT were in fact covered by curriculum materials and by instruction. Several chapters provide necessary background. Chapter 1 by Diana Pullin gives the reader a legal analysis of the *Debra P.* case. (The full decision of the district court and the Fifth Circuit Court are reproduced in Appendix A and B and the petition for Rehearing En Banc in Appendix C) Several chapter authors — George F. Madaus (2), Walt Haney (3), Robert Calfee (4), Robert L. Linn (5), and William H. Schmidt, Andrew C. Porter, John R. Schwille, Robert E. Floden, and Donald J. Freeman (6) — discuss general issues of validity.

Techniques to analyze the match between textbooks and test material are described by Schmidt and his colleagues (6) and Gaea Leinhardt (7). These chapters also describe techniques that have been used to analyze the match between instruction and material covered on tests. Calfee (4) and Linn (5) describe techniques that can be used to explore differences between groups on item-response patterns. Jeanne S. Chall (10) describes techniques to analyze the reading-difficulty levels associated both with textbooks and with MCTs. Roger W.

Shuy (11) offers a linguistic analysis of issues related to test validity. Decker F. Walker (8) and Richard L. Venezky (9) discuss aspects of the curriculum and school environment that must be present if pupils can be said to have had an adequate opportunity to learn.

There was no attempt to arrive at a consensus on what steps should be followed in evaluating the curriculum or instructional validity of MCTs used for certification. The hope is that after reading this book, readers will be able to draw up their own agendas for evaluating the extent to which pupils have had a fair opportunity to acquire the skills measured by such tests.

Acknowledgments

I am indebted to a number of people for their assistance in producing this book. First I wish to express my appreciation to the officers of the Ford Foundation for their financial support. Marjorie Martus, while working as a program officer at the Ford Foundation, was particularly helpful in planning the conference. Edward Meade of the Ford Foundation supported efforts to organize and edit the manuscript. I also wish to thank the Carnegie Corporation of New York for its financial support. Fritz Mosher of the Carnegie Corporation was particularly helpful throughout the entire process.

Boston College also offered a great deal of support. For assistance at various stages of the writing process, I am indebted to Dean Mary Griffin of the School of Education and to Joseph Pedulla of the Center for the Study of Testing, Evaluation, and Educational Policy.

Diana Pullin was extremely helpful in planning the conference. My thanks go to Robert Linn, Jason Millman, and Daniel Stufflebeam for chairing the group discussions at the conference. Peter Airasian and Paul Weckstein offered summaries of all papers from a measurement and legal view, respectively, which helped to focus the group discussions. Robert Calfee offered excellent suggestions on what might be included in the third section of Chapter 2. Joseph Foley of Boston State College was of enormous help to me in reacting to and editing my chapter. My thanks to Philip Jones of Kluwer-Nijhoff Publishing for speeding up the steps in production in order to publish this book as soon as possible. To my wife Anne, my thanks for all of her patient help.

For their assistance at the conference, I am indebted to Paul Lucas and Rita Comtois. To Carolyn Pike, Catherine Bransfield I extend my thanks for the many patient hours they gave during the process.

Last, but by no means least, special thanks go to each of the conference participants for their time, consideration, and substantial contributions and to the chapter authors for an excellent job and for their patience.

The Courts, Validity, and Minimum Competency Testing

1 DEBRA P. v. TURLINGTON:
Judicial Standards for Assessing the Validity of Minimum Competency Tests

Diana Pullin

The educational equity issues presented by the use of minimum competency tests (MCTs) to deny high school diplomas are addressed in *Debra P.* v. *Turlington*,[1] a lawsuit addressing the state of Florida's use of a functional literacy examination to determine the award of regular high school diplomas. The litigation provided the first judicial forum for addressing issues concerning the fairness of MCT programs used to make critical determinations about students. In addition, the court decisions entered in the case present new challenges to education and testing professionals concerned about the validity of criterion-reflected tests used to certify a student's successful completion of a program of elementary and secondary education.

The author gratefully acknowledges the assistance of her colleague at the Center for Law and Education, Paul Weckstein, in the preparation of this article. The author, however, remains solely responsible for the contents, which express her own views and are not necessarily the views of either the Center or the clients it represents.

History of the Case

In *Debra P.,* the student plaintiffs challenged Florida's implementation of a 1976 statute that required students to demonstrate proficiency in "functional literacy" in order to receive a standard high school diploma. Students who failed a functional literacy test (FLT) but had met all other graduation requirements were to receive a "certificate of completion" in lieu of a diploma. The new test-for-diploma requirement was, under the 1976 legislation, to be imposed for the first time on the students who would be candidates for graduation in spring 1979. The Florida Department of Education was, under the legislation, given the task of defining functional literacy and preparing an examination to assess it. In February 1977, the definition was formalized as follows:

> functional literacy is the satisfactory application of basic skills in reading, writing, and arithmetic, to problems and tasks of a practical nature as encountered in everyday life.[2]

In the summer of 1977, the specific functional literacy skills identified by the state for assessment on the test were distributed to the local schools. When the FLT was first administered in October 1977, 36% of the students failed either the math or communications section of the FLT or both.

The impact of the test on black students was even more startling. On the first administration of the FLT, 77% of the black students failed the FLT compared to 24% of the white students. The first graduating class subjected to the test-for-diploma requirement, the class of 1979, was given three chances to pass the test. Following the third administration of the test, 1.9% of the white seniors and 20% of the black seniors were to be denied high school diplomas. In short, a black high school senior in Florida in spring of 1979 had a ten-times-greater chance of failing to receive a diploma on the basis of FLT performance than did a white student.

The Florida MCT litigation was initiated in October 1978, by ten named plaintiffs who sought, on behalf of themselves and all other Florida students who failed or would fail the test, to challenge Florida's FLT. The original plaintiffs, all of whom were black, received the permission of the court to file their claims anonymously to protect themselves from further public stigmatization; although the court and all parties to the litigation knew the identities of the students, their names were not made public. In March of 1979, the trial court judge ruled that the case could proceed as a class action on behalf of all students in Florida who had failed, or might in the future fail, the test. Class action status allowed the proof offered at trial to focus in a general way on statewide practices concerning the testing program and race relations rather than to look at the educational histories of each individual student who failed the test. In addition, class action certification meant that any remedy or relief the court ordered would extend to all students across the state who failed the test, relieving students of having to go to court on an individual basis to obtain redress.

The trial court heard evidence from both sides for approximately four weeks in late spring 1979. Plaintiffs presented lengthy evidence of past and ongoing racial discrimination in Florida schools; this evidence was not rebutted by the defendants. Plaintiffs also devoted considerable time to a challenge to the validity and reliability of the test itself; these claims were contested by the defendants.

The Florida litigation focused on two major sets of legal claims: first, claims that a test-for-diploma scheme with a disproportionate impact on blacks denied constitutional and statutory guarantees of equal protection of the laws; and, second, constitutional claims, brought on behalf of all students, that the entire test-for-diploma program was unfair bacause the test instrument was inadequate and the diploma sanction was imposed too hastily. One other challenge concerned violations of the due process and equal protection clauses resulting from the fact that a test-for-diploma scheme with a disproportionate impact on blacks denied

After the trial, the federal district court placed a four-year moratorium, until 1982–1983 school year, on the use of the state FLT as a diploma requirement; administration of the test for other purposes could continue. The moratorium was based upon determinations that the plaintiffs were correct in both their race discrimination and due process claims. The trial court found that

> . . . in light of the evidence relating to the necessary period of time to orient the students and teachers to the new functional literacy objectives, and to eliminate the taint on educational development which accompanied segregation . . . the state should be enjoined from requiring passage of the [test] as a requirement for graduation for a period of four (4) years.[4]

Following the trial court decision, both sides declared a victory; then both appealed to the United States Circuit Court of Appeals for the Fifth Circuit.

At the court of appeals level, no new evidence is considered. The case is decided on the basis of the evidence and testimony offered to the trial court, plus written briefs on points of law and disputed facts as well as thirty minutes of oral argument by each side to a panel of three appellate judges. In *Debra P.*, there were also *amicus curiae,* or "friend of the court," briefs submitted in support of the positions taken by the students filed by the United States Department of Justice and the Florida Teaching Profession/National Education Association.

The appellate court panel issued a decision favorable to the students that sent the matter back to the trial court with instructions that Florida should not be allowed to

> deprive its high school seniors of the economic and educational benefits of a high school diploma until it has demonstrated that the [test] is a fair test of that which is taught in its classrooms and that the racially discriminatory impact is not due to the educational deprivation in the "dual school" years.[5]

Following the decisioin by the panel, the Fifth Circuit Court of Appeals apparently partially reopened the appeal of the *Debra P*. case without the knowledge of the parties to the lawsuit. Under a seldom-used rule, one of the judges of the circuit court asked for a rehearing of the appeal in the case, with the rehearing to be conducted *en banc,* before the entire panel of circuit judges. The request for a rehearing was denied by the entire court, although dissents to that denial were filed by two judges.

The Debra P. Decisions

The claims brought by the students overlapped substantially, in both theoretical underpinnings and factual detail, particularly in areas addressing race discrimination. For example, allegations of race bias in the test instrument were made both under the constitutional and statutory race discrimination claims and the due process and equal protection challenges to the fairness of the test. For ease of discussion only, the race and nonrace legal theories and proof offered in the case are set forth separately as follows.

Discrimination on the Basis of Race

Many students who face MCT requirements as part of new graduation requirements imposed in the late 1970s and early 1980s are students who have not had the benefit of twelve full years of racially integrated education. Those black students who today face a test-for-diploma requirement and who were previously placed in racially isolated schools are disadvantaged on examination day because they were previously subjected to inferior educational opportunities. For over twenty-five years, this nation's courts have, under constitutional standards, deemed inferior the education that black students received in segregated schools. This constitutional doctrine was first enunciated by the United States Supreme Court in *Brown* v. *Board of Education* in a declaration that is as apt for the present as it was in 1954:

> Today, education is perhaps the most important function of state and local governments . . . In these days it is doubtful that any child may reasonably be expected to succeed in life if he is denied the opportunity of an education. Such an opportunity, where the state has undertaken to provide it, is a right which must be made available to all on equal terms . . . We conclude that in the field of public education, the doctrine of separate but equal has no place. Separate educational facilities are inherently unequal.[6]

It is from this foundation, built upon the federal constitution by the *Brown* decision, that the case law and federal statutory provisions prohibiting discrimination on the basis of race in our schools has been built. The statutory provisions are embodied primarily in Title VI of the Civil Rights Act of 1964, which prohibits discrimination on the basis of race in programs and activities receiving federal financial assistance. The case law concerning racial discrimination in the schools has been based upon both this statute and federal constitutional guarantees of equal protection of the laws. The case law concerns not only a standard that prohibits segregation on the basis of race in the school but also a presumption that desegregation, to be successful, should result in the elimination of underachievement among black students.[7]

Both the spirit and the letter of this legal history was heavily relied upon by the students who brought the *Debra P*. litigation. The use of the MCT to deny high school diplomas was, according to the students, both a new act of racial discrimination in itself, as well as a mechanism that determined diploma awards on the basis of information that black students may not have had a fair opportunity to learn because of the inferior education that they had received from the schools in the past.

The constitutional standard upon which the students relied is the Constitution's prohibition against discrimination on the basis of race, which is contained in the equal protection clause of the Fourteenth Amendment. The equal protection clause prohibits a state from denying "to any person within its jurisdiction the equal protection of the laws." The clause does not prohibit a state from sorting or classifying individuals or groups of persons into categories, but it does require that such classifications be done rationally, fairly, and with adequate justification. When an equal protection challenge to a particular state action is raised, the nature of the proof that will be scrutinized by the court considering the challenge will vary according to the nature of the interest affected by the government action. The more important the interest, the closer will be the court's scrutiny of the challenged practice. Courts will look most closely at fundamental interests, such as the right to vote, or at classifications that are suspect, such as those that sort people on the basis of race. These types of classification schemes will only prevail if the state can show a compelling reason for its program and no available alternative that would achieve the state's purpose.

Until dismantled under court orders in the early 1970s, Florida's public school systems were segregated on the basis of race. This dual school system was perpetuated through the policies and practices of local boards of education and by state statutes and the Florida Constitution. The trial court in *Debra P*. found overwhelming evidence that the segregated schools that black students had been forced to attend through 1971 were inferior in their physical facilities, course offerings, instructional materials, and equipment. The trial judge also indicated that these disparities in resources created an atmosphere that was not as conducive to learning as that found in white schools, resulting in a serious impairment to black students' chances to learn, particularly in the critical early years of schooling.[8] Black students in the graduating class of 1979 spent their first three or four years of school in segregated classrooms and buildings and were denied the benefits of integrated education in their important, formative years.

The trial court determined that "the principle effect of the dual school system was the inferior education given black school children" and that "the results on three administrations of the SSAT II evidence this fact."[9] That court found equal protection denials to black students as a result. In addition, the trial court scrutinized the students' race claims under federal civil rights statutes and regulations.

The students' statutory challenges arose from the fact that programs that receive federal financial assistance are obligated to comply with several sets of statutes and regulations prohibiting discrimination on the basis of race, sex, national origin, color, or handicap. In the *Debra P.* case, these statutory challenges were based upon Title VI of the Civil Rights Act of 1964[10] and the Equal Educational Opportunity Act (EEOA).[11] Title VI is a broad nondiscrimination statute prohibiting discrimination on the basis of race in programs receiving federal financial assistance. Title VII of the same act[12] has been widely used to challenge race discrimination in employment testing. The EEOA prohibits states from denying equal educational opportunity on the basis of race and requires education officials to take steps to alleviate the problems caused by previous denials of equal educational opportunity.

The use of the constitutional and Title VI theories to scrutinize an educational testing practice has been employed recently, with perhaps even more far-reaching implications than the Florida case, by a federal court in California. The California case, *Larry P.* v. *Riles,*[13] involved the use of I.Q. tests to place students in classes for the educable mentally retarded (EMR). Classes for EMR students were populated with a large percentage of black students, a percentage considerably higher than the proportion of blacks in the total school population. The court in *Larry P.* traced the history of the development and use of intelligence tests, particularly the intentional racial bias built into the tests and their use. The court found it unlawful to rely upon I.Q. tests to determine EMR placement when those tests are invalid and unreliable for use with black students and the state could not prove that use of the tests or resultant disproportionate class placements furthered the purpose of providing the best educational opportunities for students.

The legal theories advanced on behalf of black students in *Debra P.* were based upon some of the same approaches used in *Larry P.* as well as those used to attack various forms of race discrimination in public education, such as racially segregated schools and isolation of the races through class placement or tracking practices. If *Debra P.* had involved employment — rather than educational — testing, a challenge under Title VII would have been possible, either by pursuing the matter through the courts or through administrative procedures under federal regulations and guidelines[14] that incorporate many of the minimum standards set forth in the joint test standards of the American Psychological Association, the American Educational Research Association, and the National Council on Measurement in Education. A number of employment testing cases pursued under Title VII of the Civil Rights Act of 1964 have relied heavily upon the *Standards* to assess test validity and reliability when complaining parties asserted that a test used by employers had a racially discriminatory impact. In their appeal to the Fifth Circuit, the *Debra P.* plaintiffs asserted that, because Title VI and Title VII are so closely linked, it would be appropriate, in assessing the Title VI claims of the students, to follow the same procedures and standards set forth under Title VII for scrutinizing the FLT. In effect, this was the approach taken by the court in the *Larry P.* case.

The primary claim by the students in *Larry P.* was the racial bias inherent in the I.Q. tests used in California. The students in *Debra P.* presented similar charges against the FLT. The evidence on bias offered at the *Debra P.* trial included little discussion of statistical indicia of racial bias in the test. Instead, the evidence focused upon a number of items on the test that required familiarity with situations and information not a part of the background of many black or low-income students.[15] Expert testimony identified a number of black students were unable to answer correctly and that involved unfamiliar material or items where the "correct" answer to the test developers was not the same answer black students would consider correct.

The trial court noted that there were several that seemed "to have factual settings unfamiliar to certain racial groups" but dismissed the matter as unimportant.[16] This failure to address the bias issue was troublesome, particularly when the bias of the items was confirmed statistically.[17] Also, the error inherent in even one item can be of critical significance when, as was the case with the FLT, substantial numbers of students would have passed the test if only one, two, or three biased items had been removed.[18]

The circuit court summarily affirmed the trial court's determination that there was no bias in the FLT items.[19] The circuit's determination that the test lacked content validity may, however, reopen the issue of bias, particularly when it relates to the particular instructional needs of black students.

Neither the trial court nor the appellate court used the *Standards* in applying the equal protection or the civil rights laws to analyze the facts in the case. The professional standards were, however, important in the courts' analyses of the students' due process claims. The violations of Title VI and the EEOA that were found in Florida resulted from the disproportionate racial impact of the test coupled with a finding that there was no improvement in the educational opportunities for black students as a result of the test-for-diploma program.

The remedy ordered by the court for the violations of the equal protection clause, Title VI, and the EEOC was the placement of a four-year moratorium on the use of the test as part of the diploma requirement. At the end of the four-year period — the end of the 1982–1983 school year — all schools in Florida will have been physically desegregated for a full twelve years; the trial court presumed that student test performance at that time would no longer be affected by the dual school system.

The black plaintiffs in the *Debra P.* litigation were unwilling to agree, however, that the harmful and unlawful impact of the test on them would automatically be remedied during the moratorium. At trial, the students had offered substantial evidence of ongoing difficulties suffered by black students as a result of state and local school policies and practices. The trial court recognized these problems and also recognized that the vestiges of the inferior education that black students received in their years of segregation were still present and still affected test performance. The relief the trial court ordered did not go beyond the four-year moratorium. Because the plaintiffs felt that more protections needed to be in place to ensure that unlawful race-based practices were not having an impact on test performance, they sought further relief from the appellate court to reassess the race issues and to consider appropriate further relief to remedy those problems.[20]

The appellate court, in briefly addressing the race issues presented in *Debra P.*, made a determination that an unlawful racial impact might well be present in a test-for-diploma scheme. The appellate court therefore ordered the trial court to reassess the racial impact of the test if that court should determine at some future date that the testing scheme might go forward because all the other legal problems with the scheme had been eliminated. If all other legal bars to the testing scheme were removed, the scheme could still not be implemented if a racial disproportion remained and the state had not effectively remedied the problem.[21]

Unfair Treatment of All Students — Denials of Equal Protection

In addition to the equal protection claims against the test brought on behalf of black students, there were also equal protection challenges asserted on behalf of all students who faced the test-for-diploma requirement. All students who took the test were subjected to a classification, or sorting, scheme that they alleged was not an accurate or fair means of identifying potential high school graduates. This equal protection claim on behalf of all students was based upon an assertion that inequality stemmed from defects in the scheme that resulted in an inaccurate sorting of students into categories of test passers and test failers. The analysis the courts used in reviewing this claim was interwoven with the analysis used to review the due process claims that were also presented.

The trial and appellate courts found that, for the purpose of both equal protection and due process analysis of the students' claims, the state's actions would be subject to rigorous standards of review. This basis for the standard for scrutiny of the state's actions was based upon a determination that the students who failed the test had important legal interests and rights at stake. The trial court found that students who failed the test at any time during their high school careers were labeled "functional illiterates" or "functional incompetents." These labels have, according to the court, a universally negative inference and lead to stigmatization of the students who failed the test. The harm to students that resulted from this labeling was substantial enough to place a considerable burden upon the state to justify the testing program and its resulting classifications of students.

The plaintiffs asserted that the use of the test was not a valid and reasonable means of making the classification decisions or for ensuring the value of a high school diploma. This equal protection challenge addressed both the validity and reliability of the test itself and the rationality of using any test-for-diploma sanction to ensure educational accountability.

The appellate court found that the use of the FLT to classify students did create denials of equal protection. The analysis the court followed in reaching that conclusion was included in its discussion of the student's due process claims.

Unfair Treatment of All Students — Denials of Due Process

The portion of the *Debra P*. litigation that has attracted the greatest attention within the education professions is not the assertion of race discrimination, but the lawsuit's claims on behalf of students of all races that the test-for-diploma scheme is constitutionally infirm under the due process and equal protection clauses of the federal Constitution. The due process challenge has three components, all of which rely upon a broad reading of the due process guarantee of "fundamental fairness" in government's treatment of individuals when the matter at issue is of critical importance to the individuals effected.[22]

Traditionally, constitutional guarantees of due process of law ensure that individuals are treated with fairness, consistency, and lack of arbitrariness by governmental agencies and employees. Due process protections are of two types: procedural and substantive. Procedural due process protections seek to ensure that the procedures used by government in dealing with individuals are fair and operate with a reasonable degree of accuracy. Procedural due process protections typically include the right to some form of notification of impending governmental action and the right to effectively influence or participate in governmental decision-making through hearings, representation by counsel, review of evidence, and so forth. Substantive due process seeks to ensure that, regardless of the procedures followed, the action undertaken by the government must be reasonable and must serve a legitimate governmental objective or purpose.

A scrutiny of state action under the due process clause will, like equal protection analyses, only be conducted if a deprivation of liberty or property is at stake. The courts found both types of denials in the Florida program. First, the courts both recognized that a student has a "property interest" at stake; the property consisted of an expectation that a high school diploma would be awarded if he/she successfully completed all required courses and met attendance requirements.[23] Second, the courts found a "liberty interest" in being free of the adverse stigma of receiving a certificate of completion rather than a regular high school diploma.[24]

Once the courts found liberty and property interests at stake in the MCT program, then procedural due process required that the state act in a fair manner when depriving some students their diplomas.

Due process — both substantive and procedural — is an elastic concept requiring different levels of protection depending on the context. The procedural protections that must be afforded a defendant in a criminal trial are much more detailed than those that must be provided a student who faces a short-term suspension from school. Similarly, the governmental objectives to be served by a statute regulating conduct through criminal sanctions will be subject to a much stricter substantive due process analysis than the objectives of a statute regulating the dress and appearance of police officers. The meaning of due process, the delineation between substantive and procedural due process, and the standards for determining what process is due in a particular situation can be somewhat blurred.

A substantive due process analysis ordinarily begins with an examination of the legitimacy of the goal of the governmental program. This analysis of the "state interest" in a program can rarely be conducted by referring to a full and clearly articulated statement by the governmental agency made at the time the program was initiated; such statements seldom exist. Instead, often a court relies upon the government's after-the-fact rationale for its program, or the court itself defines what it feels a legitimate interest or goal might be. A substantive due process analysis therefore begins with scrutiny of the goals — either explicit or implied — of a testing program. Next, if the governmental goals are legitimate (and courts almost always find that they are), the means of achieving the goal will be examined.

A second series of questions relating to the fundamental fairness of an educational program or practice concerns the manner in which the program or practice was implemented. These questions are sometimes treated as procedural-due-process issues, sometimes as substantive due process issues. The implementation of a new program or practice presents fairness issues that relate both to the sufficiency of advance notice of the change and to the extent to which the implementation scheme reasonably and rationally furthers a legitimate educational purpose. The students' due process claims were, therefore, of three types: first, that there must be sufficient advance notice of the diploma requirement and test objectives so that students may have a fair opportunity to prepare to pass the examination; second, in order for a test to be used as a measure of the successful completion of twelve years of schooling, the test should only measure that which the schooling has in fact offered students; third, in order for a state to be able to use a test, it must prove that its test *fairly* sorts passers from failers, the "literate" from the "illiterate," and diploma recipients from those to be denied diplomas. This proof requires that the state establish the validity and reliability of the test.

Both the trial and appellate courts refused to question the legitimacy of Florida's goal of attempting to foster educational accountability. But the courts found that the implementation of the testing program was not fair.

The first type of due process violations found were those involving the timing of the program. Both courts agreed that there was insufficient time between the initiation of the program and the testing. Time was needed to match curriculum and instruction to the functional literacy objectives and to prepare students to pass the test. Two years' notice of the implementation of a statewide testing program is inadequate for students where there has been no statewide curriculum, there has not been adequate instruction in all the skills and objectives measured on the test, and students do not know during the time of their instruction which skills will be required to be learned prior to graduation from high school. As the trial judge stated:

> The Plaintiffs, after spending ten years in schools where their attendance was compelled, were informed of a requirement concerning skills, which, if taught, should have taught in grades they had long since completed. While it is impossible to determine if all the skills were taught to all the students, it is obvious that the instruction given was not presented in an educational atmosphere directed by the existence of specific objectives stimulated throughout the period of instruction by a diploma sanction.[25]

A due process violation was found because there are other constitutionally acceptable and less onerous alternatives to implementation of the test requirement two years after the statute was enacted. Phased-in introduction of the objectives in all grades without the diploma sanction, the use of longer-term remediation programs to bring students up to the standards, and a longer time period between implementation of the statute and administration of the test would have been more fair.[26]

As for the test itself, the trial court found that, although there were "errors of considerable magnitude" in the test, those errors did not, either individually or collectively, amount to problems of sufficient magnitude to constitute constitutional infirmities. The test was, the trial court found, a valid test. The phase-in time for implementation of the test and the proof of match between the test and the curriculum to which students had been exposed were, however, found to be so inadequate that a due process deprivation resulted from use of the test to deny a diploma. In short, the trial court found that the test had "content validity." This determination was made in spite of the court's determination that the test failed to meet the "curricular match" standard many would consider a critical component of content validity.

The appellate court found that the due process guarantee against arbitrary and capricious governmental action included, in the Florida context, an entitlement to a test with content validity. The circuit court includes a requirement of proof of curricular match as part of proof of content validity. The trial court's determination that the Florida test had content validity was, according to the appeals panel, "clearly erroneous" because "the record is simply insufficient in proof that the test administered measures what was actually taught in the schools of Florida."[27]

Test Fairness and
the Judges' Curricular Match Requirement

If all MCTs simply attempted to assess the most fundamental "basic" skills of reading and mathematics, the problem of curricular match would perhaps be of less concern. One must assume that most schools teach most students the very fundamental skills. This is not the case in all schools, or in all classes, or for all students, however, so the issue of curricular match used to make critical decisions about students is an important concern in every MCT context and becomes more important, and more difficult, as the skills being tested become more complex. When MCTs go so far as to purport to measure "functional literacy" or other more global notions of competence, the issue becomes exceedingly difficult — particularly when the skills involved have not traditionally been a part of the required school curriculum for all students.

An effort to assess curricular match must begin by focusing upon an evaluation of the clarity with which the skills and objectives to be taught are defined. Unless the minimum competency skills and objectives are clearly and specifically defined, teachers will not know what to teach, students will not know what to study, testers will not know what knowledge to measure, and the public will not know the nature of the educational end products it is receiving. An exact sense of the nature and extent of curricular match is impossible without clear definitions of the skills and objectives covered in the teaching-testing program. Each skill and objective to be covered on the test should be defined so that it is possible to know both the dimensions of the skill and the level of proficiency of the skill. If the tests to be given will only assess part of a skill area or will only conduct an assessment at a limited level of difficulty, that information should be made known. An examination of some of the functional literacy objectives used in Florida is illustrative of the significance of clear definitions for use in the teaching-testing process. The regulations of the state board of education setting forth the functional literacy objectives include two objectives in the communications skills area:

> The student will, in a real world situation, determine the inferred cause and effect of an action.

> The student will include the necessary information when writing letters to supply or request information.[28]

In the mathematics skills area, the objectives include a requirement that:

> The student will determine the solution to real world problems involving comparison shopping.[29]

These objectives are representative of all of the Florida functional literacy objectives in terms of degree of specificity.

The objective requiring students to infer cause and effect of an action might refer to questions involving matters as complex as nuclear physics or as easy as following a road map. In fact, the items linked to this objective that were included in one early version of the FLT involved such tasks as choosing which among four sample letters would be the best for ordering concert tickets; determining what was most likely to occur if an employee consistently broke company rules; or understanding the warning label on a medicine bottle. A student who failed to answer any one of these items might be labeled incompetent. This label would be placed on the student even if he/she knew such cause and effect relationships as the sanctions that might be imposed for failure to complete and turn in homework assignments or to return the family car before curfew after a Saturday-night date.

A related problem is the level of proficiency required to meet each objective. This level of proficiency concerns both the actual definition of the objective and the actual difficulty of the test and the instruction. Understanding nuclear physics involves a higher order of skills than does knowing how to follow a road map. Recognizing the correct letter from among four samples is probably not as challenging as is making an inference from a sample of written company rules.

In Florida, the test was not developed to reflect a standardized statewide curriculum that was in use in the past. Rather than the curriculum's defining the test, the FLT will, over time, begin to define the curriculum in Florida schools. This will occur not through educators' review of the FLT objectives, but because they are so general, through a review of past test items. An initial difficulty with such efforts to achieve curricular match arises from the state's determination that the tests — even old forms — should be maintained as secure documents. There are, of course, many methods that educators and students might employ to obtain copies of test items, or parallel versions of such items, even if the test is "secure." Fairness would mandate that less troublesome alternatives be made available.

Other difficulties arise from the practice of relying on test items as the basis for assessing curricular match. Because items change with each administration of the test, curriculum and instruction may also need to change. The new curriculum, however, would not be available until after the test has already been given, a process that clearly violates the constitutional requirements concerning notice. In sum, an analysis of curricular match is not meaningful unless curricular and test objectives are clearly and specifically articulated — well before the administration of the test.

What Should the Standards Be?

The overall nature and scope of the evidence to be offered on curricular match for students of all races also depends upon how the teaching-learning process is defined by a court of law. To "measure what is actually taught" will require a standard of measurement that can somehow "quantify" the teaching process so we can be assured that students are being fairly exposed to all of the material covered on the test.

The goal must be to develop standards that set forth means for satisfying a court — and ourselves — that students have had a fair opportunity to learn. The standards must afford a reasonable mechanism for making this determination. These standards, in their most detailed application, must serve in a court of law as a means of assessing match or mismatch, and can also be used as guidelines for educators, parents, and students who are conducting self-evaluations. Without imposing too much bureaucratic detail, the standards must reach as far as possible toward assessing not only curricular issues but also these instructional matters that, together, constitute the provision by a school system of a fair opportunity to learn. Again, this is not to say that schools, under the Constitution, will be held responsible for ensuring that all of their educational efforts are effective. Yet these standards are not simply "nuts and bolts" exercises; the standards will probably also have to examine some less easily quantifiable learning factors — particularly as these relate to the education of minority and low-income youth in a system controlled primarily by white, middle-class professionals.

The burden is upon the educators implementing the test-for-diploma requirement to prove that curricular match exists. This burden is both constitutionally justified because of the importance of the student rights and interests at stake in the program and reasonable in light of the context in which the burden arises. In *Debra P.*, as is the case in most education litigation, court action was initiated only because formal and informal efforts to change professional practices failed. Judicial intervention in educational affairs was almost directly the result of a failure by educators to practice professional self-governance. There is no evidence that professionals initiating the program or developing or administering the test sought to comply with the *Standards*. Even if the relevant professional code had been followed, the standards set forth are in part insufficient to address all of the issues presented by a test-for-diploma scheme.

We are not without judicial guidance, however, in addressing the task of developing standards for fair teaching and testing practices in the MCT context. The trial court judge in *Debra P.* set forth in his decision several standards for defining fair teaching and an adequate opportunity to learn. None of these is unusual; most, if not all, involve educational strategies that have long been recognized as critical for effective teaching and learning.

Judicial guidance is more sparse concerning standards for determining the validity of a MCT used to determine the award of high school diplomas. Here lies the more substantial challenge for the educational community — a challenge that might well begin with an inquiry directed at determining whether any standard of validity is high enough that educators would comfortably support the use of a single test to make such critical determinations about students.

The attempt to determine standards for assessing the validity of MCTs that will withstand judicial scrutiny should begin, therefore, with a review of what the courts have said about the teaching component of the teaching-testing process and an outline of the types of questions that must be answered about the tests themselves.

MCT and Standards for Teaching

There are some more clear criteria, given a fair test, for determining whether a student has been offered a fair opportunity to learn the knowledge and skills covered on a MCT. These criteria are contained in the trial court's discussion of the due process protections to which students are entitled in a test-for-diploma program.[30] The trial court lists the following components of a constitutionally fair teaching program:

1. Students must be told the specific objectives that will be covered on the test used for graduation. This announcement must occur at the time of instruction in the objectives.
2. The curriculum offered to students must include instruction in the objectives covered on the test.
3. The acquisition of skills is a cumulative process. Students must be offered instruction in a rational and orderly sequence that affords them an opportunity to acquire proficiency through an appropriate developmental process.
4. The amount of time spent on instruction of a particular skill or unit of knowledge is important.
5. The timing of the instruction received by students is important. In addition to receiving sufficient instruction in a skill, students must be provided instruction, or a review of prior instruction, at a time just prior to administration of the test.
6. The teaching process must include some mechanism for identifying whether objectives are being learned by individual students, because teaching and learning are not always coterminous.
7. Students must be offered an opportunity for remedial instruction if they have not mastered an objective.

MCT and Standards for Test Validation

As a result of the *Debra P.* decisions, the testing profession is now being asked to establish the validity of its MCT efforts and to provide more evidence of the curricular and instructional validity, or curricular match, of tests used to make critical decisions about students. Some of the questions confronting the profession include the following:

1. What is the standard for, and definition of, ''content validity'' for MCTs used to determine the award of high school diplomas and MCTs used to make other critical decisions about students?
2. Does ''content validity,'' as we have defined it, include ''curricular validity'' or ''instructional validity''? Does it include the court's requirement that the test ''should measure what its actually taught''?
3. To what extent can curricular match determinations be made for an entire group of students (for example, the certified class in the *Debra P.* case) rather than on an individual, case-by-case basis? Are both types of analysis necessary?
4. What is the methodology for making determinations that a test fairly measures things that were ''actually taught'' to students?

Conclusion

The articulation by federal courts considering the case *Debra P.* v. *Turlington* of standards for assessing the fairness of MCT programs used to make critical decisions about students establish important standards for educators. These standards, concerning the fair testing and appropriate teaching for all students and the particular needs of black students, should guide future efforts to achieve educational accountability.

Notes

1.   474 F. Supp. 244 (M.D. Fla. 1979), *affd, in part, revd, in part*, 644 F.2d 397 (5th Cir. 1981), *petition for rehg, and petition for rehg, en banc denied*, 644 F.2d 397 (5th Cir. Sept. 4, 1981).

2.   474 F. Supp. at 259.

3.   Plaintiffs alleged that the failure to require the test for potential private high school graduates violated the constitutional guarantees in two ways. First, they charged that the exemption had the effect of sorting students on the basis of race because most of the private schools had all white or predominantly white enrollments. Plaintiffs asserted that these enrollments were the result of black students' financial inability to attend private schools as well as the attempts of white parents to use private schools to shield their children from the desegregation of the public schools. The trial court found that the private school exemption was constitutional. The issue was not raised during the appeal of the case.

4.   474 F. Supp. at 256.

5.   644 F.2d at 408.

6.   347 U.S. 483 (1954).

7.   McNeal v. Tate, 508 F.2d 1017 (5th Cir. 1970).

8.   474 F. Supp. at 252.

9.   474 F. Supp. at 256–257.

10.   42 U.S.C. §2000d.

11.   20 U.S.C. §1703.

12.   42 U.S.C. §2000e.

13.   495 F. Supp. 926 (N.D. Cal. 1979).

14.   Uniform Guidelines on Employee Selection Procedures (of the Equal Employment Opportunity Commission, U.S. Civil Service Commission, Department of Labor, and Department of Justice), 33 Fed. Reg. 12,333 (1978) (formally codified at 29 C.F.R. pt. 1607 (1979)).

15.   Presumably, the high failure rate on these items meant the material was not taught in school either — a unique problem of curricular match (or lack thereof) for black students taking the FLT.

16.   474 F. Supp. at 261–262.

17.   Madaus, G.F. and Pedulla, J.J. "An Examination of Item Bias in the Florida Functional Literacy Test" A paper prepared for the Center for Law and Education, Cambridge, Mass., June 1980. The work on the paper was supported by the Ford Foundation.

18.   Testimony of Professor Robert Linn, *National Institute of Education Issues Clarification Hearing on Minimum Competency Testing*, Washington, D.C., July 9, 1981. The data are also available in unpublished form from Professor Linn at the University of Illinois, Champaign.

19.   644 F.2d at 406.

20.   *Id.* at 408.

21.   For a discussion of the legal issues concerning MCT that provides more detail than space allows here, see McClung, *Competency Testing Programs: Legal and Educational Issues*, 47 Fordham L. Rev. 651, (1979).

22.   474 F. Supp. at 266, 644 F.2d at 404.

23.   *Id.*

24.   474 F. Supp. at 267.

25.   474 F. Supp. at 266, 644 F.2d at 404.

26.   644 F.2d at 405.

27.   474 F. Supp. at 259.

28.   *Id.*

29.   *Id.* at 264.

30.   474 F.Supp. at 264.

2 MINIMUM COMPETENCY TESTING FOR CERTIFICATION: *The Evolution and Evaluation of Test Validity*

George F. Madaus

The purpose of this chapter is three-fold. The first aim is to trace the evolution of the concepts of curriculum and instructional validity and their relationships to what has become more widely known as content validity. It took jurists to clear away the underbrush surrounding the various conceptualizations of content validity. The Fifth Circuit's insistence in the *Debra P.* case that the validity of a certification test be evaluated in terms of what was taught needs to be put in the broader historical context of changing perspectives on the validity of achievement tests. The second aim is to describe several issues related to minimum competency testing (MCT) that affect an evaluation of the validity not only of the test but also of the certification program itself. The third aim of the chapter is to outline what state departments of education and local educational authorities might do in order to demonstrate that an MCT used for graduation or promotion decisions measures what was actually taught.

Evolution of the Concepts of Curriculum and Instructional Validity

Conflicting Views of Content Validity at the Trial

This section looks at the history of the concepts of curricular and instructional validity and the way in which these early conceptualizations concerning the

21

validity of achievement tests virtually disappeared under the rubric of content validity only to reappear in the annals of the court. We shall start, therefore, with the *Debra P.* trial and examine the different ways in which content validity was interpreted during the trial, setting the stage for the Fifth Circuit's restoration of curricular and instructional validity. Next, we shall describe why the concept of content validity has proved so popular. We then conduct our historical survey.

The Debra P. v. Turlington *Trial*

Curriculum, examinations, commencement, and degrees are all part of a long tradition dating back to the twelfth century when admission to the guild of masters or professors was through an examination of academic attainment in several subjects of study. Until one passed the examination, one could be only a student. Thereafter one was a master, in rank if not occupation; one had passed out of the journeyman stage into the guild of scholars with a license to teach. Since those earliest days, certification examinations in education have presupposed "a body of material upon which the candidate is examined, usually a set of standard textbooks, and this in turn implies systematic teaching and a minimum period of study" (Neill 1957, p. 126). Even a cursory reading of the Fifth Circuit's decision shows agreement with this historical description of examination for certification. For the court, the linkage between examinations, curriculum, and teaching was essential, even obvious. Reading the Fifth Circuit panel's opinion, one gets the feeling that when all was said and done the judges acted out of a "strong gut feeling" of fairness:[1]

> The due process violation potentially goes deeper than deprivation of property rights without adequate notice. When it encroaches upon concepts of justice lying at the basis of our civil and political institutions, the state is obligated to avoid action which is arbitrary and capricious, does not achieve or even frustrates a legitimate state interest, or is fundamentally unfair . . . We believe that the state administered a test that was, at least on record before us, fundamentally unfair in that it *may* have covered matters not taught in the schools of the state.[2]

What was it that led the Fifth Circuit panel to this "gut feeling" that the test *might* have been unfair because the material tested *may* not have been taught? In the appellate court, judges do not make their own factual determinations but rely instead on the parties in the case to place before them the facts relevant to the issues on appeal. Facts that are not contained within the "four corners of the record," with few exceptions, do not exist (Greenhouse 1982). However, judicial actions can also be based on inferences that depend on experience and common sense (Greenhouse 1982). Judge Skelly Wright refers to straightforward moral and constitutional arithmetic that figures into many decisions.[3] The finding that fairness requires that the material tested be material taught probably emerged in part from the judges' ordinary experience with schools and tests, and from common sense. But it also must have emerged in part from reading a record that contained within its "four corners" the quite different meanings attributed to content validity by plaintiffs and defendants. How exactly did the two sides differ?

For the state, expert witnesses argued that content validity was limited to a determination that the sample of items making up a test adequately represent the domain of defined objectives. They argued that it was not necessary to explicitly connect the defined domain with either curricular material or instruction in evaluating a test's content validity. Content validity was a closed circle limited by the boundary of the defined domain. This conceptualization of content validity is perhaps best typified by the following somewhat convoluted statement and the ensuing exchange:

> Witness: . . . If it were to be determined that high school graduation would depend on knowledge of Greek, if that were the state law, then a person building a test that had content validity, in order to make inferences about whether the person had an adequate knowledge of Greek, would indeed have to write a test that measured that.

Whereupon the lawyer for the plaintiffs asked:

> And that would be regardless of whether or not those students who are going to be denied a diploma on the basis of that test had been taught Greek . . . ?

To which the witness, William Mehrens, replied:

> Well, [the test] would still have content validity if it had been determined that the test was to measure these objectives.[4]

Mehrens went on to amend his statement by pointing out that content validity refers to the match between the objectives and the items; that the question of whether the objectives were in fact appropriate was not a measurement matter but an educational one. He indicated that as an educator he would not want to see an MCT measure things one did not reasonably expect students to be able to do after instruction. This subtle but crucial distinction between a measurement issue and an educational issue — in defining the proper domain for the test — may have been lost on the judge. The thrust of the testimony, and the issue under contention, dealt with a *measurement* question — that is, the test's content validity.

For the plaintiffs, the experts had a different view of content validity. They argued that the first question that needed to be answered when evaluating the content validity of a test was this: Is the domain in question the correct one given the purposes for which the test is to be used? Since the Florida State Student Assessment Test-Part II (SSAT II) — more commonly known as the functional literacy test (FLT) or Funci Lit — was to be used for certification, the correct domain was a subset of that which had been taught. This question about the legitimacy of the domain was as much a measurement/validity issue as it was an educational one. The record shows that the plaintiffs' experts repeatedly argued that the pupils should have received instruction on the domain tested if the certification test was to be valid.

The following exchange between one of the plaintiffs' lawyers and Ralph Tyler exemplifies the thrust of this argument:

> Q: Doctor, is there a preferred method to develop [a testing program for certification] in conjunction with [the] curriculum . . .?
>
> A: If a child is to be judged in terms of whether he is learning what the school is trying to teach, the test should parallel what it is he is being taught. It would be considered unfair to say "I can't get my diploma because I haven't learned something that was not in the curriculum and was not taught me."[5]

A number of times plaintiffs' experts cited the findings of a state commission:

> [Students] were suddenly required to pass a test constructed under pressure of time covering content that was presumed to be elementary but that their schools may or may not have taught them recently, well, or perhaps at all . . . Prior to 1977, when the test was first given, some Florida schools probably did not offer sufficiently good and recent instruction in the skills covered by the test to expect all students to demonstrate them (Task Force on Educational Assessment Program 1979, p. 4).

The trial court agreed with Florida's ideas of content validity — that is, that the items match the domain of objectives — and the court seemed to divorce whether the domain was correct or not from an evaluation of content validity. The court ruled that the SSAT II was, in fact, content valid. What is interesting is that while in one section of the opinion the court found that the test had content validity, in another it found serious educational problems resulted from a mismatch between what the test measured and what was taught. For example, it observed that the design and implementation of instructional programs, and the selection of textbooks, were mainly the tasks of individual counties; that until recently there was a lack of uniformity among districts in their selection of instructional materials; and that even with state-approved textbooks, several texts would have to be used by a district if all the material on the test were to be covered. The court went on to admit that there was evidence that certain skills were not taught in Florida's public schools. The judge then assumed *in arguendo* that the skills were taught but observed that the atmosphere of the instruction prior to implementation of the test did not emphasize either the FLT or the diploma sanction. The court argued that the acquisition of functional literacy skills was a cumulative process and that these skills were not taught in any specific grade, in any specific class, or by any specific teacher. At the end of this discussion about instruction, the judge agreed with the observation of one of the plaintiffs' witnesses that the "functional literacy program was a test looking for a plan of instruction."[6]

Despite an acknowledgment of these educational and instructional short-comings, the court nonetheless ruled that the Florida test was content valid. However, after reviewing the record, the Fifth Circuit rejected as "clearly erroneous"[7] this finding of fact. The appellate court in effect seemed to link the appropriateness of the domain tested to an evaluation of a test's validity. The court noted that in competency testing "an important component of content validity is curricular validity defined by defendant's expert Dr. Foster [sic] as 'things that are currently taught.' "[8] However, the court failed to clearly distinguish between and among content, curricular, and instructional validity. It talked about content validity and observed that an important aspect was curricular validity, and then without mentioning it specifically went on to describe instructional validity. The court's description of *content* validity — including as it does a reference to *curricular* validity — in fact implicitly incorporates McClung's (1978, 1979) earlier descriptions of *instructional* validity:[9]

> Even if the curricular objectives of the school correspond with the competency test objectives, there must be some measure of whether the school district's stated objectives were translated into topics actually taught in the district's classrooms. While a measure of curricular validity is a measure of the theoretical validity of the competency test as a test instrument to assess the success of students, instructional validity is an actual measure of whether the schools are providing students with instruction in the knowledge and skills measured by the test (1979, pp. 682–683).

At the conference, Roger Rice, one of the plaintiff's lawyers, related the following incident. One of the appellate judges early in the hearing asked a lawyer for the state if Florida could give a test on country-club etiquette and use it for a graduation standard. Receiving an affirmative answer, the judge then asked, what about Greek? (This was perhaps a reference to the portion of the trial transcript quoted earlier.) The lawyer again indicated that this would be all right. The judge then remarked that he had a big problem with that because it was not fair. On hearing the exchange, a second judge indicated that he had the same problem about fairness and went on to say that if they both had the same problem, then the state's lawyers had a problem. Fundamental fairness had raised its comely head.

Reasons for the Popularity of Content Validity

Over the past five years or so, a number of people in the measurement community have argued that validity is a unitary concept (Cronbach 1980*a*, 1980*c*, 1980*d;* Dunnette and Borman 1979; Guion 1977*a*, 1977*b*, 1978*a*, 1978*b*, 1980; Linn 1980; also see Linn's Chapter 5 for an excellent discussion of this topic; Messick 1975, 1980*a*, 1980*b*, 1981; Tenopyr 1977). However, the field in general, and test users in particular, have been slow to adopt a unitary conceptualization of validity.

An example close at hand was the assertion by Florida in the *Debra P*. case that content validity was the only type of validity that needed to be considered when evaluating the SSAT-II. For a much longer time — certainly since *The Technical Recommendations* (APA 1954; AERA/NCMUE 1955) — validity has been compartmentalized into at least three distinct components: content, criterion-related, and construct validity. Guion (1980) colorfully describes this compartmentalization "as a holy trinity representing three different roads to psychometric salvation" (p. 386). For achievement testing the road to Damascus has always been by way of content validation, and it would be sacrilegious in the minds of some to argue otherwise. Why this singular devotion to content validity when evaluating achievement tests? At least four general reasons can be discerned.

First, using *content* as an adjective modifying the noun *validity* conjures up the image of subject matter coverage rather than hypothetical constructs — particularly in the minds of administrators and teachers, the largest users of achievement tests. The word *content* is defined as subject matter, or topics treated in books; the matter dealt with in a field of study, the subject matter of a discipline or educational course (*Webster's Third New International* 1976). This common and popular use of the word forms a mind-set for many achievement test users when they see or hear the phrase content validity. The broader implications of the word *content* in the measurement literature are quickly forgotten (Cronbach 1971).

Second, publishers of standardized achievement tests emphasize content validity in their manuals. They describe how they survey the most widely used textbooks and curriculum guides, review the syllabi of large city school districts, and consult teachers and subject-matter specialists to arrive at a table of specifications for their test. While such a table of specifications may cross content topics with categories of skills needed to deal with the topics, the impression left with many users reinforces the subject-matter emphasis associated with content, an emphasis with which most users have always been more comfortable.

Third, while skills have always been emphasized in achievement testing (that is, reading comprehension, writing, computation, problem-solving, and so forth), they have not generally been viewed in the educational community as theoretical propositions or constructs at all. For many, it is perfectly clear from the public performance of the task whether one has the skill in question — be it reading a passage and then answering a multiple-choice question, or writing an essay on "How I Spent my Summer Vacation." There was never a need to evoke constructs or talk about construct validation (Messick 1980*b*); content was enough.

Finally, there were some very practical reasons for a singular emphasis on content validity. If one could show a test was content valid — that is, the items represented the test domain — then the test was viewed as content valid for all kinds of persons. (Cronbach 1971) — regardless of the ethnic or racial status of the examinees, where they happened to go to school, or the instruction they received. Further, since an evaluation of content validity traditionally involved consensual judgment about the match between the test content and test domain, it was a cheap, feasible, and relatively simple procedure. Construct and criterion-related validity, on the other hand, are rooted in empirical investigations and as such are seen as difficult, costly, bothersome, and time-consuming.

For these reasons content validity has been the popular validation method of choice over the years when educators have considered achievement testing. The court's decision to broaden the meaning of content validity to include evidence that pupils had been taught the materials on a certification test adds an important new dimension to the validation process. If the test is to be used as a graduation requirement, then the court is asking the state for evidence that the test is measuring things that pupils had fair opportunity to learn.

Early Conceptualizations of the Validity of Achievement Tests

The Fifth Circuit's fairness test is not entirely new to the measurement profession. From the late 1920s into the 1970s content validity has often been described with various levels of precision as the process of relating test items to the objectives of curriculum *and* relating them to instruction. (Ruch 1929; Woody and Sangren, 1933; Lee 1936; Odell, 1938; Greene, Jorgensen, and Gerberich 1943, 1954; Cureton 1951; Ross and Stanley 1954; Wrightstone, Justman, and Robbins 1956; Ebel 1956; Noll 1957; Furst 1958; Stanley and Hopkins 1972) Those writing on the subject clearly took for granted — and why not? — that the domain of interest in educational achievement testing was the curricular *and* instructional emphasis of a teacher or of a school. Keep in mind that diploma denial based on a test score was not at issue. For example, in 1929 Ruch wrote that "validity is in general the degree to which a test parallels the curriculum and good teaching practice" (p. 28). Almost forty years later Stanley and Hopkins described content validity as a process of logical analysis where test items are examined "in relation to the objectives and *instruction* [in order to] make the following professional judgments:

1. Does the test content parallel the curricular objectives in content and processes, and
2. Are the test and curricular emphasis in proper balance?" (p. 102) [emphasis added]

In fact it was not unusual to use the terms *curricular validity* and *content validity* interchangeably (for example, Cureton 1951, p. 669). Nor was it uncommon for writers even to use the terms *curricular validity* or *curricular relevance* rather than *content validity* when discussing the validity of achievement tests (for example, Cureton 1951; Furst 1958; Greene, Jorgenson, and Gerberich 1954; Wrightstone, Justman, and Robbins 1956). What was different was that certification was not the issue — and that alone is much of the story. The discussion about content validity was either in the more benign contexts of teacher-made tests, or of teachers selecting a standardized test. Therefore, one frequently found that instruction and/or teaching was mentioned as a component in evaluating curricular or content validity. For example, consider the following passages:

> The best check for the teacher in judging the validity of the test is to be sure that the items selected (1) measure objectives of the course as nearly as possible, (2) are the more important ones of the course, (3) *parallel the actual teaching which has been done,* and (4) *represent a wide sampling of the materials taught* (Lee 1936, p. 324) [emphasis added].

> Content should be *similar but not identical with* that content (problems, reading selections, musical compositions, etc.) used for instructional purposes. *The crucial elements and relationships, however, should be those which were at the focus of instruction,* rather than concepts, principles, and relationships which were already a part of the student's general information and comprehension. Otherwise the content will lack curricular relevance.

> Moreover, the mental operations to be done with the content must also be consistent with the instructional goals. Otherwise they, too, will lack curricular relevance. *It is unreasonable to expect students to perform sophisticated mental operations if they have not had instruction along those lines.* (Furst 1958, p. 219.) [Emphasis in the original in the first paragraph, added in the second.]

Running throughout the literature is a belief that the teachers were best able to determine curricular validity since they knew that materials had actually been taught (for example, Lee 1936; Greene, Jorgensen, and Gerberich 1943; Furst 1958).

The links between content and curriculum on the one hand and instruction on the other, were never free of ambiguity. While acknowledging that it was important to show that the test covered the material taught, often it was simply assumed, or implied, that the stated goals or objectives of instruction were actually taught. We now know that such assumptions are not necessarily valid (Feldhausen, Hynes, and Ames 1976; see also Chapter 6 by Schmidt and his colleagues, and Chapter 7 by Leinhardt). An example of this ambiguity can be seen in Cureton's (1951) discussion of curricular relevance. He first points out that the teacher is the best judge of whether the materials or operations measured by a particular test were identical with the ones taught. Later he seems satisfied with a match between the test and the *stated* objectives when he argues that "if the materials, situations, and performances themselves represent all of the pertinent specific objectives of instruction, no futher evidence of [the test's] curricular relevance is required" (1951, p. 670).

Ambiguity can also be found in the assertion that curricular validity involves a determination of the extent to which the test measured the major objectives and/or the most common and important material found in popular textbooks and courses of study (for example, Greene, Jorgensen, and Gerberich 1954; Noll 1957). Again, the implicit assumption is that pupils received instruction on those objectives that were common to the texts or courses of study surveyed.

A final example of ambiguity is that validity somehow adhered to the test itself and the items that comprised it, rather than being a function of the test scores and inferences made from these scores (Lennon 1956; Messick 1975). We shall return to this point in more detail presently.

In summary, early conceptualizations of the validity of achievement tests clearly included "curricular" validity. Curricular validity is not a recent concept, and it certainly is not unique to the Fifth Circuit decision. Over the past fifty years or so, this concept can be found throughout the literature on achievement testing. It has generally been described as involving a judgment on the match of what was tested and the objectives of a curriculum; however, more often than not, explicit mention was also made of the match between what was tested and what was actually taught in a particular course — what McClung (1978, 1979) calls instructional validity. However, when reference was made to a match between the content and what was taught, it was in the context of a teacher-made test or of teachers selecting a standardized test for use in their classes and certainly not in the context of an external test used for certification.

The Technical Recommendations

In 1954, the American Psychological Association (APA), through its Committee on Test Standards, published *Technical Recommendations for Psychological Tests*. The document distinguished four kinds of validity: content, predictive, concurrent, and construct. We shall concentrate on the first of these since the *Technical Recommendations* began the formal enshrinement of content validity.

Content validity was seen as particularly important for achievement tests or proficiency measures and was evaluated "by showing how well the content or the test samples the class of situation or subject matter about which conclusions are to be drawn" (APA 1954, p. 13). While not specifically discussing the question of whether the domain or universe is correct or appropriate for a given use, this concern could be implied from a recommendation that the universe of situations be discussed and that the manual clearly indicate what universe is represented.

A year later, the American Educational Research Association (AERA) and the National Council on Measurements Used in Education (NCMUE)[10] published *Technical Recommendations for Achievement Tests* (1955). That document adopted the APA committee's fourfold classification of validity. Content validity involved "sampling of a specified universe of content" (p. 16). In an example showing when it was appropriate to determine content validity, the committee incorporated both curricular and instructional concerns. When a science teacher wished to measure a teaching objective on interpretative reading in science, the content validity question was this: "Does the test present the types of situations to which the teacher is trying to teach students to respond?" (p. 16).

Like its APA counterpart, the AERA-NCMUE committee was also concerned that the universe be clearly described, but they also made an important distinction not found in the APA *Technical Recommendations:*

> . . . for instructional uses of achievement tests (diagnosis and analysis of achievement, planning of remedial work, and determination of supervisory needs of the teacher) content validity is important. For administrative uses of the test scores (classification of pupils, promotion, and school records of achievement) it is only the concurrent and construct validity that are important. It is the measure of the accuracy of the inferences which determine administrative decisions. In such cases content validity is important primarily as it lends logical support to concurrent or construct validity. (p. 19)

While the committee did not explain why the accuracy of inferences is not an issue for instructional uses also, it is interesting to note that many present-day MCTs fall into the 1954 category of administrative uses of test scores (that is, classification and promotion of pupils). At issue is the validity of such administrative inferences about pupils as competent or incompetent; pass or fail; and such administrative decisions as awarding a diploma or certificate of attendance and promotion or retention of a student in grade. In these situations — according to the *Technical Recommendations* — content validity would be important only insofar as it supports arguments for concurrent or construct validity; contemporary commentators on validity would agree (for example, Cronbach 1980c; Linn, 1980; also see Linn, Chapter 5; Messick 1980a, 1980b, 1981).

In commenting on the two versions of the *Technical Recommendations,* Lennon (1956) noted content validity was a linear descendant of logical or the venerable curricular validity. He argued that in the *Technical Recommendations* the sense in which content validity was to be interpreted was "the extent to which a subject's responses to the items of a test may be considered to be a representative sample of his responses to a real or hypothetical universe of situations which together constitute the area of concern to a person interpreting the test" (p. 295). Lennon's argument that content validity inheres in the examinee's responses, not in the test items themselves, went virtually unheeded for almost twenty-five years. (Anastasi is an exception. Her text has the following interesting, but isolated, observation: Content validity depends on the relevance of the individual's test responses to the behavior area under consideration, rather than on the apparent relevance of item content [1976, p. 135].) Lennon recognized the problem of ascribing validity to the test questions per se rather than to interpretations from test performance. He argued that since a test user wishes to make inferences about a behavioral universe, the items must sample examinee behaviors, which in fact are the examinee's modes of response and the responses themselves. He went on to argue that since "items on the test lend themselves to response via different processes for various examinees, the possibility exists that [the test's] content validity differs from one examinee to another, even though the test questions are identical for all subjects" (p. 296). In other words, content validity is idiosyncratic. Lennon's exegesis of the *Technical Recommendations'* treatment of content validity is interesting for three other reasons.

First, he was ahead of his time in expressing reservations about limiting the conceptualization of content validity to a consideration of the test items and the universe description and about evaluating content validity without considering the persons tested. If content validity involves only a consideration of the match between the universe description and the test items, one can begin to see why Florida argued that it was the *only* validity consideration needed; that construct and criterion-related validity of the SSAT-II (the FLT) were not germane. Once the test content was shown to be validly selected from the universe, the test was then content valid for persons of all kinds (Cronbach 1971). Further, as already noted, since the determination of content validity is basically a logical rather than empirical process, it is much easier to establish than either construct or criterion-related validity and certainly much less expensive and bothersome.

Second, Lennon argued that while content validity inheres in an examinee's responses to the test items, it is not at all clear how to determine what process was used by different examinees in answering an item. Naturally, persons asked to judge content validity cannot observe each student taking a test and divine the intellectual functioning for each question. At best, judges can attempt to determine — from their experience of students, from curricular materials supplied them, and from an examination of the question — what process most students would most likely have employed in answering a particular question. Judges would need to keep in mind that the intellectual ability actually used for answering a particular question might have been very different from what the examiner had hoped it would be in framing the question. For example, the examiner might have hoped that a question would require a student to apply a principle in a new situation — for example, the application level in Bloom's *Taxonomy of Education Objectives* (1956). Some student might have anticipated the question and committed the answer to memory; for others, the situation may not have been new. In either case the item functioned at the level of knowledge. In short, the judges' ratings would have to focus on *estimates* of the level at which students functioned, rather than focus on the level intended by the test developer (Madaus and Macnamara 1970). The most appropriate persons to make estimates of the level of response would be teachers since they would know most about the instruction pupils received.

There is a still more fundamental problem involved in efforts to divine the mental process actually used by a pupil in answering a question. Even the best of item writers cannot anticipate all of the nuances of perception, background, and attitude that influence the way in which examinees answer an item (Taylor and Willie 1979). In addition, the content or the format of the item can vary the process brought into play by an examinee in answering it (Loevinger 1965; Linn 1980; see also Chapter 5 by Linn for a concrete example). Further, answering a single item involves numerous behavioral processes rather than a single one (Cronbach 1971).

A third implication of Lennon's conceptualization of content validity flows from the second and has direct relevance to the issue raised by the Fifth Circuit Court — that is, whether the material tested had actually been taught. If content validity is to be evaluated according to whether an item measures material and behavior actually taught pupils, then it will almost by necessity differ from one examinee to another even though the test questions are identical for all. Again, content validity becomes idiosyncratic. A test may lack content validity for one person because of missing the instruction associated with a given item; for another, because of lacking the prerequisites to benefit from the instruction received; for another, because the instruction given the group he/she was part of may have been personally inappropriate; for still another, because the group used an out-of-level textbook or followed a self-pacing plan and certain material was not "covered." All this may occur despite the fact that the test is identical across all these individuals. That content validity is idiosyncratic — a function of the items that form the test and examinees' educational and personal background — is a concept that is difficult for many in testing simply because there never before was an urgent need to deal with it.

Challenges to the appropriateness of a test for a particular individual would likely surface after the individual had failed the test, not during test development. If the pupil passed, the point that several items on the test measured material or behaviors that had not been taught recently, well, or at all, would probably not be pursued. (False positives are never an issue in MCT programs.) However, given the arbitrary nature of cut scores on a MCT, a student who failed by only a few items may very well argue that the items involved material not taught. When only the tiny tilt of a few items prevents a pupil from reaching the all-important cut score, it would be naive to think that no challenge would be directed toward the offending items. The idea of challenges to particular items by particular individuals who fail an MCT seems to open Pandora's box. This was an issue that came up, without resolution, several times in group discussions at the conference. Yet as Walker points out (Chapter 9), a sense of fairness and decency dictates that it is not enough to show that on average throughout the state adequate opportunity was provided to learn the offending items, if in fact a particular pupil could show that he/she did not have such opportunity.

In light of the several implications of Lennon's 1956 critique of content validity, it is interesting to consider Florida's response to the Fifth Circuit's decision. The state has proposed that a student who felt that he/she had not been taught material covered on the test be granted an administrative hearing. The administrative tribunal would determine whether the material tested had been taught. At the hearing the superintendent would assume the burden of proof, "that the material tested by the SSAT-II was covered in the schools to which the student had been assigned."[11] The problem with such a proposal is that it may be determined that a pupil was in fact assigned to a school that covered the material tested, but that does not guarantee that the individual had an opportunity to learn the material; nor, given the opportunity, does it guarantee that the instruction was appropriate for that individual. If, on the other hand, the district must show that an individual was actually taught the material on an item-by-item basis, then a system of record keeping in anticipation of such challenges would need to be installed. Even with such a system, the issue of whether the instruction was "appropriate" would remain unresolved.

At the administrative hearing, the district may be tempted to introduce evidence about a pupil's motivation, discipline, or attitude in an attempt to discredit a claim. Such an attempt could deprive the pupil of the sacred benefit of the doubt, shifting the burden of proof back on to the pupil. How to balance the responsibility for learning between pupils and the school during an administrative hearing needs very careful consideration. In short, the individual hearing route has a number of troublesome pitfalls.

The Test Standards

The rather cryptic treatment of content validity contained in the *Technical Recommendations* remained the only statement from the three professional organizations on the subject for the next twelve years. It was a much less hectic, less contentious, and less litigious era for the measurement community. In 1966 a Joint AERA, APA, and NCME Committee revised the *Technical Recommendations* and issued the *Standards for Educational and Psychological Tests and Manuals*. This document represented a consensus of professional opinion about what information test developers should supply to test consumers.

The joint committee described three kinds of validity coefficients: content, criterion-related, and construct. Content validity was at issue when "the test user wishes to determine how an individual performs at present in a universe of situations that the test situation is claimed to represent" (APA 1966, p. 12). The committee described the universe of situations for an achievement test as "a certain phase of educational achievement or certain educational objectives" (p. 12). Evaluating content validity involved demonstrating how well the test items sampled the class of situations, or subject matter, about which conclusions were to be drawn. The committee never explicitly mentioned teaching or instruction but instead talked about the test universe in terms of educational objectives, or the types of aptitudes, skills, and knowledge that the school *wishes* to develop in the students. The emphasis was on instructional *intentions* or *stated* objectives. Since it talked about the "coverage of the subject" (p. 15), one might infer that the committee assumed that the pupils would receive instruction on the educational objectives that formed the universe that the test user wished to evaluate. However, a narrower view might be that the appropriateness of the universe of tasks could be considered solely in terms of stated intents rather than in terms of what was actually covered by instruction. It simply is not clear.

Because the 1966 *Standards* were found wanting in court cases involving the use of tests in employment settings, they were revised in 1974. The revision, entitled *Standards For Educational and Psychological Tests,* pointed out that validity referred to "the appropriateness of the inferences from test scores or other forms of assessment" (p. 25). The measuring instrument was seen as an operational definition of a specified domain. The 1974 committee saw various methods of validation, but all of them required a definition of what was to be inferred from the scores and data to show that there was an acceptable basis for such inferences. For convenience sake only, criterion-related, content, and construct validity were discussed independently; but all three were seen to be interrelated operationally and logically. Unfortunately, the added clause "only rarely is one of them alone important in a particular situation" (p. 26) tended to undermine a unitary conceptualization of validity; too many people considered their case as one of those rare occasions. With benefit of hindsight, one can see that this bow to convenience was a serious mistake. It led some test useres to argue that only one of the three aspects of validity was appropriate for their test, and the remaining two were ignored (see Cronbach 1980*b,* and Guion 1977*a,* 1978*a,* 1980 for a further description of this point). Not surprisingly, content validity was the aspect most often selected for attention at the expense of the other two. For example, witness the assertion by Florida in the *Debra P.* case that construct and criterion-related validity were not appropriate.

The discussion of content validity in the 1974 *Standards* is confusing and contradictory (Guion 1977*a,* 1977*b*). For example, the *Standards* state that

> To demonstrate the content validity of a set of test scores, one must show that the behaviors demonstrated in testing constitute a representative sample of behaviors to be exhibited in a desired performance domain (p. 28).

This emphasis on behavior is reminiscent of Lennon's thesis that the test samples behaviors, and that the behaviors are the examinee's modes of response and the responses themselves. One might therefore interpret that statement as meaning that content validity inheres in the responses of the examinee rather than in the items. There is, however, no further explanation of this statement and to my knowledge it has never been interpreted in Lennon's sense. Further, consider the confusion between the terms *domain* and *universe* in this sentence: ". . . a definition of the performance domain of interest must always be provided by the test user so that the content of a test may be checked against an appropriate task universe" (p. 28).

While the 1974 *Standards* never tied content validity directly to instruction, instructional objectives were specifically mentioned. In 1974, as in 1966, the focus was on *intentions* rather than on what was actually taught. The committee offered the example of a test used to estimate achievement in American History. The performance domain was described as the pooled judgments of authorities, experienced teachers, and competent curriculum makers, about the instructional objectives appropriate for twelfth-grade American History. The committee went on to note that "an achievement test so constructed would not necessarily constitute a representative sample of the skills, facts and concepts taught by any particular teacher during any particular year" (p. 28); this constituted a recognition, no doubt, of the wide variation in coverage between teachers teaching the same subject. In this vignette the committee probably had in mind a standardized norm-referenced survey test that could be chosen by a school district or teacher. It is safe to say that the committee did not refer to a test reflecting a mandated statewide curriculum of syllabus, such as the New York Regents Exam in American History, or to a mandated certification test used for graduation, such as Florida's SSAT-II (the FLT).

Previously, we saw that experts for the plaintiffs and the state in the *Debra P.* case disagreed on the question of whether one had to first justify the universe selected in terms of the use of the test for certification. The *Standards* do say that the test developer (or user) is accountable for the adequacy of the definition of the universe. This might be interpreted to mean that consideration of the universe in terms of the test use is required. This interpretation is strengthened by the statement that "an employer cannot justify an employment test on grounds of content validity if he cannot demonstrate that the content universe includes all, or nearly all, important parts of the job" (p. 29). Analogously, we could say that a state cannot justify a test used for graduation decision on grounds of content validity alone if it cannot demonstrate that the content universe encompasses material and skills actually emphasized in instruction in high school. But, again, the 1974 *Standards* — like those of 1966 — were never explicit on the question of the appropriateness of the universe for the decision being made.

Content Validity and Employment Testing

The 1966 *Standards* were revised in part to correct deficiencies in that document's treatment of the use of tests in selection for employment. Rather than clarifying these issues, the *1974 Standards* made some more opaque (Guion 197*a*, 1977*b*, 1978*a*, 1978*b*, 1980; Cronbach 1980*b*). As a result, the issues of test validity in the employment setting received extensive treatment in the literature from about 1976 onward. This section briefly reviews that portion of the literature that has implications for issues related to the Fifth Circuit Court's decision. For a more detailed review of the testing issues in the employment area, the reader is referred to *Ability Testing: Uses, Consequences, and Controversies* by the Committee on Ability Testing, National Academy of Science (Wigdor and Garner 1982).

The concept of content validity in the employment setting was borrowed directly from educational measurement (Guion 1978*b*, 1980). Guion's description of content validity in education is interesting; a test is considered content valid when the content of the test matches in general proportions the material to be covered in the curriculum. The match is between test content and educational *intents*, not between test content and what was actually taught in the classroom. Further, there is an assumption that the test represents the curriculum in proper proportion. We will return to this latter point presently.

The adaptation of the concept of content validity from education to the employment setting was not without its problems. While the job replaced the curriculum as the target domain of the test, the 1974 *Standards* talked only about the match between the test content domain and the test items. ''There was no talk at all about the relationship of a test content domain to a job content domain'' (Guion 1977*b*, p. 409). A determination that a test is a good sample of some domain does not necessarily mean it is a job-related test; there must be a logical and empirical basis for calling a test domain job-related (Guion 1977*b*). An important aspect of the evaluation of the content validity of a test in an employment setting therefore involves evaluation of whether the test domain is relevant in terms of the use to which the results will be put — for example, selecting someone for a *particular* job (Guion 1977*a*, 1977*b;* Shimberg 1981; Cronbach 1980*c*).

The issue of the *correctness* or *appropriateness* of the test domain relative to test use clearly falls within the sphere of content validity. For example, in describing how one might demonstrate the content validity of a test used to select candidates for the police force, Green (1981) points out that a police officer's job can be analyzed into particulars. Evaluating the content validity of a test used to select police officers therefore involves matching the particulars of the job to the test items.

The courts have agreed that content validity in the employment setting involves a demonstration that the test domain is appropriate for the selection being made. In the *United States* v. *City of St. Louis*[12] the court held that a multiple-choice test used to select fire captains was not content valid because it assessed skills that were too dissimilar to those used by fire captains on the job (Bershoff 1981). In *Guardians Association of New York City* v. *Civil Service Commission*[13] the court found that content validation could be used to justify a test only if it could be shown that the abilities being measured by the test were job-related (Bershoff 1981). This acceptance by courts that an evaluation of content validity involves first a determination of the appropriateness of the test domain to the test use, and only then a determination of the match of test items to the domain goes to the heart of the disagreement between experts for the defendants and plaintiffs over the meaning of content validity in the *Debra P.* case. Plaintiffs argued that it had to be determined that a certification test measures material taught before one addresses the issue of the match between items and the domain.

Until recently in education content validity was usually considered in terms of commercially marketed achievement tests. In this more traditional context, there were two evaluations of the test content that needed to be made: first, whether the items fit the *developer's* blueprint, and second, whether the test user would have selected the same blueprint (Cronbach 1971). Here the test developer and test user are distinct. The user is considering the purchase of a test developed for national use. In the context of using a test for certification purposes in education we have a different situation — one more analogous to the employment area. The agency that mandates the use of a test for certification often is, in fact, the test developer. While mandating authority may contract with a test company to build its certification test, as the developer it is ultimately responsible to see to it that the test is valid for the proposed use. Even when the agency selects a test from a commercial source, the test must be justified as appropriate for certification. At the same time the mandating authority is also the test user; old and comfortable distinctions between test developer and test user are blurred. As is often the case in the employment setting, separation of the test developer from the test user, (or of development from use) makes little sense. In short, the developer must justify the test domain in terms of test use — be it selection for employment or educational certification. In this regard, the Fifth Circuit's decision that a certification test must measure things taught in the schools seems to mirror court decisions that tests in employment selection measure important aspects of the job.

Another aspect of the literature on validity in the employment setting that has implications for certification testing has been the insistence there that test validity is concerned with the correctness of interpretations, descriptions, or decisions made from test scores. Several writers have pointed out that *content* validation, on the other hand, traditionally focused on test items, or test forms — that is, on test construction rather than on scores or interpretations from them (Messick 1975; Guion 1978*a*, 1978*b*, 1980; Cronbach 1980*c*). "Content validity contributes to the basic meaning only insofar as it provides assurance of care and competence in test construction" (Guion 1977*b*, p. 410). A demonstration that a certification test has content validity is not sufficient to justify many of the inferences associated with such tests. Inferences are often made about competence, functional literacy, mastery, ability to survive as adults, and so forth. Failure to reach the cut score on a certification test that can be shown to be related to instruction, or adequate opportunity to learn, does not by itself justify inferences that the pupil is incompetent, functionally illiterate, lacking basic skills, and so on. Such constructs are not dichotomous but continuous variables; such inferences can only be justified after ruling out competing explanations for low scores (Messick 1975, 1980*a,* 1980*b,* 1981).

While curricular or instructional relatedness in the educational setting is somewhat analogous to job relatedness in the employment setting, the analogy is far from perfect. The Uniform Guidelines on Employee Selection Procedures (EEOC) (United States Equal Employment Opportunity Commission 1978) state that to demonstrate the content validity of a selection procedure a user should:

> . . . show that the behavior(s) demonstrated in the selection procedure provides a representative sample of the behavior(s) of the job in question or that the selection procedure provides a representative sample of the work product of the job (p. 38302).

This implies that in the test materials, stimulus and response should not depart substantially from the stimulus and response mode in the job situation. Further, it implies that the test samples the critical elements of the job domain. In other words, the test is a sample rather than a sign; one is interested in the behavior manifested by the test performance in its own right rather than as a sign of some other behavior (Lennon 1956). Guion (1978*b*), discussing content validity, describes this close relationship between the stimulus and response associated with the test and the domain this way:

> If the whole domain is called Y, and the part is X, then X and Y are the same variables, that is, X is a *sample,* not a *function,* of Y (p. 500).

When trying to apply Guion's logic or the EEOC definition to the Fifth Circuit's finding about the validity of certification tests, one immediately runs into problems. It would be nice, for example, to be able to adapt the EEOC description of content validity to include a curricular and instructional aspect as follows: to demonstrate the content validity of an educational certification test the developer/user should show that the behavior(s) demonstrated in the certification procedure(s) provides a representative sample of the behaviors actually taught at the particular level of education in question. Unfortunately, however, such a determination would not be as straightforward as in the employment setting. First, the principal duties associated with jobs like those of police or fire officers are relatively uniform from one city or town to the next. Curriculum and instruction are not nearly as uniform among districts nor, within districts, among teachers teaching the same course or subject. Curriculum and instruction are more complex and more difficult to analyze than any particular job. Second, in the employment setting one should show that the test items represent, in proper proportion, the critical aspects of the job. However, the case of an MCT built for certification, the key determination to be made is whether or not the test content is adequately covered by either the curriculum (cf. Calfee Chapter 4) or by instruction (cf. Leinhardt Chapter 7), not that the curriculum or instruction are adequately covered or represented by the test.

In its decision, the Fifth Circuit explicitly distinguished between content and curricular validity but only implicitly between those two and instructional validity. ("An important component of content validity is curricular validity defined by defendant's expert Dr. Foster [sic], as 'things that are currently taught.' "[14]) These three faces of validity are clearly distinguishable. Schmidt and his associates (cf. Chapter 6) describe the domains associated with content, curricular, and instructional validity. The appropriate domain for content validity is a set of instructional objectives. For curricular validity, the domain is the curricular materials, textbooks, workbooks, and so on, used in the schools. For instructional validity, the domain of interest is the instruction actually delivered. (The reader is referred to Schmidt *et al.*, Chapter 6 for a discussion of the relationships among the three domains.)

Given the nature of these three distinct domains, it makes sense to talk about the test being *representative* of the objectives domain but not of the other two. The curricular and instructional domains are too large and complex to think of building an MCT that would be representative. To insist on a requirement of representativeness could limit both domains to that which is measured by the test. Of course, if the test has important sanctions associated with it, a serious danger is that the test narrows and confines both curriculum and instruction to those things measured by the test (Madaus and Macnamara 1970; Madaus and Airasian 1977; Madaus and McDonagh 1979; Madaus and Greaney 1982).

Curricular or instructional validity of a test is judged not on how well the test represents the curriculum or instruction but instead on the basis of whether or not the students had sufficient opportunity to learn (cf. Schmidt *et al.*, Chapter 6). That is, curricular or instructional validity involves a determination *not* that test is representative but that the test material is covered by either the curriculum or by instruction.

Finally, to use Guion terminology, the *X* that represents the stimulus and response associated with an achievement test is not necessarily a sample of the instructional domain *Y;* it may instead be a function of *Y*. This is particularly true for the multiple-choice format; used primarily because such tests can be machine-scored, an important consideration in any statewide testing program. A great deal of teaching involves getting pupils to supply answers rather than select them, produce a written passage rather than recognize errors in one presented, and read material and put it in their own words rather than read a passage and choose an answer that describes its meaning. This is not to imply that the multiple-choice format is not useful, but instead to point out that many instructional objectives can be measured through methods more directly connected to teaching and learning.

The point is that the appropriateness of using a particular mode of assessing an educational objective or skill needs to be validated against other modes of assessment.

One negative aspect associated with certification tests is that the testing mode often dictates teaching and study. For example, in a number of states instructional material or worksheets increasingly take the form of multiple-choice exercises. There are even commercially available materials that coach students to pass test items similar to those found in some MCTs. These practices are one of the consequences of certification testing that must be considered before a decision is made to proceed. Such practices can seriously narrow instruction, and while they might help to raise substantially the numbers falling above the cut score on a test consisting of similar exercises, the actual skills or constructs or interest might not in fact be substantially improved. The problem is that test-taking exercises can displace instruction geared to developing a more generalized application of the skills in question. (Ct. Calfee Chapter 4, and Shuy Chapter 11 for a further discussion of the problems associated with teaching to the test.)

This excursion through the literature on content validity shows that while there was consensus in the measurement community that content validity involved a match between the test items and the test domain, there was always some ambivalence over what constituted the domain. Over the years, the domain for achievement tests was identified in the educational literature — sometimes explicitly, sometimes implicity — with what was taught. More often, however, it was explicitly linked to instructional intent. This ambivalence deepened when employment testing borrowed content validity from educational measurement. The *Standards,* particularly the 1974 emphasis on employment testing, clouded the meaning of content validity further by failing to discuss specifically the issue of the relevance of the test domain to either the job domain in employment or to the curricular or instructional domains in education.

The content validity of achievement tests throughout most of the literature — in the *Technical Recommendations* and in the *Standards* — was described in terms of developing teacher-made tests or selecting standardized tests. It took the *Debra P.* trial to wrench content validity into the arena of educational certification. Experts for the state argued that based on the 1974 *Standards,* content validity was the only validity at issue; these experts maintained that content validity was limited to showing that there was a match between the items and the test domain — for example, the educational objectives defined by Florida. Plaintiffs countered that first there needed to be a determination that the test domain as defined by Florida was correct in terms of the decision to be made — for example, award or denial of diploma. They argued that the objective should have been taught and, further, that the construct validity of the test needed to be evaluated.

It took the cauldron of the courts to bring the issues surrounding certification testing into clear distillation; fundamental fairness required that such a test measure things actually taught. The court made explicit what had been implied in some discussions of content validity — namely, that an achievement test should measure things taught.

Content, curricular, and instructional validity have always been conceptually separable. This is not to say that they were always clearly separated in the literature. In fact, the curriculum and instrucational facets were overshadowed by content validity. The more recent literature on validity reminds us that all three facets contribute to a determination of validity only insofar as they reflect on the meaning of the *scores,* the inferences from the *scores,* or the correctness of the decisions made from the *scores.* Validity inheres in the test scores and use of scores, not in the items themselves. In the case of MCT for certification, all three facets speak to the fairness of the decision about an individual; therefore, all are relevant, along with other logical and empirical evidence, to an evaluation of the test's validity.

The Fifth Circuit saw as the heart of the matter the fairness of the test in terms of its proposed use. The court, however, did not address the question how such a determination was to be made either on average, or for an individual — only that it must be made. The court has turned the ''how'' back to the educational and measurement communities. The third section of this chapter, and the remaining chapters, offer specific suggestions on what might be done and by whom. Before turning to these suggestions, however, there are several additional issues related to MCT that need to be considered in any determinations of the test's validity.

MCT Programs: Issues Related to Test Validity

There are several issues endemic to MCT programs that need to be considered in any discussion of the validity of the test itself. These issues impinge upon validity related to the genesis of such programs, the populations at risk in such programs, the level of schooling involved, what the tests try to measure, the belief that the tests give diagnostic information, and the inferences people attempt to make from a MCT score.

The Genesis of MCT Programs

The movement is based in essence on the perception that proficiency in basic skills in this country is declining; that pupils are being promoted from grade to grade solely on the basis of seat time; and that pupils are receiving high school diplomas without having the skills necessary to survive in society. These perceptions are based in part on complaints from businesses, colleges, and the military that disturbing numbers of high school graduates lack both literacy and numeracy skills — that graduates cannot fill out applications correctly, read directions, write letters, or perform basic calculations (Lerner 1981*a,* 1981*b;* Madaus 1981). If it is assumed that most children should and can master these minimal skills, then significant numbers of children, particularly among the poor and minorities, were ill served by the instruction they received.

There was little that policymakers could do to reform instruction. It was impossible to mandate a better technology of instruction, assuming one were available. Instead, policymakers turned to an available, well-developed, and relatively cheap technology — testing — to solve the problem. The test became an administrative mechanism in a policy aimed at improving basic skills. By mandating that all pupils must pass a test in order to receive a high school diploma, the issue of dealing directly with instruction is effectively sidestepped. Students are held accountable and history shows that when the penalties associated with failing a certification test are severe enough, instruction and study will adjust to prepare pupils to pass it (Madaus and Airasian 1977; Madaus and McDonagh 1979; Madaus and Macnamara 1970).

The test becomes a coercive device to influence both the curriulum and instruction (Benjes, Heubert, and O'Brien 1980). If there is fear that the diploma will be denied or promotion refused, then this hobgoblin will bully the instructional delivery system into line. The test, rather than being an acolyte serving instruction, becomes an engine driving it. The test was also seen as a coercive device to motivate lazy or recalcitrant students. To paraphrase Dr. Johnson, there is nothing like the threat of denying a diploma to concentrate the mind wonderfully. The policy of MCT implicitly assumes therefore that an effective educational program, and attainment of proficiency in the basic skills on the part of individuals, depend upon the machinery for diploma denial (McClung 1979) —an assumption contradicted by the school effectiveness literature (Austin 1981; Madaus, Airasian, and Kellaghan 1980).

Further, the policy assumes that the testing technology is sufficient to the task. The validity of this assumption has been called into question by the National Academy of Education's (1978) Committee on Testing and Basic Skills, which concluded in part:

> Any setting of state-wide minimum competency standards for awarding the high school diploma — however understandable the public clamor which has produced the current movement and expectation — is basically unworkable, exceeds the present measurement arts of the teaching profession, and will create more social problems than it can conceivably solve . . .

> The effort to determine and assure minimum competency standards for high school graduation will . . . fail of its own weight, for the scaffolding of existing test designs is too weak to carry such an emotionally-laden and ambiguous burden. Continuing extensive efforts and funds in this direction is wasteful and takes attention away from the major tasks of improving out schools (p. 9).

There is another problem associated with the reasoning that underlies the enactment of many MCT programs — namely, that the sanctions that propel the
program are directed primarily at students. The Fifth Circuit's decisions require
that the test measure that which has actually been taught, which in turn implies that

> all persons involved in the educational system should bear responsibility for improving it;
> students, who have the least power to protest and the least power to alter the quality of
> public education, should not be forced to bear alone the blame for educational short-
> comings (Benjes, Heubert, and O'Brien 1980, p. 539).

Underlying the use of MCT results as an administrative mechanism in a policy of
basic skills improvement is the unexamined assumption that test performance is an
appropriate indicator of the extent and quality of service provided by the schools,
of the quality of teaching, and of the skills and knowledge acquired by pupils
(Lipsky 1979). Donald Campbell's warning is relevant here:

> The more any quantitative social indicator is used for social decision-making, the more
> subject it will be to corruption pressures and the more apt it will be to distort and corrupt
> the social processes it is intended to monitor (1975, p. 35).

Holmes (1911), writing in the context of using public examinations in Great
Britain, recognized the danger later articulated by Campbell:

> Whenever the outward standard of reality (examination results) has established itself at
> the expense of the inward, the ease with which worth (or what passes for such) can be
> measured is ever tending to become in itself the chief, if not sole, measure of worth. And
> in proportion, as we tend to value the results of education for their measurableness, so we
> tend to undervalue and at last to ignore those results which are too intrinsically valuable to
> be measured (p. 128).

Despite reservations about the wisdom of using MCTs for certification, such
programs are nevertheless mandated. They have symbolic or emblematic value,
providing policymakers with reassurances that the goal of improving basic skills
will be met, thereby deflecting the criticism that led to the policy in the first place
(Lipsky 1979). The problem is that the test is mandated without an accompanying
statewide curriculum or syllabus. MCT programs are not geared to specific
academic subject areas like algebra, history, physics, and so on, as is the case with
external examinations in Great Britain and in Ireland. Messick (1979) has commented that one of the sources of confusion in interpreting MCT scores derives
from the educational program in which the concept is embedded; however, the real
problem is precisely that MCT programs are too often *not* embedded in any
educational program. This is particularly true for programs of the secondary level.
As Calfee puts it (cf. Chapter 5), policymakers have put the cart squarely in front
of the horse — that is, the test before the educational program.

Given a common statewide test without a common syllabus, an evaluation of
the fairness of the test must involve a determination of another type of validity

related to a determination of curricular and instructional validity — namely, external validity (Cronbach 1980*b*, 1980*d*). To what degree is the test a fair measure of what is taught across the various school districts within a state, and, within a district, across the various schools? During the first few years of the program, it will be difficult to generalize about the MCTs' curricular and instructional validity. Predictably, the curriculum and instruction in many districts will not cover all the things measured by the test. As the program begins to bite, however, the curriculum and instruction will almost certainly adjust to prepare the pupils for the test, thereby making it simpler to show that the test has the necessary curricular and instructional validity within each district.

This concession to external validity can be a mixed blessing. The danger is that the test can distort the process it was meant to improve (Campbell 1975). For example, Mathew Arnold, commenting on the 1863 revised code in England, described it as:

> . . . A game of mechanical contrivance in which teachers will and must learn how to beat us, it is found possible by ingenious preparation to get children through the revised code examination in reading, writing and ciphering without their really knowing how to read, write and cipher (Sutherland 1971, p. 52).

In this country, in 1888 E. E. White, the Superintendent of Schools in Cincinnati, after surveying districts which used written exams for promotion decisions concluded:

> The tests have perverted the best efforts of teachers and grooved their instruction; they have occasioned and made well-nigh imperative the use of mechanical and rote methods of teaching; they have occasioned cramming and the most vicious habits of study . . . they have tempted both teachers and pupils to dishonesty (p. 518).

There are indications that this narrowing of instruction is already taking place in states with MCT certification programs. Testimony at the 1981 National Institute of Education (NIE) Clarification Hearings on MCT included a great deal of testimony that in many places teaching had been replaced by test preparation. This was particularly true in so-called remedial programs designed to help those who initially failed the test. The NIE hearing also demonstrated that eventually the percentage of pupils passing MCTs rises dramatically. When the pass rate goes up dramatically, one of two things happens: Either the issue of test fairness becomes moot since almost everyone passes, or there is a clamor on the part of segments in the community to make the test more difficult.

Populations at Risk in MCT Programs

Despite the unhappiness over basic skills attainment in our schools, the vast majority of pupils pass MCTs on the first try. However, about 20 percent of the pupils, most of whom have long-standing academic problems, are at risk. These pupils tend to be poor or members of a minority group. A determination that these pupils at risk have had a fair opportunity to learn the material tested is most important. Joseph Pedulla has suggested that validation efforts center on these pupils and that they be monitored and tracked very carefully. In evaluating the curricular or instructional validity of the test for these pupils, remedial programs need to be viewed with suspicion. A pupil should not have to fail a test in grade 10 or 11 to receive proper instruction. Further, as noted earlier, such remedial programs often consist of merely giving pupils practice taking multiple-choice exercises modeled after those on the test. While such coaching may indeed push many pupils over the magic cut score, it probably does little to improve their basic skills.

The Level of Schooling and MCT Programs

Most statewide certification programs are aimed at high school graduation, while most local programs are geared to the grade-to-grade promotion. Haney (Chapter 3) and Calfee (Chapter 4) describe the problems associated with secondary level programs in some detail and the reader is referred to these chapters for a further discussion. Suffice it to say here that instruction at the high school level is not organized around basic skills but instead around specific subject areas and is further differentiated by tracks (that is, accelerated, college level, business, technical, and so forth). The organization of American high schools therefore complicates the problem of establishing the curricular and instructional validity of state-mandated basic skills tests used as a graduation requirement.

What MCTs Measure

We have already noted that the high schools do not specifically teach basic skills so the test is not defined by a specific course. The relevant experiences that a student has had in algebra I, or American history, can be more easily identified than the experiences that are relevant when the test is trying to measure the application of basic skills to the real world situations or basic survival skills or functional literacy. When a test in grade 6 measures basic skills taught at that grade level, the test is an achievement test. But if in the eleventh grade the test measures basic skills taught in the sixth grade the test may in fact be an aptitude test. MCTs used at grade 11 are generally measuring older learning, making it more difficult to establish the curricular and instructional validity of the test.

Popham and Lindheim (1981) argue that if the test domain is described in generalities it should be relatively easy to match the domain to curriculum and instruction, but if the test domain is spelled out with great care and specificity, it will be more difficult to find a curricular and instructional match. However, the level of specificity of the *domain definition* is a separate issue from the level of transferability of the skill or construct the test is trying to measure. The more general and transferable the skills, the harder it may be to match them with any specific course or with any specific instruction. Tenopyr (1977) points out that licensing or certification tests for employment are often treated as pure achievement tests. They purport to assure prospective employees, or the public, that a person has the minimum skills needed to practice the trade or profession. However, such an assurance has a predictive aspect; those not possessing the minimum skills will do a poorer job than those who do. Similarly, MCTs are often treated as if they were pure achievement tests when, in fact, there is an implicit predictive cast to interpretations made on the basis of test performance — that is, the student does not possess the skills necessary to function successfully in society. These implicit and explicit predictive claims associated with MCTs need to be evaluated empirically. This is an aspect of validity associated with MCTs that is often ignored.

The Diagnostic Use of MCTs

Endemic to many MCT programs is an implicit assumption that such tests are diagnostic and that pupils who fail an MCT can be given proper remediation. Using MCT results to place a pupil in a remedial class involves a prediction about the performance of the student — that is, as a result of the placement the student basic skills will improve. However, at best, a MCT merely categorizes an individual as falling below a predetermined cut score. The test does not describe "the process by which learning facility and disability proceed in a given individual so that it is possible to describe developmental treatment if necessary (Gordon and Terrell 1981, p. 1170). Glaser (1981) further reminds us that "there is a little empirically derived and conceptually understood relationship between test score information and specific instruction activity" (p. 924). MCTs do not guide specific instructional practice except, as we have already noted, to narrow instruction to test preparation through *repeated* exposure of pupils to similar multiple-choice exercises.

If the MCT is publicized as having a diagnostic remedial dimension it would need to test all of the components that go into the skills measured. Further, after a pupil fails a MCT there should be individual assessment by trained specialists (Cleary, Humphreys, Kendrick, and Westman 1975). Both ingredients would add a great deal of expense to any MCT program; it is not surprising, therefore, that they are absent.

Inferences From MCT Results

A final issue that needs to be considered in evaluating the validity of a MCT program relates to the inferences that people make from these tests. If a pupil fails an MCT, a common inference is that he or she is incompetent; if a pupil fails a test that purports to measure skills that are needed to survive as an adult, then he or she does not have adult survival skills. Messick (1975, 1980*b*, 1981) points out that such inferences first require the elimination of a number of plausible rival hypotheses that might explain a low test score. There can be any number of cognitive, motivational, attitudinal, affective, health, nutritional, social, and ecological reasons for poor performance that would have to be ruled out before making such inferences (Scarr 1981; Gordon and Terrell 1981). The whole psychodynamics of the testing situation can also influence performance (Loevinger 1957; Scarr 1981).

> [S]ensitivity to these factors becomes especially important if assessment seeks to determine not just whether a particular criterion of performance is met, but also how it is met or why it is not met. In a society committed to the democratization of opportunity, or simply to the optimal development of all its human resources, answering these latter questions becomes an appropriate goal of assessment (Gordon and Terrell 1981, p. 1170).

The problem of the inference one makes from an MCT is confused further by what Messick (1980*b*, 1981) calls compounding of the assessment models — that is, interpreting a test score in terms of *minimum competency* in a *basic skill* like *reading comprehension:*

> The three components of minimum competency, basic skills, and reading comprehension tap into different nomological networks, leading to confusion as to which nomological network to reference (or which part of a composite network) as well as to confusion about the kinds of evidence needed for the construct validity of the compound interpretation (1981, p. 16).

Nomological networks, construct validity, and inference apart, the names associated with MCTs need to be very carefully considered. There can be great harm associated with the choice of a particular test name. Judge Carr's remarks (Appendix A) on the Functional Literacy Test in Florida illustrate this danger:

> What is functional literacy to one person may not be functional literacy to another person, but it is clear that the term ''functional illiterate'' has a universally negative inference and connotation. While ''illiteracy'' is itself a negative and impact ladened word, ''functional illiteracy'' further compounds these implications by focusing on the individual's inability to operate effectively in society. The categorizing of an individual without reference to a specific standard can be detrimental and debilitating without justification. As one of the Plaintiff's experts comments, students who fail the functional literacy test perceive of themselves as ''global failures.'' Another of the Plaintiff's experts testified

that the biggest flaw in the Florida program was its name alone. The Court is in complete agreement. Beyond the economic and academic implications of failure on the test the stigma associated with the term functional illiteracy is the most substantial harm presented (p. 258).

In the minds of "consumers, users, and victims" a test name, or a test construct name can take on quite different meaning from that intended by the test developer (Carroll 1980, p. 26). Therefore, in naming a test to be used as part of the certification process in the schools, the choice should be made with an eye toward any potentially negative and damaging connotations (Carroll 1980; Messick 1981). Putting the words "functional literate" in parentheses will not solve the problem; nor will giving the test a totally nondescript name like the State Student Assessment Test-II. A neutral name that *nonetheless* conveys meaning such as a test of basic skills in reading, mathematics, or writing is preferable.

All of these issues need to be considered in any assessment of the validity of a MCT used as a graduation or promotion requirement. Much of what was discussed previously involves a consideration of the consequences of using an MCT this way. Such consequential evidence should be evaluated before a decision is made to proceed with the program (Messick 1980*b*, 1981). However, since many programs are enacted without such consideration, these issues should be addressed as part of any ongoing evaluation. The final section of this chapter describes specific steps that state departments of education and local educational authorities can take to evaluate curricular and instructional validity.

What Can Be Done to Evaluate Curricular and Instructional Validity? Tasks for the State Department of Education and The Local Education Authorities

What practical steps can a state department of education (SEA) or a local educational authority (LEA) take to ensure that a test mandated for certification meets the court's requirement that it be a fair measure of what was taught? What evidence should parents or advocate groups concerned with children and their rights reasonably ask for, and expect to receive, when they attempt to evaluate an MCT program used for graduation or promotion decisions? In the following pages, we will attempt to answer these questions in outline form, relying heavily on material in subsequent chapters and on transcripts of previous discussions. The reader is referred throughout to these subsequent chapters and/or to other sources for more details.

Some caveats are in order. First, my starting point is a decision by the state or local authority to use an MCT as a graduation or promotion requirement. Outlining the steps that might be followed to show that a certification test has sufficient content, curricular, and instructional validity should not be taken as an endorsement of such a decision, nor of such programs. Before making such a decision, serious consideration should be given to the consequences of such testing and the kinds of test interpretations that might be made (Messick 1981). At the very least, the ancient medical admonition *primus non nocere* — first of all, do no harm — should be satisfied. Given the important uncompromising individual decisions to be made on the basis of these test scores, and the possible impact of the test and its associated sanctions on the curriculum and on teaching, the risk both for individuals and the schools needs to be carefully considered.

While test performance can play a legitimate part in making certification decisions, it should never be used by itself. Failing an MCT should trigger a review of a student's abilities; the results of a single episodic test should not result in automatic retention in grade or denial of diploma. Other information should be used by teachers and administrators in conjunction with the test scores in making such important decisions. These decisions should be the result of a professional's judgment informed by all available data. The decisions should not be a fait accompli based on a fallible test score. This concern is doubled-edged: Among students who "pass" the test (false positives), there may be some who might benefit from retention in grade or remediation, as indicated by other information.

This position may be considered naive for at least two reasons. First, a distrust of teacher judgments about pupil ability has been one important motivation behind the institution of MCT programs. Altogether too many pupils have been promoted solely on the basis of seat time, without mastering important skills, and this practice needs to change; but the teachers and administrators are nevertheless the ones who need to make decisions about promotion and graduation. Not to do so is to have their professional status diminished. Second, the so-called trigger mechanism may not work, may not result in the needed review of student abilities. The seductive administrative convenience of using only the test score may be too strong to resist. In New Jersey, where such a trigger mechanism is part of the formal policy, the review seldom takes place. Instead, falling below the cut score automatically results in the pupils' being pulled out of their regular class and put in a separate remedial program (NIE 1981).

A second caveat is that each of the following procedures suggested has difficulties, limitations, flaws, or drawbacks associated with it. No single suggestion taken alone is sufficient. However, collectively, they would certainly constitute a good faith effort to document the fairness of the program, and the content, curricular, and instructional validity of the test.

A third caveat is that a state-level program is assumed here in outlining the steps that might be taken to gather different kinds of complementary and supplementary evidence on test validity. This approach was taken for the sake of convenience. It permits a discussion of the respective roles of the SEA and LEA in the process.

However, what follows is also applicable to an MCT program designed and put in place by an LEA. The LEA would simply assume the tasks assigned to the SEA.

The final caveat concerns the point that in adhering to the following steps, the SEA with help from the LEAs, is validating not only the test but the entire certification process. Such an evaluation involves not just the gathering of data to support the program and the test (Cronbach 1980*a,* 1980*b,* 1980*c,* and 1980*d*). Counter interpretations, arguments of critics, or challenges to the program or test that appear credible to others should be seriously investigated (Cronbach 1980*b*). Cronbach reminds us that validation is forensic as well as investigative and offers this sound advice:

> Professionals who think of their work as scientific and objective are pained by references to consensus, persuasion, and plausible reasoning. The bad news is that we will not achieve unequivocal, perfect evidence of validity. The good news is that no one expects or demands it, save as a rhetorical ploy. The world turns on judgmental weighing of uncertainties (1980*b,* p. 45).

Funding the investigation of plausible challenges to a statewide MCT certification program may cause some state department officials a serious problem. They are often charged with implementing legislation or a state board of education policy. The immediate job is to get the program into operation within the time and budget restraints written into the legislation or policy. There is little room to struggle with the fallibility of the program.

There is another reality with which SEA officials must deal. The MCT program is often viewed by policymakers as a panacea — a way to restore standards, give meaning to the diploma, eliminate promotion based on seat time, motivate recalcitrant students, and ensure that students have adequate command of the basic skills before they leave school. All of these are laudatory goals. Given a belief that something must be done to correct what is viewed as an intolerable situation, and given the personal investment by those behind the program, it is psychologically difficult to consider spending money to investigate plausible arguments from critics or to seek out the faults in the test or the program. It takes no small degree of courage for civil servants to argue the need for such studies with legislative or policy bodies. It takes an unusual degree of foresight and an absence of smugness to fund such efforts.

These caveats provide a necessary background for the steps to be outlined. It should be noted that the state department of education should have the responsibility to develop a systematic audit trail. This audit trail, which is analogous to a test manual, permits concerned outsiders to evaluate the fairness of the entire process. Developing such an audit trail involves defining clearly the specific tasks that the state department will itself undertake and those it will delegate to the LEAs. With regard to tasks of the LEAs, the state department should structure the tasks so that districts can do work themselves or collaborate with other districts without the need to hire private contractors. This requirement means that the state must develop a program to train district personnel to gather, analyze, and document the necessary information. Further, the state department needs to monitor the work of the LEAs in the validation process.

An important issue that needs to be faced squarely is who must assume the costs of work done by the LEAs. There are costs in dollars, personnel time, and effort when LEAs take part in the validation of a MCT program enacted by the state. Failure to consider these costs could cause great hardship, not to mention resentment. There are nine steps in the process as follows.

1. The SEA should develop a specific definition of the domain to be tested. The content, skills, and format limits of what will be tested must be clearly specified. (For an excellent discussion of domain specifications the reader is referred to Millman 1974.) The need for clear domain and item specifications came up repeatedly at the conference. There is an emphatic need for a description of the domain written in language understandable not only by professional educators, but by parents, students, and the general public. The SEA should see to it that representatives of the major groups affected by the program are involved in the process of domain definition. The manner in which these representatives are chosen should become part of the audit trail. How decisions were made, and by whom, regarding the definition of the domain and item specifications should also be part of the audit trail. Wiley (1981), in discussing the content specifications for the Scholastic Aptitude Test (SAT), makes an important point applicable to MCTs:

> The central issues concerning the role and importance of skills assessed do not lie with the content specifications . . . rather they lie with the openness and thoughtfulness with which the content decisions are made and a realization that these decisions are not merely technical, they are educational and political ones which reflect our conception of [education] and the role it plays in the society (p. 35).

If the state is to show that the test has content validity — that is, the items on the test represent the domain; and if the LEAs are to show that the test covered areas in their curriculum materials and textbooks; and if the local schools within the district are to show that the content of the test was actually taught, then it is essential that the test domain be clearly specified and understandable. (Cf. Schmidt et al., Chapter 6, for a discussion of these three aspects of test validity.)

2. The domain should be widely publicized. The SEA should make available items, or even a sample test, that should be disseminated by the LEAs to all parents and pupils affected by the program as well as to the general community. The audit trail should show that the LEAs have distributed the domain and sample items. The SEA should also require districts to hold meetings for parents and students to explain what will be tested, how and when it will be tested, and the consequences of failing the test. Clearly flagging and publicizing what is important and what will be tested is an essential part of the process (cf. Walker, Chapter 8; Pullin, Chapter 1; and Judge Carr's decision, Appendix A). Once the test has been administered several times, a tradition of past exams will develop (Madaus and McDonagh 1979); however, the flagging process cannot await the development of this tradition. There needs to be widespread, immediate dissemination of the domain specification, item specifications, and a sample test.

3. The SEA should document the steps taken to ensure that standards of good test development were followed. Several aspects of the test-development process need additional comment. Test items should be piloted and then pretested on appropriate populations. These tryouts help to determine how the linguistic meaning of the items may vary among different populations. How the items are handled by pupils thought to be at risk should be determined by having such students "think out loud" when answering. Such a procedure will give the test developer insight into the students' thought processes and reveal how some students can get the wrong answer for perfectly logical reasons or the right answer for wrong reasons (cf. Shuy, Chapter 11).

Hills and Denmark (1978) worked closely with pupils to see why they missed items on the math portion of Florida's SSAT-II (Functional Literacy Test [FLT]). They concluded in part, "that students simply were not learning adequately how to deal with practical problems by translating the wording of the problem situations into an orderly sequence of mathematical operations" (p. 44). Their work is similar to Brown and Burton's (1978) analyses of why pupils get arithmetic items wrong and why teachers have difficulty remediating errors. They found that teachers often did not perceive the nature of the pupil's misconceptions, a prerequisite for successful remediation. Such analyses raise questions about instruction; if done before a certification test were to become operational, such analyses would call into question the test's instructional validity and point to changes in the instruction (cf. Haney, Chapter 3).

When field testing identifies populations at risk, an analysis of the difficulty level of the reading material to which such pupils have been exposed should be carried out. Because of interclass or intraclass grouping practices, use of out-of-level textbooks, or selfpacing, pupils may not have had sufficient practice in reading material of the same difficulty as that found in the test (Chall et al., Chapter 10). This is an area where the instructional validity for an individual becomes intertwined with instructional validity for groups of pupils. If field testing shows that students at risk are more apt to have experienced easier reading material than that associated with the test items, then questions need to be raised about the curricular and the instructional validity of the test for those individuals. (Cf. Chall, Chapter 10 for further discussion of the importance of knowing the reading difficulty of both the textbooks and the tests.)

4. The LEA should determine that the test is a fair measure of what is taught.
There are three components that need to be evaluated:

1. a content component
2. a curricular component
3. an instructional component

The content component is most easily evaluated by the SEA. This can be done in two complementary ways. The first is to obtain consensual judgments about the representativeness of the items relative to the domain appropriate for the given use. (Cf. Walker, Chapter 8, and Calfee, Chapter 4 on some problems associated with consensual judgments.) The second is to have two teams independently use the domain and item specifications to build separate tests. Any person's score on the two versions should be within the limits of sampling error "if the test content is fully defined by the written statement of the construction rule" (Cronbach 1971, p. 456; also see Walker, Chapter 8).

The state department should prepare a model of how LEAs might investigate curricular and instructional components of test validity. McClung (1979) has argued that the ultimate responsibility for evaluating the curricular and instructional validity of an MCT used for graduation decisions lies with the LEAs. MCTs are put in place without a statewide curriculum or syllabus. The choice of curriculum materials and the delivery of instruction are both left entirely to the local districts. The LEAs are therefore in the best position to evaluate the degree to which the state test has been covered by their curriculum materials and by instruction.

The SEA needs to develop a model for the LEAs to follow in matching the test with their curriculum and instruction. The SEA should field-test techniques suggested by Schmidt et al. (Chapter 6) and by Leinhardt (Chapter 7) to determine whether the teachers and administrators can be trained to use them. The SEA should provide the LEAs with the necessary training and assistance to implement the process.

The LEAs would need to examine textbooks, curriculum materials, and guides employed over a number of grades in order to document the scope and sequence involved in developing the basic skills measured by the MCT. The LEA would also need to show that the pupil had access to the material and that the material gave the pupil sufficient chance to practice the skills measured by the test reasonably close to the test date. The curricular match therefore involves evaluation of dimensions of depth of coverage, longitudinal coverage, and proximity of coverage.

The LEAs' task should be to show that the content and skills measured by the MCT are covered by the regular curriculum. In evaluating the curricular and the instructional validity of an MCT, remediation programs geared to the test should be viewed with suspicion, particularly at the secondary level. As we have noted, some so-called remediation programs simply involve teaching to the test. This kind of coaching "develops highly restricted skills that may be of little use in life activities . . . [and] . . . tends to concentrate on the particular sample of skills and knowledge covered by the test, rather than on the broader knowledge domain that the test tries to assess" (Anastasi 1981, p. 1089).

On examination, an LEA may find that a particular subset of the MCT items were not adequately covered either across the grades or with sufficient depth or recency. If this were to happen, then the LEA would need time to adjust its curriculum and instruction. Unless the state policy were flexible enough to accommodate this situation, pupils would be penalized unfairly. Any phase-in period should be designed to give LEAs sufficient time to adjust their curriculum and instruction to cover the material and skills measured by the MCT.

5. *The SEA should design a standard record-keeping system.* The record-keeping system would be used by all districts to document each pupil's relevant educational history. During discussions at the conference several points related to the need for a better system of monitoring and recording the progress of each pupil came up. First, the skills measured by MCTs, particularly at the high school level, form part of a continuous instructional strand extending back a number of years (cf. Venezky, Chapter 9, Walker, Chapter 8, and Haney, Chapter 3). Because of this, a developmental record of student progress is necessary. Second, pupils should be given sufficient time on task and repetition over the years to enable them to develop the skills in question (cf. Venezky, Chapter 9, Walker, Chapter 8, Haney, Chapter 3, and Linn, Chapter 5). The availability of such opportunities needs to be documented. Third, there should be continuous monitoring of a pupil's progress toward mastery of basics, including, when applicable, the use of skills in so-called real life situations. This monitoring and its results need to be documented. Finally, pupils having difficulty along the way should receive proper remediation, which also needs to be documented.

A standard cumulative record card would give districts a way to record, at appropriate grade levels, the student's mastery of those skills and objectives the MCT will eventually measure. The record card would be one piece of evidence — an individual's educational history — which when systematically shared with parents would help assure that pupils had an opportunity to learn the skills in question. A well-designed cumulative record system would give a clear picture of a student's strengths and weaknesses in particular areas for particular objectives or skills. With greater clarity than a single overall grade, such reports identify areas in which teachers and parents can help pupils improve. Further, the cumulative nature of record systems gives teachers in succeeding years information about the instructional and remedial needs of students (Bloom, Madaus, and Hastings 1981). Such a system should identify quite early pupils at risk and help assure that proper remediation is given long before these students sit for the certification test.

If at grade 11 or 12 the pupil failed the MCT and the cumulative record card showed mastery of all skills at each grade, and if alternative explanations for failure (for example, poor motivation, illness, anxiety, and so on) are ruled out, certain questions would have to be asked. Was the instruction appropriate? Did pupils have the necessary prerequisites to benefit from the instruction? Was the appraisal of performance along the way accurate? (South Carolina [1981] has developed a suggested record-keeping system to assure continuous monitoring of individual student progress in relation to that state's minimum standards for achievement in reading, math, and writing.)

Pupils transferring into the system would need careful consideration. An immediate assessment of their skills might be made and entered into the cumulative record. The closer the transfer to the time of the test, however, the more difficult it would be to assess the instructional validity of the test for such pupils.

If designed properly, the record-keeping system should not prove onerous; in a given year, entries should not be too numerous. The principal should be responsible for seeing that the record is kept accurately and that pupils falling behind receive the aid they need. The principal should also assess the validity of the record; if it indicates that a pupil has mastered the objective or skill in question, then other indicators should confirm this judgment.

The record-keeping tasks would be much easier if the MCT were given at the end of the elementary grades rather than at the end of high school. Basic skills are an integral part of the elementary curriculum and are taught there directly each year in more or less self-contained classrooms by one or two teachers. It is not clear which teacher at the secondary level would be responsible for keeping a record of student progress in basic skills.

6. *The SEA should conduct criterion-related validity studies of the MCT.* At the very least, the state department should collect data on how the MCT correlates with other tests purporting to measure similar skills. Most school districts have their own standardized testing program. How do the results on the MCT correlate with these measures? Teacher grades or independent assessments of their pupils on the skills measured by the MCT should also be correlated with the MCT scores (cf. Haney, Chapter 3). The Kansas Competency Testing Program is an excellent example of how such criterion-related studies can be managed statewide on a sampling basis (Poggio and Glasnapp 1980).

Criterion-related studies should also be designed to examine how well standardized tests, or other tests of basic skills, administered at earlier grades predict success on the MCT used at a later stage for graduation or promotion decisions. Such studies would allow the state and the LEAs to determine early in the process the degree to which current testing programs help identify pupils at risk. Scores on standardized tests and other tests of basic skills might be included as part of the statewide cumulative record system described previously.

7. *The SEA should analyze item-response patterns by districts, schools within a district, or by student characteristics, (for example, race, sex, curriculum tracks in high school, and so on).* After the test has been administered, a number of methods can be used to identify either students for whom the test is inappropriate or schools in which the curriculum or the instruction do not match the test content. These techniques offer the state department a powerful tool to look *ex post facto* at how items function across districts, or across schools within a district, and/or how uniform the instruction is across districts or schools relative to the items. (For a further discussion of the potential of pattern analysis of items see Chapter 5 by Linn; also Harnisch and Linn 1981; and Airasian and Madaus 1978).

Pattern analysis should also be used as a triggering mechanism. Schools or districts that have an unusually large number of failures on particular objectives should be inspected closely to see if the pupils had adequate opportunity to learn the material tested. If patterns of incorrect answers emerge — for example, a large percent of pupils in one district fail a certain type of item that pupils in another district pass — then several questions need to be asked by the SEA and LEA. Were the pupils taught the material? Did they receive enough instruction or time on task? Was the instruction too far removed from the testing time? Was the instruction appropriate?

8. *The SEA should plan and carry out a series of small-scale evaluations on the impact of the program on the curriculum and on teaching.* The impact of MCTs on what is taught and how it is taught should be undertaken. Further studies should be carried out to investigate whether performance on the MCT — particularly a gain in performance — is reflected in other indicators of the same constructs and skills.

9. *The SEA should set up a mechanism that allows students to question the accuracy of their scores and to see the test, their answer sheet, and the answer key.* Students should also be able to appeal any perceived irregularities in administering the test.

The SEA and each LEA share the responsibility of showing that a MCT used for graduation or promotion decisions is a fair measure of what was taught. However, the SEA should take the lead in providing the technical assistance needed by the LEAs to carry out their responsibilities. The SEA should provide models of what the LEAs are to do, along with necessary training to implement the models. In addition, the SEA needs to monitor, evaluate, and check the entire process both at the state and at the local level. The emphasis has been on ensuring that both the SEA and LEA leave an audit trail so that an evaluation can be made of the fairness of the process in general, and in individual cases. The preceding was an outline of what might be done. In the chapters that follow, the obligations of the SEA and LEA in determining the validity of the entire certification process are considered in more depth.

Notes

1. This observation was made by Christiane Citron during the conference.
2. Debra P. v. Turlington, 644 F.2d 397, 404 (5th Cir. 1981).
3. Hobson v. Hansen, 327 F. Supp. 844, 859 (D.D.C. 1971).
4. Debra P. v. Turlington, No. 78-892 Civ. T-C (M.D. Fla. July 12, 1979) at 2380.
5. 78-892 Civ. T-C at 2108.
6. Debra P. v. Turlington, 474 F. Supp. 244, 265 (M.D. Fla. 1979).
7. 644 F.2d at 405.
8. 644 F.2d at 405.
9. The recent report of the National Academy of Sciences (see Wigdor and Garner 1982) defines instructional validity quite differently from the way in which McClung defines it or from the way it is used in this book. In that report, instructional validity relates to the educational soundness of using ability tests to group or classify students or for individualizing instruction. In this definition, instructional validity relates to the use of tests to choose among alternative teaching programs the one most appropriate to a given student's mental traits or abilities and to assess current learning status as it relates to more complex learning tasks (p. 179). Thus instructional validity in this sense involves a predictive element not found in McClung or in the Fifth Circuit's sense. In the Fifth Circuit's conceptualization and as used in this book, instructional validity involves an evaluation of whether or not the material and skills measured by the test were covered by instruction.
10. NCMUE is now the National Council on Measurement in Education (NCME).
11. Debra P. v. Turlington, No. 78-892 (N-T M.D. Florida, January 18, 1982) at 6.
12. Firefighters Institute v. City of St. Louis, 616 F.2d 350 (8th Cir. 1980), *cert. denied sub nom.* United States v. City of St. Louis, 49 U.S.L.W. 3931 (June 15, 1981).
13. Guardian Association of New York v. Civil Service Commission, 630 F.2d 79 (2d Cir. 1980), *cert. denied,* 49 U.S.L.W. 3932 (June 15, 1981).
14. 644 F.2d at 405.

References

Airasian, P.W., and Madaus, G.F. "A Post Hoc Technique for Identifying between Program Differences in Achievement." *Evaluation Studies,* 1978, 4, No. 1, 1–3.

American Educational Research Association & National Council on Measurements Used in Education. *Technical Recommendations for Achievement Tests.* Washington, D.C.: 1955.

American Psychological Association. *Technical Recommendations for Psychological Tests and Diagnostic Techniques.* Washington, D.C.: 1954.

American Psychological Association. *Standards for Educational and Psychological Tests and Manuals.* Washington, D.C.: 1966.

American Psychological Association. *Standards for Educational and Psychological Tests.* Washington, D.C.: 1974.

Anastasi, A. *Psychological Testing.* 4th ed. New York: Macmillan Publishing Co., 1976.

Anastasi, A. "Coaching, Test Sophistication and Developed Abilities." *American Psychologist,* 1981, 36, No. 10, 1086–1093.

Austin, G.R. "Exemplary Schools and Their Identification." *New Directions for Testing and Measurement,* 1981, 10, 31–47.

Benjes, J., Heubert, J., and O'Brien, M. "The Legality of Minimum Competency Test Programs under Title VI of the Civil Rights Act of 1964." *Harvard Civil Rights & Civil Liberties Law Review,* 1980, 15, No. 3, 537–622.

Bersoff, D.N. "Testing and the Law." *American Psychologist,* 1981, 36, No. 10, 1047–1056.

Bloom, B.S., Englehart, M.D., Furst, E.J., Hill, W.H., and Krathwohl, D.R. *Taxonomy of Educational Objectives: Handbook I, Cognitive Domain.* London: Longmans Green & Co., 1956.

Bloom, B.J., Madaus, G.F., and Hastings, T.J. *Evaluation To Improve Learning.* New York: McGraw-Hill, 1981.

Brown, J.S., and Burton, R.R. "Diagnostic Models for Procedural Bugs in Basic Mathematical Skills." *Cognitive Science,* 1978, 2, 155–192.

Campbell, D.T. "Assessing the Impact of Planned Social Change." In G.M. Lyons, ed., *Social Research and Public Policies: The Dartmouth/OECD Conference.* Hanover, N.H.: Dartmouth College, Public Affairs Center, 1975.

Carroll, J.B. "Measurement of Abilities Constructs in Educational and Psychological Measurement." In A.P. Maslow, ed., *Construct Validity in Psychological Measurement: Proceedings of a Colloquium on Theory and Application in Education and Employment.* Princeton, N.J.: U.S. Office of Personnel Management and Educational Testing Service, 1980.

Cleary, A.T., Humphreys, L.G., Kendrick, S.A., and Westman, A. "Educational Uses of Tests with Disadvantaged Students." *American Psychologist,* 1975, 30, No. 1, 15–41.

Cronbach, L.J. "Test Validation." In R.L. Thorndike, ed., *Educational Measurement.* Washington, D.C.: American Council on Education, 1971.

Cronbach, L.J. "Panel Discussion in Cultural Issues." In A.P. Maslow, ed., *Construct Validity in Psychological Measurement: Proceedings of a Colloquium on Theory and Application in Education and Employment.* Princeton, N.J.: U.S. Office of Personnel Management and Educational Testing Service, 1980*a*.

Cronbach, L.J. "Selection Theory for a Political World." *Public Personnel Management,* 1980*b*, 9, 37–50.

Cronbach, L.J. "Validity on Parole: How Can We Go Straight?" In W.B. Schrader, ed., *Measuring Achievement Progress over a Decade. Proceedings of the 1979 ETS Invitational Conference in New Directions for Testing and Measurement.* San Francisco: Jossey-Bass Publishers, 1980*c*.

Cronbach, L.J., and associates. *Toward Reform of Program Evaluation.* San Francisco: Jossey-Bass Publishers, 1980*d*.

Cureton, E.E. "Validity." In E.F. Lindquist, ed., *Educational Measurement.* Washington, D.C.: American Council on Education, 1951.

Dunnette, M.D., and Borman, W.C. "Personnel Selection and Classification Systems." *Annual Review of Psychology,* 1979, 30, 477–525.

Ebel, R.L. "Obtaining and Reporting Evidence on Content Validity. *"Educational and Psychological Measurement,* 1956, 16, 294–304.

Feldhausen, J.F., Hynes, K., and Maes, C.A. "Is a Lack of Instructional Validity Contributing to the Decline of Achievement Test Scores:" *Educational Technology,* 1976, 16 No. 7, 13–16.

Furst, E.J. *Constructing Evaluation Instruments.* New York, London, and Toronto: Longmans Green & Co., 1958.

Glaser, R. "The Future of Testing: A Research Agenda for Cognitive Psychology and Psychometrics." *American Psychologist,* 1981, 36, No. 9, 923–936.

Gordon, W., and Terrell, M.D. "The Changed Social Context of Testing." *American Psychologist,* 1981, 36, No. 10, 1167–1171.

Green, B.F. "A Primer of Testing." *American Psychologist,* 1981, 36, No. 10, 1001–1011.

Greene, H., Jorgensen, A., and Gerberich, J. *Measurement and Evaluation in the Secondary School.* New York, London, and Toronto: Longmans Green & Co., 1943.

Greene, H., Jorgensen, A., & and Gerberich, J. *Measurement and Evaluation in the Secondary School.* New York, London, and Toronto: Longmans Green & Co., 1954.

Greenhouse, L. "Even the High Court Discovers That Not All the Facts Are in the Record." *New York Times.* February 21, 1982.

Guion, R.M. "Content Validity — The Source of My Discontent." *Applied Psychological Measurement,* 1977a, 1, No. 1, 1–10.

Guion, R.M. "Content Validity: Three Years of Talk — What's the action?" *Public Personnel Management,* 1977b, 6, 407–414.

Guion, R.M. "Content Validity in Moderation." *Personnel Psychology,* 1978a, 31, 205–213.

Guion, R.M. "Scoring of Content Domain Samples: The Problems of Fairness." *Journal of Applied Psychology,* 1978b, 63, No. 4, 499–506.

Guion, R.M. "On Trinitarian Doctrines of Validity." *Professional Psychology,* 1980, 11, No. 3, 385–398.

Harnisch, D.L., and Linn, R.L. "Analysis of Item Response Patterns: Questionable Test Data and Dissimilar Curriculum Practices." *Journal of Educational Measurement,* 1981, 18, No. 3, 133–146.

Hills, J.R., and Denmark, T. "Functional Literacy in Mathematics." Proposal submitted to the Florida State Department of Education, 1978.

Holmes, E.G.A. *What Is and What Might Be: A Study of Education in General and Elementary in Particular.* London: Constable & Co., 1911.

Lee, J.M. *A Guide to Measurement in the Secondary School.* New York, and London: D. Appleton Century Co., 1936.

Lennon, R.T. "Assumptions Underlying the Use of Content Validity." *Educational and Psychological Measurement,* 1956, 3, 294–303.

Lerner, B. "The Minimum Competency Testing Movement: Social, Scientific and Legal Implications." *American Psychologist,* 1981a, 36, No. 10, 1057–1066.

Lerner, B. "Vouchers for Literacy: Second Chance Legislation." *Phi Delta Kappan,* 1981b, 62, 252–255.

Linn, R.L. "Issues of Validity for Criterion-Referenced Measures." *Applied Psychological Measurement,* 1980, 4, No. 4, 547–561.

Lipsky, M. "Accountability in Urban Society." In S. Green, ed., *Accountability in Urban Society: Public Agencies under Fire.* Beverly Hills, Calif.: Sage Publications, 1979.

Loevinger, J. "Objective Tests as Instruments of Psychological Theory." *Psychological Reports,* 1957, 3, 635–694.

Loevinger, J. "Person and Population as Psychometric Concepts." *Psychology Review,* 1965, 72, No. 2, 143–155.

Madaus, G.F. "Miminum Competency Testing: A Critical Overview." Paper presented at the 46th Annual Education Conference of Educational Records Bureau, New York, October 1981. Mimeographed.

Madaus, G.F., and Airasian, P.W. "Issues in Evaluating Student Outcomes in Competency-Based Graduation Programs." *Journal of Research and Development in Education,* 1977, 10, No. 3, 79–91.

Madaus, G.F., Airasian, P.W., and Kellaghan, T. *School Effectiveness: A Reassessment of the Evidence.* New York: McGraw-Hill, 1980.

Madaus, G.F., and Greaney, V. *Competency Testing: A Case Study of the Irish Primary Certificate Examination.* Occasional Paper Series. Cambridge, Mass.: National Consortium on Testing, 1982.

Madaus, G.F., and Macnamara, J. *Public Examinations: A Study of the Irish Leaving Certificate.* Dublin: St. Patrick's College, Educational Research Centre, 1970.

Madaus, G.F., and McDonagh J. "Minimum Competency Testing: Unexamined Assumptions and Unexplored Negative Outcomes. In R. Lennon, ed., *Impactive Changes in Measurement: New Directions for Testing and Measurement.* New Directions, 1979, 3, 1–14.

McClung, M.S. "Are Competency Testing Programs Fair? Legal?" *Phi Delta Kappan,* 1978, 59, 397–400.

McClung, M.S. "Competency Testing Programs: Legal and Educational Issues." *Fordham Law Review,* 1979, 47, 652–712.

Messick, S. "The Standard Problems: Meaning and Values in Measurement and Evaluation." *American Psychologist.* 1975, 30, 955–966.

Messick, S. "Constructs and Their Vicissitudes in Educational and Psychological Measurement. In A.P. Maslow, ed., *Construct Validity in Psychological Measurement: Proceedings of a Colloquium on Theory and Application in Education and Employment.* Princeton, N.J.: U.S. Office of Personnel Management and Educational Testing Service, 1980*a.*

Messick, S. "Test Validity and the Ethics of Assessment." *American Psychologist,* 1980*b,* 35, No. 11, 1028–1055.

Messick, S. "Evidence and Ethics in the Evaluation of Tests." *Educational Research,* 1981, 10, No. 9, 9–20.

Millman, J. "Criterion-Referenced Measurement." In J. Popham, ed., *Evaluation in Education: Current Applications.* Berkeley, Calif.: McCutchan Publishing Corp, 1974.

National Academy of Education. *Improving Education Achievement: Report of the National Academy of Education Committee on Testing and Basic Skills.* Washington, D.C.: Assistant Secretary for Education, 1978.

National Institute of Education. *Transcript of Minimum Competency Testing Clarification Hearings, Washington, D.C., July 8–10, 1981.* Washington, D.C.: Alderson Reporting Co., 1981.

Neill, T.P. *Readings in the History of Western Civilization.* vol. 1. Westminster, Md.: The Newman Press, 1957.

Noll, V.H. *Introduction to Educational Measurement.* Boston: Houghton Mifflin, 1957.

Odell, C.W. *Traditional Examinations and New Type Tests.* New York and London: D. Appleton Co., 1938.

Poggio, J.P., and Glasnapp, D.R. *Report of Research Findings: The Kansas Competency Testing Program, 1980.* Lawrence, Kansas, University of Kansas, School of Education, Department of Educational Psychology and Research, December 1980.

Popham, J.W., and Lindheim, E. "Implications of a Landmark Ruling on Florida's Minimum Competency Test." *Phi Delta Kappan,* 1981, 63, No. 1, 18–20.

Ross, C.C., and Stanley, J.C. *Measurement in Today's Schools.* 3rd ed. New York: Prentice-Hall, 1954.

Ruch, G.M. *The Objective or New Type Examination: An Introduction to Educational Measurement.* Chicago, Atlanta, and New York: Scott-Foresman, 1929.

Scarr, S. "Testing *for* Children: Assessment and the Many Determinants of Intellectual Competence." *American Psychologist,* 1981, 36, No. 10, 1159–1166.

Shimberg, B. "Testing for Licensure and Certification." *American Psychologist,* 1981, 36, No. 10, 1138–1146.

South Carolina State Department of Education. "Basic Skills Assessment Program: A Suggested Record Keeping System." Columbia, South Carolina, Basic skills section Office of General Education, 1981.

Stanley, J.C., and Hopkins, K.D. *Educational and Psychological Measurement and Evaluation.* Englewood Cliffs, N.J.: Prentice-Hall, 1972.

Sutherland, G. *Elementary Education in the Nineteenth Century.* London: London Historical Association, 1971.

Task Force on Educational Assessment Programs. *Competency Testing in Florida: Report to the Florida Cabinet, Part I.* Tallahassee, Fla. 1979.

Taylor, E.F., and Willie, N.A. "Categorical Test Validation." Newton, Mass.: *Project TORQUE Education Development Center,* October 1979.

Tenopyr, M. "Content — Construction Confusion." *Personnel Psychology,* 1977, 30, 47–54.

U.S. Equal Employment Opportunity Commission, Civil Service Commission, U.S. Department of Labor, U.S. Department of Justice, "Uniform Guidelines on Employee Selection Procedures." *Federal Register,* August 1978, 25, 38290–38315.

Webster's Third New International Dictionary. Springfield, Mass.: G & C Merriam Co., 1976.

White, E.E. "Examinations and Promotions." *Education,* 1888, 8, 517–522.

Wigdor, A., and Garner, A. *"Ability Testing: Uses, Consequences, and Controversies."* Washington, D.C.: National Academy Press, 1982.

Wiley, D.E. "Vicious and the Virtuous: ETS and College Admissions." Unpublished manuscript. Chicago, Ill.: Northwestern University, 1981.

Woody, C., and Sangren, P.V. *Administration of the Testing Program.* New York: World Book Co., 1933.

Wrightstone, W.J., Justmen, J., and Robbins, I. *Evaluation in Modern Education.* New York: American Book Co., 1956.

3 VALIDITY AND COMPETENCY TESTS: *The* Debra P. *Case, Conceptions of Validity, and Strategies for the Future*

Walt Haney

Introduction

Both competency testing and test validity have been receiving considerable attention in recent months. But the relationship between the two remains unclear. Indeed, as more attention has focused on the issue of competency tests' validity, the more disagreement there appears to be among people billed as experts on testing and who might have been presumed to bring some coherent professional opinion to bear on the matter. But where the experts — given to usually abstract disputation — seem to have fostered complexity and provided more questions than answers, lawyers and judges — given more to dealing in the particulars of law and cases at hand — are producing some firm answers on the question of competency tests' validity. It remains uncertain whether the clash between the disputation of testing experts and the decision-making of the courts is consistently making for better law, but it is at least leading to more direct attention to practical issues of test validity. This chapter's purposes include the following:

1. To describe major points of dispute over competency test validity as evidenced in arguments in the *Debra P.* case.
2. To summarize how courts have made sense of such disputation in reaching their decisions.

3.   To suggest some of the ways in which the relationship between a test and what is covered in school might be conceived.

4.   To suggest some practical strategies for examining the validity of competency tests.

There are two reasons for concentrating on the *Debra P*. case. First, the Florida test that was the subject of the *Debra P*. case has probably received the closest judicial scrutiny of any current competency testing program, and certainly the most national publicity of any statewide competency testing program. Second, more testimony and documentation concerning the Florida test are available as a result of the *Debra P*. case than are available with respect to any other statewide competency test.

Who Said What about Validity in the *Debra P.* Case?

To determine who said what in the *Debra P*. case, expert testimony and a variety of documents submitted into the trial record — specifically, the portions of the trial transcript and documents collected together into two fat volumes of briefing papers by the Center for Law and Education for a seminar entitled *Minimum Competency Testing: A Case Study of the Florida Functional Literacy Examination,* in February and April 1980 — were reviewed. The briefing papers contain copies of transcripts of testimony by both plaintiffs' and defendants' expert witnesses on testing and test development and include documentary evidence as well.

For the purposes of this discussion, testimony on issues such as cut-score setting, bias, equating, and reliability are ignored. Such issues obviously do bear on the issue of validity, but the present discussion will focus only on testimony directly aimed at the validity issue.

The major characters offering testimony regarding validity were as follows. For the plaintiffs: George Madaus, John Walsh, Ann Cleary, and Peter Airasian. For the defendants, major witnesses on the validity issue were: William Mehrens, Thomas Fisher, and James Popham. Several other witnesses touched on test validity in the course of testimony on other issues (for example, Asa Hilliard testified on bias for the plaintiffs, and Sherry Rubenstein testified on test development for the defense), but for the sake of brevity, this chapter will concentrate on the arguments of the witnesses offering fuller testimony on the validity issue.

In the trial, the following eight different types of validity were referred to:

Construct validity
Content validity
Criterion-related validity
Concurrent validity

Predictive validity
Face validity
Curriculum validity
Instructional validity

Witnesses differed markedly in opinion as to the relevance of different forms of validity to the Florida test, the relationship among the different forms of validity, and the adequacy of evidence pertaining to them. Because the main points in contention dealt with construct, content, curriculum and instructional validity, we will dispense with the minor validity themes quickly. The only witness to give much attention to face validity was Fisher, who offered the following:

> There is a term in psychometric circles known as face validity. A test ought to look like what it's supposed to be. An item that is an application item to be attractive to the subject or to the student needs to have something that will catch his eye and be attractive. [2721.][1]

Fisher did not have much more to say about face validity, except to note that "in one of our test development operations, we had a retired Army officer who kept writing items related to how many mortar shells it would take to invade some island in the Pacific, and we didn't think that was particularly germane to the average high school student's sphere of interest [2721–2722.]."

Other types of validity that received relatively little attention were criterion-related validity, concurrent validity, and predictive validity. Concurrent and predictive validity are, of course, now widely acknowledged to be variants of criterion-related validity, and there was no dispute on this question in the *Debra P.* trial. There was, however, some dispute over the relevance of criterion-related validity to the Florida literacy test. This dispute was only a variation on a much larger theme — namely, the relevance of anything other than content validity to the Florida test. Let us turn to the larger validity issues under dispute in the *Debra P.* trial. The major points in dispute in terms of two questions are as follows:

1. Is any type of validity evidence other than content validity required for the Florida high school graduation test?
2. Is evidence pertaining to the match of test content with test specifications sufficient for showing content validity?.

In brief, answers to these questions were as follows:

1. Witnesses for plaintiffs: Yes
   Witnesses for defendants: No
2. Witnesses for plaintiffs: No
   Witnesses for defendants: Yes

The plaintiffs' and defendants' expert witnesses reasoned in the following manner. For the plaintiffs, Madaus testified that for a test such as the Florida one, "construct and content validity overlap," and "you can't separate the two" (1777). He maintained specifically that "Adequate validation of a test requires the integration of construct validity studies, criterion validity studies and content validity studies (1732)." Questioned as to his reaction concerning the validity evidence he had seen concerning the Florida high school graduation test, Walsh commented:

> I am distressed by the contention which I found so often in the literature dealing with the functional literacy test that content validity is the only type of validity which is relevant to a test of this type. I would seriously challenge the legitimacy of that statement . . . The concept of functional literacy itself is an almost perfect example of what we mean by a construct . . . Construct validation procedures should have been employed. [1526–1527.]

Cleary commented that "I could find nothing in the documents that I was given with respect to Florida to indicate that the curriculum had ever covered the things that were being assessed (1548)." In a similar vein, Airasian observed:

> . . . the justification that has been provided for this test, the validity of this test, the whole question of instruction whether kids have been exposed to the kinds of applications or similar kinds of applications has been neglected. (1822.)

Asked whether it is necessary in validating a criterion-referenced test like the Florida one that aims at measuring students' success in achieving certain instruction to look "not only at the test items themselves, but [also] to whether or not students actually received instruction sufficient to allow them to perform successfully on those items," Airasian answered simply, "that absolutely is essential (1822)."

Expert witnesses for the defense countered these arguments by maintaining that content validity evidence is the only form required for a test like the Florida test. Here, for example, is Mehrens' testimony on this point:

Q. Now with respect to validity, what kind of validity does an achievement test have to have?

A. An achievement test needs content validity. And I don't know if you wish me to expand as to . . .

Q. Well, how important would it be to demonstrate construct validity, predictability, or any other kind of validity with respect to achievement tests?

A. Well, achievement tests would not need predictive validity unless one wanted to use the results of that test to predict some subsequent performance. (2224–2225.)

Q. How important would it be to demonstrate construct validity with reference to the functional literacy test?

A. Well, under my premise that it is an achievement test, construct validity would not be that important. (2227.)

Similarly, Popham testified that content validity is "the principal type of validity that bears on this type of test. The other types of validity that are approved by the professions bear less relevance (3157)." Fisher said almost exactly the same thing, with only a minor wrinkle regarding face validity.

A.   I think the primary emphasis should be on the content validity of the test.

Q.   Is that the only kind of validity this test needs to have?

A.   As far as I'm concerned, it's the only kind it needs to have other than, as I mentioned, some people talk about face validity, which is generally not mentioned too much. (2743.)

So, in answer to the question, "Is any type of validity evidence other than content validity required for the high school graduation test?" plaintiffs' expert witnesses unanimously answered in the affirmative, but defendants' experts unanimously answered in the negative.

The only point of implicit agreement between both sets of experts was that content validity is very important with respect to a test like the Florida high school graduation test. This of course brings us to the question of what constitutes content valdity evidence. Witnesses for the state maintained essentially that the content validity of the Florida test was entirely satisfactory. The colloquy between Mehrens and the defense counsel on the issue of content validity follows.

Q.   Now with respect to the general area of content validity, would the test development process that was used there yield a content valid test as a measure of the skills and objectives and the standards, as adopted by the State Board of Education on the functional literacy examination?

A.   Well, yes. The procedures if followed would necessarily lead to a content valid test. Because content validity again speaks to whether the test is actually measuring those objectives. [2223.]

And slightly later:

Q.   Does the content validity of this test meet with acceptable standards of your profession?

A.   It would be my judgment that it does, yes, for reasons that I think I really explained with respect to following of the objectives. [2229.]

Another defense witness, Rubenstein, offered a similar interpretation of content validity in the following exchange:

Q.   What procedures are used to establish content validity for a test like this?

A.   Well, the content validity procedures are procedures which are, I believe, now well established in the field to be a matter of close analysis of the parameters to be provided by the specifications for the skill. [2636.]

Rubenstein went on to describe two steps for ensuring content validity: first, review by measurement specialists and subject-matter specialists, and second, statistical analysis using point biserial correlations to show whether "the way students respond to one of the items in the set is the same way in which they tended to respond to the others (2637)."

Defense witness Popham offered the following assessment of the content validity of the Florida test:

> The content validity of the test I would say is equal to or superior to the content validity found in typical achievement tests of this type. [3172.]

Expert witnesses for the plaintiffs took clear exception to those interpretations, arguing that content validity encompasses more than the relationship between test items and test specifications or objectives. Here is how Madaus addressed the issue:

> The content validity of a test, as I understand the issue the State is making is that all you have to show is that the items on the test adequately fit the specifications that you had for the test.
>
> Now that is not what is meant by content validity . . .
>
> That's part of it. But there are several prior questions. The first question is: Do you have the right domain? Do you have the right content to begin with?
>
> I mean if Florida had decided to build a test on open heart surgery to give to 11th graders and show that the items in the test matched the specifications, you wouldn't say that that had content validity for the purpose it's being used. [1733.]

Quoting the joint *Standards,* Madaus maintained that "any content-referenced interpretation should clearly indicate the domain to which one can generalize it (1771)." In Madaus's view, this prior question had not been adequately addressed in the process of developing the Florida test:

> But the question really becomes — the first question is: Is it the correct domain for the purpose we're using the test for? And the purpose you're using this test for is to certify the successful completion of secondary school.
>
> The McCarry Commission raises this question of whether it is the right domain. And they say, "No, it's not." Because they say the stuff was not taught in the schools adequately well recently and perhaps not at all. [1734.]

Other expert witnesses for the plaintiffs raised similar questions about the relationship between test content and what is taught in Florida's schools. Questioned as to the content validity of the Florida test, Cleary responded as follows:

> There are really two options in this. Usually when achievement test or educational tests are administered to students in school to determine whether or not they will pass onto another grade or to determine whether or not they will graduate, it is usual to base that examination on what the students have had in their instruction.
>
> Now, I don't see that this is the case here. On the other hand, one could say in the Educational Accountability Act the legislature said they wanted something else, that they

wanted functional literacy, which is the ability to operate somehow outside the schools
— but if that were the case, it seems to me you would have to demonstrate the validity of
this test in terms of a sampling from real-life situations.

It seems to me that neither of these criteria [has] have been met. [1594–1595.]

As previously noted, Airasian testified that "the whole question of instruction, whether kids have been exposed to the kinds of applications on similar kinds of applications[,] has been neglected."

Numerous details have been omitted in summarizing this conflicting testimony regarding content validity. Nevertheless, the trial transcript suggests that the major point of contention between the two sets of experts was that although defense experts maintained that content validity dealt with the match between test items and specifications or objectives, the plaintiffs' experts held that this formulation was too narrow. In general,[2] the plaintiffs' witnesses held that in the case of the Florida high school graduation test, content validity also should encompass the question of whether the test specifications and objectives (and implicitly the test items) cover material in the school curriculum and that students have been taught.

This dispute seems to have been a key one in affecting court decisions regarding validity, as we will see. To illustrate the significance of the dispute over the definition of content validity, let us first recount the following exchange between plaintiffs' counsel Diana Pullin, defense witness Mehrens, and the court during cross-examination.[3]

Pullin first stated her understanding that Mehrens' position was that assessment of the content validity of a test requires simply an examination of the extent to which the test items reflect the test specifications. Mehrens affirmed that this was a correct understanding of his position. To clarify the point in dispute regarding the definition of content validity, Pullin then presented the following example. Suppose one constructed a test for determining award of high school diplomas that was based upon ability to answer questions in Pakistani or Greek. Pullin then asked if the test items matched the test specifications, would that test still have content validity? Mehrens said yes, as long as the specifications had been accepted. Pullin proceeded to ask whether such a test would have content validity regardless of whether students had ever been taught Pakistani or Greek. Mehrens answered: "Well[,] it would still have content validity if it had been determined that the test was to measure those objectives." After a few more exchanges and some prodding from both Pullin and the court, Mehrens made the following distinction:

The content validity talks about the match between the objectives and the items. The question of whether the objectives are in fact appropriate is a different matter. That's really not a measurement issue in and of itself. If I were speaking as an educator, it would seem to me that one would not want to build a test of minimal competency over things that you did not reasonably expect the students could do based on their instruction. [2383–2384.]

In other words, when pressed, Mehrens seemed to acknowledge the legitimacy of the plaintiffs' expert witnesses' concerns over what they called curricular or instructional validity. He simply did not define content validity to include such concerns.

Which Experts Did the Courts Believe?

Before attempting to answer this question, let us note that the discussion is focusing strictly on disputation regarding the validity of the Florida high school graduation test. Overall, of course, both the trial court and the appeals court ruled in favor of the plaintiff's case. But on the validity issue, court opinion was clearly split.

District Court Decision

In section IV E of the trial court decision (474 F. Supp. 244, 257–261 [1979]), District Judge Carr considered ''the manner in which the test was developed and its validity from both a constitutional and a professional testing perspective.'' In it, Judge Carr ruled that the Florida test had adequate content and construct validity and bore rational relationship to valid state interest. In other words, in the judge's opinion, though the plaintiffs won the war over the *Debra P*. case overall, they lost the battle over validity. Elsewhere in his decision, Judge Carr noted that ''there is evidence that certain skills were not taught in Florida public schools'' (264), but his ruling that the test had adequate content validity clearly implied his acceptance of the defendants' narrow definition of content validity and rejection of the contention by plaintiffs' experts that curriculum and instructional validity are relevant aspects of content validity for a test such as the Florida high school graduation test.

Appeals Court Decision

If they lost the battle over validity in the district court's decision, the plaintiffs won a fair amount of it back in the appeals court decision (644 F.2d 397 [1981]). The three-member panel of judges ruled as follows:

> The trial court apparently found that the test had adequate content validity, but we find that holding upon the record before us to be clearly erroneous. In the field of competency testing, an important component of content validity is curricular validity defined by

defendants' expert Dr. Foster as "things that are currently taught." This record is simply insufficient in proof that the test administered measures what is actually taught in the schools of Florida [*Id*. at 405].

In short, unlike the trial court, the appeals court clearly accepted the plaintiffs' contention that for a competency test like the Florida one, curricular validity — defined as things that are currently taught — is an important component of content validity.

On the issue of construct validity, however, the appeals court equivocated somewhat:

> In analyzing the constitutionality of the examination under the Equal Protection Clause, the trial court stated, "[i]f the test by dividing students into two categories, passers and failers, did so without a rational relation to the purpose for which it was designed, then the Court would be compelled to find the test unconstitutional." 474 F. Supp. at 260. Analyzing the test from the viewpoint of its objectives, the court found that is does have adequate construct validity, that is, it does test functional literacy as defined by the Board. We accept this finding and affirm that part of the trial court's opinion holding that having a functional literacy examination bears a rational relation to a valid state interest. That finding is, however, subject to a further finding on remand that the test is a fair test which was taught. If the test is not fair, it cannot be said to be rationally related to a state interest. [*Id*. at 406.]

So from the perspective of the validity arguments presented in trial by the plaintiffs' expert witnesses, the appeals court's decision was something like two-thirds of a victory. The appeals court agreed with the plaintiffs contentions that:

1. The issue of the content validity of the Florida test encompassed the question of whether the test covered what was taught in Florida schools.
2. Insufficient evidence was available to demonstrate whether or not the test covered such material (that is, had curricular validity).

But in affirming, at least tentatively, the lower court's ruling that the Florida functional literacy test (FLT) had adequate construct validity, the appeals court rejected the contrary contentions of the plaintiffs' expert witnesses. The construct validity of the Florida test as a measure of "functional literacy" was, however, actually seen by the court as a moot issue, as indicated in the following portion of Judge Carr's original ruling:

> The test as legislatively created was to be one of functional literacy. Functional literacy has not been defined in a way which is acceptable to either all educational academicians or the public. The testimony, in fact, indicates that there are at least eleven known definitions of functional literacy. . . . . The categorizing of an individual without reference to a specific standard can be both detrimental and debilitating without justification. As one of the Plaintiffs' experts commented, students who fail the functional literacy test perceive of themselves as

''global failures.'' Another of the Plaintiffs' experts testified that the biggest flaw in the Florida program was its name alone. The Court is in complete agreement. Beyond the economic and academic implications of failure on the test, the stigma associated with the term functional illiteracy is the most substantial harm presented.

While the Court recognizes this program, it cannot be oblivious to the definition of functional literacy provided by the DOE, ratified by the State Board of Education, and legislatively approved. While the meaning of functional literacy is clear to the reader of the amended statute or the Rules of the State Board of Education, it is not to the Florida public. In an attempt to escape the impact of the terminology utilized in the original statute, the State Board of Education adopted a new name for the functional literacy test: the State Student Assessment Test II (SSAT II). Still the test remains the Florida functional literacy examination in the mind of the public and the name change has not dispelled the implications of the original denomination. Regardless of how the public perceives the test, the Court must analyze it from the definition provided by the state in conjunction with the twenty-four objectives. The court must not permit public perceptions to be the guide for statutory interpretations. [474 F. Supp. at 258–259.]

One other point is worth noting about the appeals court decision. Though the *Debra P.* trial saw much testimony from expert testing witnesses — including lengthy disputation over technical terms and interpretation of professional standards and prevailing professional practice — it seems clear that the appeals court did not rely very heavily on such professional expertise. The appeals court decision mentions the joint test *Standards* only in passing in a footnote (644 F.2d at 405), for example, and does not cite a single plaintiffs' expert witness by name. One of the defendants' expert witnesses — namely, Thomas Fisher — is even once incorrectly referred to as Dr. Foster (*Id.* at 405). Given the wide-ranging conflict of opinion among the testing experts, it is understandable that the court may have been reluctant to rely on one set of experts rather than another. Instead of relying heavily on expert testimony, the appeals court appears to have relied more upon the legal profession's standards of due process and the court's own sense of fairness. In the text of its decision, for example, the appeals court opined: ''We think . . . that fundamental fairness requires that the state be put to test on the issue of whether the students were tested on material they were or were not taught'' (*Id.* at 406). In conclusion, without a reference to test validity or professional test standards, the court wrote simply:

> We hold, however, that the State may not deprive its high school seniors of the economic and educational benefits of a high school diploma until it has demonstrated that the SSAT II is a fair test of that which is taught in its classrooms . . . [*Id.* at 408.]

The contrast between expert testimony and the appeals court opinion is worth pondering. The experts on both sides of the case seem to have been far less inclined than was the appeals court to step beyond the bounds of technical issues regarding test validity and prevailing testing practices to address the broader issue of the fairness of the Florida testing program. The contrast is surely partly due to the roles that experts and courts are given in litigation. Also, some observers have already interpreted the appeals court decision as an instance of unwarranted judicial intervention in educational policy. After the appeals court decision in the *Debra P.* case was filed in May 1981, one circuit court judge requested a rehearing of the appeal *en banc* — that is, before the entire circuit court — rather than before the three-judge panel that originally heard the appeal. The request for the *en banc* rehearing was denied, but in response to this denial, two judges filed dissents charging that the appeals court's decision was in error, and in fact constituted unwarranted judicial intervention in educational policy (*Debra P.* v. *Turlington, petition for reh'g and petition for reh'g en banc denied,* 644 F.2d 397, Sept. 4, 1981, at 10,854–10,866). Both dissenting judges, Tjoflat and Hill, made such charges of unwarranted judicial intervention, with Tjoflat arguing that the appeals court decision created strong disincentives for state officials who were trying to improve educational quality in the schools of Florida, and Hill suggesting that it "established a constitutional basis for the judiciary to assume the role of state educators" (*Id.* at 10,865).

These dissents have considerable merit. Nevertheless, if professional testing experts responsible for development of the Florida testing program had confined themselves less to the strictures of prevailing testing practice and attended more to broader educational issues and to the question of the fundamental fairness of the testing program, the *Debra P.* case might never have been brought to trial, and the occasion for judicial intervention might possibly never have arisen.

Regardless of what might have been, the charge from the appeals court is now clear. It remanded the *Debra P.* case to the lower court for a determination of whether the Florida high school graduation test covers material that students were or were not taught. How to make such a determination is, however, far less clear than is the charge itself, so the next sections of this chapter will describe, and attempt to evaluate a variety of strategies for addressing this question.

Does the Test Cover What Was Taught or Not?

How can one go about determining whether the material in the test was taught or not? In oral argument before the appeals court, counsel for the state of Florida assured the court that "the state could prove that the test covered things actually taught in the classrooms" (644 F.2d at 405). However, such proof cannot be easily accomplished. Why? To illustrate the potential complexity of the problem, refer to figure 3–1.

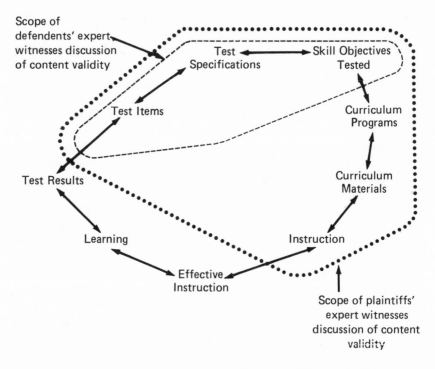

Figure 3–1. Terms with Which to Address the Question of Whether the Test Covers
Material Actually Taught.

This figure shows the different terms that might be used to address the court's
question. With only one exception, these terms represent language used in the
Debra P. trial to address, either explicitly or implicitly, the question of whether the
Florida test covers what was taught in the schools. The terms in figure 3–1 are
organized to show terms that are most often directly compared with one another in
adjacent, or at least nearby, positions. For example, in discussing content validity
in the *Debra P*. trial, defendants' expert witnesses typically talked about the
relationship between objectives tested and test specifications and between test
specifications and test items. Hence, these terms are shown next to one another.
Figure 3–1 also indicates the general scopes of the plaintiffs' and defendants'
discussions of content validity (with the former indicated within dotted lines and
the latter within dashed lines). As the illustration shows, the plaintiffs' formulation
of content validity was considerably broader than was that of the defendants. Also,
as already noted, the plaintiffs' formulation was the one embraced by the appeals court.

Before talking about the various possible relationships among the terms shown in figure 3–1 much less how to bring systematic evidence to bear on each of them, let us first see why each of these terms is relevant to the seemingly simple question put to the appeals court: Does the test cover what was taught or not taught?

Skill Objectives

As early as February 1977, after considerable internal debate about the meaning of functional literacy, the Florida State Department of Education (DOE) had determined the following:

> For the purposes of compliance with the Accountability Act of 1976 functional literacy is the satisfactory application of basic skills in reading, writing and arithmetic, to problems and tasks of a practical nature as encountered in every day life. [Cited in 474 F. Supp. at 258.]

Though, as previously noted, functional literacy has been officially dropped from the title of the Florida high school graduation test, the skills identified subsequent to this definition have apparently remained as objectives guiding development of the Florida test, now known as the SSAT II. Among the three basic skills mentioned, skill objectives are distributed as follows:

Communications	Total: 11
Reading:	8
Writing:	3[5]
Mathematics	Total: 13

Without describing each of the twenty-four skill objectives, let me note simply that they all focus on skills applied in "real world," everyday, practical situations. Thus two dimensions are implied in the Florida definition of skill objectives: that of particular skills and subskills and that of practical application of such skills. The latter dimension complicates enormously the task of determining the content validity of the Florida test in any formal deductive way. For as Acland (1976) noted in his critique of the Adult Performance Level test (a test similar to the Florida test in its intent to assess real-life applications, and one which was investigated by Florida officials in developing their own instrument), there are two fundamental problems in the real-world approach. Acland maintained: (1) in real life, different people tend to face quite different problems, and (2) there are a variety of ways, often involving quite different skills, of solving any particular problem.[6] Consider, for example, just one of the Florida reading skill objectives:

> The student will in a real world situation determine the inferred cause and effect of an action.

Though testing specialists frequently speak of defining relevant domains in order to develop content valid tests, how can a reasonable domain possibly be specified for such an objective? Would it include or exclude such issues common in newspapers nowadays as the inferred causes of cancer or the inferred effects of selling AWACs planes to Saudi Arabia?

Item Specifications

To help test developers make the jump from skill objectives to actual test items, the device of item specifications often is employed. Though there was some dispute in the Florida case about whether this intermediary device was initially employed (specifications appear to have been developed *after* items for the first form of the high school graduation test), this device now apparently forms the base for development of new test items. For example, for the skills objective already mentioned, the *Debra P.* trial record indicates that for the 1977–1978 test, the following specifications were given:

Maximum reading level: 7
Stimulus Characteristics
    A.   Stimulus is statement of an action.
    B.   Action is clearly described.
    C.   Stimulus is either a sentence, a paragraph, or a passage of no more than three hundred words.
    D.   Stimulus is an actual or believeable statement based on situations familiar to high school students.
    E.   Possibilities.
        1.   Description of traffic violation, school experience.

Stem Characteristics
    A.   See stimulus and stem characteristics.

Option Characteristics
    A.   Keyed option contains the only logical cause or effect that can be inferred from the stated action.
    B.   Distractors contain illogical effects in relation to a stated action or illogical causes in relation to stated effect.

Directions Characteristics
    The student is told to read the stimulus and choose the option that best describes the logical cause or effect of the particular action.[7]

Now these specifications clearly do somewhat circumscribe the range of uncertainty over what is involved in determining the inferred cause or effect of an action in a real situation. The action is to be described in no more than 300 words, and the reading level of the description is to be no more than level 7, which appears to mean grade 7 in terms of one of several readability formulae available for determining readibility levels. But note two things about these specifications. First, in circumscribing the range of uncertainty, these specifications clearly change the nature of the skill described in important respects. For example, the term *real situation* is interpreted to mean a situation familiar to high school students. Obviously, there are many so-called real situations that are *not* familiar to high school students. Also, the item specifications clearly imply that this skill objective is to be assessed through use of multiple-choice items. Second, note that those specifications, though restricting potential items to the multiple-choice form and to stimuli of no more than 300 words certainly do not restrict very greatly the range of uncertainty with respect to what is to be assessed. What, for example, is encompassed in the phrase "situations familiar to high school students?" Certainly, it is far more than the two possibilities mentioned — that is, traffic violations and school experience. Also, the restriction on item stimuli to passages of no more than three hundred words at maximum reading level of 7 seems to encompass a wide range of reading skills. For instance, are passages of say, 5 to 25 words not generally easier to read than passages of 250 to 300 words? Moreover, don't the specifications regarding keyed and distractor options, suggesting that the former are "logical" whereas the latter are "illogical" suggest that items meeting these specifications may be measures of logical ability as much as of applied reading skills? At a minimum, the specification regarding distractors fails to meet Cronbach's (1971, p. 454) prescription that "For a multiple choice test, the specifications should go beyond a statement of topical categories to state the general characteristics of misleading alternatives (distractors) . . . [since] the content of an item can be altered radically by changing the distractors, while keeping the correct response the same."

Test Items

If there is a considerable range of uncertainty implicit in the Florida test specifications, what then were the items that were derived from such specifications? It is difficult to answer this question because the Florida test is secure and not generally available for public scrutiny.[8]

Since the Florida test is a secure one, only a few items were described in the course of the *Debra P.* trial (see, for example, the testimony of Asa Hilliard, at 2032–2048, discussing items that were potentially biased against low-income black students.) However, because these items are not described in the transcript in the exact manner in which they appeared on the test, let us instead focus on an example given in conjunction with the test specifications already cited, concerning the inferring cause and effect objective:

Read the following statement and choose the sentence that best describes why the action occurred.

1. The teacher gave John an "A" in social studies.

    a. John behaved and therefore scored 100% on tests.
    b. John studied hard and scored very high on a test.
    c. John did not study and flunked the tests.
    d. John studied and flunked the tests. [CT 112, p. 6.]

Three things stike me about this item. First, although the specifications for which this item is an example suggest that the item stimulus should have no more than three hundred words, the stimulus for this item has only nine. Second, each of the options contains *two* potential causes of the stated action; behaving, studying, or not studying on one hand; and scoring 100% on tests, scoring very high on one test, or flunking tests on the other. Third, one cannot help but wonder whether individuals' responses to this item — in particular whether they choose option A or B — may have more to do with their own experience in observing why teachers give grades than with the *reading* skill that this item is purported to assess.

It is probably not worth speculating further on this item because it is only an example and not an actual operational item from the Florida test. But the more general point that is worth making is that if this is a fair example of the Florida test items, then even the narrow construction of content validity offered by defendants' expert witnesses — namely, that it concerns only the extent to which items match specifications and skill objectives — surely should not be taken for granted. At a minimum, the Florida test specifications and items seem to me very likely to fail the sort of experimental verification that Cronbach (1971, p. 456) suggested. He advised that

> . . . a second team of equally competent writers and reviewers . . . work independently of the first team [of item developers], according to the same plan. They would be aided by the same definition of relevant content, sampling rules, instructions to reviewers, and specifications for tryout and interpretation of data as were provided to the first team. If the universe description and the sampling are ideally refined, the first and second tests will be entirely equivalent. Any person's score will be the same on both tests, within the limits of sampling error (Cronbach 1971, p. 456).

In fairness though, it should be acknowledged that this test of the relationship between specifications and items may be honored more in theory than in practice. It is likely very rarely used to test the adequacy of item specifications.

So far, this discussion has been confined mainly to the three terms encompassing the narrow formulation of content validity that the appeals court rejected in saying that for competency tests, an important aspect of content validity is curricular validity. So what of the other terms shown in figure 3–1?

Curriculum Program

The first observation here is that no high school curriculum programs are known to be specifically organized around the three general skill areas of the Florida program — namely, reading, writing, and math — much less around the twenty-four applied skill objectives that serve as a framework for the Florida high school graduation test.

No information at all was presented in the *Debra P.* trial about the nature of the curriculum programs offered in Florida public schools. Nevertheless, it seems safe to assume that at the high school level, Florida schools, like most high school systems across the nation, offer three broad types of programs — namely, academic or college preparatory programs, general programs, and vocational programs. Data from the National Longitudinal Survey of the Young Americans indicate that approximately 54% of those surveyed nationwide in 1979 reported being in a general high school program, 30% in a college preparatory program, and 16% in a vocational program.[9] It is doubtful whether these exact proportions pertain to enrollments in Florida high schools, but it seems safe to assume that substantial proportions of Florida high school students are enrolled in each of these three broad curriculum program areas. Data recently reported by the National Center for Educational Statistics (NCES 1980), for example, indicate that over 200,000 eleventh and twelfth graders in Florida were enrolled in vocational programs in 1978–1979, and around 100,000 were in occupationally specific vocational education programs. Thus in pursuing the question of whether the Florida high school graduation test covers what is taught in the schools, it would seem pertinent to inquire into how well the Florida test matches what is taught in these three broad types of high school curriculum programs.

Curriculum Materials

A curriculum program such as vocational education does not, however, do much to define a course of study. Within vocational education programs at the high school level, for example, frequently there are six or more different occupational specialty programs. Moreover, one school's vocational or college preparatory program can vary markedly from that of another school. Therefore a more refined way of examining the match between a test and the curriculum would be to look at curriculum materials actually used: for example, textbooks and workbooks used in the schools. There is even something of a tradition of inquiry in this area. Some researchers have performed readability analyses to compare textual materials and tests (for example, Chall 1977; Britton and Lumpkin 1978). Other researchers at the University of Illinois, have shown that there are notable differences in the content coverage of standardized reading tests and commercial reading curriculum materials (Armbruster, Stevens, and Rosenshine 1977; Jenkins and Pany 1976). Porter and his colleagues at Michigan State University also have carried out comparative analyses of the math problems presented in textbooks and in standardized tests (Porter 1978; Porter et al. 1978) and found that the test-text coverage varied considerably.

Examining curriculum materials certainly would seem to be one fairly direct way of addressing the concern expressed frequently in the *Debra P.* case over the curriculum validity of the Florida test. But note that this is not what seems to be implied in the court's citation of Fischer's definition of curriculum validity as "things that are currently taught." This definition seems closer to what McClung (1977) called "instructional validity" as opposed to curriculum validity. Moreover, the case of *Anderson* v. *Banks* clearly illustrates the potential importance of the distinction that McClung drew between curriulum and instructional validity. In the *Anderson* case, the issue under dispute was whether it was legal for the Tattnall County Georgia School Board to institute a requirement of a 9.0 grade equivalent score on the California Achievement Test for receipt of a high school diploma.

> The school system hired an expert witness — an employee of McGraw-Hill, the CAT developer — to demonstrate the close link between the CAT and the curriculum taught in Tattnall county. The Court, however, placed "little weight on her results," because she assumed the use of a particular set of curriculum materials (the Scott-Foresman series) throughout the Tattnall County schools. As the court pointed out, there were a multitude of problems with this assumption. For example, the Scott-Foresman program was phased in over a number of years; thus, during some period of their education, only portions of the classes of 1978, 1979, and 1980 had been exposed to the Scott-Foresman curriculum. In addition, there was evidence that about a third of the students in the Tattnall County schools were not exposed to the Scott-Foresman curriculum at all. Moreover, even those students who took some courses with the Scott-Foresman materials probably were not exposed to the full Scott-Foresman curriculum. [Flygare 1981, p. 135.]

Instruction

This finding clearly suggests the importance of looking more closely at whether test content was covered in the course of *instruction* received by students, or as the appeals court put it, the test covers things that are currently taught. Teachers, school administrators, and even students might, for example, be surveyed regarding whether and to what extent skill objectives around which the test is organized are actually covered in particular schools or courses. Similarly, schools and classrooms could be observed to determine whether teachers are actually using relevant curriculum materials and instructional methods. Past research indicates that such techniques can be useful in documenting the relationship between what is tested and what is taught. Karlson and Stodolsky (1973), for example, showed that observations of child behavior in preschool programs can be used to explain changes in I.Q. scores. Soar (1973) and Stallings and Kaskowitz (1974) showed systematic observations of instructional practice to be significantly related to changes in student test performance in the national Follow Through Program in first through third grades. Lewy (1972) and Anderson (1975) both showed that opportunity to learn defined in terms of teachers' reports of material taught has a significant positive association with student achievement. More recently, Leinhardt and Seewald (1981) have reported on efforts to use teachers' ratings of material covered in class as a predictor of student test performance. They found that teachers' ratings of whether students have been taught information required to answer test items and have been exposed to the format of items explain significant amounts of variance in posttest scores above and beyond that explained by pretest scores.

Such studies indicate that the relationship between what is tested and what is taught (whether measured by teacher ratings or by classroom observation) is significantly related to how students perform on tests. Though none of this research was brought into evidence in the *Debra P.* case, it certainly provides a broad base of evidence[10] to substantiate the appeals court's concern over the relationship between what is taught in the Florida schools and what is tested in the high-school-graduation test.

Effective Instruction

It may not be enough, however, to merely inquire into the question of instruction; instead, it may be appropriate to investigate whether students are given adequate or effective instruction. After all, the real issue is not whether students have simply been exposed to teachers' going through the motions of covering a prescribed text, but instead whether students have been afforded instruction from which, if willing and attentive, they could reasonably be expected to learn what is covered on the test. Indeed, this distinction between instruction and adequate or effective instruction seems to be clearly drawn in some of the documentary materials submitted in the *Debra P.* case itself. For example, it is implicit in the observations of the McCrary Commission that in the graduation test, students were examined on content ''that was presumed to be elementary, but that their schools may or may not have taught them *well,* recently or at all'' (McCrary Commission Report, CT 25, p. 4) [emphasis added]. In their study of the math portion of the Florida test with students who had failed the exam, Hills and Denmark also raise the issue of effective instruction, as follows:

Apparently students are not familiar with the idea of thinking of a model, such as a clock face, or a calendar, as they try to solve these kinds of problems. When we suggested such a model, it was sometimes surprising how effectively the examinee could see it. Perhaps more instruction along these lines would make a real difference in Functional Literacy Tests scores. [J. Hills and T. Denmark, "Functional Literacy in Mathematics," CT 140, pp. 43–44.]

Also, in much of the research previously cited, determinations of what was taught (defined variously in terms of curriculum materials, direct observations of teachings, or teachers' reports) were organized around assumptions, either explicit or implicit, of what should be taught.

This approach to answering the question of the appeals court — namely, by studying the extent to which students are given effective instruction covering the content of the Florida test, of course, would raise a host of problems. Because there is no statewide prescribed *curriculum* in Florida schools, it is hardly possible to conceive of how a statewide definition of effective instructional practice could be arrived at, much less operationally specified so as to allow empirical investigation of the match between test content and student's receipt of effective instruction concerning that content.

Learning

From concerns for effective instruction, it is of course only a small step to the issue of student learning. For the test of effective instruction is surely most widely acknowledged to be whether or not students learn. Indeed, if one starts from a premise like that of Benjamin Bloom and others that *all* students (save perhaps those with severe physical or mental handicaps) — if given time and appropriate instruction — can learn the sort of basic skills covered on the Florida test, then it is reasonable to conclude that the fact that 20% of black high school seniors and nearly 6% of all high school seniors in Florida had not passed the graduation test by spring 1979 — after as many as three tries — is prima facie evidence that *many* Florida students are *not* receiving effective instruction concerning the skills tested. In other words, if the Florida test results are taken as valid indicators of student learning, an argument could be easily advanced that the test results themselves indicate that the graduation test covers material that is *not* effectively taught currently in Florida's schools. The validity of such a sweeping conclusion is doubtful for two reasons. First, as indicated already, the quality of the Florida test seems doubtful even within the narrow formulation of content validity espoused by the defendants' expert witnesses. More generally, it is questionable whether ability to apply basic skills in real-life settings can be adequately measured with multiple choice items, the item format exclusively relied upon in the Florida test.

Second, even if we put aside the testing issue, it seems that good teaching may sometimes not result in student learning — at least not the sort anticipated. Surely, good teaching should generally promote student learning, but individual students may fail to learn what is intended for a variety of reasons, including occasional obstinacy, disinterest, inability, or attention to other matters. Student learning is doubtless an important general indicator of good teaching, but I doubt that it could or should be the sole criterion of good teaching.

Too Complex a Question?

So where does this leave us? We have seen that there are a host of ways in which one can conceptualize how to go about answering the question of whether the Florida test covers what is taught. Specifically, the question could variously be addressed in terms of the interrelationships among the following: test items; test specifications; skill objectives; curriculum programs; curriculum materials; instruction; effective instruction; learning; and test results.

If one undertook to study the correspondence of such terms on just a pairwise basis, one would have thirty-six different potential comparisons (that is $_9C_2$). But this analysis really does not begin to convey the difficulty of the task. For if one can raise doubts about the validity of the Florida test, surely one could also raise questions about the validity of any means of assessing such things as curriculum materials, instruction, and effective instruction. Indeed, even if we restrict ourselves to only narrow formulation of content validity advocated by the expert witnesses for the defendants in the *Debra P.* trial, previous research indicates that the job of assessing the content validity of the Florida test is almost impossible to accomplish in any definitive way. To illustrate this point, let us refer briefly to Bloom et al.'s (1956) *Taxonomy of Educational Objectives*. This taxonomy is probably the most widely known framework in terms of which educational objectives and skills that U.S. schools seek to impart to students have been analyzed. Also, Bloom's *Taxonomy* is fairly widely used by commercial-test publishers in describing the content and skill areas covered by their tests. Yet Seddon's (1978) review of studies using this taxonomy in classifying test items indicates clearly how difficult it is to reliably classify the skills tapped by particular test items. Seddon (1978) reports that the extent of agreement among judges on the skill classification of test items in terms of Bloom's *Taxonomy* varies inversely with the number of judges doing the classification. Among the studies reviewed by Seddon (1978), the extent of perfect agreement ranged from a high of 90% with two judges to a low of 0% with twenty-two judges. Lack of agreement between judges regarding skills classifications of test items surely may be attributed partially to the fallibility of human judgment. But there also is an important substantive reason for such disagreement. As Bloom et al. warned, "Before the reader can classify a particular test exercise [in terms of the taxonomy], he must know or at least make some assumptions about the learning situations which have preceded the test" (Bloom et al. 1956, p. 51).

Let us see a practical example of what this means. Recall the sample Florida test question already discussed regarding why the teacher gave Johnny an "A" in social studies. This item was shown to a small unsystematic sample of individuals who were all high school graduates. One individual selected option A: "John behaved and therefore scored 100% on tests." This option was ostensibly incorrect, but the choice was explained as follows:

> In my experience, kids get good grades as much for behaving in school as for anything else.

In other words, for the individual who provided this rationale, option selection was dependent on previous personal experience (or in Bloom et al.'s language, "learning situations" preceding the test exercise), rather than on reading skill per se. Thus, even if one attempts to focus solely on the narrow formulation of content validity (as the match between test items and skill objectives ostensibly tested), one is quickly drawn into other realms suggested in figure 3–1 — namely, instruction and learning.

Another large problem in answering the seemingly simple question asked by the appeals court is the temporal one. The skills intended to be assessed by the Florida test are basic ones of reading, writing, and math. However, because these skills are not the focus of instruction in most high school programs, answering the question of whether the test covers what has been taught likely would require an investigation not simply of high school programs, but also of prehigh school instruction. Determining what it was that the high school class of 1980 or 1981 was taught in the way of reading, writing, and math skills ten years ago, when students were in elementary school, would be an almost impossible task.

These problems only hint at the potential difficulties of answering the court's seemingly simple question. Should we try to assess whether the graduation test covers things taught to students in Florida *generally,* or students in particular *districts,* or for all *individual* students who are required to take the test? Regardless of the level of inquiry at which such investigation is undertaken, how much would it cost, and could not resources be better devoted to teaching students?

There are many more such questions, both practical and theoretical, that could be raised about how to address the court's concern. Enough questions have been identified already to make it clear that answering the court's question, "Does the test cover what is taught?" is exceedingly difficult to do in any detailed way and altogether impossible to accomplish in a way that could not easily be challenged. Therefore instead of expanding further on potential problems, let us turn in the next section to address the practical question of what could reasonably be done to illuminate the court's concern in ways that are both practical and potentially useful in serving ends other than the resolution of the *Debra P.* litigation.

What Can Be Done?

The preceding section fostered more complexity than may be useful for purposes of guiding action. In this vein, Lee Cronbach's comment regarding George Madaus's testimony in the *Debra P.* trial is equally apropos of the argument set out in the section titled "Does the Test Cover What Was or Was Not Taught?". Recall that Madaus had testified that adequate validation of a test to be used for important decisions about individuals — such as whether or not they should receive a high school diploma — "requires the integration of construct validity studies, criterion validity studies and content validity studies." Cronbach observed that if Madaus's testimony "were taken seriously, testing would be impossible."[11] Similarly, the chain of inquiry described in "Does the Test Cover What Was or Was Not Taught?," regarding how to answer the appeals court's question of whether the Florida test covers what was actually taught in Florida schools, seems as a practical matter to be almost impossible to carry out in any timely or definitive way. A wide range of useful investigation surely could be carried out on the relationship between the Florida test and curriculum programs, curriculum materials, instructional practices, and student learning. Certainly it would be relevant, for example, to inquire into whether or not curriculum materials used in Florida schools provide students with practice in the sort of "real-life" applications that form the basis of the high school graduation test. Also, systematic observations or surveys regarding instructional practices in Florida schools might well provide information useful in improving instruction.

But such inquiries very likely have little utility for two reasons. First, it is doubtful that such inquiries would provide a very efficient means of addressing the appeals court's concern over the "fundamental fairness" of the high school graduation test — that is, whether high school seniors are being deprived of "the economic and social benefits of a high school diploma" by an instrument that is a fair test of that which is taught in Florida classrooms. Second, the quality of the Florida test itself should not be taken for granted. Although relatively little information on the Florida test is available in the record of the *Debra P.* case, that which is available (for example, the specifications for the 1977–1978 instrument) suggests that the instrument may not be a particularly good one. So what can be done? The remainder of this section will discuss two strategies for illuminating the concerns raised by the appeals court. The strategies are practical in that they would require no new data gathering or additional testing. Also, they do not aim directly at answering the question of the court regarding the content and curricular validity of the Florida test. But such indirect approaches, skirting the specific question posed by the appeals court, do address both the broader question of the "fundamental fairness" of the high school graduation test and what seem to be the ultimate concerns of both the plaintiffs and the defendants in the *Debra P.* case — namely, how to improve instruction in the schools without unfairly penalizing students who may have been inadequately taught in the past or unfairly tested in the present.

First, graduation test results themselves provide a potentially useful source of information. Patterns of achievement on different parts of the graduation test (defined in terms of either item content or format) among students in different schools or districts may provide initial clues regarding coverage of instruction. Harnish and Linn (1981) provide a review of techniques that can be used to identify anomalous patterns of performance on test items. Also, Harnish and Linn illustrate the use of such techniques in identifying large school-to-school variations, after adjusting for overall school performance, on different items in the mathematics test of the Illinois statewide assessment program. The authors suggest that large variations in performance on particular types of items may indicate weaknesses in the teaching of math skills in certain schools and districts. Such a method for examining patterns of teaching has one overriding virtue in that it is relatively easy and requires no additional data gathering, instead relying upon statewide test results themselves to provide clues regarding patterns of teaching. This approach has two severe drawbacks, however. First, it relies exclusively on results of the test itself, and if serious doubts exist about the validity of the test — as is the case for the Florida graduation test — then the potential is obviously limited. Second, this technique can be applied only for groups of students (within district schools, or perhaps in some circumstances within classes), not for individual students. Because teaching coverage and test results vary substantially within districts and schools, and because the appeals' court's questions about whether the Florida test covers what was taught derives from the due process concerns about *individual* rights, this is obviously an important limitation.

What else, then, might reasonably be done? A second approach would be to examine the relationship between graduation test results and what might be called the common currency of school evaluation — that is, things such as course grades and grade promotions. Thus, for example, if a student were found to have been regularly promoted through the twelve grades of elementary and secondary school and to have maintained, say, a C average in course grades but to have failed the high school graduation test, it would be reasonable to conclude that something was fundamentally unfair about this situation. The problem might derive from the quality of instruction received, from the grading practices and promotion practices of the schools he or she attended, or from the graduation test itself. Nevertheless, such a disproportion between an individual's school record and his or her graduation test performance would clearly provide *prima facie* evidence that something was wrong.

There is, of course, an obvious objection to such a strategy for examining the question asked by the appeals court. Minimum competency tests (MCT) have been advocated and introduced as a means of bolstering educational standards, and in particular as a mechanism for remedying such perceived ills as social promotion and grade inflation. Thus it might seem at first somewhat perverse to examine the results of a high school graduation test in terms of school grades whose low standards the test was introduced to bolster. Nevertheless, it seems that such an examination could help to clarify the issues of fundamental fairness that the *Debra P.* case raises. Course grades and grade promotion are probably the most common currency of evaluation in U.S. schools. If a student has performed satisfactorily in terms of these evaluative criteria over the course of a school career, it is fundamentally unfair to deny the student "the economic and educational benefits of a high school diploma" on the basis of a graduation test. Such a state of affairs would, of course, also serve to raise questions about the prevailing standards of evaluation in the schools, but it is likely that such an analysis would at least begin to sort out the balance of responsibility for things. Thus if a student performs satisfactorily in terms of course grades and grade promotion but fails the graduation test, then the problem may be not so much with the student's inability or unwillingness to learn as with the standards of the school system itself — including the graduation test.

Is there any evidence to suggest that such a state of affairs, (that is, a student performing satisfactorily in terms of school records but still failing the graduation test) does in fact exist? Unfortunately, there was not much evidence along these lines presented in the *Debra P.* trial. But at least two pieces of evidence are clearly suggestive: first in Hills and Denmark's study entitled "Functional Literacy in Mathematics" (CT 140). In this study carried out in the summer of 1978, the authors investigated student performance on the mathematics section of the Florida graduation test by interviewing students regarding how they went about solving the math problems on the test. Among other observations, Hills and Denmark offered the following:

> [T]he group of advanced students we tested in one urban high-school were surprisingly ineffective with some of these problems, too. These students were in a class in which a number of different topics were being taught, such as trigonometry, advanced algebra, and solid geometry, on an individual basis. The students were definitely not having difficulty with mathematics per se. Still they were relatively unsuccessful in dealing with comparison shopping problems that asked the student to compare, with converting square feet to square yards, and at subtracting one time from another or determining elapsed time when regrouping was necessary. This is more evidence that these applica-

tions of basic skills just are not being learned even by the good students. [Hills and Denmark, "Functional Literacy in Mathematics," CT 140 p. 52.]

Another document available in the record of the *Debra P*. case similarly indicates that there may be important discrepancies between performance on the high school graduation test and school-record data. An investigation of the relationship between students' grade point averages (GPAs) and FLT scores apparently was prepared by the Orange County Public Schools Research and Evaluation Office.[12] The investigation was based on the records of a systematic sample of two hundred eleventh grade students in the school system studied. The report of the study shows the correlations between FLT scores and student GPAs, table 3–1.

These data show the correlations between GPAs and FLT scores to be relatively low. Not a single one of the correlations between GPAs and graduation test scores reached the 0.50 level. In other words, GPAs explain no more than 25% of the variance in FLT scores. The authors suggest that these "moderately low" correlations may result from a number of factors:

> First the possibility of grade instability exists. That is, there could be variability in grading procedures from subject-to-subject, teacher-to-teacher, and school-to-school. Second, the elements being assessed by . . . the Functional Literacy Test may not be sufficiently covered by the curricula of the courses. Third, the reliability and validity of [this test is] still in the process of being determined. [*Id*. at 5.]

The authors of this report properly point out that there are several alternative explanations for the moderately low correlations between the graduation test and students' GPAs. Indeed, other explanations are worth mentioning: for example, restriction of range on the graduation test results (with the majority of students scoring above 70%). Nevertheless, these data, together with the findings of Hills

Table 3–1.   Correlations (Pearson *r*) and Partial Correlations between Functional Literacy and GPA's, Eleventh Grade

	Correlation Coefficients		
Test Section GPA	*Pearson r*	*Race Partialled Out*	*Sex Partialled Out*
Communications/English	.3865	.3793	.3896
Mathematics/Mathematics	.4651	.4553	.4827
Total/Total	.4715	.4668	.4963

Source: Research and Evaluation Office, "An Investigation of the Basic Skills and Functional Literacy Test of the Statewide Assessment Program," October 1978, CT 103, p. 3.

and Denmark, clearly suggest that important discrepancies may exist between traditional school record evaluations of student performance and results on the graduation test.

This brings us back to two observations concerning the appeals court's concern over fundamental fairness and the broader utility of any investigations of the relationship between what is taught in Florida schools and the high school graduation test. On the first point, if we are concerned about the fundamental fairness of a high-school-graduation testing program, we should be concerned with not just whether students have been taught material covered by the test, but also with the methods by which they have previously been evaluated on what they have been taught. For if it is unfair to withhold students' high school diplomas on the basis of a test that covers that which has not been taught, surely it is also unfair to do so when they have been told in terms of grades and other regular school evaluations that they have satisfactorily learned what they have been taught. In other words, even if the test *does* cover what has been taught, it would seem fundamentally unfair to evaluate students by one set of criteria in regular school evaluations and by a more stringent or altogether different standard only for the purpose of awarding high school diplomas.

Beyond the fairness issue, however, is the question of what can be done to improve instruction and learning. Here again, it seems that investigation of the relationships between regular school evaluations of student performance and graduation test results may be advisable. It may indeed be that grading and promotion standards are too lax. If so, inquiry into the relationship between such matters and graduation test results should help to reveal this and at least indirectly provide guidance for improvement without unfairly penalizing individual students. For example, given the disproportionate failure rate of blacks on the high school graduation test in Florida, it would seem pertinent to inquire into whether black students in Florida are receiving substantially inferior education and as a result are being evaluated by standards that leave them less well prepared both to succeed on the graduation test and to attain functional literacy skills. In advocating this approach — both to illuminate the concerns of the court and to provide information useful in identifying localities, programs, and populations particularly in need of better instruction — the point should be reemphasized that, given the currently available information, the quality of the graduation test itself should not be taken for granted. If important discrepancies exist between ongoing school evaluation and graduation test results, it should not be assumed that they derive strictly from instructional programs and internal school evaluations; they may also derive from inadequacies in the graduation test itself.

The two approaches just suggested — namely, seeking out anomalous patterns of performance on the Florida test and examining the relationship between test results and individuals' school records — obviously do not directly address the court's concern in the *Debra P.* case over whether the graduation test does or does not cover what was taught in Florida schools. As noted already, other approaches (such as analyses of curriculum materials, surveys of teachers and students regarding what is taught, or observation of what is taught) may have real value in addressing the concerns of the court. Nevertheless, these approaches are limited, whereas the two methods that have been emphasized are less handicapped for three reasons.

First, it seems clear that expert testimony and research evidence have relatively little impact on the court's deliberations. This in turn suggests that means for influencing the judicial considerations and, indeed, for influencing public policy on education more generally will have more persuasive power if they are straight-forward and deal in data that are already accepted. Thus data such as school grades and promotion histories, which are recognized indicators of school performance, may have more persuasive power than newly gathered data based on classroom observations or teacher ratings. Second, it is clear that judicial concern over the Florida testing program might easily evaporate as a result of administrative changes in the program that would leave the educational issues largely intact. If, for example, high school diplomas were not *denied* on the basis of the Florida test, but instead high school diplomas continued to be awarded on previously existing bases and passing or failing of the Florida test was noted through some *new* administrative procedure, then the legal basis for the *Debra P.* case would almost completely disappear. Third, it is likely that inquiry aimed directly at answering the appeals court's questions regarding the match between what is tested and what is taught, probably would fail to address the larger concerns of both the plaintiffs and the defendants in the *Debra P.* case — namely, how to improve instruction in Florida's schools. In this regard, unless we assume that tests like the Florida competency test are to completely supercede traditional means of education such as course grades and yearly promotions, then MCT results might fruitfully be employed in critical comparisons with such indicators as a means of examining both the relevance of competency test results to past school practice and the possibilities for improving school practice in the future. If MCTs have been instituted at least partly as a means of remedying perceived ills of social promotion and grade inflation, it is high time to take a closer look at the relationship between competency test results and both school grades and promotion practices. Such inquiry surely would not yield any panaceas, but it would at least offer a reasonable way to begin sorting out the nature of the problem regarding what is taught, how learning is regularly evaluated in the schools, and how both learning and teaching are reflected in the statewide test results.

Notes

1. This number and subsequent ones in parentheses not otherwise identified refer to pages in the *Debra P.* trial transcript. Numbers preceded by the letters "CT" refer to documents entered into the court's transcript of the trial.

2. The only apparent exception among plaintiffs' experts was Cleary, who as noted, suggested that the notion of functional literacy — if taken seriously and defined "in terms of sampling from real-life situations" — could have been used as a basis for establishing the content validity of the Florida test.

3. I summarize the exchange here merely for the sake of brevity. The full exchange can be found on pp. 2379–2384 of the trial transcript.

4. For anyone who was as puzzled as was I by the sudden appearance of a "Dr. Foster" in this story, it is worth noting that the reference should have been to "Dr. Fisher."

5. It is worth noting that two of the three Florida writing objectives do not deal with what most English teachers would construe as writing skill — namely, to "complete a check and its stub accurately" and to "accurately complete forms used to apply for a driver's license, employment, entrance to a school or training program, insurance and credit."

6. I highly recommend "The Barometer Story" (Calandra, 1964/1971) as a delightful account that makes the point that there are a variety of ways to solve a problem — namely, a physics examination.

7. Document CT 112 in the *Debra P.* trial record.

8. I am somewhat surprised that the issue of security *after* test administration was not raised during the Florida trial. It seems that because it is a major instrument of public policy developed with public funds and having a clear impact on individuals' educational and other social opportunities, a much stronger case could be developed for the public release of the Florida test after its administration than was developed with respect to postsecondary admissions tests, which led to passage of the New York Truth-in-Testing law. But to avoid diverging into a discussion of arguments regarding the virtues and vices of what might be called open versus secure testing, I will not elaborate on this issue.

9. Calculated from data provided in Woods and Haney, 1981, appendix A.

10. Probably the best review of research on the relationship between what is taught (as indicated both by curriculum materials and teachers reports) is Walker and Schaffarzick (1974). Although this research is somewhat outdated, these reviewers found essentially what has been confirmed in subsequent studies — namely, that "different curricula are associated with different patterns of achievement" (p. 97).

11. Seminar on the Florida Functional Literacy Examination, Center for Law and Education, Cambridge, Mass., February 1980. With regard to Cronbach's comment, it is worth noting that virtually none of the widely used commercially prepared standardized achievement tests have the wide-ranging validity evidence that Madaus said is necessary for adequate validation. With regard to Madaus's original point, it should be noted as well that the end Cronbach identified was in a way exactly what Madaus sought, for he maintained that no test should be used as the sole or determining criterion of important decisions about individuals.

12. This document — CT 103 — dated October 1978, does not contain thorough bibliographic information but was apparently carried out in Orange County, Fla.

References

Acland, H. "If Reading Scores Are Irrelevant, Do We Have Anything Better?" *Educational Technology* 16:7, (July 1976) 25–29.

Anderson, L. "Opportunity To Learn, Test Bias, and School Effects." Paper presented at the annual meeting of the National Council of Measurement in Education, Washington, D.C., 1975.

Armbruster, B., Stevens, R., and Rosenshine, B. *Analyzing Content Coverage and Emphasis: A Study of Three Curricula and Two Tests*. Urbana, Ill.: University of Illinois at Urbana-Champaign, 1977.

Bloom, B.S., ed. *Taxonomy of Educational Objectives: Cognitive Domain*. New York: Longman, Inc., 1956.

Britton, G., and Lumpkin, M. "Readability Labeling: An Answer to the Middle Grade Slump." *Reading Improvement* 15:3, (Fall 1978) 162–169.

Calandra, A. "The Barometer Story." *Current Science, Teacher's Edition*. 49, No. 14, (January 1964). Reprinted in *Project Physics Course reader 3*. New York: Hold, Rinehart & Winston, 1971, p. 45.

Center for Law and Education, *Minimum Competency Testing: A Case Study of the Florida Functional Literacy Test*. 2 vols. (A compilation of testimony and documentary evidence submitted in the *Debra P.* case) Cambridge, Mass.: Center for Law and Education, Harvard Graduate School of Education, 1980.

Chall, J. *An Analysis of Textbooks in Relation to Declining SAT Scores*. Princeton, N.J.: College Board, June 1977.

Cronbach, L. "Test Validation," in T. Thorndike ed., *Educational Measurement* (Washington, D.C.: American Council on Education, 1971), pp. 443–507.

Debra P. v. *Turlington*. On petition for rehearing and petition for rehearing *en banc*. U.S. Court of Appeals, 5th Circuit, September 4, 1981.

Debra P. v. *Turlington*. United States Court of Appeals, 5th Circuit. 644 F.2d 397, May 4, 1981.

Debra P. v. *Turlington*. United States District Court, Middle District of Florida. 474 F. Supp. 244, 1979.

Flygare, T. "Graduation Competency Testing Fails in Georgia." *Phi Delta Kappan* 63;2, (October 1981), 134–135.

Harnish, D., and Linn, R. "Analysis of Item Response Patterns: Questionable Test Data and Dissimilar Curriculum Practices." *Journal of Educational Measurement*. 18, (1981), 133–146.

Jenkins, J., and Pany, D. *Curriculum Biases in Reading Achievement Tests*. Urbana, Ill.: University of Illinois at Urbana-Champaign, Center for the Study of Reading, 1976.

Karlson, A., and Stodolsky, S. "Predicting School Outcomes from Observations of Child Behavior in Classrooms." Paper presented at annual meeting of the American Education Research Association, New Orleans, La., February 1973.

Leinhardt, G., and Seewald, A. "Overlap: What's Tested, What's Taught?" *Journal of Educational Measurement*. 18:2, (1981), 85–96.

Lewy, A. "Opportunity To Learn and Achievement in Three Subject Matter Areas." *Journal of Experimental Education.* 41 1972, 68–73.

McClung, M. "Competency Testing: Potential for Discrimination." *Clearinghouse Review* 2. (1977), 439–448.

Porter, A. *Relationships between Testing and the Curriculum.* East Lansing, Mich.: Institute for Research on Teaching, Michigan State University, 1978.

Porter, A., et al. "Practical Significance in Program Evaluation." *American Educational Research Journal,.* 15, No. 4, (1978), 529–539.

Seddon, G. "The Properties of Bloom's Taxonomy of Educational Objectives for the Cognitive Domain." *Review of Educational Research.* 48 No. 2, (Spring 1978), 303–323.

Soar, R.S. *Final Report. Follow Through Classroom Process Measurement and Pupil Growth (1970–1971).* Gainesville, Fla.: College of Education, University of Florida, June 1973, 231 pp. Also *Appendix E: Sponsor Differences in Classroom Process,* June 1976, 29 pp.

Stallings, J.A., Kaskowitz, D.H., et al. *Follow Through Classroom Observation Evaluation 1972–1972.* Menlo Park, Calif.: Stanford Research Institute. August 1974, ca. 600 pp. ED 104 891.

Walker, D., and Schaffarzick, J. "Comparing Curricula." *Review of Educational Research.* 44, (1974), 83–112.

Woods, E., and Haney, W. *Does Vocational Education Make A Difference?* A review of *Previous Research and Reanalyses of National Longitudinal Data Sets.* Cambridge, Mass.: the Huron Institute, September 1981.

4 ESTABLISHING INSTRUCTIONAL VALIDITY FOR MINIMUM COMPETENCY PROGRAMS

Robert Calfee
with the assistance of Edmund Lau and Lynne Sutter

Back in the Old Days . . .

Effective education depends on a proper working relation between instruction and assessment — the linkage between teaching and testing is essential. A few decades ago, the ties between what was taught and what was tested seemed fairly direct. The teacher was responsible for both activities. Tests were often short essays. In math, it was important to "show your work." Exams came regularly, often once a week, covering recent material from lectures and assignments. Final exams were more comprehensive and required students to review and integrate what they had been taught.

The system was not perfect. Students sometimes felt that a question covered material that had not been taught, but they usually lost the argument. It is unclear what passed through the teacher's mind in such cases, but the task of testing for transfer of knowledge is surely a difficult one. The good teacher does not attempt to teach students everything they need to know; this is an impossible task, and in attempting it the teacher will not help the student learn to handle new situations. By the same token, the teacher should ensure that the student has had a fair chance to learn the relevant facts and principles. Education is a continuing exchange, a struggle, a game, wherein ideally both student and teacher learn from each encounter.

As I look back on my high school days, I am convinced that sometimes there really was a bad match between the curriculum and the exam. Algebra provides an example. Our text consisted of a series of lessons, each dealing with equations of a particular type. Each lesson began with a description of the type of equation, then

95

showed how to solve this type, and ended with a problem set. The teacher reviewed the lesson, worked through the examples, adding a few along the way, and then assigned homework from the problem set. Success on the assignment (a form of test) required diligence, but basically students had only to follow the pattern in the examples. Then came the final exam, and surprisingly, the game had changed. Different problem types were scrambled together, and suddenly what was most important was the ability to distinguish the different problem types. Students may have memorized the solution techniques for every problem type, but what was really needed was something that had not been taught — that is, how to tell one problem type from another.

How Does the State Give a Final Exam?

The United States Court of Appeals (Fifth Circuit) ruled on May 4, 1981 in the *Debra P*. case that ''. . . the State many not deprive its high school seniors of the economic and educational benefits of a high school diploma until it has demonstrated that the SSAT II (the Florida minimum competency test) is a fair test of that which is taught in its classrooms . . . (*Debra P*. v. *Turlington*, 1981).'' The court's judgment was consistent with analyses put forward by a number of scholars (Haney and Madaus 1978, p. 478, and references therein; McClung 1977). The court went on to state that ''Just as a teacher in a particular test gives the final exam on what he or she has taught, so should the state give its final exam on what has been taught in its classrooms (*Debra P*. v. *Turlington*, 1981).''

This idea sounds straightforward, but we know it is not. As already noted, it is difficult for teachers to ensure that what they test is reasonably related to what they teach. At least the individual teacher can focus on a limited and well-defined matter — the content of a particular course as taught by that particular teacher. The issue takes on different dimensions when the state gives a final exam — the tone of the quotation from *Debra P*. v. *Turlington* properly suggests that the state does not teach students — at least not yet.

What does it mean then for a state (or a district) to give a ''final exam''? In answering this question, we will reflect in turn on the purpose, coverage, and timing of a test.

Purpose

Although purposes vary, we can distinguish between the need to certify and the need to rank (for discussion of the role of tests for certification, and references on this topic, see the papers by Hecht and Pottinger in Bunda and Sanders 1979). States administer tests designed to certify an individual as competent to drive a car, to act as an attorney, to perform brain surgery, or to serve as classroom teacher, among other skills and occupations. Everyone passing the bar exam receives a license to practice law, regardless of whether that person will excel or is just above the cutoff point. Certification tests are generally created under the auspices of the appropriate professional organization, and judgment about the cutoff point for granting a license is also a matter of expert opinion.

Ranking is a different matter. A group of individuals may be competing for a limited number of jobs, in which case the purpose of assessment is to decide which individuals are most capable to perform the job. Civil service jobs, admission to elite universities, and selection for management training positions exemplify situations wherein ranking is of paramount concern. Because of the need to make fine-grained decisions all along the scale, the psychometric characteristics of the test become critical, and the psychometrist may have more to say than the content expert about the final version of the test.

Coverage

The domain to be covered is the starting point for determining validity. Any test is a sample of performance from a much larger domain — the tester uses the sample to make judgments about how the individual is likely to perform throughout the domain as a whole. The domain of generalization may be more or less well defined. For instance, suppose we need to determine whether a soldier can disassemble, clean, and reassemble an M-1 rifle. The content of the domain is fairly clear-cut: the "curriculum" has relatively few elements to it, and there is likely to be consensus on the structure of the content. Other facets of the domain are more difficult to spell out or may be intractable for testing: the environment in which the task is to be performed (for example, at a work table, out in a field, or hip deep in a swamp on a dark night), the method of assessment (for example, paper and pencil, multiple-choice, or actual performance), and the condition of the individual (for example, well rested, or having endured forty-eight hours without sleep).

In the case of a high school exit exam, the domain of generalization is much less definite. The content is fuzzy, it varies over individuals, the observed performance may depend on the conditions of assessment, and the extent and direction of transfer of the knowledge is debatable. This phase of the *Debra P.* case may prove to be of special significance insofar as it forces educators and other concerned citizens to reflect on what we expect from a high school education. One group of voices (for example, Popham and Lindheim 1981; Popham 1981) defines that course of study in relatively detailed and down-to-earth language, akin to specific training tasks such as rifle assembly. Other voices call for a broader scope (for example, Broudy 1980): when they discuss preparation for life, they consider the person's ability to act as a responsible citizen, not just to be able to successfully interpret a want ad.

Timing

Finally, there is the timing of a test. How much time may intervene between instruction and assessment? Should testing be distributed over time (lots of "little" tests interspersed with teaching) or concentrated within a single occasion (the final exam)? How long will it take for students to find out how they did, what is going to happen, and what they can do in response?

More could be said about the relevance of the temporal dimension; take this paragraph and the preceding one as placeholders to say that people live from moment to moment, from day to day, and from year to year; as a recognition that teaching and learning take time; and as a reminder that the *when* of testing can be as significant as the *why* and *what*.

Some Typical Test Packages

Present-day testing practices can be viewed as a constellation of packages defined by purpose, coverage, and timing. For instance, many schools have adopted "management systems" in reading and math. These systems are actually test packages — each test is designed to cover a limited domain within the area of reading or math, suited for frequent administration (often using a multiple-choice format for efficiency) and for the purpose of deciding whether the student has learned the material within the domain. These systems are especially popular for dealing with students in need of remediation. Unfortunately, these systems are quite piecemeal and prone to Ralph Tyler's criticism that they emphasize "small answers to small questions (McKenna 1977)."

Many high school teachers still give old-fashioned final exams at the end of the course. The purpose is both *to certify* (that is, students must score higher than an "F" to receive certification that they have taken the course) and *to rank* (students with "A" grades are ranked higher than students with "B"'s, and so on). The coverage is the content of the syllabus, as defined by the teacher, within the typically broad mandates of the school and district. The students generally have to be ready to handle a substantial amount of material within the domain of the course and may be required to demonstrate productive ability such as writing an essay or working out a math problem.

Another package takes such forms as the Scholastic Aptitude Test (SAT), the New York Regent's Exam, or any of the various standardized achievement tests. Here, the purpose is clearly to rank individuals, the coverage is broad and unabashedly academic and measures outcomes that span several years of instruction. Both teacher and student may receive the test results in relatively short order, but there is little that either can do about it.

Finally, there are the "new guys on the block" — minimum competency tests (MCTs). These devices come in a variety of shapes and sizes, but certain generalizations can be drawn. The purpose is certification — pass or fail, diploma or no diploma. Like the standardized tests just mentioned, the MCTs have coverage that is broad and diffuse. The instruments are often constructed from lists of specific objectives and are generally "criterion-referenced." They may or may not focus on the academic curriculum; quite often, the idea is to have students demonstrate their ability to apply academic skills to practical life situations. The end effect is to increase the coverage of the test.

Like standardized tests, competency tests are designed to measure the long-term effects of schooling. Although many states and districts have mandated "early-warning" tests in the elementary and middle-school grades, the consequences of failing these are less clear-cut; retention in grade and assignment to remedial programs may ensue, but the policies are far from uniform. For the high school student, the meaning of the competency test is clear — success is required for receipt of the diploma (that is, for certification as a high school graduate). The action is akin to receiving a license. Unlike other licensing programs, however, the decision has broad consequences and affects all citizens (the motor-vehicle operation examination has similar features). The individual chooses to seek certification as a lawyer, beautician, or plumber; the state requires that everyone attend school through the twelfth grade. This mandate, in combination with the provision of free public high school education, implies that everyone is expected to acquire a high school diploma. *Not* to receive this certification carries a stigma — whether or not the individual considers the high school education an important personal goal. If an individual does not pass the bar exam, this failure entails no bias should he or she thereafter attempt a civil service exam. Failure to receive a high school diploma, in contrast, can deny the individual entry to postsecondary education, as well as a wide array of job opportunities (Dearman and Plisko 1981, p. 232). High school dropouts have substantially higher unemployment rates and are far less likely to enter high-prestige jobs. Incidentally, the proportion of adolescents failing to receive a high school diploma, which peaked at 23.7% in 1969, has increased slowly but steadily over the past decade until it now stands at 26% (Dearman and Plisko 1981, p. 112).

Should We Teach What We Test?

Investigations of several minimum competency programs provide convincing evidence that the cart has been placed firmly in front of the horse: states and school districts, in the absence of a clear and defensible conception of the educational goals for their students, have imposed standardized tests and uniform criteria for graduation. Those familiar with philosophy of science have a new example of the consequences of unbridled operationalism: *A high school education is whatever is measured by a high school competency test.*

The controversy about whether tests should lead or follow the curriculum is a long-standing one (for example, McClung 1979, esp. p. 668, and references therein). Those who hold that "the responsibility of the schools is to *educate first*, to validate learning second (Turnbull 1978)" deserve support. Yet a local associate superintendent has this to say about the curriculum for students who have had trouble with the competency test:

> We have a learning center, to which students may go to receive packets of material for each of those competencies that was developed by teachers and we have three or four packets for each competency. Students can go to the aide in there and say I need some help in learning fractions, I can get a packet to study on my own, or get help from their parents. When they feel they know it, they can take the test again. [Hardy, 1981]

Technology is no barrier to constructing tests that measure something, even though we may not be sure what the "something" is. Validity has always taken a back seat to reliability in test construction; it has always been easier to state the precision and consistency of an educational test than to describe with certainty what is being measured (Buros 1977; Messick 1980). The softness in validation procedures has had few serious consequences in the past. For one thing, face validity has been respected by practitioners, if not always honored by theoreticians. For another thing, the results of a single test have seldom been used to make significant decisions about individuals or educational programs.

With the growth of competency testing programs, we are in a new ball game. First, implementation of these programs has fallen chiefly into the hands of test designers, administrators, curriculum designers, and instructional specialists, and teachers have played a less important role (Bardon and Robinette 1980). Second, face validity has suffered because of the way in which the domain has been defined. High school instructors know little, if anything, about basic skills in reading and math, nor are they expert in the area of functional application of basic skills. Reading and math are elementary school topics, and it is not clear whether anyone could be reliably identified as expert in the skills needed for "life after school." Tom Fisher certainly had trouble wrestling with this issue in Florida

(Center for Law and Education 1980, CT64). In any event, psychometricians, along with teachers from English, algebra, social studies, science, and other subject-matter fields, are being asked to make judgments about the face validity of test items in domains outside of their professional expertise. Third, test results are now being taken quite seriously. High school youngsters are being denied diplomas — even though they have successfully completed a course of study — because they do poorly on a test. Equally important, youngsters are being placed in remedial programs on the basis of test performance; such remedial programs are clear-cut examples of the design of instructional programs being determined by the characteristics of the test, rather than the other way around. The management systems used in many elementary schools for reading and mathematics instruction illustrate the same phenomenon. These and other like examples represent a disastrous educational strategy: design an examination based on what test constructors find to be convenient and conventional, and then shape the high school curriculum to match the content and format of the test.

To be sure, it is quite reasonable for a curriculum to include opportunities to learn test-taking skills. Law students, just before they take the bar exam, spend some time studying the mechanics of the bar exam. Students who want to practice for the SAT, the graduate record exam (GRE), the law school admission test (LSAT), and so on, can find materials and programs to familiarize them with the format and content of the tests. Although the effectiveness of such programs is not clear-cut, it appears that the additional training improves performance for some students.

No one believes that such test-taking exercises substitute for the "real" curriculum. Consider, by way of analogy, an automobile's gas gauge. The gauge, when hooked up and operating properly, serves as a valid and reliable indicator of how much gas is available to propel the automobile. It does not per se power the car. One can invalidate the gauge; for example, one might install a knob on the dashboard, so that whenever one wants to show a full tank of gas, one needs only turn the knob to "full." Although such a device may make the driver "feel good" in the short run, reality must eventually be reckoned with: the car will stop if the tank is empty, no matter what the gauge reads.

In like manner, practice in test taking may be a reasonable exercise for many students, but these exercises must not be substituted for genuine curriculum goals. Even if such exercises help the student over the minimum competency hurdle, a more fundamental reality will be lacking. To doubt this conclusion is to question the value of secondary education. Eventually, students will run out of gas. Unfortunately, they will make the discovery and pay the price long after they have left school — the "mechanic" who installed the quick fix will not be penalized and will be unaware of the long-term consequences.

The Structure of the High School Curriculum

What are the educational goals of the comprehensive high school in the United States? First, the high school curriculum is organized around several reasonably well-defined disciplines: English literature, mathematics, social studies, natural sciences, fine arts, practical arts, and athletics, to name a few. Each teacher specializes in one of these disciplines; teachers cluster in professional groups according to discipline.

Second, schools arrange student programs around tracks that reflect combinations of ability and interest. A track can be thought of as a focused subset of disciplines. To be sure, certain core elements are required of all students, and there is even some effort to ensure that every student has contact with every discipline. The distinctive character of the comprehensive high school comes about, in theory at least, because the combination of a broad array of student types and instructional disciplines facilitates a fuller and richer experience than is possible in more specialized educational environments.

Naturally, the common requirements and the optional courses are not the same for everyone. Every student may be required to take English, but a youngster in the college-bound track is likely to be in different courses than is one in a vocational track. Likewise, everyone may be required to take physical education, fine arts, and home economics, but depending on the significance of the disciplines to their program, the individual student is likely to encounter quite different experiences in each of these areas. The student who has prospects of becoming a professional baseball player properly seeks a different balance among disciplines than does the youngster who aims toward becoming a carpenter or an astronaut.

Finally, the comprehensive high school has been generally oriented toward intellectual growth. This emphasis may be developmentally appropriate. Piaget (1971) has described adolescence as the time of growth in "formal operational thought" — the ability to reflect and analyze at an abstract, conceptual level. In fact, it is a chicken-and-egg situation. Youngsters may become able in their teenage years to think more abstractly, or the demands and opportunities of the secondary curriculum may promote such thought. Recent years have evidenced a spate of anti-intellectualism. Under the guise of relevance and personal freedom, some teachers have disavowed abstract and principled knowledge. But the so-called classical high school curriculum still places a premium on understanding. Whether the subject being taught is trigonometry or typing, the emphasis is on the development of thought, in contrast to a stress on the acquisition of facts and skills.

In summary, the curriculum of the comprehensive high school can be painted in the following broad strokes: it is built upon a collection of disciplines, each acting as an independent entity. Students are generally organized into tracks, each built to give the student experience with each discipline, with the intensity and content of that experience shaped to match the student's track. The underlying theme across tracks and disciplines is the intellectual focus of the curriculum, the stress on understanding, on conceptual levels of thought, and on general skills in problem-solving. The high school provides the student with general preparation for life — college, apprenticeship, and the personal and social demands of young adulthood. The high school prepares adolescents to deal intellectually with the role of spouse or parent; it does *not* introduce them to either activity by direct personal and emotional experience. It prepares youngsters to benefit from a program of apprentice training as firemen; it does *not* train them to be firemen. It prepares students to figure out the long version of the 1040A federal income tax form when and if that becomes necessary; it does *not* include the details of how to fill out the form. An English professor puts it in a nutshell: "... the principal effect of an education is to make us wiser and more intelligent. ... the measure of an education is what remains after the facts have been forgotten (Rice 1981)."

The Structure of Competency Tests

Minimum-standard tests for high school graduation are a recent development and scarcely have a tradition as such. In addition, there is considerable variation in practice from one locale to another. Nonetheless, some general trends can be observed that may help in thinking about the match between the curriculum and the test.

Some structural features of competency tests reflect the mandates establishing them. First, the emphasis is generally on the basic skills of reading and mathematics or on the application of these skills in practical life settings. Second, the usual practice is to establish a common test and a common set of standards for all students within a state or district. Local districts in some states (for example, California) are free to decide how to implement competency testing, but the implicit or explicit understanding is a standard procedure for all students, regardless of the program they have pursued in high school. Third, the mandates focus on minimum levels of competence, without being precise about what is being minimized. Rhetoric alluding to the minimum performance needed to survive in our society overlooks the fact that students face quite different challenges in life after school, and that what seems bare survival to one may seem quite elegant to another. Competency test design is presently faced with a three-fold dilemma — the content of the high school curriculum, the basic skills of reading and mathematics, and the pragmatics of life after school. The last of these alternatives is difficult, if not impossible, to pin down and is not seriously considered in this chapter.

The legislative and bureaucratic mandates place limits on the design of competency tests, but the test constructors further restrict themselves because of conventions and notions of efficiency. For instance, it is taken for granted that a test instrument necessarily entails group administration and a multiple-choice format (three or four alternatives, most likely). It is virtually inconceivable that one could design a test any other way.

Most competency tests use an "objective" or "domain" approach for design (for example, Hambleton and Eignor 1980). This technique, with wellsprings in the "behavioral objectives" philosophy of the early 1960s, emphasizes the specific operational characteristics of what is to be measured and gives little attention to the structure of the discipline. Every discipline has a structure. Even experts may not be able to articulate this structure, but reason dictates that a coherent organization of some kind must exist (Simon 1981). An analogy may help explain the importance of emphasizing the organizing principles of a complex system. A steer has structure. Biologists and butchers differ in how they describe this structure, but the animal is not "incoherent." Suppose that I slaughter the steer, grind the entire carcass into hamburger, and present this to a biologist for reconstruction — let us assume that the biologist is from Mars, and thus has no prior knowledge about how a steer is built. The task will be impossible. By chopping the animal into little pieces, I have destroyed the clues to the overall structure. In like manner, test designers who rely on the behavioral-objectives approach as their primary design technique are likely to destroy the disciplinary structure which they are trying to assess. The disrespect of the structure can have several consequences. For one thing, students (and others) may concentrate on the details and never pick up the main themes — they may fail the task of reconstruction. It is also hard to establish priorities in any rational fashion — one piece of hamburger looks pretty much like another. The tendency is to strain at gnats and swallow camels.

The design of competency tests also reflects the typical reliance on consensus judgment by a wide variety of interested parties (Ganopole 1980). Administrators proudly report the number and diversity of individuals who "provided input" on the test objectives. These groups generally have little awareness of the limits governing their charge: all students will be assessed by the same group-administered, multiple-choice test; the objectives will be specified by a highly particularized format; item writing, statistical analysis, and final item selection will be carried out by procedures that they do not understand and that affect test design in ways that they cannot appreciate.

The chief problems with the consensus-by-committee approach are that expertise is diluted and clarity is compromised. Just because someone happens to know a great deal about curriculum and instruction in a discipline is no guarantee that the person's voice will stand out in the crowd — loudness and insistence can be more important than expertise. When dissenting opinions do arise, the easiest solution is to find compromising language, which leaves even more to the discretion of the item writers.

Another indicator of the structure of competency tests comes from factor analysis of student performance. The typical standardized test comprises two or more subtests. Many tests have been "objectivized" — the test publisher can provide a list of specific objectives and can identify the items corresponding to each objective. Despite the subtest and objective labels, most achievement tests can be described quite adequately by a single underlying trait —a beguilingly simple structure. The correlation among subtests is about as high as it can be, given the reliability of the individual subtests. In fact, the correlation between different disciplines (for example, reading and mathematics) is often quite high, approaching 1.0 when corrected for attenuation. Although standardized tests have a number of strong points, they are poorly designed to measure patterns of strength and weakness in the subject-matter areas (Buros 1977).

The statement that test performance reflects a single trait means that the total test score, aggregated over *all* items, is a reliable measure. What about validity? What does the test measure? Validity probably judges the student's overall reaction to schooling and to the format of the standardized testing situation. The statement also means that any profile of differences between subtests and objectives is *not* a reliable index, that test performance cannot be used to describe relative strengths and weaknesses (Calfee and Drum 1979).

These remarks hold for standardized tests; but what about MCT? The documentation for most such tests is rather limited, and it is not easy to find the data needed to answer the question. However, four sets of competency test data (none of these are from Florida) — two in reading and two in math — are available. These tests have characteristics similar to norm-referenced tests (Mandinach, Lau, Calfee and Capell 1982). They are likely to include a few items that are "bad" by the usual conventions — for instance, the percentage of students passing an item may exceed 90%, which means the item is weak at discriminating among students. Nonetheless, we find that the tests have high internal consistency (that is, they are reliable), and the subtests are highly correlated. Notwithstanding the complex and carefully orchestrated selection of objectives, an individual student's performance is adequately summarized by the total score. Differential success or failure on specific objectives is mainly due to error of measurement; using test results to decide on student assignments is unlikely to help students pass specific objectives unless there is a close match in format, style, and content between test items and work sheets. Such a practice seems an undesirable instance of "teaching to the test."

In short, analyses to date suggest that competency tests measure generalized achievement; competency tests measure the same thing as standardized tests, whatever that may be. Regardless of the overlay of subtest labels and specific objectives, these tests have a simple underlying structure. To the extent that the designers of competency tests have attempted to create assessment systems that highlight specific strengths and weaknesses, their efforts have been of little avail; the same is true of standardized tests (Resnick 1981).

Conclusions

Let me now summarize the main conclusion from this section on the structure of competency tests — generalizations that apply with full force to the Florida competency project. First, legislative and regulatory mandates place various constraints on the design of competency tests — that is, on the content, the format, and the decision that a single test shall be used to assess all students. These mandates often reflect conventional practice. Second, the process of design is determined more by psychometric experts than by curriculum specialists. The latter may be members of the advisory committee, but in the consensus process, their voices are seldom given special weight. The result is an omnibus design not unlike existing standardized tests. Third — and not surprisingly — empirical analysis shows that, as is true for standardized tests, competency tests can be adequately described by a single underlying trait. The student's total score, aggregated over objectives, is a reliable measure. Differences in success and failure for specific objectives are not trustworthy patterns and are poor guides for making specific curriculum assignments.

Is There a Match between the Test and the Curriculum?
An Educational Answer

The previous sections have laid a foundation for answering questions of primary concern: how might the state of Florida demonstrate the degree of correspondence between the competency test and the curriculum, and what are the strengths and weaknesses of various approaches? From the analyses in the preceding section, a *substantive* examination will reveal fundamental mismatches between the high school curriculum and the test. This section will first give some examples of what is meant by "substantive examination" of the linkage between test and curriculum. The next section will describe an accounting approach, with pros and cons, that might be considered by Florida.

Let us consider substantive approaches to instructional validity by posing a contrast: should instructional validity mean that (1) the content of a test is adequately covered by the curriculum, or that (2) the curriculum (or some subset of the curriculum) is adequately covered by the test?

The first approach assumes that the test represents outcomes that have value in their own right and that the curriculum is adequate in that it teaches students what they need to do well on the test. This approach is quite reasonable in some situations. For instance, airline pilots receive a fairly extensive assessment at the end of their training, including tests of performance as well as knowledge. The domain is well defined, and the test is sufficiently broad and rich that it seems reasonable to require that the curriculum be evaluated against the content and format of the test. One might challenge curriculum elements that did not contribute to improved test performance.

One can imagine a test for graduation from elementary school that could serve as a standard for evaluating the curriculum in reading and math. The instrument would need to be more extensive and more performance-based than the multiple-choice tests now in use (Haney and Madaus 1978, p. 471 *ff.*, make the point that direct measures of achievement are not necessarily correlated with multiple-choice measures). Moreover, such an assessment would need to emphasize students' ability to apply their skills and knowledge to facets of elementary education other than reading and math. Whenever a test of limited scope is established as a standard, there is the risk of neglecting important aims that fall outside that scope.

The second approach — requiring that the test provide adequate coverage of a curriculum — focuses on the curriculum and places the burden of adequacy on the test. This interpretation makes more sense when the goal is schooling. It is not the goal of secondary education to turn out competent airline pilots, but rather to educate broadly so that people have a good chance to achieve competence in the various fields they aspire to after graduation. The focus is not on the actual postgraduate activities — these are too numerous and too idiosyncratic. Schools should concentrate on teaching skills and knowledge that are broadly applicable in a variety of contexts; in school, students should be learning to learn.

These remarks do not imply that a single curriculum for all students is appropriate. As already mentioned, the curriculum in reading and mathematics for elementary students is so fundamental that it may be viewed as a fixed requirement for all students. However, any serious effort to certify a test as adequate coverage of the high school curriculum quickly confronts what appears to be an insurmountable difficulty — that is, the curriculum is diverse. There is no significant core that is identical in content, form, and level for all students. One may protest that all students should be able to read "simple" materials, and to compute "simple" problems, but what is "simple" for one high school may have little relation to what is simple for another. The earlier discussion of secondary education in the United States leads to the conclusion that the high school curriculum does not include a common core for all students nor should it. To repeat an earlier point, it does make sense to certify that all elementary students attain a level of performance in basic skills that ensures they can benefit from instruction at the secondary level; this should be done *before* they graduate from elementary school. On the other hand, if we take the high school curriculum as the focus and require a single competency test that covers a significant "common core" of the curriculum, the test will fail its intended purpose.

A second facet for determining the substantive match between teaching and testing centers around the question of what is meant by "teaching" (McClung, 1977, has referred to this as the instructional validity of a test; Amarel, 1980, suggests that "the notion of curriculum should include the practice as well as the content of instruction"). From an administrative perspective, a convenient index is whether something is "on the books"; is it listed on the scope-and-sequence chart that provides the official account of what is "taught" in the district or in the school? But is it reasonable to say that something has been taught if the teacher does not assign it or if the student never encounters it? Should not teachers be held responsible for presenting those elements of the curriculum identified as essential for success on a competency test? Anyone familiar with the standardized curricula followed in some countries (and in some elementary programs in the United States) may balk at the implications of this remark; one way to ensure accountability is to establish a set routine, in which on any given day and hour administrators know what is being taught in the core courses.

Exposure is only one issue under the "Was it *really* taught?" banner. One can also ask: "How much?" "How recently?" "How well?" (*Debra P.* v. *Turlington* 1981, p. 404). The issue of *how much* is a question of reasonable proportions. Given that we reach agreement about how to divide up a curriculum into workable elements (that task can be done — behavioral objectives are generally not the most appropriate units), the goal is to relate the amount of coverage in the curriculum to the number of items on the test. For example, if half the items on a reading test assess vocabulary knowledge, and only 5% of the lessons in the reading course deal with word meaning, this would seem to be an intolerable mismatch.

The *how recently* question was raised as an explicit issue in the Florida case (Haney and Madaus 1978, p. 469). Parents (and presumably their children) reportedly complained that many items tested skills that had not been studied since the primary grades. Refresher courses might be a remedy, but these should be justified on other grounds than the need to test on skills and knowledge in which students have already demonstrated their competence. Time is a precious resource in schooling.

How well is a difficult and complex issue. It is reasonable to expect teachers to do a good job in the classroom. We cannot condone situations wherein students have trouble learning because they are badly taught and wherein they have to bear the burden of that failure. Effective teacher evaluation is difficult to implement because of problems that are partly conceptual, partly technical, and partly political (Millman 1981). These problems are solvable, though it is hard to point to exemplary programs.

Incidentally, we are likely to see renewed efforts to tie teacher evaluation to student outcomes (Britell 1980; Bardon and Robinette 1980; Tyler 1978; Glass 1973). The same pressures that cause some students to be denied diplomas will probably lead to demands to fire some teachers. For the moment, the strongest arguments lead to the conclusion that teachers should be evaluated according to their classroom performance and not according to their students' test performance. This principle will be maintained, it is hoped, during the rough seas ahead.

The questions just raised should be addressed in any substantive attempt to establish the match between what is taught and what is tested. Finding answers to these questions is a challenge, but one that can be met. The answers are critical if schools are to meet the challenge of providing an adequate education for all youngsters, while maintaining a standard of excellence for those students who are able and inclined (Cohen and Haney 1980).

A "Minimum-Accounting" Strategy for Measuring the Match between What Is Tested and What Is Taught.

It is unlikely that school administrators in Florida (or anywhere else) will respond to a court mandate to show that they "teach what they test" by pursuing the kinds of questions raised in the previous section. Given their backgrounds, the time and resources, and the demands of the situation, they will probably search for a minimum accounting that will satisfy the court. Such a practical strategy is both defensible and understandable, but just as minimum test standards have led to problems, so a minimum approach to a test-to-curriculum match has inherent flaws.

The minimum-accounting strategy is carried out by the test administrators — they designed the test, it is their "baby," and it is under fire. The structure used to construct the test — typically, behavioral objectives — is the primary mechanism for establishing the match. The objectives structure has features that make accounting quite workable. Each objective appears relatively discrete and simple. The number of objectives is sufficiently great that no single objective receives serious attention. Finally, the list lacks clear priorities; all objectives are more or less equally important. These features simplify the counting process; instructional goals can be handled as though they were so many apples or oranges.

The next step in the process is to collect all materials used for instruction. Special attention is given to materials with an objectives-based structure. Literature texts and library books may be used to teach reading, but they are not properly "indexed" for accounting, and so they will be disregarded.

Once the materials have been collected, the matching process begins. The task is simple and requires relatively little expertise; one simply searches through the index of objectives in the materials for correspondences with the test objectives. Whenever one finds a match, one tallies the relevant pages for that objective on the accounting sheet. The goal is to show that for each objective on the test, there is *at least one* corresponding element somewhere in the curriculum materials. This provides the evidence that every student, sometime and somehow, may have been exposed to instruction on every test objective.

The accounting strategy has several strengths that are administratively attractive. It places little burden on the instructional staff — that is, teachers need not play any role. It is objective, and so-called expert judgment is not needed. It is quantitative — that is, a term like "main idea" may appear under a variety of labels, but once certain equivalences are established, tallying can be reliably carried out by virtually anyone.

The accounting approach can be enhanced in various ways. For instance, the people doing the tally may examine the materials to ensure that objectives are covered in nontrivial ways. They can search for exercises not indexed but relevant to an objective. The materials can be analyzed to see how closely the content and format of the instructional exercises match the content and format of the competency test. These and other enhancements do not alter the strategy in any fundamental way; it remains a bureaucratic response to a bureaucratic mandate.

What are the weaknesses in this approach? First, simply establishing that a test objective is "on the books" is no assurance that it has been taught — no matter how teaching is defined. As long as high schools provide variety in programs and some freedom of choice, it is possible for students to miss large chunks of material that may cover critical objectives. Second, the matching process is of questionable validity. Although the process may seem "natural" to administrators and might appear satisfactory at first glance to the courts, the other people involved are likely to pursue the validity issue in one form or another. As long as some students are denied diplomas or others seem to be receiving a poor education, questions will be raised about the effectiveness of the curriculum, the appropriateness of the tests, and the match between testing and teaching. Students and parents, along with their advocates, will turn to curriculum specialists and instructional experts for advice, and more thorough examinations of competency tests and instructional programs will raise questions about the accounting strategy — questions of sufficient concern that eventually the courts will reject the strategy.

There is the danger that administrators will try to "validate" the strategy by altering the instructional program to match the test. We may be experiencing this today under the rubric of "remedial programs" (Amarel 1980). Many districts have prepared "individualized programs" for students who fail the competency test. These programs are usually work-sheet packets, organized according to the test objectives. The instructional program is simple: the teacher gives the student a set of work sheets corresponding to the failed objectives; the student studies the work sheets until he or she can pass the objectives. From an accounting perspective, the match between testing and teaching is perfect. From an instructional perspective, there are serious questions about whether students are learning anything beyond the specifics of particular test items. The peril is that this conception of secondary education may prove so attractive to administrators that it is extended to cover all students, not just those unfortunate enough to be assigned to remedial programs.

What Can Florida Do?

The Florida State Department of Education has three options for responding to the court's mandate to show they are teaching what is tested on their high school competency test. One option has already been described. The Department of Education can argue that the objectives on the present test have been at least minimally taught. The court will likely reject this option; most judges will conclude that it is not enough simply to show that what a student needs to learn is in a book somewhere in the school. Instead, schools will have to demonstrate that a reasonable effort has been made to educate the student.

A second option is for the state to examine the curriculum more closely, determine what is being taught, and assign to curriculum specialists within the state the task of deciding the extent to which the test is an appropriate measure of what is being taught. If the foregoing analysis is correct, the diversity inherent in the secondary curriculum will emerge as a dominant consideration, and it will prove impossible to assess student performance in a reasonable and valid manner with a single test. This option has the disadvantage that administrators (and possibly even legislators) may have to rethink their positions and actions. As noted earlier, it is feasible to design a minimum competence program for graduation from sixth grade, guaranteeing that any student entering junior high school is reasonably literate and has the skills needed to benefit from secondary education. The elementary curriculum has a coherence that allows it to be covered by a standard test; it should be relatively straightforward to validate such a test against what is taught in elementary school and what is needed for progress in secondary school.

A third option, which has much to recommend it but probably is the least satisfactory from an administrative perspective, is to disavow the competency test approach and return to a strengthened track-course-grade approach as the basis for high school graduation. A variation of this approach incorporates a standard examination for one or more of the tracks. This option may seem conservative and retrogressive, and perhaps it is. This perspective can also look forward to a stronger and more equitable curriculum. In the short run, this option is probably not a viable alternative. In the long run, however, it may be that competency testing will provide the leverage for more careful examination of the U.S. high school (Broudy 1980). If so, this so-called testing fad ultimately may prove valuable.

References

Amarel, M. "Comments on H. Broudy's Impact of Minimum Competency Testing on Curriculum," in R.C. Jaeger and C.K. Tittle eds., *Minimum Competency Achievement Testing: Motives, Models, Measures, and Consequences.* Berkeley, Calif.: McCutchan Publishing Corporation, 1980.

Bardon, J.I., and Robinette, C.L. "Minimum Competency Testing of Pupils: Psychological Implications for Teachers." In R.C. Jaeger and C.K. Tittle eds., *Minimum Competency Achievement Testing: Motives, Models, Measures, and Consequences.* Berkeley, Calif.: McCutchan Publishing Corporation, 1980.

Britell, J.K. "Competence and Excellence: The Search for an Egalitarian Standard, the Demand for a Universal Gurarantee." In R.C. Jaeger and C.K. Tittle eds., *Minimum Competency Achievement Testing: Motives, Models, Measures, and Consequences.* Berkeley, Calif.: McCutchan Publishing Corporation, 1980.

Broudy, H.S. "Impact of Minimum Competency Testing on Curriculum." In R.C. Jaeger and C.K. Tittle eds., *Minimum Competency Achievement Testing: Motives, Models, Measures, and Consequences.* Berkeley, Calif.: McCutchan Publishing Corporation, 1980.

Bunda, M.A., and Sanders, J.R., eds. *Practices & Problems in Competency-Based Measurement.* Washington, D.C.: National Council on Measurement in Education, 1979.

Buros, O.K. "Fifty Years in Testing: Some Reminiscences, Criticisms, and Suggestions." *Educational Researcher.* 6 (1977), 9–15.

Calfee, R.C., and Drum, P.A. "How the Researcher Can Help the Reading Teacher with Classroom Assessment." In L.B. Resnick and P.A. Weaver eds., *Theory and Practice of early Reading* (Vol 2). Hillsdale, N.J.: Lawrence Erlbaum Associates, Inc., 1979.

Center for Law and Education. "Minimum Competency Testing: A Case Study of the Florida Functional Literacy Examination." Briefing paper for two seminars. Cambridge, Mass.: Center for Law and Education, Inc., 1980.

Cohen, D.K., and Haney, W. "Minimum Competency Testing and Social Policy." In R.C. Jaeger and C.K. Tittle eds., *Minimum Competency Achievement Testing: Motives, Models, Measures, and Consequences.* Berkeley, Calif.: McCutchan Publishing Corporation, 1980.

Dearman, N.B., and Plisko, V.W. *The Condition of Education.* Statistical report, National Center for Education Statistics. Washington, D.C.: U.S. Department of Education, 1981.

Debra P. v. Turlington, 644 F.2d 397 (5th Cir. 1981).

Ganopole, S.J. "Using Performance and Preference Data in Setting Standards for Minimum Competency Assessment Programs." In R.C. Jaeger and C.K. Tittle eds., *Minimum Competency Achievement Testing: Motives, Models, Measures, and Consequences.* Berkeley, Calif.: McCutchan Publishing Corporation, 1980.

Glass, G.V. "Statistical Measurement Problems in Implementing the Stull Act." In N.L. Gage ed., *Mandated Evaluation of Educators: A Conference on California's Stull Act.* Washington, D.C.: Educational Resources Division, Capitol Publications, 1973.

Hambleton, R.K., and Eignor, D.R. "Competency Test Development, Validation, and Standard Setting." In R.C. Jaeger and C.K. Tittle eds., *Minimum Competency Achievement Testing: Motives, Models, Measures, and Consequences.* Berkeley, Calif.: McCutchan Publishing Corporation, 1980.

Haney, W., and Madaus, G. "Making Sense of the Competency Testing Movement." *Harvard Educational Review.* 48 (1978), 462–484.

Hardy, C.C. "Basic Tests Called Improvement in Education." *San Francisco Examiner,* November 23, 1981.

Mandinach, E., Lau, E., Calfee, R., and Capell, F. "Test Structure, Information Content, and Curriculum Linkages in Minimum Competency Tests." Paper presented at American Educational Research Conference, March 1982.

McClung, M. "Competency Testing: Potential for Discrimination." *Clearinghouse Review.* 2 (1977), 439–448.

McClung, M.S. "Competency Testing Programs: Legal and Educational Issues." *Fordham Law Review.* 47 (1978–1979), 651–712.

McKenna, B. "What's Wrong with Standardized Testing?" *Today's Education* (March-April, 1977) (reprint).

Messick, S. "Test Validity and the Ethics of Assessment." *American Psychologist.* 35 (1980), 1012–1027.

Millman, J., ed., *Handbook of Teacher Evaluation.* Beverly Hills, Calif.: Sage Publications, 1981.

Piaget, J. *Science of Education and Psychology of the Child.* New York: Viking Press, 1971.

Popham, W.J. *Modern Educational Measurement.* Englewood Cliffs, N.J.: Prentice-Hall, Inc. 1981.

Popham, W.J., and Lindheim, E. "Implications of a Landmark Ruling on Florida's Minimum Competency Test." *Phi Delta Kappan.* 63 (1981), 18–20.

Resnick, L.B. Introduction: Research To Inform a Debate. *Phi Delta Kappan,* 62 (1981), 623–624.

Rice, S. "Educators Have Failed To Plead the Case for Education." *San Jose News,* August 31, 1981.

Simon, H.A. *The Sciences of the Artificial* (2nd ed.). Cambridge, Mass.: The MIT Press, 1981.

Turnbull, W.W. "Issues in Assessment of Basic Skills." Paper for presentation at the Southern Regional Meeting of the College Board, Myrtle Beach, S.C., February 1978.

Tyler, R.W., Lapan, S.D., Moore, J.C., Rivers, L.W., and Skibo, D.B. *The Florida Accountability Program: An Evaluation of Its Educational Soundness and Implementation.* Washington, D.C.: National Educational Association, 1978.

5 CURRICULAR VALIDITY:
Convincing the Courts That It Was Taught without Precluding the Possibility of Measuring It

Robert L. Linn

The decision of the Fifth Circuit Court of Appeals to require Florida to submit ''proof of the circular validity of the test''[1] before making the award of a diploma contingent upon passing it was in keeping with recommendations made by McClung (1977, 1978). McClung suggested that the courts should require curricular and instructional validity for competency tests used to deny high school diplomas. He distinguished between the concepts of curricular validity and instructional validity with the former referring to the degree to which ''test items represent objectives of the curriculum'' (1979, p. 682) and the latter referring to the degree to which the topics measured by the test were actually taught. McClung argued that minimum competency tests (MCTs) need both curricular and instructional validity but that instructional validity should be the central concern.

Although the appellate court used the term *curricular vaildity,* it is clear that the main thrust of the court's decision is most consistent with McClung's definition of instructional validity. That is, the emphasis is on determining whether the topics that are on the test are actually taught in the schools. The possibility that the test may have covered matters not taught in the schools was apparently of paramount importance in the court's decision, where it is stated that ''We believe that the state administered a test that was, at least on the record before us, fundamentally unfair in that it *may* have covered matters not taught in the schools of the state.''[2]

The requirement that the state submit "proof of the curricular validity of the test" raises a host of legal, educational, and psychometric questions. The legal analysis will be left to legal scholars, but this chapter will attempt to address some of the salient educational and psychometric issues that result from this requirement. First, this chapter will review some recent work on the general concept of validity and try to place the requirement within the context of that conceptual framework. Then the discussion will turn to a consideration of the type of evidence that should, or might, be required to support claims of curricular or instructional validity. Finally, the chapter will discuss some implications of various requirements for "testing, teaching and learning."[3]

The Concept of Validity

Curricular validity is not a new term in the measurement literature, but neither is it a common one. The term is sprinkled here and there in some measurement texts (for example, Ebel 1972; Ross and Stanley 1954) but not others. Even when mentioned, the terms seldom receives much attention. McClung, whom the appellate court cites, refers to the second edition of Cronbach's (1960) *Essentials of Psychological Testing,* but interestingly, that brief discussion occurs, not in the chapter on validity, but in the one on proficiency tests, which was dropped from the third edition (Cronbach 1970).[4]

The terms *curricular* and *instructional* are two among a long list of modifiers of the term *validity.* Messick (1980), for example, listed seventeen validity terms or descriptive modifiers of validity. In addition to the "Holy Trinity" (Guion 1980) of content, construct, and criterion, Messick listed such modifiers as task, population, trait, and ecological. In reviewing the substantive points associated with each of the terms, Messick forcefully argued that, with the possible exception of construct validity, "none of the concepts qualify for the accolade of validity, for at best they are only one facet of validity and at worst, as in the case of content coverage, they are not validity at all (p. 1015)."

Although not on Messick's list of modifiers, his arguments also apply to the one the court of appeals decided to underscore in *Debra P.* v. *Turlington.* Indeed, the court identified curricular validity as a component of content validity. According to the court: "In the field of competency, an important component of content validity is curricular validity."[5] It is, of course, content validity that Messick singled out in stating that content is "not validity at all."

It appears somewhat ironic that at a time when a number of people in the measurement community have been arguing against the division of validity into types (Cronbach 1980; Dunnette and Borman 1979; Guion 1977, 1978, 1980; Linn 1980; Messick 1975, 1980; Tenopyr 1977), the court seems to be adding yet another type. The irony is illusory however. To argue that "all validation is one" (Cronbach 1980, p. 99) is, in fact, quite compatible with the demand of the court that there be evidence that the matters covered on the test were actually taught. The court started with a relatively noncontroversial premise: it is inappropriate and unfair to establish a requirement without providing an opportunity to meet it. There was no challenge of the right of the state to determine the content to be covered or the level of the score needed to pass. But whatever the content, that content must be taught or the test is inappropriate for use as a requirement for receipt of a diploma.

A test may validly measure how well certain content has been mastered — whether or not the test takers have been provided with an opportunity to learn the material covered by the test. It may be a highly valid measure of degree of content mastery at a given point in time. Because the test has good validity for that interpretation, however, does not mean that it has adequate validity for some other interpretation or use. Test validity is specific to the interpretation and use of the test scores. For any specific use, a validity claim involves an "overall evaluative judgment" (Messick 1980, p. 1023) of the adequacy *and* appropriateness of the measure for that purpose. The court has simply stated one of the requirements for a test to be considered appropriate for a particular use. This requirement expands the validation task, but it does not alter the basic logic. It merely gives salience to a particular type of evidence in reaching the overall judgment of adequacy and appropriateness for a particular use.

Having said this, of course, leaves unanswered many crucial questions about how this should be done, about what will count as evidence, and about how much evidence will be required. For example, if the material is covered in an assigned textbook, does that mean it has been taught? If students are taught to compute X % or Y, does that mean that a question asking them to determine the sales tax on an $8.30 purchase when the tax rate is 4% would meet the curricular validity standard? These and similar questions have no universal answers. Judgment as well as evidence will be required in arriving at a conclusion that the court's curricular validity has been satisfied. But that is true of all aspects of the validation process.

Although the match between what is tested and what is taught may be seen as a reasonable concern, it may also appear rather far removed from most theoretical discussions of validity. Construct validity usually occupies center stage in the latter discussions (for example, Guion 1977; Linn 1979; Messick 1975, 1980; Tenopyr 1977). Messick, for example, (1980) concluded that "construct validity is the evidential basis of test interpretation" and went on to state that "the evidential basis of test use is also construct validity — but elaborated to determine the relevance of the construct to the applied purpose and the utility of the measure in the applied setting. (p. 1019)"

In the case of competency tests used for the award of high school diplomas, that elaboration must include evidence that the construct is relevant to what is actually taught. But mere relevance may not be sufficient if the idea of a match between instruction and the test is taken literally. Despite the more stringent requirement implied by the term *match* in comparison to Messick's relevance, construct validation is still the fundamental underpinning that is needed for competency tests used for awarding diplomas — just as it is for other test uses. Content validity, even including good evidence that the test has a high degree of curricluar and instructional validity, is not sufficient for a competency test — or any other test for that matter (Linn 1979; Messick 1975, 1980). As the following discussion will rely on only content validation — including its "important component," curricular validity — can lead to educational distortions and subvert the alleged purpose of the tests, which is increased competence, not merely higher test scores.

Although arguing that construct validity, elaborated by evidence of relevance to what is taught and the utility of the test when used to award diplomas, is the fundamental concern, it is important to heed the warnings of Lerner (1976) and Cronbach (1980) about the need for more than the academic discussions typically associated with construct validity. As both of these authors have noted, the line of argument concerning validity of a particular use and interpretation of a test needs to be made reasonable to nonscientists, and, as typically discussed, "construct validation is a better topic for the seminar room than for the public arena (Cronbach 1980, p. 100)." The rationale and logic of construct validation are needed, but they must be presented in less esoteric terms.

In this regard, it is interesting to note that in the *Debra P*. case, the appellate court concurred with the trial court's finding that "the Florida test has adequate construct validity."[6] Although I personally do not believe that the evidence and logical analysis support such a conclusion, the finding is quite understandable in view of the abstractness of the concept of construct validity as well as the lack of consensus about its relevance in this case and the lack of any clear perscription about how to do the construct validation of the test. Messick's (1980, p. 1019) call for a determination of "the relevance of the construct to the applied purpose and the utility of the measure in the applied setting" surely was not satisfied, however.

Evidence of Curricular Validity

The following discussion will adopt the courts use of the term *curricular validity,* which includes what McClung (1979) has labeled instructional validity. McClung's distinction between curricular validity — that is, the degree to which the "test items represent the objectives of the curriculum" (p. 687) — and instructional validity — that is, "an actual measure of whether schools are providing students with instruction in the knowledge and skills measured by the test'' (p. 683) — is important. But, as already noted, the court clearly included the notion of instructional validity when it used the term *curricular validity*. McClung's instructional validation is obviously much more demanding than is his curricular validation, for it focuses not just on the intent — that is, the match to the objectives — but on the reality of what actually takes place in the classroom (Popham and Lindheim 1981). Meeting this more demanding standard set by the court will be the primary concern.

Types of Evidence

Popham and Lindheim (1981) identified two types of data that might be used as evidence that the material covered by the test has actually been taught. The first is derived from an analysis of the instructional materials, including not only textbooks but course syllabi and teachers' lesson plans. The second category consists of data on actual classroom transactions. Whether the lesson-plan data is based on actual classroom observations or much simpler, and probably more feasible, reports by teachers and students, it is apparent that evidence regarding classroom transactions will be more difficult to accumulate than evidence derived from existing instructional materials. Classroom-transaction data may also be more important, however. Indeed, the appellate court had before it some instructional materials that the state had placed in evidence but dismissed that evidence with the comment that ''at least one teacher . . . testified that he did not cover the whole book in class.''[7] This statement suggests that classroom-transaction evidence may be an essential part of the ''proof'' that the test has curricular validity. If the statement is interpreted to imply a necesasary requirement, it also suggests a clearly unattainable standard because surely the state could not provide evidence that *every* teacher covered *all* the material in the designated curriculum to which the test is keyed. Practicality will necessitate acceptance of a less stringent requirement.

Video recordings and direct observations by independent parties may provide the most compelling evidence regarding classroom transactions, but they are not very practical for large-scale use — certainly not for the relevant classes attended by *all* students. Yet Pullin (1981 p. 21) has asserted that ''the courts have decided that proof of fairness of a test requires evidence that *all* students have had a fair opportunity to learn the skills and knowledge covered by the test.'' Nonetheless, practicality rules out the possibility of obtaining direct evidence for all students.

Even analyses of curriculum materials and surveys of teachers to ascertain content coverage and overlap with the test is apt to prove to be a very demanding job. The work of researchers at the Institute for Research on Teaching (for example, Porter, Schmidt, Floden, and Freeman, 1978; Schmidt 1978; Schmidt, Porter, Schwille, Floden and Freeman 1981) has highlighted the potential importance of the match between what is taught and what is tested and has shown that superficially similar tests vary greatly in the specifics of content coverage. This work has also illustrated the difficulty of the problem and suggests that substantial time and effort need to be devoted to the analysis of content coverage on the test, in the curriculum and in the classroom.

Although somewhat of a bureaucratic nightmare, teacher reports for all classrooms or for the ones wherein material covered by the test is supposed to be taught, are conceivable. Recent work that has used teacher reports of whether the content of specific items has been taught (for example, Leinhart 1981; Leinhart and Seewald 1981; Leinhart, Zigmond, and Cooley 1981; Poyner 1978) suggests that this approach has potential utility. It is difficult to evaluate, however, the degree to which the context of a MCT program would alter the validity of teacher reports. In any event, teacher reports would be much stronger if buttressed by evidence from special studies of samples of classrooms demonstrating the correspondence between teachers reports and direct observation by independent observers.

Form and Level of Evidence

Whether teacher reports, direct observations, analyses of instructional materials, and/or other evidence is used, the form and level of detail of the evidence that may be required is quite unclear. Popham and Lindheim (1981, p. 19) claim that "any effort to establish a match between what is tested and what is taught must rely on the description of the content of the test." They go on to argue that this will be much easier, albeit less convincing, when the description is general than when they have the type of precision that Popham (1978) and other proponents of criterion-referenced testing have argued. It would appear, however, that the test description, whether general or precise, may not be the key issue for the courts. Just as the emphasis on the instructional side is on the *reality* of what is actually taught rather than the *intent* as found in the curricular objectives, the emphasis for the test will probably have to be on the reality of the actual test items and what they measure rather than only on the intent as stated in the test specifications.

Although it seems essential to focus on the actual test items in order to judge the curricular validity of the test, doing so poses several problems. Test security is a critical concern for any test that is used in making an important decision such as the awarding of a high school diploma. Widespread review of the actual form of a test prior to its administration would be foolhardy. The almost-certain breaks in test security would render it useless and fundamentally unfair.

Not being able to rely on widespread teacher review of a specific test form prior to administration leaves two alternatives. Either the test can be reviewed after the fact or a much larger pool of items and/or specific item generation rules used to construct specific test forms may be reviewed. The former approach risks the possibility that at least some of the items will be judged to lack curricular validity. The latter approach avoids that risk and has other desirable features but makes the task much more demanding.

Complete specification of an item domain that would allow the random selection of items from the domain is more often an ideal than a reality. Random generation of arithemetic items is still the most common example. There are some exceptions, however, for example, Millman 1980; Millman and Outlaw 1978. The more complete the specification, the easier it will be to judge whether the material has been taught prior to examining the individual test items. Detailed specifications have several advantages, some of which are due to the fact that such specifications provide the basis for making the testing process more public. Good, understandable specifications can be used to tell parents, teachers, and pupils what is expected. The release of previously used exams would provide the means of elaborating the specifications as well as checking on the extent to which they are followed.

Review of a test form immediately following administration could be practical if the operational system allowed for the elimination of specific test items prior to scoring and reporting. This would be technically feasible, but the rules to be used to determine when an item should be deleted will be difficult to establish and defend. New forms for each administration would also be required; this requirement is desirable, if not mandatory, even without widespread review.

The development of a new test form for each administration is an expensive proposition. The forms must meet high standards of test equivalence and relatively large numbers of them will be required. Form-to-form equivalence is fundamental to fairness. The form of the test should be a matter of indifference to both the test taker and the user of the test results. Otherwise, some test takers are put at an unfair disadvantage relative to others. The requirement of many forms is dictated by the need to give students multiple opportunities to pass the test.[8]

Judging the Match

Possibly one of the most difficult judgments in evaluating curricular validity will be determining what constitutes a match between the matters covered by the test and those actually taught. At one ludicrous extreme, the actual test items could be given to students along with feedback on the correct answers. Clearly, this extreme was not endorsed by the court, which acknowledged that "in composing items for a test, the writer is dealing with applications of knowledge, and therefore the form of the test question would not necessarily be the same as the form of the information taught in class."[9]

This conclusion is certainly sensible because the real educational concern is not with test performance per se but only inasmuch as this performance is indicative of skills and knowledge of the student. Furthermore, if the goal is application of knowledge to new problems, then the measurement value of an application question is destroyed by teaching that specific application. On the other hand, there is evidence that even seemingly trivial format changes can lead to substantial differences in test results. Whether addition problems are presented horizontally or vertically not only affects test outcomes, but the effect depends on the match between the test format and the way problems are presented in the instructional program (Alderman, Swinton, and Braswell 1979; Glass 1978; see also Cronbach's 1980, comments on this issue). Still larger effects can be anticipated for larger variations in form.

Completion of an income tax form requires a variety of skills, to say nothing of tolerance for lengthy instructions. Among other skills, this task requires the application of basic addition, subtraction, and division skills. But as Pullin (1981, p. 21) suggested, "a student who has never seen a federal income tax form may well be so confused by it that he or she will be unable to demonstrate the basic ability to add, subtract, or divide." Whether the completion of a tax form is a desirable task for a test depends, in part, on the importance attached to this application of a combination of skills and on the generality of this type of application to other important applications. What evidence would be needed to satisfy a court that this application is a fair test of what was taught is a matter for speculation, but cautious test givers will surely opt for giving students practice in filling out tax forms if the test is to include such items. To do otherwise invites litigation, the outcome of which would be quite uncertain.

School or Regional Differences

Harnisch and Linn (1981) found large school-to-school variations on certain categories of items after adjusting for overall school performance on the mathematics test of the Illinois statewide assessment program. For example, students at one school performed consistently better than expected on items using geometric figures to represent fractions whereas they performed worse than expected on numeration questions. In contrast, students at another school did better than expected on definition items but worse than expected on figural representation of fraction items. A third school had a strong showing on story problems dealing with money (for example, "Mary earned $1.00 raking leaves. Candy bars cost 15¢. How many candy bars can she buy with her money?") but relatively poor showing on calculation items. Even within the category of story problems, there were sizable school-to-school contrasts in the relative performance on those involving money and those involving some other application (for example, time or amounts of physical quantities).

Fairness, as viewed by the court, would seem to require assurance that all these topics were taught, and as Judge Tjoflat suggested, "perhaps taught well,"[10] for the test to be used for purposes of awarding a diploma. Yet such school-to-school differences raise doubts about this or at least about the uniformity of emphasis. In fact, the test analyzed by Harnisch and Linn is not used for awarding diplomas. Hence, it is reasonable to anticipate that it has less impact on classroom practice than does a test that is used for such important decisions. Nonetheless, uniformity of coverage of material on the test from school to school or classroom to classroom is apt to be a serious concern.

Even for such a clearly important area as reading — to which every school system surely devotes substantial instructional efforts — questions can be raised about whether instruction matches the test better for some students than for others. The importance of prior knowledge is well documented by a large body of research on reading comprehension (see, for example, Anderson 1977; Bransford 1979; Spiro 1980). Schema theory suggests that prior knowledge is crucial to the organization and storage of textual information as well as in the retrieval of information. The lack of appropriate schema resulting from background knowledge can lead to reading failure (Spiro 1980). Furthermore, the amount of prior knowledge that a reader has on the specific topic of the text can influence an individual's reading comprehension score (Johnston 1981). Thus, an individual's relative performance can be expected to vary as a function of the match between the content of the passages selected for the test and his or her prior knowledge about a topic.

Results of a study by Johnston (1981) show that the effect of passage choice and consequently the match to prior knowledge can be substantial. Some results based on his study are illustrated in figure 5–1, which shows a disordinal interaction between the community in which a school is located (rural or urban) and the type of passage. The rural sample outperformed the urban sample on a passage dealing with the specialization of corn in the United States, whereas the urban sample did significantly better than the rural sample on a passage dealing with the financial problems of the Chicago Regional Transit Authority (RTA). Still more striking differences at an individual student level were found by Johnston when prior knowledge was assessed by passage-specific vocabulary items.

Interactions such as the one illustrated in figure 5–1 are not new to the measurement literature. Test constructors usually try to minimize such effects in two ways. First, materials that are suspected of being much more familiar to some identifiable subpopulations than to others are avoided. Second, there is an attempt to balance passages in the hope that the relative advantages and disadvantages for a particular group will tend to cancel out.

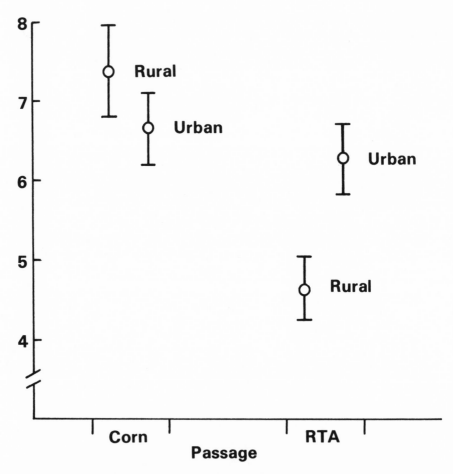

Figure 5–1. Means (o) and 95% Confidence Limits on Two Reading Comprehension Test Passages for a Rural (N = 101) and an Urban Sample (N =
106) (based on Johnston 1981).

Within the context of the court's curricular validity requirement, it may be
necessary to show that all students have been taught background material that is
judged important to comprehending a particular passage. Mere balance across the
set of passages seems to fall short of the implied standard that none of the items
cover materials that were not taught to all students. If such an interpretation is
correct, then Judge Tjoflat's conclusion in his dissenting opinion that the "holding
places a very onerous burden on the state"[11] seems appropriate. On the other hand,
without assurance of adequate instruction in the topics tested, the state is placing
an onerous burden on students.

Impact on Instruction

Test-Driven Curriculum

Without arguing the merits of having the curriculum shaped by the tests, some shaping is an inevitable effect of introducing a MCT requirement. The court's demand for curricular validity only reinforces this effect. Madaus and Greaney (1981) not only provide evidence that such testing requirements in Ireland influenced the curriculum, but that there was a narrowing of the curriculum and a concomitant narrowing of instruction. Teachers devoted their time to training students to do well on the tests — sometimes with little apparent regard for achieving any real understanding.

Important examinations necessarily exert an influence over the curriculum. This is evident in the British external examination program (Madaus and McDonagh 1979). It is also apparent in Florida where remediation for students failing the 1977 Functional Literacy Test (FLT) was found to consist of coaching "on the specific skills represented by questions . . . missed on the 1977 test" (Task Force on Educational Assessment Programs 1979, p. 10).

Of course, not all in the measurement community would agree that a test-driven curriculum is undesirable. On the contrary, some would argue that the test provides the means of making agreed-upon objectives clear and precise. An important goal of instruction should be the achievement of those objectives as demonstrated by performance on the test. Nowhere is this more apparent than in description of one of the oldest and most prestigious statewide testing programs — the New York Regents examinations. According to Tinkleton (1966, p. 88), "once the decision is made that a student will pursue a Regents-type course, then the decision has automatically been made that he will take the Regents examination at the end of the course. In essence, the Regents examination is part of the course." Old exams that had been used in previous administrations were widely available. The tradition of the exams largely defined the specifications to be used in constructing future exams and the material to be covered in the classroom. The Regents exams, of course, had a tradition quite different from MCT. They have been intended for what Tinkleman referred to as "first-track courses." But the link between an important certification test and the curriculum is much the same.

Having quoted Tinkleman regarding the close correspondence between test and curriculum, it seems worthwhile to call attention to another of his observations in the same paper. He concluded that "The same examination is not appropriate for all students, any more than the same curriculum is appropriate for all students (Tinkleman 1966, p. 88)." Admittedly, Tinlkeman had in mind more specialized and more advanced topics than are found on MCT. His observation seems relevant nonetheless.

Although it is clear that some educators see the shaping of the curriculum by the test as a desirable outcome, others perceive it as a danger because it represents a distortion of more fundamental goals. Regardless of one's views on this issue, it is crucial that a distinction be made between teaching the test and teaching the skills and knowledge that the test is intended to measure.

Teaching the Test

Dyer (1973, p. 89) related a story about a former colleague of his, a sixth-grade teacher, who took it upon herself to boost her students' I.Q.s

> Her method was simple. She had got hold of all four forms of the old *Otis Self-Administered Test of Mental Ability,* and, in all good conscience, she used the items of the test as exercises in a unit on intelligent thinking. This she conducted strictly in the drill-and-practice mode of instruction — minus, of course, any aid from a computer, since computers had not yet arrived on the scene. The gains in IQ she produced in her pupils were breath-taking in their magnitude and beautiful in their upward flight,.

> Clearly, that sixth grade teacher was not playing according to the rules of the testing game. But this was because, like many of her present-day counterparts, she was simply unaware of the rules. On the other hand, had she known what the rules were, she would probably have thought them an irksome constraint on what she regarded as effective teaching. Given her pedagogical frame of reference, she would have had a rather good point. For it was the frame of reference that included the old formula — lately revived in some forms of programmed instruction: "test, teach, test, teach, test, and teach to mastery." And where else than those old *Otis Tests* would she have found such well worked out exercises for applying the formula to the teaching of intelligence? The trouble was she got the teaching mixed up with the testing. What she did not realize — and what I'm afraid many people still do not realize — is that if you use the test exercises as an instrument of teaching you destroy the usefulness of the test as an instrument for measuring the effects of teaching.

Dyer's illustration has considerable relevance for current MCT programs, especially in light of the new pressure that the court has placed on such programs to provide proof of curricular validity. The pressure is great to ensure that instruction includes practice on materials that match the test. What better match could there be than the items themselves. Barring that, the next best thing would be items from old versions of the test or ones constructed by the teacher that mimic as nearly as possible those that are anticipated to be on the test.

Spending large portions of instructional time taking practice tests may not be all that great a change from much current practice. Durkin (1978–1979), for example, found teachers devoting more time to questioning than to direct instruction. She also found that the manuals of five major basal readers devoted more attention to assessement and practice exercises than to "direct explicit instruction (Durkin 1981, p. 45)." In a similar vein, Jenkins and Pany (1978, p. 12) stated that "It is tempting to conclude that comprehension instruction consists primarily of repeated testing with feedback." If these accounts are correct, then the major change resulting from the curricular validity requirement may be only a substitution of new practice exercises that more nearly mimic the test items. Now, practice on similar test items may in some circumstances prove to be a relatively effective form of instruction. But before accepting such a conclusion, one would surely want evidence of the generalizability of the results to other nontest situations. In other words, evidence is needed that the construct validity of the test has not been destroyed by the instructional practices.

Cronbach (1963) made a related point in a different context some years ago. He was writing about curriculum evaluation rather than MCT, but his observations are quite relevant in either context. He argued as follows:

> The demand that tests be closely matched to the aims of a course reflects awareness that examinations of the usual sort "determine what is taught." If questions are known in advance, students give more attention to learning their answers than to learning other aspects of the course. This is not necessarily detrimental. Whenever it is critically important to master certain content, the knowledge that it will be tested produces a desirable concentration of effort. On the other hand, learning the answer to a set of questions is by no means the same as acquiring understanding of whatever topic that question represents. [Cronback 1963, p. 681].

If too close a match between the instructional materials and the test is forced, the capacity to measure such important constructs as the understanding of a topic may be lost.

Cheating

Dyer's teacher, although possibly misguided, was not intentionally cheating. Neither would the vast majority of today's teachers be purposely cheating; it would be naive, however, to assume that all teachers are so scrupulous. For some of those who are philosophically opposed to a MCT requirement for graduation, cheating may be seen as a case of the ends justifying the means.

Although seldom discussed, the problem of assuring that tests are administered in a uniform manner and that some test takers are not given an unfair advantage by the administration is an old problem. It is a problem that led Rice (1897), before the turn of the century, to reject the spelling-test results that he initially collected for some 16,000 students when he "learned from many sources that the unusually favorable results in certain class-rooms did not represent the natural conditions, but were due to the peculiar manner in which the examinations had been conducted (Rice 1897, p. 165).'' To avoid this problem, Rice resorted to personally directing the administration of his second test to some 13,000 students — a rather monumental task, but one that was small by comparison to testing all the students in a given grade for a large state.

Conclusion

Literal match of instruction and testing in the sense of practice on the items that appear on the test destroys the measurement value of the test. Inferences about skills and knowledge that are made on the basis of test results become suspect when the match becomes too close. To accurately test whether a student can apply skills and knowledge to solve a new problem requires that the problem be new. Practice on the problem as part of instruction ensures match and may improve scores but eliminates any conclusions regarding problem-solving. The demand for curricular validity thus poses a dilemma. On the one hand, we can ensure a match but in doing so we risk a reduction in the importance of learning to apply skills and knowledge to new problems. On the other hand, we can emphasize application and problem-solving by presenting new problems on the test but risk failing the court's curricular validity test.

The conceptual framework for resolving the dilemma is that of construct validation. It provides the needed logic for attacking the problem, but it does not provide a blueprint. What is needed is support for the judgment that students have been provided with instruction in and ample opportunity to learn the skills and knowledge measured by the test — but not the actual items.

Cronbach (1980, p. 103) has argued, ''The job of validation is not to support an interpretation, but to find out what is wrong with it. A proposition deserves some degree of trust only when it has survived serious attempts to falsify it.'' In the case of the Florida MCTs, the court has concluded that the proposition that all students have been provided with an adequate opportunity to learn the material on the test does not deserve to be trusted. To gain this trust, serious attempts will be needed to find schools where the material has not been taught or where insufficient attention has been given to topics that are tested. Judgment will be required to decide whether something has or has not been taught adequately, and judges will surely disagree. The validation goal cannot be to prove with certainty that all students have had a fair chance to learn what is measured by the test. We can only hope to make a reasonable case based on serious attempts to find schools where students have not been provided with instruction considered necessary. Opposing critics may wish to demonstrate that, although students have been coached to give the required responses to the test items, they lack the skills and knowledge that the test purports to measure. There will be uncertainties and ambiguities on both sides of the argument. But this is generally true of matters of public policy. In the case of the curricular validity requirement, the challenge will be to convince the courts that knowledge was taught — without precluding the possibility of measuring it.

Notes

1. Debra P. v. Turlington, 644 F.2d 397, 6765 (5th Cir. 1981).
2. 644 F.2d at 6770.
3. The phrase "testing, teaching and learning" was borrowed from Tyler and White (1979).
4. Cronbach notes that the chapter, "Proficiency Tests," was dropped from the third edition "for the paradoxical reason that there is just too much to say on that subject" (1970, p. xxx).
5. 644 F.2d at 6770.
6. Debra P. v. Turlington, 474 F. Supp. at 261.
7. 644 F.2d at 6771.
8. There is general agreement that students who fail should be given opportunities to retake the test. Once the student has passed, however, repeat testing is not expected. This asymmetry suggests that the error of failing a student who should pass is considered more serious than passing one who should fail. Although certainly understandable, this asymmetry makes one wonder about the outrage that is expressed by some proponents of these programs concerning "counterfeit diplomas" and the claim that MCT will eliminate them.
9. 644 F.2d at 6771.
10. 644 F.2d at 10,858.
11. 644 F.2d at 10,858.

References

Alderman, D.L., Swinton, S.S., and Braswell, J.S. "Assessing Basic Arithmetic Skills and Understanding across Curricula: Computer-Assisted Instruction and Compensatory Education." *The Journal of Children's Mathematical Behavior,* 2 (1979), 3–28.

Anderson, R.C. *Schema-Directed Processes in Language Comprehension* (Technical Report No. 50). Urbana, Ill.; University of Illinois, Center for the Study of Reading, July 1977. (ERIC Document Reproduction Service No. ED 142 977.)

Bransford, J.D. *Human Cognition: Learning, Understanding and Remembering.* Belmont, Calif. Wadsworth, 1979.

Cronbach, L.J. *Essentials of Psychological Testing, 2d ed.* New York: Harper Brothers, 1960.

Cronbach, L.J. "Course Improvements through Evaulation." *Teachers College Record* 64 (1963), 672–683.

Cronbach, L.J. *Essentials of Psychological Testing, 3rd ed.* New York: Harper Brothers, 1970.

Cronbach, L.J. "Validity on Parole: How Can We Go Straight?" *New Directions for Testing and Measurement* (San Francisco, Calif.: Jossey-Bass Inc., 1980, no. 5, 99–108.

Durkin, D. "What Classroom Observations Reveal about Reading Comprehension Instruction." *Reading Research Quarterly.* 14 (1978–1979), 481–533.

Durkin, D. *Reading Comprehension Instruction in Five Basal Reader Series* (Reading Education Report No. 26). Urbana, Ill.: University of Illinois, Center for the Study of Reading, 1981.

Dyer, H.S. *Recycling the Problems in Testing. Proceedings of the 1972 Invitational Conference on Testing Problems.* Princeton, N.J.: Educational Testing Service, 1973.

Dunnette, M.D. and Borman, W.C. "Personnel Selection and Classification Systems." *Annual Review of Psychology.* 30 (1979), 477–525.

Ebel, R.L. *Essentials of Educational Measurement.* Englewood Cliffs, N.J.: Prentice-Hall, 1972.

Glass, G.V. "Minimum Competence and Incompetence in Florida." *Phi Delta Kappan.* 59 (1978), 602–605.

Guion, R.M. "Content Validity, the Source of My Discontent." *Applied Psychological Measurement.* 1 (1977), 1–10.

Guion, R.M. "Content Validity in Moderation." *Personnel Psychology.* 31 (1978), 205–214.

Guion, R.M. "On Trinitarian Doctrines of Validity." *Professional Psychology.* 11 (1980), 385–398.

Harnish, D.L., and Linn, R.L. "Analysis of Items Response Patterns: Questionable Test Data and Dissimilar Curriculum Practices." *Journal of Educational Measurement.* 18 (1981), 133–146.

Jenkins, J.R., and Pany, D. *Teaching Reading Comprehension in the Middle Grades* (Reading Education Report No. 4). Urbana, Ill.: University of Illinois, Center for the Study of Reading, 1978. (ERIC Document Reproduction Service No. ED 151 756.)

Johnston, P.H. *"Prior Knowledge and Reading Comprehension Test Bias."* Ph.D. dissertation, University of Illinois, 1981.

Leinhart, G. "Overlap: Testing Whether It's Taught." Paper presented at the Ford Foundation Conference on the Courts and Contents Validity of Minimum Competency Tests, Boston College, Chestnut Hill, Mass., October 1981.

Leinhart, G., and Seewald, A.M. "Overlap: What's Tested, What's Taught?" *Journal of Educational Measurement.* 18 (1981), 85–96.

Leinhart, G., Zigmond, N., and Cooley, W.W. "Reading Instruction and Its Effects." *American Educational Research Journal.* 18 (1981), 343–361.

Lerner, B. "Washington v. Davis: Quantity, Quality and Equality in Employment Testing." In P. Kurland (ed.), *1976 Supreme Court Review,* pp. 263–316.

Linn, R.L. "Issues of Validity in Measurement for Competency-Based Programs." In M.A. Bunda and J.R. Sanders (eds.), *Practices and Problem in Competency-Based Measurement,* Washington, D.C.: National Council on Measurement in Education, 1979.

Linn, R.L. "Issues of Validity for Criterion-Referenced Measures." *Applied Psychological Measurement.* 14 (1980), 547–561.

Madaus, G., and McDonagh, J. "Minimum Competency Testing: Unexamined Assumptions and Unexplored Negative Outcomes. In R. Lennon (ed.), *Impactive Changes in Measurement: New Directions for Testing and Measurement.* Vol. 3 1979, no. 3, pp. 1–14.

Madaus, G.F., and Greaney, V. "Competency Testing: A Case Study of the Irish Primary Certificate Examination." Unpublished manuscript, 1981.

McClung, M.S. "Competency Testing: Potential for Discrimination." *Clearinghouse Review.* 11 (1977), 439–448.

McClung, M.S. "Competency Testing Programs: Legal and Educational Issues." *Fordham Law Review.* 47 (1979), 651–712.

Messick, S. "The Standard Problem: Meaning and Values in Measurement and Evaluation." *American Psychologist.* 30 (1975), 955–966.

Messick, S. "Test Vaildity and the Ethics of Assessment." *American Psychologist.* 30 (1980), 1012–1027.

Millman, J. "Computer Based Item Generation." In R.A. Berk (ed.), *Criterion-Referenced Measurement: The State of the Art.* Baltimore, Md.: Johns Hopkins University Press, 1980.

Millman, J, and Outlaw, W.S. "Testing by Computer." *AEDS Journal.* 11 (1978), 57–72.

Popham, W.J. *Criterion-Referenced Measurement.* Englewood Cliffs, N.J.: Prentice-Hall, 1978.

Popham, W.J., and Lindheim, E.L. "Implications of a Landmark Ruling in Florida's Minimum Competency Test." *Phi Delta Kappan.* 63 (1981), 18–20.

Porter, A.C., Schmidt, W.H., Floden, R.E., and Freeman, D.J. *Impact on What?: The Importance of Content Covered* (Research Series, Report, No. 2). East Lansing, Mich.: Michigan State University, The Institute for Research on Teaching, 1978.

Poyner, L. "Instructional Dimensions Study: Data Management Procedures as Exemplified by Curriculum Analysis." Paper presented at the annual meeting of the American Educational Research Association, Toronto, Ontario, Canada, 1978.

Pullin, D. "Minimum Competency Testing and the Demand for Accountability." *Phi Delta Kappan.* 63 (1981), 20–27.

Rice, J.M. "The Futility of the Spelling Grind: I." *Forum.* 23 (1897), 63–72.

Ross, C.C., and Stanley, J.C. *Measurement in Today's Schools.* Englewood Cliffs, N.J.: Prentice-Hall, 1954.

Schmidt, W.H. *Measuring the Content of Instruction* (Research Series Report No. 35). East Lansing, Mich.: Michigan State University, the Institute for Research on Teaching, 1978.

Schmidt, W.H., Porter, A.C., Schwille, J.R., Floden, R., and Freeman, D. "Validity as a Variable: Can the Same Certification Test Be Valid for All Students?" Paper presented at the Ford Foundation Conference on the Courts and the Content Validity of Minimum Competency Tests, Boston College, Chestnut Hill, Mass., October 1981.

Spiro, R.J. *Schema Theory and Reading Comprehension: New Directions* (Technical Report No. 191). Urbana, Ill.: University of Illinois, Center for the Study of Reading, December 1980.

Task Force on Educational Assessment Programs, *"Competency testing in Florida: Report to the Florida Cabinet, Part I."* Tallahassee, Fla., 1979.

Tinkleman, S.N. *Regents Examinations in New York State after 100 Years. Proceedings of the Invitational Conference on Testing Problems.* Princeton, N.J.: Educational Testing Service, 1966.

Tyler, R.W., and White, S.H. *Testing, Teaching and Learning: Report on a Conference on Research on Testing, August 17–26, 1979.* Washington, D.C.: National Institute of Education, 1979.

Tynopyr, M.L. "Content Construct Confusion." *Personnel Psychology.* 30 (1977), 47–54.

6 VALIDITY AS A VARIABLE:
Can the Same Certification Test Be Valid for All Students?

William H. Schmidt, Andrew C. Porter,
John R. Schwille, Robert E. Floden,
and Donald J. Freeman

Introduction

In the judicial case of *Debra P*. v. *Turlington,* the courts addressed the concept of validity as it pertained to the Florida Functional Literacy examination. Because the test was to be used in certifying functional literacy required for high school graduation, much was at stake. Out of the controversy surrounding the examination and its use, two new types of validity emerged; curricular validity and instructional validity. The purpose of this chapter is to explore the meaning of these two new types of validity, to show where they fit within the psychometrics tradition, and to touch on some of the practical considerations involved with determining the extent to which a test has curricular and/or instructional validity.

The work reported herein was sponsored by the Institute for Research on Teaching, College of Education, Michigan State University. The Institute for Research on Teaching is funded primarily by the Program on Teaching and Instruction, National Institute of Education, United States Department of Education. The opinions expressed in this paper do not necessarily reflect the position, policy, or endorsement of the National Institute of Education. (Contract No. 400–76–0073.)

Three Types of Content Validity

This book is concerned not with validity in general, but more narrowly with the concept of content validity. The APA (1974) defines content validity as the situation in which the behaviors measured in a test constitute a representative sample of the behaviors to be exhibited in the desired performance domain. However, the case of *Debra P*. v. *Turlington* raises a complication not addressed in this definition. For while the lower court found that the test had reasonable content validity with respect to the skill objectives developed by the state board of education, the appellate court maintained that there was an additional question of curricular validity. The contributors to this book have added to the complexity by introducing still another term: instructional validity. What do these terms mean and what are their implications for tests of certification?

Defining the Three Terms

Most large-scale testing programs such as state assessment, minimum competency tests (MCTs), and certification tests have used a set of instructional objectives as "the desired performance domain" against which to judge content validity.

As for curricular validity, the judges seemed to be concerned with using the schools' curricular materials as the domain against which to judge a test. By the same token, instructional validity can be defined as content validity with the domain of interest being the instructional content actually delivered by teachers in school.

The term *content validity* as used by the trial court in *Debra P*. v. *Turlington* referred to the extent to which the test accurately reflected the domain specified for development of the test — namely, the set of skill objectives defined by state legislation and operationalized by the state board of education. Curricular validity asks whether the test, established as valid with respect to the domain of objectives, is also consistent with the curricular materials used in the school system wherein it is to be administered. Similarly, instructional validity is a matter of whether the test — however valid with respect to the objectives — adequately samples the instructional content actually taught to the students. In the following discussion, we refer to these three domains as the *objectives domain,* the *curricular materials domain,* and the *instructional content domain.*

Relationship of the Three Domains

If one were to think of each domain as a set, the interrelationships among the types of validity can be seen through Venn diagrams such as that portrayed in figure 6–1. If content validity were equated with validity for the objectives domain, as in the

Florida case, the test must adequately sample subsets A, B, E, and F. However, subset A represents content that students taking the test were not instructed in or content that was not included in the materials used by the schools.

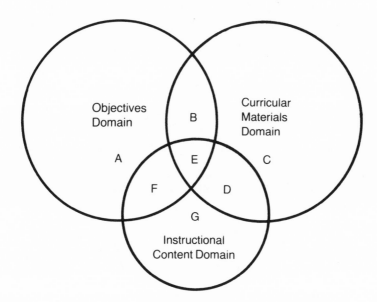

Figure 6–1.   Venn Diagram Showing Interrelationship Between Types of Content Validity.

If a test has content validity with respect to both objectives and instructional content, then it is likely that the relationship shown in figure 6–2 would be obtained. In this case, the objectives domain is a proper subset of the instructional content domain. This arrangement seems reasonable inasmuch as certification tests are commonly based on minimal competencies. The instructional domain is large in scope, reflecting a lack of restriction to minimal competencies. The domain of curricular materials need not be coincidental with either of the other two domains, however. Further, because different children may receive different content, it is quite conceivable that the model of figure 6–2 would change across children within the same classroom as well as children in different classrooms.

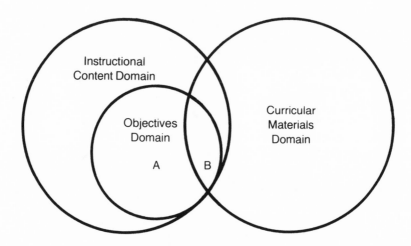

Figure 6–2.   Venn Diagram Showing Relationship Between Objectives and Instructional Content.

If the test has content validity with respect to both objectives and curricular materials, then the objectives domain is likely a proper subset of the curricular materials domain, suggesting a situation similar to the one given previously in which a test of minimal competencies is being used.

Problems in Defining Domains

One of the problems in defining a domain is the level of detail to be contained in that domain. The domain should be at a fine enough level to make important distinctions but not to such a fine level of detail so as to classify everything within the subject matter as being different. This, of course, is the trick of being knowledgeable about (1) the subject matter and (2) the amount of transfer in learning that can occur among the topics contained in the domain. For if transfer of learning is straightforward between two topics — for example, instruction on how to solve a problem such as "5 + 3" enables one to correctly do the problem "4 + 3" — then a taxonomy that makes such distinctions might be overly detailed. On the other hand, it is obvious that at a very high level of generality, most all topics are similar — for example, all items on a mathematics test deal with mathematics, so that moving in this direction too far is similarly not of any great value.

Another problem in specifying domains is tied more closely to the instructional content domain and the curricular materials domain. This is the question of topic emphasis: is it sufficient for a topic to be included in the domain if it is covered in the school one time on one day or if it is found in one problem in the textbook? If this is not the case, then what number of hours, days, or problems is sufficient in order for the topic to be included in the domain?

Making the Test Representative

Figures 6–1 and 6–2 do not address one aspect of the traditional definition of content validity — namely, that the test be a *representative* sample of behaviors from the domain. When one considers the objectives domain alone, this property seems clearly desirable. Otherwise, one objective (for example, a computation objective in mathematics) might be overemphasized to the detriment of another (for example, an applications objective in mathematics). It is not as clear that the original motivation for introducing the terms *curricular validity* and *instructional validity* are best served, however, by retaining the requirement of representativeness. If we consider a test of minimal competencies, for example, the requirement for representativeness could be interpreted to mean that the content of the curriculum materials and the content of instruction must be limited to minimal competencies for the test to have curricular validity or instructional validity. Otherwise, there would be content in the materials and content in the instruction not represented on the test. To be restrictive in this way seems undesirable. The concepts of curricular validity and instructional validity serve in the eyes of the court and the contributors to this book to provide assurance that test content is also covered in curriculum materials and in class. The requirement for representativeness could change the concept of curricular and instructional validity from an assurance of sufficient coverage to a limitation on coverage.

If the requirement for representativeness is dropped, then in a strict sense, curricular validity and instructional validity cannot be thought of as specific types of content on a par with objectives validity. Rather, they should be thought of as characteristics of interest for tests that have first been judged to be valid with respect to the objectives domain, which could once again be equated with content validity. Because validity is a matter of degree rather than a dichotomous state, curricular validity and instructional validity would, in practice, need to be judged directly against the test rather than against the objectives domain.

On the other hand, the merit of requiring representativeness as a criterion for curricular or instructional validity is that this criterion would guard against a test giving too much weight to topics that are minor or trivial aspects of instruction. For example, a test of minimal competencies might be devoted entirely to basic number facts. Would this test be considered to have curricular or instructional validity solely on the basis that number facts were covered in the materials or in the classroom — even if other important aspects of the materials or classroom coverage were entirely neglected?

Thus the question of representativeness seems to revolve around the issue of whether curriculum materials and classroom instructions are considered worthy indicators of content priorities in their own right or, alternatively, whether the objectives domain is considered a sufficient criterion of content priorities with the curriculum materials and classroom instruction being taken not as indicators of content priorities but as indexes of sufficient student opportunity to learn. There may be no general answer to this question because in part it is dependent upon the extent to which the objectives are viewed as authoritative. Presumably, the greater the overlap among the three domains, the more authoritative each would be viewed as a guide for what should be tested.

A discussion of our attempts to measure the overlap between tests, curriculum materials, and classroom instruction that follows later in this chapter will serve to further illustrate these issues. Given the general nature of state assessment, MCTs and certification tests and the issues before the courts the answer for these types of tests seems to be the latter — that is, to not require representativeness for a test to have curricular and instructional validity.

What Type of Validity for What Type of Test?

For general aptitude or general achievement tests, we would argue the main concern should be content validity with respect to the domain upon which the test is to be based.

For tests of certification, it is not enough that a test have validity with respect to the objectives domain. It should also have content validity with respect to instructional content, but not necessarily in a representative fashion. In other words, some acceptably large percentage of the items sampled from the objectives domain must also be covered by every student in every classroom (see figure 6–2). This is the issue of sufficient student opportunity.

If tests without instructional validity are being used for certification, the students who fail such tests are being penalized for the failures of the schools and teachers — and not for their own inadequacies. The rational basis for judging student performance in school is undermined.

If a test has instructional validity, it can be argued that curricular validity has little importance and is superfluous. In fact, at least two arguments can be made for curricular validity. One is that curriculum materials can serve to reinforce classroom coverage of all the content on the test. The other argument, developed in the following sections, involves the greater difficulty of measuring instructional validity as opposed to curricular validity, the possibility of using the curricular validity as a surrogate for instructional validity, and the relative ease of controlling curricular validity as opposed to instructional validity.

Prototype Measurement of
Curricular and Instructional Validity

This discussion sets forth a system to be considered for use in the area of content validation. Suggestions here are the result of work in elementary school mathematics. It is hoped that some of what has been learned in this context might be generally applicable to other subject matters and to other grade levels as well.

A Taxonomy for Measuring Content Validity

In our research on the determinants of content coverage in the classroom, we were interested in developing an instrument that would enable us to measure the content of instruction, tests, and curricular materials. It is our proposal that such a device could also be used to establish the content validity of a test with respect to any of the domains discussed in this chapter. A taxonomy that enables one to map the items of a test into their content specifications for fourth-grade mathematics could be used to characterize the content domains represented by that test. This taxonomy could also be applied to the other domains. For example, the domain specified by the objectives on which the test is to be constructed could be content analyzed using this taxonomy. Because this could also be done for the tests, a way to establish the content validity of the tests is to determine the degree to which the test item map can be subsumed under the objective map.

This same strategy could be followed with respect to curricular materials. The various curricular materials could similarly be content analyzed using the taxonomy and a map developed that suggests the range of topics that are represented in the domain covered by the textbook or other curricular materials. Similarly, the same thing could be done with respect to the content of the actual classroom instruction. A later section of this chapter addresses the additional problem of how one takes the actual classroom instruction and maps that into the taxonomy.

Description of a Taxonomy for Elementary School Mathematics

The taxonomy discussed here takes the form of a three-dimensional matrix. The three dimensions are: (1) the general intent of the lesson (for example, conceptual understanding or application), (2) the nature of the material presented to students (for example, measurement or decimals), and (3) the operation students must perform (for example, estimate or multiply). Developed in conjunction with this taxonomy is a set of rules to operationalize the cell boundaries. The application of the taxonomy to tests and textbook exercises is relatively staightforward, suscept-ible to being replicated, and results in high interrater reliability (Freeman et al. 1981).

Application of the Taxonomy to Tests

Each item on the test is examined and classified according to the taxonomy. The data from such an analysis can be represented by a mark on the taxonomy that indicates which of the cells in the taxonomy are covered. After the entire test has been mapped onto the taxonomy, the result is a visual representation of the areas covered by that test. This process is illustrated in figure 6–3, which portrays the results of the content analysis of the Stanford Achievement Test (SAT). It illus-trates the flexibility of the taxonomy in describing content at different levels of detail. Specific topics are represented by the cells of the classification matrix (for example, 3 of the 112 Stanford items focus on the skill of column addition of multiple-digit numbers). More general topics can also be addressed by summing across cells to obtain marginal totals (for example, 7 of the 112 items deal with column addition).

Application of the Taxonomy to Curricular Materials

The use of the taxonomy to content analyze curricular materials is much more difficult than it is for tests. Lessons in textbooks contain two distinct components: instructional activities directed by the teacher and practice exercises assigned to students. Our analyses of textbooks were limited to items in the student exercise portion of each lesson. The number of items to be classified for the student exercise portions of the three textbooks we have worked with range from a low of 4,288 items in the Addison-Wesley textbook to a high of 6,968 items in the Houghton Mifflin text. These figures show that the amount of content classification involved in curricular materials such as textbooks is extensive and time-consuming.

To illustrate the results of applying the taxonomy to curricular materials, we provide the results from the content analysis of three fourth-grade textbooks: *Mathematics in Our World,* Addison-Wesley Publishing Co., 1978; *Mathematics,* Houghton Mifflin Co., 1978; and *Mathematics Around Us,* Scott, Foresman and Co., 1978.

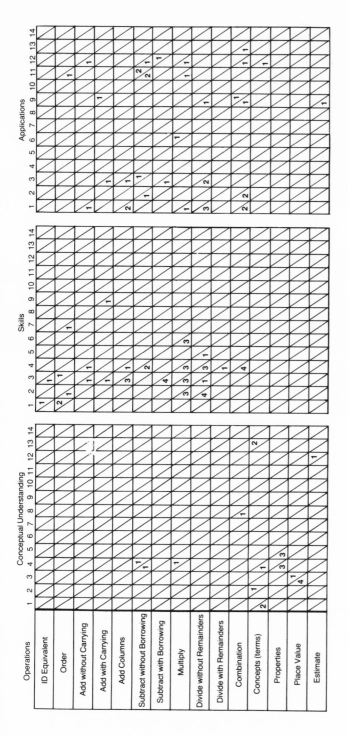

Figure 6-3. Content Analysis of Stanford Achievement Test (Intermediate Level/ Grades 4.5–5.6), 1973.

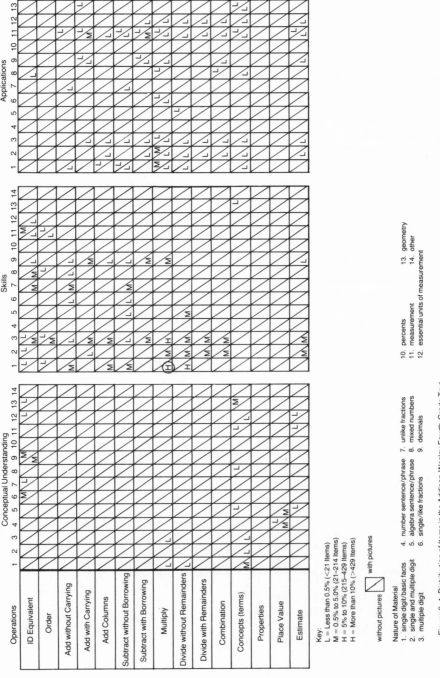

Figure 6–4 Distribution of Items in the Addison-Wesley Fourth-Grade Text.

An analysis of content at the *cell* level within the taxonomy provides a basis for comparing the treatment of specific topics within textbooks (for example, applications involving the multiplication of single-digit numbers). Figure 6–4 depicts the concentration of items representing specific topics within one of the three texts. Four general categories are used to depict the relative frequency of items in each cell of the taxonomy. The symbol "H" denotes high-frequency cells in which 5 to 10% of the items fall. When the "H" is circled, over 10% of the items in the text are concentrated in that cell. An "M" designates cells containing a moderate concentration of items (0.5% to 5.0%), and "L" indicates cells containing a low frequency of items (less than 0.5%). Cells that have no symbols are "empty," meaning that content does not occur in the textbook.

Each textbook's distribution of specific topics across the categories of concepts, skills, and applications is presented in table 6–1. From table 6–1, it can be seen that of the 293 topics included in one or more of the three books, 51% were included in the Addison-Wesley text, 57% in the Houghton Mifflin text, and 67% in the Scott, Foresman text. Because there was overlap in topic coverage — that is, some topics were covered in two or three of the books — the cell frequencies in table 6–1 sum to more than 293. Nevertheless, this analysis reveals that any given book covers only a little more than half the topics presented in all three books collectively.

Table 6–1. Distribution of Specific Topics across Concepts, Skills, and Applications

	Addison-Wesley	Houghton Mifflin	Scott, Foresman
Concepts	23	42	56
Skills	53	52	66
Applications	72	73	75
Totals	148	167	197

The Establishment of Curricular Validity: Textbooks

This section illustrates the way in which curricular validity can be established by examining the map between the several tests and the textbooks illustrated in the previous section. In order to put this in the context that has been considered, assume that the test's content validity with respect to the objectives domain has already been established and that what is being considered here is the additional question of the degree to which the test has curricular validity with respect to the textbook's being used in that particular district.

For purposes of illustration, data are presented contrasting the content domain specified by the five most frequently used standardized tests in mathematics and three textbooks. With these data, we can ask what % of the topics on a test are covered in a given textbook. The three columns labeled "T" in table 6–2 describe the % of topics in each test that served as the focus of at least one item in the student exercises in each book. In interpreting these figures, it is important to remember that at least 4,000 items were classified for each book. The percent of tested topics covered in a given book ranged from a low of 52.8% for the SAT and Houghton Mifflin text to a high of 73.7% for the Metropolitan Achievement Test (MAT) and Houghton Mifflin textbook. Thus only about one-half of the topics that were considered in the SAT were covered by one or more of the 6,986 items in the student exercise portions of the Houghton Mifflin text.

Table 6–2.   Percent of Tested Topics Covered in Each Textbook*

	Addison-Wesley		Houghton Mifflin		Scott, Foresman	
	T	$T\dagger$	T	$T\dagger$	T	$T\dagger$
	$(N = 148)$	$(n = 42)$	$(N = 167)$	$(n = 49)$	$(N = 197)$	$(n = 50)$
MAT (n = 38 topics)	63.2	31.6	73.7	39.5	73.7	42.1
SAT (n = 72 topics)	54.1	22.2	52.8	20.8	62.5	22.2
IOWA (n = 66 topics)	54.5	25.8	72.7	31.8	71.2	25.8
CTBS I (n = 53 topics)	56.6	32.1	64.2	37.7	64.2	35.8
CTBS II (n = 61 topics)	60.7	27.9	59.0	37.7	67.2	34.4

*T = Topics covered by at least 1 item in the book

T† = Topics covered by at least 20 items in the book

The columns labeled "T†" in table 6–2 describe the percent of test topics that served as the focus of at least twenty items in each book. If one assumes that this subset of book topics represents content students will have had an adequate opportunity to learn or to practice during the preceding academic year, these figures should provide reasonable estimates of the relation between test content and the content of instruction suggested by the book. These values ranged from a low of 20.8% for the SAT and Houghton Mifflin text to a high of 42.1% for the MAT and Scott, Foresman text. In other words, the proportion of topics presented on a standardized test that received more than cursory treatment in each textbook was never higher than 50%.

The Establishment of Curricular Validity: District Objectives

Still another example of an examination of curricular validity is presented with respect to the mathematcal objectives used in a district that we call Knoxport. The full strand of mathematical objectives excluding those dealing with enrichment was subjected to a content analysis. This mapping of the objectives was then contrasted with the SAT, which also happens to be the standardized test administered in that district.

The content specified by the objectives is not all covered on the SAT; nor for that matter are the topics tested on the SAT all present in the district objectives. There is a fair amount of overlap between the two sources, but this is in no sense complete.

One way to suggest this comparison is in terms of the objectives used by the school district. Of the total number of objectives 56% have content that is tested on the SAT. These fifty-two objectives, however, do not represent distinct topics as defined by the taxonomy. In fact, the fifty-two objectives are classified into twenty-four cells of the taxonomy. Another way to think of this lack of consistency is to point out that 44% of the topics covered by the district objectives are topics that are also tested by the SAT. Either figure implies only one-half of the content covered by the objectives is tested by the SAT.

Another way to look at the lack of consistency between the two is to consider it from the other point of view. The items on the SAT represent sixty-one cells, or topics, in terms of the taxonomy. Again remembering that twenty-four topics are covered by both the district objectives and the SAT implies that approximately 40% of all topics covered by the SAT are also similarly covered in terms of the district objectives. From this perspective, there is even greater discrepancy. The SAT items deal with many topics not covered by the district objectives.

Establishment of Instructional Validity

The application of the taxonomy to instructional content is a much more difficult task. Tests and curricular materials are almost always expressed in written form and hence are rather easily subjected to a content analysis using the taxonomy. The content of instruction, however, is more elusive as it represents an ongoing process that is presented to the students in an interactive vein with the teacher. Obtaining data on instruction and detailing the content of that instruction is a difficult task.

At the Institute for Research on Teaching (IRT), we have used various forms for the collection of such information. The most costly is field observation. In this approach, trained observers record during the course of the day what topics are covered and for what periods of time. A cheaper and more straightforward approach to the problem is to have teachers keep daily logs on which they record the content of their instruction.

An important question is the degree to which logs kept by teachers are accurate representation of topic coverage. In one project at the IRT, we found that teachers in general were able to keep fairly accurate logs. An analysis of the measurement error inherent in the process is being conducted and preliminary results suggest that in the aggregate (that is, averaged over days), the amount of error in using the logs to represent content/time allocations of teachers is not unacceptably large.

Hence, the instructional validity of a test can be established here as was illustrated with respect to curricular validity — the only difference being that within this context the content profile of the test is contrasted with the content profile derived from the log analysis. The degree to which the two are consistent with each other is the extent to which instructional validity is present for the test and for the students in that particular class. None of the data from our study were in a complete enough form to provide us with an illustration contrasting content coverage against one of the standardized tests. We can, however, discuss more generally examples of teachers who used the same materials but whose content coverage varied.

During the 1979–1980 school year, we collected extensive data on seven teachers in three different districts. We interviewed the teachers weekly, observed their classroom instruction, and had them keep daily logs recording their fourth-grade mathematics instruction.

In the Sawyer district, we observed two teachers whom we shall call Wilma and Jacqueline. The Sawyer district had a mandated mathematics textbook series (Holt) that all teachers were required to use. Teachers were not told they had to teach all topics from the book, however. In order to place the observations made in this study into the context of this paper, imagine that this district is considering a MCT for promotion from fourth to fifth grade and that we are concerned with the mathematics section (this is a totally hypothetical situation). Let us further assume that the superintendent and curriculum director have specified the domain on which this test is to be developed and that through a careful analysis of the Holt text, they have decided that the domain specified by the objectives is a proper subset of the domain of topics generated by the Holt textbook: in other words, the test has curricular validity. But would it also have instructional validity? One might think that having established curricular validity and also having a standardized textbook so as to assure curricular validity for all students in the district would assure that all students would receive instruction on every topic contained in the domain specified by the objectives. In other words, this would ensure instructional validity. In Sawyer, however, the two teachers we observed treated the textbooks in very different ways. For Jacqueline, the textbook essentially defined for this particular year at least the content of her instruction. She followed the textbook in an almost linear fashion, covering it page by page until she ran out of time at the end of the year (at chapter 9). A test such as the hypothetical promotion test just suggested would have had instructional validity for Jacqueline's class-room if it contained the same content as did the first nine chapters of the textbook.

Two caveats need mentioning. Three students in Jacqueline's classroom were put into a special subgroup that used the third-grade Holt book because these students were all below grade level. Obviously, a mathematics test that matched the fourth-grade text would not have had instructional validity for these students. It is also interesting to note that if the material covered in the test were not concen-trated at the beginning of the textbook but were found throughout the textbook, then the issue of how far the students went in the textbook does detemine whether the test would have instructional validity. In other words, if the test examines domain topics covered in the back sections of the book, then Jacqueline's students would not have been instructed in them and the certification tests would not have been instructionally valid for those students.

The other teacher in this district, Wilma, did not follow the textbook in any staightforward fashion. In fact, this teacher had her own conception of what should be covered in fourth-grade mathematics. This conception not only included a detailing of the topics that should be covered but also a time schedule as to when these topics should be covered. As a result of this, Wilma did not cover the textbook. She rearranged the order in which she covered things in the textbook, skipped sections of the book that she did not find consistent with her own conception of what should be covered, and added to the instruction topics that were not contained in the book.

In this case, it is clear that although the textbook was mandated the teacher chose to use it in her own fashion. If any of the topics that she chose to skip were a part of the domain on which the test was based, then, despite the fact that the test had curricular validity, it would not totally have had instructional validity for the students in Wilma's class. In general, our data show that students in this district using the same mandated textbook in mathematics received different instructional content.

The implication of this is that the hypothetical promotion-certification test would have had content validity with respect to both the objectives and the curricular material for all students in the district, but for the students in Jacque-line's class the test would additionally have had better content validity regarding the domain of instructional content than would have been the case for students in Wilma's class.

Consider one last example. In Knoxport, a detailed strand of objectives for mathematics was required for use by all teachers. Associated with this set of mathematical objectives was a management system that included locater tests, pretests, and mastery tests. Teachers kept records on the objectives that students had passed. In fact — although to the best of our knowledge it was never invoked — there was a policy that teachers could be released from their job if they did not use the MBO system and have the students in their class work through the objectives. Interestingly, even in this district with paper sanctions for not following the system, we found among the three teachers studied in this district a lack of consistency in terms of their students covering the objectives. One of the teachers, Andy, almost totally followed the MBO system and had his students work systematically through the objectives, one by one, until they passed the mastery tests. For students in his class, any test for advancement made consistent with the objectives would have been valid with respect to instructional content — at least for some students — but would have varied student by student because not all were able to progress through all the objectives for that grade level due to self pacing.

In the same district, two other teachers, however — Terry and Lucy —did not follow nearly as closely the MBO system for their mathematics instruction. Lucy provided two mathematics sessions, one of which was devoted to regular mathematics instruction and the other of which was devoted to using the individualized objectives system. The other teacher, Terry, rarely used the MBO system and in fact by the end of the year the students had spent very little time in the system. For the students in Terry's class — although they are from the same district — a test consistent with the objectives would not necessarily have been instructionally valid.

The Three Types of Content Validity and Implications for Curriculum Policy Making

Study results indicate that if no efforts are made to assure curricular or instructional validity, a test that has content validity with respect to the objectives domain would vary in its curricular and instructional validity for different students. Consider, for example, a test that has curricular validity — that is, the test has content validity, both with respect to the domain of objectives and with respect to the domain defined by the curricular materials. A test will not have this characteristic unless the materials have been standardized for the population being tested (for example, the state or district). Otherwise, one must talk about curricular validity in relationship to some district, school, or building. In this way, validity becomes a variable and is not a constant characteristic of the test itself as it is in classical test theory and in the case of content validity based on a set of objectives. To have curricular validity in general, the curricular materials must be uniform among the population for which the test is designed. For example, statewide adoptions of textbooks would assure that a test based on the objectives and consistent with the textbook would have content validity, both with respect to the objectives domain and the curricular materials domain.

Many educators assume all basic textbooks in a certain subject matter area cover the same basic content and are in fact interchangeable. This would imply that the test would have curricular validity with respect to any one of these textbooks.

In work that has been done with three fourth-grade mathematics textbooks — including Scott, Foresman, Houghton Mifflin, and Addison-Wesley — substantial differences have been found that imply that these books are not interchangeable with respect to their definition of a curricular domain. One cannot assume that any book within a certain subject matter will guarantee curricular validity. Once the content domain with respect to the objectives is specified, careful analysis of the major textbooks in the field must be undertaken so as to guarantee that the content domain specified by the objectives is in fact coincidental or at least a subset of the domain defined by the curricular material.

At this point, it is reasonable to ask why anyone would be particularly concerned with the notion of a test's having curricular validity. One reason is the belief by many educators that the materials do in fact specify the actual instruction that takes place in the classroom — that is, by assuring that a test has curricular validity, one is also simultaneously assuring instructional validity.

Also on the practical side, policies to ensure curricular validity are more easily established than is the case for instructional validity. For example, it is relatively straightforward for a district superintendent or state superintendent to mandate textbooks or curricular materials to be used in the schools within that unit. This is not the case for mandating the actual content of instruction. It is also easier to establish whether a test has content validity with respect to the curricular materials domain. The establishment of instructional validity is much more difficult and time-consuming.

Even when certain course materials are required within a district or building, the content in those curricular materials will not necessarily be covered in every classroom. Many teachers operate relatively autonomously in defining the content of their instruction. At least this was found to be the case for fourth-grade mathematics. Some teachers follow textbooks and other curricular materials to the letter, whereas other teachers in those same districts and under the same mandates will not necessarily cover nor follow the textbooks. Consider the cases of Jacqueline and Wilma as reported previously. Hence it appears that the use of the consistency between test items and the curricular domain does not ensure consistency between the test items and the instructional content domain. Because (1) consistency between test items and instructional content domain is the desired standard, (2) consistency between test items and the curricular domain would only be useful when it could serve as a surrogate for (1). Research results certainly challenge the expectation that this would occur frequently.

How could curricular validity serve as a reasonable surrogate for instructional validity? If management systems such as the MBO system used in Knoxport were to have associated stringent rewards and punishments that assure that all children will cover the objectives, and if a test has curricular validity with respect to the objectives, this system might guarantee instructional validity.

Why Does Instructional Validity Vary?

One might ask why it is that all students — even within the same classroom — do not receive identical instructional content. Research suggests two reasons. The first deals with grouping strategies. If the class is always taught as a whole, then all children within that classroom will receive the same basic content. Hence, for this situation, a test has instructional validity for all students within the classroom. If the instruction within the classroom is provided on a subgroup or individual basis, identical instructional content is not necessarily assured across all individuals or subgroups of students. This implies that even within the same classroom a test might have instructional validity with respect to one subgroup of individuals but not with respect to others.

Many of the certification or diploma tests measure cumulative types of educational experiences. A second reason for instructional validity's nonguaranteed status for all students in the same classroom is that content assumed to have been covered in a previous grade level and hence that is not covered in the present grade might not have been covered by all individuals (for example, because of the classroom from which they came). This would leave certain content uncovered for some students. To the extent to which this happens, this exacerbates the problem of guaranteeing instructional validity for all children.

The point of this section is that instructional validity will not occur naturally. One way to encourage it is to establish a system whereby certain curricular materials that are consistent with the domain specified by the objectives are required and, in fact, sanctions are included so as to require teachers to actually cover those objectives using the instructional materials provided. One also wonders if the long-held notion of teaching to the test might have a positive effect in encouraging instructional validity.

When the test is first administered (and assuming it is valid with respect to the objectives), one cannot necessarily expect the objectives domain to be a subset of the instructional content domain for all students unless one puts some constraints on what is taught. One reasonable constraint is to require some level of performance on the test as a criterion for graduation. Requiring that this test have instructional validity before it can be used (as some researchers have argued) is a "catch 22" because instructional validity is only likely after such a testing practice has been in place for a while.

If a test that is to be used for certification is administered for several years prior to its planned use for certification decisions and if careful content analyses of the objectives domain on which the test is based at the level of detail suggested by our taxonomy is made available to the teachers, teachers would likely begin to teach to the test, which would provide for greater instructional validity.

Another way of ensuring instructional validity is to give the test initially as a diagnostic device and then give remediation to students on the topics they fail. This is in fact the intended application of the New York Regents Competency Test. The test is first given in ninth-grade; students who fail are put in a special-help class. They can take the test as many times as needed to pass.

Summary

This chapter has examined the concepts of content validity, instructional validity, and curricular validity. All three concepts deal with content validity, but the domain differs among the three. Certification tests must have instructional validity, which means that the test must be valid both with respect to the domain used to define the minimum competencies and with regard to the instructional content domain, (that is, what is taught in the schools). Further, the test items must be representative of the objectives domain but not necessarily representative of the instructional content domain.

Whether a test has content validity with respect to the domain specified by the curricular materials is important only insofar as it is a surrogate for instructional validity. Some theoreticians might maintain that an analysis of the curricular materials tells us what it is that is covered in the schools. Current research suggests that this is far from true. Teachers in the United States generally operate as fairly autonomous decision-makers in defining the content of their insruction. They are influenced by many sources other than curricular materials such as tests, school administrators, and other teachers. It is for this reason that curricular validity should not be used when attempting to establish the instructional validity of a certification test. For tests of certification, there must be some other way to assure that a relatively large percentage of the items represent topics that are covered by all students in the district and/or state — that is, to assure that certification tests have instructional validity.

References

American Psychological Association. *Standards for Educational and Psychological Tests.* Washington, D.C.: American Psychological Association, 1974.

Freeman, D., and Belli, G. "Influence of Differences in Textbook Use on the Match in Content Covered by Textbooks and Standardized Tests." Paper presented at the annual conference of the National Counsel on Measurement and Education, Los Angeles, Calif., April 1981.

7 OVERLAP:
Testing Whether It Is Taught
Gaea Leinhardt

Children spend around fifteen thousand hours in schoolrooms being taught and learning a vast amount of material. They spend at least one hundred hours being tested (assuming fall and spring standardized testing). The degree to which those tests sample appropriately from the many hours of instruction is important. When the tests decide graduation status, they are of momentous consequence. But before discussions of content versus curricular validity are launched, the underlying and more difficult issue must be addressed, if only to remind us of its existence. Serious reasoned thought must be given to the content of those fifteen thousand hours and the content of tests, regardless of the use of the tests. Narrow restrictions on which brand of science or religion can and cannot be taught in the schools are not the heart of the issue; daring to design a core of meaningful goals and objectives for each grade, for each subject, for each educational unit, and for the total educational experience surely is. What the level of such planning should be (school, district, state, et cetera) is unclear; that it needs to go on is clear. When that task is addressed, issues of testing will be more directly resolved. What must be avoided is the test driving the curriculum.

The original work on overlap was done with Andrea Mar Seewald. Her thoughts and critiques are reflected in this chapter as well. William Cooley has also helped tremendously in discussing earlier drafts. Errors are, of course, the author's own responsibility. The research on which this paper was based was supported in part by the National Institute of Education.

Validity of a test is dependent upon the use of the test. Most tests are valid for something; the issue is whether a particular test is valid for the purpose to which it is put. With respect to the Florida test, we can envision issues of validity being discussed with respect to the future predictability: are the presence of these skills predictive of life success? Validity can be discussed in terms of the present reality or verity of the items: do you need to understand percentage of discounts in order to avoid being cheated? And, finally, one can discuss the validity in terms of fairness with respect to past events: did students have an adequate opportunity to learn the material covered by the test? It is this last issue that this chapter addresses.

In confronting the more restricted issue of techniques that may help to establish or reject the curricular validity of the Florida test, six assumptions are made. The first is that any educational system has the right to test its students for purposes of placement, assessment, promotion, and certification. The second assumption is that tests may include material previously taught if the student knows that is to be the case and if the material is not factual trivia but has educational significance and meaning. A third assumption is that the test may require some reasonable level of generalizations across settings (for example, if the student were taught road-map reading for Florida, the test item could be from Massachusetts). Fourth, tests designed to assess knowledge acquired should reflect not merely the content of what was taught but should also mirror the emphasis given that content in instruction. Emphasis can be achieved overtly by stating its importance or inferentially through repetition. Fifth, for the purpose of this chapter, the term *curricular validity* refers to the degree to which a specific test reflects the content in a curriculum; the term *instructional validity* refers to the degree to which a test reflects the content of text material and oral presentation. The issue of fairness for an individual or group of students refers essentially to their opportunity to learn the material tested; it is clear, however, that the process of learning specific content may be easier for one group than for another because opportunity to learn occurs *both* at home and at school. Sixth, I assume that honest and sincere efforts have been made to make the Florida test a good one; that is, items have been field tested, and each item is clearly written and has a correct answer. Failure to do these things is not an issue of validity — although it surely affects it — it is an issue of poor craftsmanship.

This chapter focuses on a narrow portion of the total problem — the overlap between test and instruction. Having a reasonable overlap is a requirement for establishing the validity of a test. Overlap is the degree to which material on a specific test has been covered by instruction (Leinhardt and Seewald 1981). Overlap can also refer to the portion of a particular curriculum that is tested; this is a much smaller area and is rarely dealt with, although it is often referred to (especially by teachers). In this chapter, unless otherwise noted, the term *overlap* refers to the degree to which test material has been taught. The chapter will describe the following: three techniques for obtaining an overlap estimate; suggestions for modifying the techniques for the Florida tests; the validity of the method using two studies done to date; and teacher thoughts while doing an overlap task will be presented as support for the validity of the techniques.

Techniques

There are many techniques available for estimating the percentage of a test that has been covered by teaching. Some of these methods are restricted to the material covered in formal curricula or textbooks; others attempt to include both text material and in-class instruction. In addition to differences in domains covered (text, text plus mimeo, and text plus mimeo plus oral and board instruction), there are considerable differences in the level at which the overlap is estimated (for example, student by item, class by item, grade by subtest, or total test). Although references will be made to each of these, the emphasis in this chapter will be on total instruction and on student-by-item analyses.

Taxonomy analysis

In response to the need to know with considerable precision the content of curricula, formal attempts have been made to deal directly with the overlap problem by identifying the best-fitting test. This has allowed informed selection of curricula and tests. The direct measurement of content can be conducted at any level of analysis considered appropriate: student, instructional group, class, or school; item, subtest, or total test. Approaches to content analysis of curricula have tended to involve matches between detailed scope and sequence charts and test descriptions of content covered (Armbruster, Stevens, and Rosenshine 1977; Everett 1976; Kugle and Clakins 1976; Pidgeon 1970). These analyses have been conducted at the levels of the entire test and total curriculum; they have not included information on how much material was actually covered in instruction by the school, class, or student. In analyses of this type, it is assumed that the same or similar labels (for example, detail, paraphrase, main idea, et cetera) refer to the same content and that different labels refer to different content. In spite of producing rather gross measures of curriculum and test content, these approaches have revealed three things. First, introductory curricula cover remarkably different content. (Beck and McCaslin 1978, showed this dramatically.) Second, tests — at least those reviewed — cover a more similar range of topics than do curricula. Third, very little of what is taught ever gets tested.

Jenkins and Pany (1976) also noted the differences between content covered in reading curricula and the content of standardized reading tests or subtests. Their analysis of seven commercial reading series and five reading achievement tests was conducted by matching the words presented in each curriculum with the words that appeared on each test. Results revealed "curriculum bias" between tests for a single curriculum as well as on a single test for different reading curricula. In their discussion of the implications of these findings for educational research, Jenkins and Pany suggest that one must either control for curricula across treatment conditions or develop tests that are curriculum-based or criterion-referenced.

More recently, researchers at the Institute for Research on Teaching have been analyzing tests and curricula in elementary mathematics (Floden, Porter, Schmidt, and Freeman 1978; Kuhs, Schmidt, Porter, Floden, Freeman, and Schwille 1979; Porter 1978; Porter, Schmidt, Floden and Freeman 1978a, 1978b; Schmidt 1978; Swhwille, Porter, and Gant 1979). From this research a detailed taxonomy of elementary mathematics topics was constructed that can be used to map out tests and curricula.

This technique is described in greater detail by Schmidt in his chapter as he and his colleagues are the primary developers of the approach. This technique involves specifying the structure of the system of knowledge to be analyzed, building a taxonomy for that structure, then specifying the elements of the taxonomy covered by text material and by tests. The taxonomy, of necessity, is at a more general level than *items* of instruction or tests and relies heavily on concepts of objectives and the equivalence of items within a domain. It does not consider the degree to which text material actually got covered; this may be of particular concern in Florida where differential coverage may be a serious problem. Further, constructing a taxonomy for an area like a fourth through twelfth-grade social studies sequence is far harder than for one grade of math. The distinct advantage to this approach is that, upon completion, a very useful map locating both text and tests results.

Text Analysis: Item Search

Recently, my colleague Andrea Mar Seewald and I have been using a technique for estimating overlap using text materials. Each item of the test is cut out, placed on a 4″ × 6″ card, and the textbooks are searched for that item. Each test item in a math search takes approximately three minutes when the search involves texts for the first through fifth grades. Obviously, one gets very fast at the process because the organization of the texts is learned quickly, as is the arrangment of sequence within domain (for example, word problems are at the end of each computational section). The matched item is written next to the test item and identifying information is catalogued. For example, given the test "52 minus 46," a computational item from a fourth-grade standardized test, no item was found to be identical in text, but a close match was discovered — "92 minus 46." Both items are two-digit subtraction in vertical form, both involve borrowing in the units column, and the units are identical; only the tens column is different. The difference in the tens column is that with borrowing the tens place, the answer is zero. Two other problems in the text series deal with that issue. Therefore the item is considered to have been taught. To estimate overlap, the search for any item must be downward from the current grade to the lowest reasonable grade and must include final location in the current grade.

Searching for a reading or language arts item is harder but follows more or less the same procedure. All words in the item need to be checked against the texts. Most items can be answered with approximately 60% of the words actually used. (For precise techniques on which words can be deleted, see Wildeman and Holland 1973.) Further, passages of similar complexity (sentence length, embedded clauses, mood, and voice), with different words need to be located. In judging whether an item has been taught, one is concerned with the essence of the material — not whether each word has been taught. The overlap estimate is the sum of the items covered by text material divided by the total number of items, times 100.

Text Analysis: Computer Search

The preceding analysis can be and has been computerized. The computer process involves developing a dictionary of information from the texts (that is, all the math items and all the vocabulary questions). The dictionary is then searched for material required for item solution as defined by the searcher. The advantage of this technique is that multiple texts can be searched simultaneously for item solutions and issues of density can be easily dealt with. (The term *density* refers to the frequency with which material is represented or reviewed in text.) The disadvantage is the laborious task of entering the texts to form the dictionary is as time-consuming and costly as a hand search when the hand search will be a one- or two-time event. The estimate is calculated in the same way as described.

Instructional Analysis: Teacher Interview

A different approach to the overlap problem has emerged from studies in which the problems of multiple (in some cases, multinational) curricula, a limited test battery, and interpretation of analytic results are part of the design. The earliest work in actually measuring overlap was done by Husen (1967), Chang and Raths (1971), and Comber and Keeves (1973). Comber and Keeves asked teachers to estimate how much of a test was covered by instruction (teacher presentation plus curriculum) in an entire school. Chang and Raths had teachers estimate the "emphasis" that their programs placed on particular items on a standardized test. These items had previously been found to discriminate between schools serving lower-class and middle-class students. As expected, the "emphasis" or overlap also varied. Husen apparently obtained slightly more detailed estimates by obtaining percentages of students who covered each test item, but the procedures were unevenly used across the study. These measures focused only on how much of the test was covered by instruction, not how much of instruction was covered by the test. The measure obtained seemed too imprecise to account adequately for variation in student performance. It was therefore not included in the analyses. It was used, however, as a guide for interpretation of results.

The technique that we have used most frequently, and continue to use, is a modification of this approach using teacher interviews. Experienced teachers (that is, those with three to four years of work experience) possess accurate information about material utilized in texts and about their own instructional practices. Essentially, there are three forms of the question as follows that can be posed to the teacher to get at that knowledge:

1. Did you teach that information this year?
2. Has Andrew been taught enough information to answer the item correctly?
3. Can Andrew get this item right?

The three forms of the question are quite close but elicit very different kinds of responses by the teacher because their fundamental structural meaning is quite different. The first question is in part "Did you do what you were supposed to do?" and in part "Did anyone at any time get taught this by you?" It is likely to be inflated in the positive direction. Question (2) focuses on a particular child and the teacher's interactions with that child as a group member and as an individual, but the question tends to reduce the teacher's impressions about the child as a person and focus more strongly on the aspect of the child as a learner being taught. The third question, on the other hand, focuses the teacher onto the child's learning personality and away from the teacher's role. It elicits answers about Andrew's attention span, areas of interest, test-taking attitudes, et cetera. Clearly, the concern in this case is whether the teacher taught the material [question (2)].

In order to obtain an overlap estimate by interviewing the teacher, the following steps are taken. A blank test is made up for each child in the class, and the teacher is asked to go through each item of the test for each child answering the question, "Has X been taught the information required to pass this item? Please deal with what has been taught, not whether X knows the material. If it seems relevant, also consider X's exposure to the test format" [question (2)]. The number of items the teacher claims has been taught divided by the total number of items on the test, times one hundred is the percentage of overlap for that class.

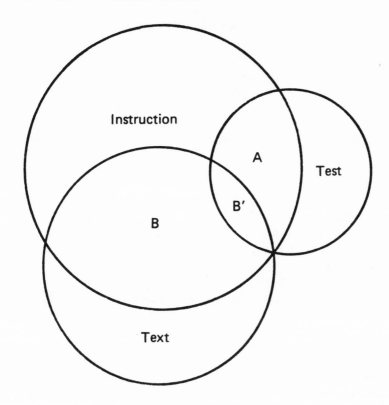

Figure 7–1. Overlap between Tests, Texts, and Instruction.

Figure 7–1 shows what various types of overlap account for. Area A plus B′ divided by the total test area is the area called instructional overlap. In figure 7–1, most of the test is covered by instruction, but less than half of the instruction is covered by the test. In curriculum-based estimates of overlap, only area B′ divided by test is considered. Figure 7–1 is drawn in a way that shows no area in which text material overlaps with test but not with instruction. It is improbable, but not impossible, that students will cover textual material that is not part of the known instruction using a standard text sequence. When teachers give extra work to some students if the students were part of the target, it would be part of area B or B′. Note that not all of the text is covered by instruction; this occurs when time runs out and when the teacher systematically deletes sections of the text. In current work we are finding that teachers rearrange text material to cover tested content first, nontested content next, and often completely delete the "challenge problems" or "projects." The deletion of sections is especially prevalent among the lower tracks.

Suggestions for Modifying Overlap Estimates for Florida

The Florida situation appears to have a number of interesting problems that would require a modification of the techniques just described. The two most important ones are that a test is given in high school that purports to assess information that could have been obtained from the fifth through eleventh grades, and second, that the state has many different curricula in place, depending on the district. If the results to date show no extensive differences between districts using different text material when socioeconomic status (SES) and race are controlled for, then the following procedure can be used. (If not, then stratification by curriculum is required.) The basic pool of teachers in social studies, language arts, and mathematics with five or more years of experience can be randomly sampled. (Sample size must be determined, probably 100 per grade per subject, ignoring district, is a minimum, given approximately 5,000 teachers per grade level. A 5% sample would be 250, given some overlap of teachers across subject matter. A sample of 200 to 300 per grade seems appropriate.) Within each teacher's roster, 6 children should be sampled and the teacher queried with respect to whether enough information has been taught to that particular student to have the student pass the item. One challenge is to select the most informative way to sum the scores over students or teachers. One way is to sum over teachers within grade and within subject. This yields a grade-by-subject overlap point, permitting easy identification of when the material is covered. Another method is to sum over teachers and over grade within a given subject or overall. This yields an overall overlap and loses the information of when in the grade sequence items were covered. It is also possible to sum overall within race, thus developing an overlap estimate for black students and white students separately. If there is reason to believe — and given the results, it seems there is — that students of different races within classes receive different instruction, this would be appropriate. An acceptable overlap would be one that falls within the standard error of measurment of the test, centered on the passing score.

This procedure uses teachers dealing with individual children, because we have found teachers to be more conservative and precise when they are discussing specific rather than hypothetical or general cases. In terms of teacher time, each item for each child takes approximately twenty seconds, or three to four items a minute. It is not a difficult task. The most serious problem with this approach is a temporal one. Essentially, this approach requires us to assume that the instruction given between sixth and eleventh grades has remained constant enough for estimates of overlap to be valid. As stated in the beginning, it is appropriate for schools to assume the retention of content over time so long as it is not trivial. It is uncertain, however, when or whether particular content was taught to a specific individual in the past. There is no way of getting that information accurately after the fact. It seems likely that those items that teachers report covering in multiple curricula and over several grades are most curricularly valid, and those taught not at all, or only once, are least valid. In other words, if no one reports teaching certain material, it clearly is not appropriate to test it. An important point is to avoid trivializing the criteria for instructional overlap.

Evidence for the Validity of the Overlap Approach

Evidence that supports the validity of the instructional and curriculum-based approaches to estimating overlap comes from two studies: "The Instructional Dimensions Study" (IDS) (Cooley and Leinhardt 1980) and "Reading Instruction and Its Effects" (Leinhardt, Zigmond, and Cooley 1981).

Instructional Dimension Study.

In IDS, the instruction-based estimate was obtained for every item of the test at the class level (Poynor 1978). Teachers were asked to estimate the percentage of students who had been taught the minimum material necessary to pass each item. The pre- and post-test in IDS was the Comprehensive Tests of Basic Skills (CTBS) (CTB/McGraw-Hill 1973). Approximately four hundred first- and third-grade classrooms were studied during reading and mathematics instruction. The means, standard deviations, correlations, and regressions of the instruction-based estimates of overlap are reported in tables 7–1 and 7–2.

As can be seen from table 7–1, three of the four means hover around 50% with 20 as a standard deviation; correlations with pretest are about .3 and with posttest about .4. Table 7–2 shows that before any program information has been included, pretest and instruction-based overlap explain considerable and significant portions of the variances. The increase in R from first to third grade is due in large part to the stronger relationship between pretest and posttest in the higher grades. This is reflected not only by the zero order correlations but also in the greater magnitude of the coefficients and the smaller standard errors. (See Cooley and Leinhardt 1980.)

Reading Instruction in Classrooms for the Learning-Disabled (L.D.).

Other examples of instruction-based estimates of overlap have been used in several instructional-effectiveness studies (Cooley et al. 1979; Leinhardt and Engel 1981; Leinhardt et al. 1981). In this approach, two components of a test item are considered — content and format. The teacher is asked to identify for each student (or a sample of students) — whether or not the student has been taught the information required to answer the item. The teacher is *not* being asked whether

Table 7–1. Means, Standard Deviations, and Correlations Using Overlap Estimates from IDS, Grades 1 and 3

| | Grade 1 | | | | Grade 3 | | | |
| | Read (n=104) | | Math (n=84) | | Read (n=109) | | Math (n=116) | |
	x̄	s.d.	x̄	s.d.	x̄	s.d.	x̄	s.d.
Pretest	29.36	5.47	18.51	3.20	29.34	8.85	33.90	8.33
Instruction-based Estimate of Overlap	50.93	18.46	27.59	12.33	51.12	21.33	56.14	19.40
Curriculum-based Estimate of Overlap	27.13	14.91	15.03	10.38	20.02	5.60	30.52	14.56
Posttest	57.93	8.94	33.38	5.73	44.38	9.62	54.17	10.96

Grade 1

	1	2	3	4
1. Pretest		.33	.21	.50
2. Instruction-based Estimate of Overlap	.32		.30	.47
3. Curriculum-based Estimate of Overlap	.33	.29		.42
4. Posttest	.39	.37	.38	

Read (above diagonal) / Math (below diagonal)

Grade 3

	1	2	3	4
1. Pretest		.34	-.05	.86
2. Instruction-based Estimate of Overlap	.41		.42	.38
3. Curriculum-based Estimate of Overlap	.30	.35		.10
4. Posttest	.78	.51	.42	

Read (above diagonal) / Math (below diagonal)

Note: Values above the diagonal represent correlations in reading while those below the diagonal represent correlations in mathematics

Table 7–2. Results of Regression of Posttest on Pretest and Overlap (IDS)*

Basis for Overlap Estimate	Grade 1 Read		Grade 1 Math		Grade 3 Read		Grade 3 Math	
	Instruction	Curriculum	Instruction	Curriculum	Instruction	Curriculum	Instruction	Curriculum
Pretest	.63	.70	.52	.52	.89	.94	.91	.95
Standard Error	(.14)	(.13)	(.19)	(.19)	(.06)	(.05)	(.08)	(.08)
Overlap	.17	.20	.13	.16	.05	.25	.13	.15
Standard Error	(.04)	(.05)	(.05)	(.06)	(.02)	(.08)	(.03)	(.04)
Adjusted R^2	.34	.34	.20	.20	.74	.75	.66	.65

*All raw regression coefficients and adjusted R^2 are significant at or below .05.

Table 7–3. Correlations and Regressions Using Overlap Estimates (LD)

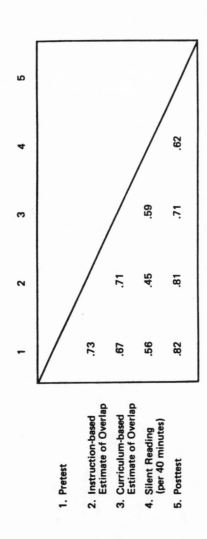

	1	2	3	4	5
1. Pretest					
2. Instruction-based Estimate of Overlap	.73				
3. Curriculum-based Estimate of Overlap	.67	.71			
4. Silent Reading (per 40 minutes)	.56	.45	.59		
5. Posttest	.82	.81	.71	.62	

	Adjusted R^2
Posttest* = 119.6 + .50 Pretest + .67 Instruction-based Estimate of Overlap (.10) (.15)	.76
Posttest = 102.1 + .64 Pretest + .92 Curriculum-based Estimate of Overlap (.10) (.34)	.71

*All raw regression coefficients and adjusted R^2 are significant at or below .05. Standard errors are in parentheses.

s/he taught the item, rather, the teacher is being asked whether the student has been taught the information the item is testing; for younger children, this includes familiarity with format. The teacher does this task for each student and each item; the time required to complete this task is minimal (approximately sixty minutes for ten children).

The results from the first year of research in reading instruction for LD children serve as an example of this method of obtaining instruction-based estimates. Overlap data were collected at the student-by-item level. Teachers were asked, for each student, to circle items (on the reading subtests of the CTBS) that contained content covered by instruction, whether the instruction was in text or classroom teaching. Overlap was the number of items circled divided by the total number of possible items, times 100. The estimates of 52 cases from the first year of study ranged from 2.70 to 100.00% (x = 59.12; s.d. = 32.73). Table 7–3 presents the correlations and regressions for the first year of study. Overlap is an important variable in predicting end-of-year test performance.

There is also evidence for the validity of the curriculum-based estimates of overlap. Although estimates of overlap based on curricula are harder to obtain than teacher estimates, they give the appearance of being more objective. The two studies just discussed — IDS and the first year of the LD reading study — also incorporated a curriculum-based estimate. The analyses from these two studies can be used to compare the two overlap procedures.

IDS

The curriculum-based estimate from IDS used teacher reports of material covered in each text for each student and matched this with test content. The results are shown in tables 7–1 and 7–2. Four interesting differences between the two estimates in tables 7–1 and 7–2 should be pointed out. First, the correlations between the two estimates range from .29 to .42. Although the two approaches cover some of the same information, it is apparent that they are not totally redundant. Second, all estimates are lower using curriculum analyses rather than instruction-based estimates. Third, although first-grade math yields the lowest estimate, it is not as dramatically different from the rest of the curriculum-based estimates as it is in those that are instruction-based. Fourth, the third-grade reading curriculum-based overlap does not correlate with either pretest or posttest. The regression coefficient is still significant, although considerably smaller than the others. This may be caused by the difficulty in estimating the content covered prior to third-grade in reading. In order to estimate item-level overlap, some assumptions must be made about the content of material that each student was exposed to prior to any given stage and level. In this case, the estimates did not involve a systematic search of earlier curricula but used nationally obtained estimates of word acquisition. As seen in table 7–2, the regression results for curriculum-based measures of overlap are almost identical to those obtained using the instruction-based estimate. Considering the substantial differences in means and the totally different process of gathering the information, this suggests that estimates are somewhat stable — regardless of technique.

LD Study

A curriculum-based measure of overlap was also included in the first year of study of reading in LD classrooms (1977–1978). In January of 1978, teachers were asked to list the major curricula used with each student. At the time of posttesting — May 1978 — that list was verified and teachers were asked where each student was in each curriculum (that is, final location). For each level in a curricular series, all words presented were entered into the computer with an identifier indicating the series, level, and unit, chapter, or page in which the word appeared. These words were then alphabetized, and duplications were deleted based on the higher-level identifiers. The remaining words then were used to compile a dictionary of unique words, including only the first presentation of each word. Separate dictionaries were compiled for each curriculum. Individual student dictionaries were compiled to include those levels completed in each curriculum the student used during the year based on the student end-of-year location given by the teacher. Dictionaries were also compiled for each level of the posttest (CTBS). The total test-by-item measure of curricular overlap had a mean of 19.65 (s.d. $= 14.73; n = 52$).

The results shown in table 7–3 again indicate that although the means are lower for curriculum-based estimates, the regression is essentially the same. These results, coupled with the IDS results, suggest that the mean curriculum-based overlap estimate is always lower than the instruction-based estimate because it automatically leaves out in-class instruction not found in textbooks. But the results also suggest that both estimates do equally well in predicting posttest. Choosing which estimate is better is a matter of philosophy or the budget of the study.

Summary of Quantitative Validity Information

Overlap has, through this and other studies, been shown to be an important variable in predicting student growth. This does several things: it demonstrates support for the notion that exposure to specific content during instruction has a powerful influence on what a student can demonstrate having learned. Clearly, students learn material not formally taught and fail to learn other material that is taught. Overlap also lends support to the reliability and relative accuracy of both procedures. There is legitimate concern, however, as to what the teacher is estimating when answering the overlap questions. In related, but not yet published work we have been investigating this issue in some depth.

Qualitative Validity

The teacher-interview approach reflects both informal in-class instruction and curriculum-based instruction, but it may also include the teacher's expectation about student competency. This problem has been addressed in two ways in other research: studying the relationship between overlap and teacher expectation and obtaining teacher protocols from sampled items for which they estimated overlap. Teacher-expectation estimates correlate with overlap estimates, but *not* in the presence of the pretest. This means that teacher overlap estimates made at the end of the year do not simply reflect teacher expectations at the beginning of the year. Further, protocol analyses indicate that although teachers claimed it was difficult to distinguish between what they taught and what they assumed students learned, they actually made this distinction easily.

Five teachers were given the overlap task and asked to "think aloud" while answering a subset of the items. Three trained observers with at least thirty hours of observation of students during reading were given the same tasks. Analysis of the protocols reveals both how the teachers conceptualized the task and how their performances differed from the novices.

The first item of the reading test on which we obtained protocols required the student to select the word "wet" from among four alternatives after having been told orally, "Find the word that tells you something has water on it." Three of the teachers responded by describing when short vowels or short "e" was taught with respect to that child. The others responded that the word was a member of word families taught. That is, they identified the unit in reading needed for correct response and assessed whether the child had the skill by checking where or when the child was taught the material. In contrast, the novices tended to emphasize the whole word and its meaning and assumed the child would have general knowledge of the meaning, ignoring the problem of how to read the word.

In assessing whether or not the child had been exposed to particular material, the teachers followed an interesting strategy. They mentally unrolled the entire curriculum text, dittoes, oral presentations. They then located the point in the curriculum where the material necessary for completing the target item had been taught. After locating the critical material, they "searched" for a student who had been, or was about to be, taught that material. They then located the target child with respect to that child. For example:

T.: She hasn't had "a-w" at all.
I.: Let me just ask you a question . . . how do you remember?

T.: I know that "a-w" comes after where she is. Robin [not target] just learned that. That's how I know that . . . Yeah, on Level 9. And that in relation to what Cheryl and Robin are studying. I knew that I just worked with "a-w" with Cheryl and Robin, and that's why I would say that . . .

This descriptive-data evidence shows that the teachers are not merely using their personal biases or opinions of the students but are seriously analyzing the task and trying to decide whether the material has been taught. The data presented earlier supports the notion that they can do this quite well.

In addition to the two measurement approaches discussed, some attention should be given to the level at which the data are collected. It is our conviction that the most accurate and easy way to collect data is on the student-by-item level. If time or cost preclude gathering the information for each student on each item, then students should be randomly sampled and data aggregated. Teacher estimates of percentages of students are undesirable because they require the teacher to think of groups of students, estimate the percentages they represent, and average (two out of thirty have all, three out of thirty have none, et cetera). This task is complex and fallible.

Conclusion

The importance of overlap in any given situation is contingent upon many elements: the accuracy of estimation; the degree to which what has been taught has been learned; the degree to which what has not been taught has not been learned; and the complexity or nonhierarchical nature of the subject-matter domain. In a case in which a student's future can be seriously influenced, then the overlap of the test to what has been taught must be established.

This chapter presents a way of assessing the degree to which a particular test has been covered by instruction over time. To the extent that a minimum competency test (MCT) is an exit requirement for formal schooling, having sufficient overlap between the test and instruction is a necessary condition for validity. To the extent that an MCT is an entrance requirement for something, the overlap must be with that something.

The more serious issues are the conclusions to be drawn from the vast differences between black and white students on the first round of the Florida tests. These differences do not suggest cultural biases as much as they suggest vastly different educational experiences for the two populations. It suggests that white children have been taught and have learned material both at home and at school that helps nearly 80% of them to get a passing score. It suggests that black children have not been taught or have not learned — and if they were not learning, someone was not watching — the material necessary to pass the test. The relative speed with which black children passed the retests suggests that they have not been taught. These inequalities will not be corrected by assessments of test validity, but obtaining estimates of differential instructional content may help to clarify the location of a portion of the problem.

References

Armbruster, B.B., Stevens, R.J., and Rosenshine, B. *Analyzing Content Coverage and Emphasis: A Study of Three Curricula and Two Tests* (Technical Report No. 26). Urbana, Ill.: University of Illinois at Urbana-Champaign, 1977.

Beck, I., and McCaslin, E. *An Analysis of Dimensions that Affect the Development of Code-Breaking Ability in Eight Beginning Reading Programs.* (LRDC Publication No. 1978/6.) Pittsburgh, Pa.: University of Pittsburgh, Learning Research and Development Center, 1978.

Chang, S.S., and Raths, J. "The School's Contribution to the Cumulating Deficit." *Journal of Educational Research,* 64, (1971), 272–276.

Cole, N.S., and Nitko, A.J. "Instrumentation and Bias: Issues in Selecting Measures for Educational Evaluation." Paper presented at the National Symposium on Educational Research, Johns Hopkins University, November 1979.

Comber, L.C., and Keeves, J.P. *Science Education in Nineteen Countries. International Studies in Evaluation I.* New York: John Wiley & Sons, 1973.

Cooley, W.W., and Leinhardt, G. *Design for the Individualized Instruction Study: A Study of the Effectiveness of Individualized Instruction in the Teaching of Reading and Mathematics in Compensatory Education Programs.* Final Report. Pittsburgh, Pa.: University of Pittsburgh, Learning Research and Development Center, 1975.

Cooley, W.W., and Leinhardt, G. "The Instructional Dimensions Study." *Educational Evaluation and Policy Analysis,* 2, No. 1 (1980), 7–25.

Cooley, W.W., Leinhardt, G., and Zigmond, N. *Explaining Reading Performance of Learning Disabled Students.* (LRDC Publications No. 1979/12.) Pittsburgh, Pa.: University of Pittsburgh, Learning Research and Development Center, 1979.

CTB/McGraw-Hill. *Comprehensive Tests of Basic Skills.* Monterey, Calif.: McGraw-Hill, 1973.

Everett, B.E. *A Preliminary Study of the Relevance of a Standardized Test for Measuring Achievement Gains in Innovative Arithmetic Programs.* Project Longstep Final Report: Volume II, Appendix Report. Palo Alto, Calif.: American Institutes for Research, 1976.

Fisher, C.E., Berliner, D.C., Filby, N.N., Marliave, R., Cahen, L.S., Dishaw, M.M., and Moore, J.E. *Teaching and Learning in the Elementary School: A Summary of the Beginning Teacher Evaluation Study.* Beginning Teacher Evaluation Study, Technical Report 7–1. San Francisco, Calif.: Far West Laboratory for Educational Research and Development, 1978.

Floden, R.E., Porter, A.C., Schmidt, W.H., and Freeman, D.J. *Don't They All Measure the Same Thing? Consequences of Selecting Standardized Tests.* East Lansing, Mich.: Institute for Research on Teaching, Michigan State University, July 1978 (Research Series No. 25.)

Husen, T., ed. *International Study of Achievement in Mathematics: A Comparison of Twelve Countries*. volume 2. New York: John Wiley & Sons, 1967.

Jenkins, J.R., and Pany, D. *Curriculum Biases in Reading Achievement Tests* (Technical Report No. 16). Urbana, Ill.: Center for the Study of Reading, University of Illinois at Urbana-Champaign, November 1976.

Kugle, C.L., and Calkins, D.S. *The Effect of Considering Student Opportunity To Learn in Teacher Behavior Research* (Research Report No. 7). Austin, Tx.: University of Texas, Research and Development Center for Teacher Education, 1976.

Kuhs, T., Schmidt, W., Porter, A., Floden, R., Freeman, D., and Schwille, J. *A Taxonomy for Classifying Elementary School Mathematics Content*. East Lansing, Mich.: Institute for Research on Teaching, Michigan State University, April 1979 (Research Series No. 4.)

Leinhardt, G., and Engel, M. "An Iterative Evaluation of NRS: Ripples in a Pond." *Evaluation Review,* 5, No. 5 (1981), 579–601.

Leinhardt, G., and Seewald, A.M. "Overlap: What's Tested, What's Taught?" *Journal of Educational Measurement,* 18, No. 2 (1981), 85–96.

Leinhardt, G., Zigmond, N., and Cooley, W.W. "Reading Instruction and Its Effects." *American Educational Research Journal,* 18, No. 3 (1981) 343–361.

Marliave, R., Fisher, C., Filby, N., and Dishaw, M. *The Development of Instrumentation for a Field of Study of Teaching*. Beginning Teacher Evaluation Study, Technical Report I-5. San Francisco, Calif.: Far West Laboratory for Educational Research and Development, 1977.

Pidgeon, D.A. *Expectation and Pupil Performance*. Stockholm: Almquist & Wiksell, 1970.

Popham, W.J. "The Case for Criterion-Referenced Measurements." *Educational Researcher,* 7, No. 11 (1978), 6–10.

Porter, A.C. *Relationships Between Testing and the Curriculum*. East Lansing, Mich.: Institute for Research on Teaching, Michigan State University, July 1978 (Occasional Paper No. 9.)

Porter, A.C., Schmidt, W.H., Floden, R.E., and Freeman, D.J. *Impact on What?: The Importance of Content Covered*. East Lansing, Mich.: Michigan State University, Institute for Research on Teaching, 1978 (Research Series No. 2.) (a).

Porter, A.C., Schmidt, W.H., Floden, R.E., and Freeman, D.J. "Practical significance in program evaluation." *American Educational Research Journal,* 15, No. 4 (1978), 529–539 (b).

Poynor, L. "Instructional Dimensions Study: Data Management Procedures as Exemplified by Curriculum Analysis." Paper presented at the annual meeting of the American Educational Research Association, Toronto, Ontario, Canada, April 1978.

Rosenshine, B. "Academic Engaged Minutes, Content Covered, and Direct Instruction." Unpublished manuscript, University of Illinois at Urbana-Champaign, 1978.

8 WHAT CONSTITUTES CURRICULAR VALIDITY IN A HIGH-SCHOOL-LEAVING EXAMINATION?

Decker F. Walker

If we as educators expect a youngster to have learned something by a certain point in his or her life, we have some obligation to make this possible. We often express this obligation by saying that we must provide all youngsters with an *opportunity to learn*.[1] But just what is an opportunity to learn? Does it mean a teacher and a textbook? Does it extend so far as to include a supportive social climate, strong incentives, and individual tutoring?

This chapter will describe some of the important specifics necessary if we educators are to say we have provided a student with an adequate opportunity to learn something. There will be several specific ingredients. The question of which ones are necessary and which ones are luxuries is a test of our values — and the reason why the *Debra P*. case is important to us all. The line the court draws in this case will define the mutual obligations of the youngster and the school. As an adviser to the parties concerned I hope to suggest the various places where a line might reasonably be drawn and to offer a rationale for these options.

An Introduction to the Curricular Issues

During the usual twelve or more years of formal instruction, a youngster is presented with millions of learning tasks. Simply to read and remember the material presented in textbooks, workbooks, films, teachers' lectures, field trips, assemblies, and so on would be an overwhelming task. Students are immersed in these myriad experiences which are interspersed with tests to see what has been retained. Then most students advance to another grade level and another collection of learning tasks. Certain students — those who do not master the material at first — may have to repeat a grade level.

Let us focus on a single fact or skill or concept presented somewhere, somehow in the series of items that students are exposed to. Unless students have some particular reason to single this item out for special attention, it is likely that many of them will fail to retain it after it has been presented. Dozens of quite normal conditions — for example, a moment of inattention, a sleepy study session, or a too-rapid presentation — could interfere with the learning of that particular item by some particular student. One important ingredient, then, in providing students with an opportunity to learn a certain item is *repeated presentation*. Another is *clearly flagging a particular item* and a reasonably small number of others as more important to learn than the remainder of items presented.

Items presented to students must also be shown in a form the student can comprehend. For example, presenting a science lesson on the climate in Urdu to schoolchildren in the United States would not generally be providing them with an adequate opportunity to learn. Similarly, presenting that lesson using mathematics too advanced for the students would not constitute adequate provision of an opportunity to learn about climate. Certain students, nevertheless, will learn from such inadequate presentations. But this entire discussion concerns expectations of the society for *all* students. All are compelled to receive an education. All are subject to the high-school-leaving examination. All should be provided with an adequate opportunity to learn.

What constitutes adequate presentation? For any given student, the only certain test of a presentation is that *that student has learned similar items from similar presentations*. We cannot assume that because a student is enrolled in the ninth-grade that student is capable of learning from a ninth-grade textbook. In fact, we know that simply reading such a presentation with comprehension would be a difficult task for about half of the ninth graders nationwide. Presumably, students affected by the Florida functional literacy test (FLT) have been successful at learning in classrooms because they will have passed all their high school courses. For them, the conventional high school classroom presentation is presumably a form of presentation from which they are capable of learning.

Communicating Expectations to Students

Learning is ultimately a result of the student's own efforts. The student must marshall his or her own personal resources of skill, knowledge, discipline, and sometimes even courage and bring them to bear on the task of learning what is required. Before the student can do that, he or she must know what is required. This means, minimally, that students should receive a detailed and specific description of all the items of skill and knowledge they will be expected to know. (These should *not* be the actual test items, of course. The question of relation of test items to test specifications will be taken up later.) A school should be able to show that printed descriptions were delivered to every student. It should also be able to show that teachers and principals were directed to go over this document with students in class to explain requirements further.

Verbal expressions are not sufficient, however. Schools always say the things they teach are important. If educators did not believe they were important, they would not be in the curriculum in the first place. Students have therefore grown accustomed to making finer discriminations. The things that are *really* important, as every student knows, are the things that appear on tests and are used in grading. Putting the item on a test clearly gets the message to students that this is important for them to learn.

Obviously, students should be told the level of performance that will be considered passing and the penalty for failing the graduation test.

Time

One of the most fundamental ingredients of opportunity to learn is time. Enough time must be provided for the student to complete the learning activities needed to teach the item in question. Enough time must be provided for review to ensure retention, for practice to ensure full control over the learned response, and for appropriate variation of stimuli to permit generalization of the learning to occur. How much time is needed depends upon the topic, the individual, and the details of the instruction. Furthermore, how the time is distributed — that is, whether in one session or many, if many how frequently, how regularly, and so on — affects the amount that will be needed. Foreign languages, mathematics, and physical skills generally benefit from regular daily periods of learning and practice, even if these are brief. Laboratory and studio learning require more massed study periods. One would expect, therefore, that such objectives as "determine the main idea" or "distinguish between facts and opinions" would require repeated teaching and regular opportunities for practice. In contrast, an objective such as "complete a check and its stub accurately" might be taught in a single session, with a few later sessions set aside for review and practice — provided, of course, students have learned prerequisite skills, including arithmetic.

To document how time has been apportioned among these objectives would be difficult. Few schools keep enough detailed records to permit a direct assessment. Teachers may remember well enough to report retrospectively, as may students. If their reports agree, one could place considerable confidence in them. The number of pages of textbook devoted to a topic is a fallible, but usable indicator of the time devoted to a topic, because teachers generally follow the textbook in this respect. (If most teachers regard the passages in question as too easy, too difficult, or less important than the rest, however, they will systematically skip pages in these sections.) Courses of study usually recommend time-interval ranges for covering various topics, and these recommendations could be documented. Each of these expedients is flawed to a significant degree. The amount of classroom time devoted to these objectives would be the most convincing evidence of providing opportunity to learn them, yet methods to document time allocations are weaker than the methods available for the other indicators of opportunity to learn. Time expenditures are therefore the weakest link in the chain of documentation that might be provided to show that the state has provided students with an adequate opportunity to learn the twenty-four objectives covered by the test.

Retention and Remediation

All of us forget what we have learned; all skills decline without use. To be prepared for a test, students must have had sufficient opportunity for review, for relearning what might have been forgotten, and for practicing important skills. For best results, such opportunities should be provided regularly from the time of first learning until the time of the test. Such a stringent requirement might be unnecessary for students whose test performance shows they have learned and retained the item. But for those whose initial learning was marginal and whose learning deteriorates between testings, provision for review, relearning, and practice is essential to lasting learning.

Students who fail to learn or to retain their mastery of a given item of knowledge or skill need another chance to learn it. Simply to tell a student that he or she has not learned something alerts the student to take advantage of the next opportunity that may come along to learn it or perhaps to try to manufacture another opportunity by rereading the book or asking a parent or friend for help. Generally speaking, however, only a small fraction of even the ablest students in secondary schools are able to independently direct their learning. One reason we provide schools for such young people is because we recognize that they need help and support in learning; they are not yet ready to learn on their own. Therefore it is unreasonable to expect a student who is failing to learn something basic to discharge such a responsibility alone. Schools should provide remediation.[2]

A preliminary list of characteristics of an adequate learning opportunity follows.

1. Repeated presentation.
2. Flagging the item as important to learn, including identifying it as likely to be tested, and actually putting it on tests.
3. Presentation in a form from which students are capable of learning.

4. Provision of adequate time for learning it.
5. Provision for retention and remediation.

Let us proceed to consider concretely what evidence a school system might provide to show it had provided an adequate learning opportunity.

The most important, frequently used channels of communication between school and student are the teacher, curriculum materials (especially textbooks), and tests. To show that an item appears in a textbook is straightforward. The only complication is the vexing but not insuperable problem of distinguishing variations in presentation of the same content and altogether new content. More will be said about recognizing equivalence of content later. To show that a teacher has presented an item of content is considerably more difficult. Reasonable evidence might include teachers' recall or rating, students' recall or rating, official guides distributed to teachers detailing district policy, records of teacher workshops provided by the district, and reports and records of supervisors and principals who monitor and evaluate teaching. To show that an item appears in tests administered by the district ought to be easy. Assessing content in teacher-made tests may be somewhat more difficult, but most teachers keep a record of the tests they develop and administer.

How frequently must an item appear in any one of these modes of presentation in order to give all students an adequate opportunity to learn? Any answer will be arbitrary to a degree, but we can at least determine a lower bound. It is widely understood among students of educational measurement that results on an immediate posttest (that is, a test administered within hours or days of presentation of the item for learning) are substantially different from results found on retention tests administered four weeks or more after initial learning. By this time, many students have forgotten. This suggests that, at minimum, an item important enough to appear in a high-school-graduation test ought to have been tested for at least twice, with an interval of at least four weeks between the two testings. Students who fail the item the second time should receive further instruction and still another test. Thus adequate provision of learning opportunity would appear to require at least three appearances of an item on tests administered to a student during the high school years.

Of course, some students will still fail to learn the item. For these students, detailed and specific diagnosis of the difficulty they are experiencing and individually tailored instruction to overcome it are required.

Summary of Indicators of Opportunity to Learn

The following list includes the summary of indicators of proper opportunity to learn:

1. The item appears in official (district/state) course of study repeatedly (at least three times), is flagged as important for teachers to teach, has adequate time allocations, and has provisions for activities facilitating retention and remediation.
2. The item appears in textbooks and other required curriculum materials repeatedly (at least three times), is emphasized there as important for students to learn, has sufficient page allotments, and is in a form students can comprehend.
3. The item appears on classroom, school, and district tests used in grading repeatedly (at least three times).
4. Teachers report providing their classes with an opportunity to learn it, spending sufficient time on it, and ensuring systematic attempts to identify and remediate learning failures.
5. Students report having been informed of test purpose and objectives before the learning opportunities had passed, having an opportunity to learn it, and spending sufficient time on it.

Equivalence Classes of Items of Content

The phrase "items of content" has been used casually throughout this chapter, implying that it is possible to recognize that different passages of text, different class activities, and different test items all somehow treat the same item of content. But such equivalence classes among instructional presentations and between instructional presentations and test items are by no means always straightforward. For instance, there is the so-called level of difficulty of the item. Common sense seems to indicate that we can present the same material at various levels of sophistication and detail. Consider the first objective on Florida's list: "determine the main idea inferred from a selection."[3] Some selections — for example, passages from the Bible, technical manuals, legal language, and annual reports to stockholders of a corporation — could make substantially more difficult demands than others. Also, some passages will be more familiar to most students than other passages. Finding the main idea in a love letter should be a lot easier for most students than finding the main idea in an insurance contract, even if the passages selected were of comparable difficulty otherwise. Specific items that may be proposed for inclusion in the equivalence class defined by this first objective could differ in many other ways that have educational significance. Among them are: length of passage, number of subordinate ideas, similarity of subordinate ideas to main idea, intrinsic interest of subject matter for students, cues that are used to mark off importance (for example, typographical, syntactic, contextual, and so forth).

Clearly we *cannot* assume that a student who is capable of finding the main idea in any one of these passages is also capable of finding it in any other. There is a sense in which the various test items and the various instructional presentations that fall under this overall objective are equivalent, but it is *not* in that they represent a single learning task such that once learned on one item is learned for all. We must imagine this objective as defining myriad items — both test items and items of curricular or instructional content — infinite in extent and highly varied along important dimensions such as those just listed.

Test developers make some sort of sampling from the infinite number of potential test items in the process of test construction. The teacher, the textbook publisher or author, and the local school district curriculum committee make judgments of a similar sort when they decide what content to include in the curriculum, how much emphasis to give to each item included, and how to present it to students. We *can* answer empirically the question of whether students attain the same scores on examinations composed of different samples of items drawn from the unlimited variety of possibilities represented by this objective. If the number of items on our test is large enough and if they have been selected in a nearly random fashion from the pool of potential items belonging in this equivalence class, then a simple analysis should show whether the items hang together or whether students' scores fall into two or more clusters relatively independent of one another. In practice, however, such determinations are rarely made with adequate data. The State Student Assessment Test I (SSAT I) is reported to contain 117 items covering 24 objectives or less than 5 items per objective.

Five items are clearly not an adequate number to verify that the many dimensions of variation of the task "find the main idea . . ." have been covered on the test. If the developers of the test had administered two different ten-item scales keyed to this objective and had been able to show that students who scored a certain way on one of these scales scored in a comparable way on the others, we might reasonably conclude that these items are representative samples from the infinite pool of such items. Without this sort of evidence, we are left to rely upon the good judgment of those who write test specifications and test items.

Clearly, it would be imprudent for a teacher to suppose that each of these twenty-four objectives defines a coherent skill that can be taught directly in a single unit of instruction. An objective like this first one — "find the main idea . . ." — must be regarded as a vast collection of instructional objectives of unspecified dimensions and extent. To teach with the aim of having students attain this objective means to provide a series of learning experiences preparing students to cope with the varied levels of difficulty, familiarity, lengths, relations of main and subordinate ideas, et cetera. Only in this way can students be equipped to answer a handful of items on the SSAT I. In short, adequate instruction for this one objective requires a strand of curriculum that must surely run from kindergarten prereading instruction to eleventh-grade content subjects and study skills. (The test is administered to eleventh-graders.) A single unit, or even two or three, on "finding the main idea" would not succeed in teaching this item of content to most students, although such a unit could be valuable for students who are prepared to profit from it by their prior education.

In brief, then, the equivalence classes for many of the objectives listed in the Florida SSAT I are so broad and encompassing as to make it impossible to verify that they have been taught simply by looking for them as a separate item of content. It would be necessary to show that they have been pursued consistently as a strand of the curriculum from kindergarten through the eleventh grade.

How would we recognize units or activities in the curriculum devoted to these objectives? The answer is, in the same way we recognize different test items as testing for the same objective. Namely, we use expert judges to consider each item of content and rate the extent to which it treats matters central to this objective. This is a crude procedure, but if it is suitable for test construction, it is suitable for curricular validation.

No one's interest would be well served by narrowing the objectives and specifying them in further detail. Broadly stated objectives such as these twenty-four have the advantage of requiring a broad and thorough educational program. With narrower, more specific, and detailed objectives, it would be possible to target instruction more directly toward the attainment of that objective but at the expense of neglecting other objectives of comparable importance. Some effort should be made, however, to identify dimensions of variation within the equivalence class of each objective. If teachers knew which types of passages presented substantially different difficulties to students, they would be able to teach in such a way as to address these dimensions of variation more effectively. Everyone would benefit.

The General and the Particular: A Dilemma

When a particular student — *Debra P.* — is tested and her performance is judged inadequate, justice would seem to require that she have had an adequate opportunity to learn the material on the test. Yet it is patently impossible for the state of Florida to verify that it, in fact, provided such an opportunity for each and every individual tested. The best educators can hope for is to show that policies and procedures have been established and followed that have led, on the average, to an adequate opportunity to learn. But is this enough? Suppose a state were to guarantee a minimum income to all adult residents. Would it be sufficient to show that a certain sum equal to the product of the number of persons below the poverty line and the minimum guaranteed income had been distributed? Or would detailed records have to be kept showing that each affected citizen had in fact been sent a check for a certain amount?

There is a monstrous disproportion between the collectivity of the state and the individuality of the person. The state builds at great expense a test instrument that seeks to surmount this obstacle and pass judgment in a uniform manner separately upon many thousands of individuals. Does the state have a corresponding obligation to go to comparable lengths to show that it has provided *each* of these individuals with an adequate opportunity to meet this test? Fairness and decency dictate that it is not enough to show that on the average throughout the state adequate opportunity has been provided. If Debra P., for example, can show that adequate opportunity was not provided in her case, that should be sufficient, in my view, to forbid the state from withholding a diploma until an adequate opportunity has been provided.

Yet I am fully aware of the cost of verifying these matters. Education budgets are already stretched beyond limits. To deflect money into verification of learning and out of provision of the opportunity to learn might well deprive everyone of important educational benefits.

If the Florida legislature and the voters are aware of these dilemmas and choose to spend their scarce educational resources on documenting provision of opportunity, that is their business. The question before the court is whether the state can test individuals without teaching them. The court seems to have decided that it cannot. The next question is whether the state can test individuals one at a time in an identical fashion although it supervises their teaching in a very loose, broad way. This dilemma does not arise with diplomas, because each school sets requirements and each teacher helps interpret them. Where there are differences in standards, there are also differences in instruction. But imposing a uniform standard although permitting variety in instruction sharply poses this dilemma of the general and the particular.

This dilemma could be partially avoided if the state's authority were not exercised so uniformly and directly. By influencing the individuals' lives with a test that affects their future in a most substantial way, the state inevitably imposes unequal hardships on these individuals. Does the state have a corresponding obligation to provide a greater opportunity to learn to those most at risk? Or is it sufficient for the state to provide a certain minimally adequate opportunity to learn to all? As the poet William Blake said, "One law for the lion and the lamb is oppression."

Ironically, imposition of a uniform and absolute standard of achievement by the state would seem to require an individualized, highly differentiated, patently unequal distribution of opportunities to learn in order to avoid imposing unreasonably unequal hardships on the most disadvantaged students. The result is very much like the mastery learning concept, with a fixed standard for all and variable programs of education leading to the attainment of the standard. The implementation of such a system statewide would be an interesting experiment indeed.

The hard choices of this dilemma can be avoided to some extent by a two-stage process of testing and instruction. The first is a broad conglomerate test like the SSAT I. On the basis of this test, some students are identified as having not achieved satisfactory mastery of the twenty-four objectives required by the state of Florida. Such students are then given enriched opportunities to learn such as those already discussed, and these additional efforts to provide greater learning opportunity are carefully documented for each student who fails to pass the first screening test.

Summary and Conclusion

To show that on the average throughout the state, schools provided students with an opportunity to learn the twenty-four objectives covered by the Florida SSAT examination would be feasible, although difficult. It would involve showing that material relevant to these objectives appeared repeatedly over a period of years in the textbooks, courses of study, and tests used by districts throughout the state. Further, it would involve showing that material relevant to these objectives was flagged as more important than other typical content, that teachers and students were informed about the test and its content early enough that they could prepare for it, and that students and teachers report having a sufficient opportunity to learn these items. Using appropriate sampling procedures, such a showing should be no more difficult, expensive, time-consuming, or subjective than the development of the test itself. Doing so presents no additional unsolved logistical, technical, or educational problems not also present with test construction itself.

On the other hand, if justice requires a showing that Debra P. herself and any other individual student deprived of a diploma by the examination was provided with an adequate opportunity to learn, serious logistical problems arise. Detailed records showing how time was spent in Debra P.'s classroom over her school career would be needed. Her teachers would need to be examined in detail, as would her test performance. The student's own testimony would be needed. The showing would be lengthy, expensive, and involved. In the future, computerized records would make such a showing quite feasible, but the record-keeping system would be costly — both in time and money.

Notes

1. *The International Study of Achievement in Mathematics* (T. Husen, ed., New York: Wiley, 1967) brought to the attention of modern educational researchers the importance of "opportunity to learn." Of all the factors within schools studied in this massive survey, only teachers' ratings of the extent to which their students had an opportunity to learn the material included on the test correlated substantially with achievement. D.F. Walker and J. Schaffarzick, ("Comparing curricula." *Review of Educational Research,* 44, (1974), 83–112, reviewing evaluation studies that compared students' achievement under different curricula, found that the pattern of achievement echoed the pattern of content inclusion and emphasis in the curriculum materials. They developed the argument that content inclusion and emphasis were likely to have powerful effects on achievement because they directed the

time, energy, and attention of students and teachers toward or away from items measured on the test. The relation between test and curriculum has been extensively studied since by a number of investigators.

2. The importance of remediation is less well established by research. The most convincing assessment of what literature currently exists is E.G. Begle's monograph, *Critical Variables in Mathematics Education* (Washington, D.C.: National Council of Teachers of Mathematics, 1979). The summaries of research in mathematics education in this volume are a most valuable guide to anyone grappling with the problem of providing opportunity for learning.

3. This quote is from "Florida Functional Literacy Test Specifications," entered as evidence in the *Debra P*. v. *Turlington* Trial, 474 F. Supp. 244, 1979 as document No. CT 112.

References

B. Armbruster, R. Stevens, and B. Rosenshine. *Analyzing Content Coverage and Emphasis: A Study of Three Curricula and Two Tests*. (Technical Report #217) Urbana, Ill.: University of Illinois at Urbana-Champaign, 1977.

R. Floden, A. Porter, C. Schmidt, and R. Freeman. "Don't they all measure the same thing? Consequences of selecting standardized tests." Institute for Research on Teaching, 1978.

G. Leinhardt and O. Seewald. "Overlap: What's Tested, What's Taught?" *Journal of Educational Meausurment,* 18, (1981), 85–96.

A. Porter. "Relationships between testing and the curriculum" Institute for Research on Teaching, Michigan State University, 1978.

9 CURRICULAR VALIDITY:
The Case for Structure and Process
Richard L. Venezky

Perspective

The following comments address two issues that were raised by the recent *Debra P.* v. *Turlington* decision:[1] first, what constitutes reasonable and valid curricular attention for a given test objective, and second, what practicable means should be employed to ascertain the existence of such curricular match. Because this chapter does not attend to the equally perplexing issues raised by minimum competency testing (MCT) per se nor the issues attendant to the design and scoring of tests, for convenience of argument the existence of acceptable MCTs will be assumed throughout. The term *acceptable tests* means tests that either have been in use long enough without challenge to be considered acceptable to all parties concerned with them or that have been declared acceptable by some legal or quasilegal body. This is not to be taken as a statement about the value of MCT nor about current practices in test construction. It is only to state that the starting point for the following discussion is one or more MCTs for which curricular validity must be demonstrated to avoid a morass of petty (and sometimes not so petty) issues related to schooling goals, we will assume that the objectives of the MCTs are objectives that by experience we know schools are capable of teaching to all or nearly all

The comments and suggestions of Carol Blumberg, Jon Magoon, and Daniel Neale on an earlier draft of this paper are gratefully acknowledged.

students, and furthermore, that these objectives are reasonable and important as determined by a rational consideration of human, community, and national needs and aspirations.

Judicial intrusion into what for centuries was considered the exclusive domain of educators is not viewed with uniform satisfaction in the United States today (see Adelson 1981). Nevertheless, the curricular validity issue of *Debra P*. v. *Turlington* raises an issue that educators and educational psychologists should have faced long ago. The court decision in this instance — muddled procedures included — provides a priceless opportunity to refocus public education on its fundamental goal of providing good instruction.

The struggle to define reasonable and adequate curricula for given educational objectives could lead to a major improvement in schooling, to a restoration of public faith in the public school system, and to an uplifting of the profession of education. But regardless of the state of research on testing, teaching, learning, communicating, or any related topic, the need for establishing curricular validity exists now and must be resolved reasonably quickly. The courts have shown an increasing willingness to mandate remedies to educational problems when educators fail within a reasonable time to find acceptable solutions on their own.[2] Needed here, as in hundreds of similar situations, is not the definitive solution but the best solution within existing constraints of knowledge, resources, and human capabilities. In other words, the challenge is to define a uniform standard, based on the assumed behavior of the reasonable man of ordinary prudence. That enforcement of such a standard, once defined, may not be practicable within existing educational practice should not deter the search for such definition. Even if the best practical approach to demonstrating curricular validity is still not adequate for meeting both legal and educational needs, both the courts and the nation's educational enterprises will have gained from the insights gathered in the quest itself.

The Nature of Instruction

A convenient starting point for demonstrating curricular match might be found in student test scores for the objectives in question. High student scores on a test objective do not constitute proof, however, of a valid curriculum, nor do low scores necessarily constitute proof of invalidity. Not all learning takes place in the classroom. Students might consolidate or even acquire some competency objectives from home or community experience — perhaps in spite of ineffective school instruction. (A case study of exactly this is reported by Feitelson 1980.) But this should not relieve the schools of responsibility for clearly defining the competencies required, monitoring their acquisition, and providing assistance to students who do not acquire them outside of school.

Potential Effects of Population Shifts

In many urban schools in the 1950s, resources (that is, time, personnel, and materials) were allocated to objectives according to the needs of the majority population. Skills that, year after year, did not need to be taught were in time neither taught nor formally monitored. Then a population shift occurred and students from different home and community environments came into these schools. Skills that were previously acquired outside of the school now needed to be taught in the schools, but some schools failed to realize this need immediately because they no longer monitored these skills. From one standpoint, the problem was in the new students' lack of academic preparation. From the standpoint of *Debra P. v. Turlington*, however, a curriculum that had no validity previously in relation to particular schooling objectives remained invalid. The shift in school population simply forced the problem to the surface. So long as even a single student fails to meet a competency test objective, the need to demonstrate curricular validity exists. But even without a single failure, schools would be foolish to assume that such a need might not arise in the future.

The converse of the high-scoring case presents a slightly more complex problem. By appealing to reason, we can conclude that a school that over a reasonably long time has a high percentage of its students failing a particular test objective either has an inadequate curriculum for that objective or has established an unattainable objective. But if the school should not be allowed to hide behind student success, the school should not be judged *a priori* at fault with student failure.

The possibility will always exist for students in a particular school and in a particular year to perform poorly on one or more competency objectives, in spite of a good curriculum. To hold the school responsible without fair hearing would be contrary to basic principles of U.S. justice. Low scores give cause for concern over curricular validity; they should not, however, be the only evidence gathered.

Classroom Practice

The terms *curricular match* or *curricular validity,* which are used interchangeably, would seem to imply *instructional validity*. The term *instruction,* however, is not well-defined operationally within the field of education. Consider, for example, the following situation: A ninth-grade social studies teachers tells her class at the beginning of each year that they are responsible on their own for recording and learning new words that occur in their social studies texts. Students are encouraged to purchase small, spiral-bound notebooks for recording words and definitions. Vocabulary words are included on quizzes and tests. Some words are defined in class at the teacher's initiative, but usually the only words discussed in class are those that students ask about or those that many students define incorrectly on a quiz or test.

Does this procedure qualify as instruction? An omnipresent classroom observer would find little direct instruction on vocabulary and no homework assignments on the topic. Vocabulary words, for the most part, would be neither introduced, practiced, nor reviewed.

Compare this to vocabulary instruction at the second-grade level, wherein words are usually introduced and discussed by the teacher before the students encounter them in their reading selections. Furthermore, many teachers use blackboard and work-sheet exercises on vocabulary, have oral vocabulary drills and reviews, and send vocabulary words home with the students for further practice. This practice leaves no doubts about the existence of instruction; the question of adequacy, however, remains unresolved.

Consider another example: At the beginning of a tenth-grade English course, students are tested on sentence diagramming, a skill that is taught in grade nine. Students who fail to exhibit mastery of this skill are given review materials to take home with a note to their parents explaining how to check the review exercises. No class time is allocated for teaching diagramming, but students must use diagramming by the third week of class.

Does this qualify as instruction? Would it qualify as instruction in grade three?

The Varying Need for Instruction

The questions raised by the examples just given center not only on instructional methods, but on the roles that school and home are expected to play in learning, and the ability of the student to teach himself or herself. Schools have limited resources and large responsibilities. Neither time nor personnel are available both to teach and reteach every objective of the curriculum. Class time, ideally, is allocated to those objectives that require the most professional attention. Topics that most students can acquire on their own need not be allocated extensive class time. Thus the amount and type of class instruction — in the broad sense — that is needed for ensuring mastery of an objective is a function of the difficulty level of the objective for the students involved.

The social studies vocabulary situation described earlier meets the test of curricular validity, given social studies vocabulary on an MCT. Students at the ninth-grade level are generally capable of looking up words in a dictionary. Furthermore, it is reasonable to assume that students at this grade level possess the required metacognitive behaviors for vocabulary learning: they can decide, within defined limits, what they need to learn; they can select from alternative learning methods; and they can detect when they are failing to learn. But this is not true, in general, for students at the second-grade level; thus such a procedure would not constitute curricular validity for second graders.

For the approach to diagramming skills, however, it would be important to know to what degree the parents were capable of assisting in the learning process. For children from middle-class homes, this approach would probably be adequate. For children of migrant farm workers, for example, it probably would not.

In both of these cases, curricular validity was not determined solely from the type and amount of instruction evidenced in the classroom. Curricular validity and instructional validity are not the same, unless instruction is interpreted in an extremely broad sense. Curricular validity depends in part upon acceptable instructional methods, but other features are also important. The United States Court of Appeals (644 F.2d 397 (5th Cir. 1981)), in upholding the United States District Court's requirement for curricular validity (474 F. Supp. 244 (M.D. Fla. 1979)), defined curricular validity as "things that are currently taught" (6770). In commenting on the positive aspects of Florida's current program for teaching basic skills, the district court's opinion gave curricular validity further definition. The court stated that ". . . present program . . . sets objectives, defines goals, evaluates achievement and, if necessary, remediates deficiencies" (474 F. Supp. at 264 ff.). By this definition, curricular validity is not established simply by declaring that certain skills are taught, nor by indicating where they are taught, nor (by inference) by stating instructional methods in the narrow sense (for example, taught inductively). Curricular validity, by the court's statements, requires at a minimum well-defined goals, instruction, evaluation of achievement, and remediation.

The Outcomes of Educational Research

Consider the following situation:

> A high school algebra teacher presents most topics deductively. Theorems and principles are stated, applications are given, and then problems are assigned. A student who flunks the course complains that the instruction was faulty, citing several studies that found induction to be superior to deduction for teaching high school algebra.

At issue here is approximately one hundred years of psychological and educational investigation. Does research tell us anything reliably about practice? The answer to this question is clearly yes, but this does not substantiate the student claim just cited.[3] First, in this particular case, the existence of purportedly better methods does not establish lack of efficacy for the method in use. Both might be above the acceptability threshold.

Second, for school-based subjects there are no definitive, all-inclusive studies on instructional methods. Worse yet, we have limited understanding on what is important for learning. Motivation is obviously important, but how it interacts with instructional methods is unknown. One of the few interesting theories of instruction we have (Stephens 1967) claims that the primary role of the instructor is to point out what is important to learn and to motivate students to learn it on their own. Content knowledge and instructional method are only marginally important in this theory.[4]

We might point to a single component of an instructional process that can be evaluated based upon the results of empirical investigations, but little can be said from the research literature on sustained learning in the classroom setting. Poor approaches to subject-matter organization might be compensated for by patient teacher assistance; poor use of exemplars might be overcome by high motivation.[5]

But if laboratory research can provide few answers, can school experience do any better? Experience appears to be the most reasonable — and possibly the only — defense schools have for their allocation of time, their selection of materials, and their instructional methods. Experience is also the only common data base related to curriculum that has potential for consistent interpretation. Schools do not always monitor and interpret experience as they should, yet they are certainly capable of doing this.

Given the limited applicability and uncertain interpretation of the research literature, it is unreasonable to expect schools to derive their curricular procedures from empirical — that is, laboratory — studies. Schools should be expected to know, however, the relationship between methods and results for the more commonly used approaches to the subjects they teach. Yet given the complexity of school-based instruction, it is questionable whether experience would be acceptable to a court as a justification for ongoing school practice. If the general principles of tort and contract law are applicable here, then experience would need to be translated into so-called minimum standards of professional competence, which shifts the issue from experience per se to the professional conduct of school personnel.

Teacher Competence

Assume that high school French students used the most respected text available, had access to a language laboratory, were assessed at reasonable intervals, and experienced all of the other procedures that might be desired for good curriculum implementation, but unfortunately had a teacher whose knowledge of French was no better than that of most of the students. Is the curriculum invalid for matching to French objectives on an MCT if any such test should include foreign language questions? The real issue here is not whether teacher incompetence can lead to a test-curriculum mismatch. That is assumed to be true. Instead, the issue is how such incompetence is to be determined.

To suggest teacher competency testing is to suggest that minimal capabilities exist, without which successful teaching of particular subjects is improbable. (This also assumes that such capabilities can be assessed reliably and validly — an issue that will not be discussed here.) If the competencies are content-related, then a relationship between instructor knowledge and student learning is required, but no such relationship has been established. High content knowledge does not always lead to high student learning. Inarticulate, insensitive, and uncaring teachers, for example, seldom teach well — regardless of how much subject-related knowledge they possess. On the other hand, highly skilled teachers can often do well teaching subjects they know little about. Therefore assessing teachers on subject knowledge alone is probably not a valid procedure for determining teacher competence.

One alternative to content testing is to assess general teaching knowledge: ability to select correct alternatives in sensitive classroom situations, familiarity with student backgrounds and interests, and so on. This might be possible, but no well-accepted approach to such testing has yet been devised, and therefore there is no information on the validity of such measures.

Another approach is to evaluate teachers in situ, through observation of teaching techniques. To do this reliably, however, requires multiple observations, which would be exceedingly costly. In addition, to evaluate data from such observations, stable relationships between teacher behaviors and student outcomes would need to be established, yet approximately one hundred years of research on teaching so far has produced little evidence that this task can be done.

A totally different approach to teacher effectiveness is to measure student outcomes, based on the difference between predicted and realized scores, where predictions are generated from student and instructional data gathered over a wide variety of classrooms. (See New York State Bureau of School Programs Evaluation 1976.) The objection to this approach is the same as one already raised — namely, that the relationship between teacher activities and student learning outcomes is not well understood.

What seems more reasonable is an evaluation system within the school that takes into account a wide range of information on teacher performance including: management and control of classroom; ability to relate to students, parents, and staff; keeping of records on student progress; and student performance itself. This, in theory, is what every principal does in making yearly teacher evaluations. Establishing curricular validity will require that this task be done adequately, and that decisions about teachers (for example, retention and assignment) be made based upon the results. This implies a major role for the principal in establishing and maintaining a valid curriculum.

Concrescence

The talmudic disputations of the previous sections lead to the conclusion that curricular validity cannot be determined solely by examination of test scores nor by investigation of instructional materials, time, or methods. Neither can it be evaluated through reference to empirical results of laboratory research. At a minimum, a valid curriculum depends upon appropriate behaviors by teachers and principals, and the evaluation of a curriculum requires knowledge of the collective experience of schooling, especially the behavior of the reasonable school person of ordinary prudence.

Within this definition, what constitutes valid instruction may differ across grade levels for the same test objective. Nevertheless, intention may rival outcomes for determining curricular validity.

The evaluation of curricular match to any test objective should, therefore, be based on the following considerations:

1.   Has the school adequately organized for teaching the objective?
2.   Are the instructional methods used either those that have worked for similar students in similar settings or those that from related experience have a high probability of working?
3.   Is the degree of responsibility for learning assigned to the pupil appropriate for the age and development level of the pupil?
4.   Is the dependence on the home and other extraschool resources realistic?

Adequate Organization

The first requirement for adequate organization is that the school make clear to students and parents what skills the students must master. This can be demonstrated at the lower elementary levels through communication with parents and at the higher elementary and at secondary level by communication with students and parents. Schools should state in unambiguous terms what they expect students to learn and how and when they expect students to engage in this learning. In the district court's terms (474 F. Supp. 244, M.D. Fla. 1979 at 264): "It is critical that at the time of instruction of a functional literacy skill the student knows that the individual skill he is being taught must be learned prior to his graduation from a Florida school." This should be interpreted for each skill.

But school administrators must also monitor how well objectives are being learned and adjust resources accordingly. In other words, if a school seriously intends to assist students in meeting major objectives, it will monitor individual progress on these objectives and take appropriate action when expected progress is not exhibited. A school that has no means for tracking student progress in critical objectives exhibits a lack of intent to ensure that these objectives are acquired. Of course, monitoring of progress implies ongoing evaluation of performance — but not necessarily formal evaluation — and allowances for providing extra help. (*How much* extra help is a function of available resources and of other demands upon these resources.) It is important, in regard to skills generally included in minimum competency exams, to keep in mind another part of the district court's opinion in the *Debra P. v. Turlington* case. "Instruction of the skills necessary to successfully complete the functional literacy test is a cumulative and time consuming process. Knowledge of how to successfully perform the functional literacy skills is not taught in any specific grade, in any specific class, or from any specific type of teacher (474 F. Supp. at 264)."

In addition to being defined and monitored, the objectives and procedures for any year or term must be *realizable*; that is, they must be feasible under the conditions that the school and the students are confronted with. To demonstrate reasonableness, a school should be able to cite similar students under similar conditions who have achieved the desired goals.

Experientially Derived Methods

A valid curriculum should be based on procedures that reasonable and informed persons would expect to work. One way to demonstrate this is to show that the same procedures previously have worked with similar students in similar situations. Another approach would be to show that a new approach contains a significant overlap with methods already found to be successful.

This appeal to experience should not be interpreted, however, as a basis for excluding experimental methods and teacher innovation. Whether implemented with cardboard and paste, stocks and bonds, or shovels and watering cans, innovative methods that include proper attention to the basic principles of instruction should be viewed as potentially valid.

The United States Court of Appeals, in upholding the requirement for curricular validity in *Debra P. v. Turlington* (644 F.2d at 6772) expressed this same concern by stating "Nor do we seek to dictate what subjects are to be taught or in what manner." To allay fears that the court's decision would stifle curricular innovation, the opinion reaffirmed the following statement from a Supreme Court decision: ". . . the judiciary is well advised to refrain from imposing on the States inflexible constitutional constraints that could circumscribe or handicap the continued research and experimentation so vital to finding even partial solutions to educational problems and to keeping abreast of ever-changing conditions." Better a loosely defined criterion that allows responsible experimentation than an exact but constraining one.

Developmentally Related Responsibility

One overriding goal of schooling is to teach students how to be independent learners. To this end, schools assign to students an increasingly larger burden in the learning process as the students progress. Young students are carefully led through most of their work; older students are required to do much of their learning autonomously. The distinction between teaching and assigning usually carries the assumption that teaching is preferred to assigning. Assigning, however, may be as desirable as direct teaching at some age levels and with some subjects.

With limited resources, the school should be required to exert only the minimum effort necessary to ensure that learning occurs. If students can, with appropriate guidance, learn on their own, they should be required to do so. A curriculum that requires students to acquire certain objectives on their own could be a valid curriculum if similar students in similar settings have demonstrated an ability to learn in this manner.

Realistic Dependence on Extraschool Resources

Schools can attempt to teach, but they have not yet been held legally responsible for student outcomes (for example, *Doe* v. *School District,* cited as: Doe v. S.F. Unified School Dist., No. 653–312 (Cal Super. Cl., Sept. 6, 1974)). Part of the reason why schools have not been held responsible is that the relationship between most schooling procedures and student learning is not understood well enough to establish conditions for negligence. Another reason is that schools cannot compel students to do homework nor can they compel parents to participate in and facilitate their children's learning. Yet both homework and parental help and encouragement are important for most school learning.

Dependence upon homework and upon home assistance should not invalidate a curriculum so long as the degree of dependence upon these factors is reasonable in view of the specific students and homes involved. Should determination of reasonableness be based upon capability or upon past practice? If parents in a certain community are not accustomed to assisting their children with homework — even though they are capable of helping — should dependence on such help invalidate a curriculum? Although this issue requires further consideration, a possible starting point is that *capability of assistance* be given primary consideration.

Liability

So far this chapter has attempted to establish that curricular validity is not simply a function of in-class activities of teachers. A curriculum is a plan for action, involving goals, organization of personnel, communications, assessment, record keeping, and instruction. Decisions about the English curriculum in a city's high schools, for example, are generally made by the school district office, the principals, and the teachers. Parents, students, community representatives, and others may advise in these matters, but decision-making authority is usually reserved for the paid employees of the school system. When a school fails to demonstrate curricular validity, the source at fault may be at any level — from the district superintendent to the classroom teacher.

The district, for example, might order the use of an outdated standardized achievement test that compares unfavorably with the state's competency requirements. Teachers might be misled by high standardized test scores and may neglect to review or reteach certain competency skills that still have not been mastered. A principal might not require skill monitoring, might fail to provide year-to-year transfer of student records, or might not allocate resources for providing extra help to students who are weak in certain objectives. Teachers might fail to carry out the school or district assessment and monitoring system, or they might teach ineffectively. All of these acts of negligence could lead to students' failure on competency exams. Therefore, *all* parties to curricular decision-making should be held responsible.

District superintendents hire and fire principals. To retain a principal who does not provide curricular leadership within his or her school is an act of negligence by the district superintendent. Similarly, for a principal to allow an ineffective teacher to remain on the job constitutes negligence. If provision of a valid curriculum is a legal responsibility of the agency that orders competency testing, then that agency must ensure that those responsible for implementing the curriculum fulfill their responsibilities. Where a significant proportion of local school funding is obtained from the state, an obvious avenue of compliance exists. But for financially independent school districts — especially those with elected superintendents — the courts probably provide the only realistic approach to enforcement of validity procedures. A brief discussion of exactly what these procedures should be and how they can be implemented without a crippling bureaucracy follows.

Practical Evaluation

There is every reason to fear that attempts to assess curricular validity on a statewide basis will lead to debilitating bureaucracy, costly administration, and a stifling of education innovation. Previous experiences in educational administration — particularly in enforcement of statewide standards — do not encourage optimism here. Nevertheless, we cannot determine the practicability of assessing test-curriculum matches until we have attempted to find the best possible validation approach.

The suggestions made earlier for defining a valid curriculum require gathering of information on such matters as clarity of curricular goals, instructional opportunities, assessment and remediation procedures, student outcomes, and teacher evaluations. One approach to validation would require that teachers, principals, district superintendents, and state educational personnel accumulate such information on a daily basis, showing for each student the educational experiences encountered and their outcomes. This is an extreme of the validation continuum and one that should be avoided — both because of the cost and the impracticality of implementing it. The other extreme — that of only periodic validation — is considerably more practical and is more consistent with traditional school validation procedures such as those reflected in accreditation assessments.[6] Schools might be required to show evidence periodically (for example, every three to four years) of how they publicize, teach, assess, and remediate competency test skills, along with data on student outcomes. This material might be evaluated as part of the accreditation procedure, or it might be reviewed primarily by state departments of education. Schools should be required to keep records for individual students on their instruction and learning of minimum competency skills. Whether such records should be kept for all students or only for students who require extra help, however, needs further consideration. Keeping records only for students needing extra help is more desirable, but this option might not satisfy a court, particularly in a negligence suit. Evidence for teacher effectiveness would be provided only through the regular means for evaluating teachers — namely, by listing the certification procedures adopted and by showing the procedures followed within districts and schools for yearly teacher evaluations and for decisions based on such evaluations.

In summary, what is suggested is a limited data-collection scheme, whereby schools would document publicly their curriculum in minimum competency skills every three to four years on a schoolwide rather than on a student-by-student basis. Emphasis would be placed on documentation of procedures along with reporting of outcomes: numbers of students passing or failing minimum competency skill assessments and preassessments and the types and amounts of remediation provided. During nonreporting years, certain of these records would be collected and retained in the schools, especially for review by parents and for defense of the school in negligence suits.

The main challenge is to find procedures that strongly encourage a sensible and effective curriculum for minimum competency skills without exhausting the schools resources and personnel. If this balance cannot be found, the use of MCTs for denial of diplomas should be abandoned.

Notes

1.   474 F. Supp. 244 (M.D. Fla. 1979), *aff'd in part, reve'd in part,* 644 F.2d 397 (5th Cir. 1981).
2.   For a review of cases in which teacher or school incompetence is involved, see *Education*

Malpractice, 124 U. Pa. L. Rev. 755–805 (1976).

3. On one aspect of the relationship between educational research and curriculum practices, see Clifford (1973).

4. A theory of instruction, in this context, is a theory that attempts to define schooling practices that induce student learning. Theories of schooling, on the other hand, generally deal with the broader issue of the role of schools in society. For a cognitive definition of the former, see Jerome S. Bruner, *Toward a Theory of Instruction.* (Cambridge, Mass.: Harvard University Press, 1966).

5. An example of this trade-off is found in Bennett (1976), which is primarily a study of the relative effects of informal (that is, open) and formal (that is, structured) methods on student learning. Whereas the informal classrooms generally were less effective than the formal ones, a "high gain, informal classroom" was nevertheless found in which a variety of techniques were used to achieve a structured, cognitive focus in spite of the "natural" tendencies of informal classrooms. For a review and discussion of studies on open classrooms, see Hurn (1978, pp. 237–247).

6. I am indebted to my colleague, Daniel Neale, for this suggestion.

References

Adelson, J. "What Happened to the Schools?" *Commentary.* 71, No. 3, (1981), 36–41.

Bennett, N. *Teaching Styles and Student Progress.* London: Open Books Publishing, 1976.

Bruner, J.S. *Toward a Theory of Instruction.* Cambridge, Mass.: Harvard University Press, 1966.

Clifford, G.J. "A History of the Impact of Research on Teaching." In R.M.W. Travers ed., *Second Handbook of Research on Teaching.* Chicago, Ill.: Rand McNally College Publishing Company, 1973.

"Educational Malpractice." *University of Pennsylvania Law Review,* 124, (1976), 755–805.

Feitelson, D. "Relating Instructional Strategies to Language Idiosyncracies in Hebrew." In J. Kavanagh and R. Venezky eds., *Orthography, Reading, and Dyslexia.* Baltimore, Md.: University Park Press, 1980.

Hurn, C.J. *The Limits and Possibilities of Schooling.* Boston, Mass.: Allyn & Bacon, 1978.

[New York State] Bureau of School Programs Evaluation. *Three Strategies for Studying the Effects of School Processes.* Albany, N.Y.: State Education Department, 1976.

Stephens, J.M. *The Process of Schooling.* New York: Holt, Rinehart & Winston, 1967.

10 MINIMUM COMPETENCY TESTING OF READING:

An Analysis of Eight Tests Designed for Grade 11

Jeanne S. Chall, Ann Freeman, and Benjamin Levy

This chapter is concerned with minimum competency testing (MCT) for reading. The discussion will address the following three questions:

1. What is minimum competency of reading at high school completion?
2. How can minimum competency be assessed?
3. How can it be determined that schools have taught for such competency?

The data came from analyses of eight minimum competency reading tests designed for the eleventh-grade: four were developed by state departments of education, and four were done by commercial test publishers. Material from an earlier survey of chief state school officers during the spring of 1978 when there was a very high interest in minimum competency testing was also drawn on (Chall 1978). Personal experiences over the past ten years on national and state advisory committees on literacy and standards of MCT were an additional source of information.

Ann Freeman and Benjamin Levy analyzed the tests. Jeanne S. Chall is the chapter author and takes sole responsibility for the views and statements in it.

197

Although the analyses reported here are on reading tests, the procedures followed are relevant also for tests in the content areas that use language for their questions and responses. Level of linguistic complexity or readability is a factor in the success or failure on tests taken by most students in math, history, and science as well as in reading.

Minimum Competency in Reading Defined

In 1975, prior to the present minimum competency movement in the states, the Reading Committee of the National Academy of Education, appointed to look into ways of solving the national reading problem, defined competency as follows:

> We take the position that the "reading problem" in the United States should not be stated as one of teaching people to read at the level of minimal literacy, but rather as one of ensuring that every person arriving at adulthood will be able to read and understand the whole spectrum of printed materials that one is likely to encounter in daily life. In terms of grade levels of difficulty, a meaningful goal would be the attainment of twelfth-grade literacy by all adults — roughly, the ability to read with understanding nearly all the material printed in a magazine like *Newsweek* (Carroll and Chall 1975).

The 1978 survey of chief state school officers found none of the states defining competency in the manner described. Indeed, the greatest problems of most of the states was in defining competency, with only 23% responding that they were able to define and measure competency. An additional 30% reported that although they were able to define competency, they had not yet been able to establish a mode of assessment for their definition. Forty % had neither defined nor established competency standards but had started to classify the skills that would be used in their competency testing. Only two states of the forty-six respondents specified a particular reading level for minimum competency — ninth-grade level for students in the twelfth grade. One state specified further that a student must be reading at a sixth-grade level in order to be graduated from eighth grade.

Generally, our survey found two types of content preferred. The first can be classified as "real-life" or survival literacy. This included application forms, labels, signs, newspaper articles, and other work-related materials.

The second type of preference was for a variety of content that included both school-oriented and so-called real-life content, with an emphasis on the reading process. The main concern here was with measuring different kinds of comprehension — that is, the critical and inferential as well as the literal and factual.

It is of interest that neither of these preference types made a statement of level. The real-life emphasis appeared to be concerned mainly with form — for example, applications and labels versus short school-type selections. The "reading process'' emphasis was concerned mainly with the type of questions asked — that is, whether they were cognitively respectable. There was little concern about the level of complexity involved. The same is true for application forms, which also range in difficulty from simple forms to the at-times complex federal income tax forms as well as for newspapers, which range from short, personal articles to analyses of international situations.

Response complexity also has limited value — if viewed without a concern for level of difficulty — for it is possible to require a highly sophisticated and original response on material at any level, whether for *Little Red Riding Hood* or *War and Peace*. One wonders why most of the definitions of reading competency lacked reference to reading level, particularly because considerable evidence from research on readability, comprehension, and test validation suggests that level of difficulty is probably the most important factor in comprehension difficulty. Some hypotheses as to why level was not mentioned follow.

The first possible reason that level was omitted is related to the general negative attitudes toward norm-referenced tests when the competency tests were first undertaken in the 1970s. Among reading specialists there was also a growing concern about the use of grade equivalent scores from norm-referenced tests. Most of the thinking of minimum competency was in terms of criterion-referenced tests and the search for those reading tasks that would define students who were or were not at a point of minimal reading competency. There seemed to be an assumption that the tests in use were partly responsible for so many reading problems. How, then, could they be effective in solving the problem?

The designation of a level may also have been viewed as politically risky because it might reveal how low the defined minimal reading competency was. Indeed, level designation might constitute an admission that a state department of education thought an elementary reading level was sufficient as a high-school-graduation standard.

Thus for many reasons it seemed easier to define literacy as form and as response — omitting the question of level of difficulty. As we shall see from the findings of the test analyses, level was a definite part of the tests.

How Can Competency Be Assessed?

To answer this question, eight MCTs for grade 11 were analyzed. The analyses covered content, response type, difficulty level, and maturity level.

The purpose of the tests as stated in their explanatory materials was to assess reading competencies, or basic skills in reading, which students will be called upon to use following high school graduation. The publication dates ranged from 1976 to 1979, with most material published in 1978 and 1979.

Aspects of Tests Analyzed

Level of Difficulty

The instrument used was the Dale-Chall readability formula, applied to each of the reading selections in the test. The formula is based on two factors — vocabulary difficulty and sentence complexity. Only the passages of connected text were analyzed for readability.

Reading Maturity

For this purpose, we analyzed each reading passage by stage level from Chall's *Reading Stages* (1979 and 1982)[1] which characterizes reading development in terms of six stages — from Stage 0 to Stage 5 — a progression based on reader characteristics as well as on those of the text and responses required.

Response or Question Complexity

For this, we used a rating scale devised for Chall, Conard, and Harris, *An Analysis of Textbooks in Relation to Declining S.A.T. Scores* (1977)[2] to judge the degree of difficulty of the questions. It is based on the *Bloom Taxonomy* (1956) and includes ideas on reading comprehension levels as defined by Ruddell (1974) and Davis (1968).

Content of Reading Selections

The content was organized on the basis of three broad classifications used by Auerback (1971) for an analysis of standardized reading tests. The first category comprised familiar experiences common in standardized tests for the primary grades; the second, expository selections on school subjects such as science, social studies, literature, music, and the like found in test selections in standardized test for grades 4 and above; the third, expository selections of everyday life and life outside of school — for example, newspaper articles, advertisements, job applications, tax forms, instructions for using appliances or tools, directions for cooking and baking, and the like.

Table 10–1 presents the findings from the analyses of the four state tests. From it we note that the average readability level of the passages of two of the tests was about seventh- to eighth-grade level and for the other two, the level was ninth to tenth grade.

Table 10-1. State High School Level Reading Minimum Competency Tests

Tests	A-1978	B-1979	C-1978/1979	D-1979
Average difficulty level (Dale-Chall Readability) of the reading passage	7–8	7–8	9–10	9–10
Reading stage level	Stage 3 — 49% Stage 2 — 51%	Stage 3 — 85% Stage 2 — 17%	Stage 3 — 83% Stage 2 — 17%	Stage 3 — 100% Stage 2 — 0%
Question complexity	Level 3 — 5% Level 2 — 33% Level 1 — 62%	Level 3 — 0% Level 2 — 37% Level 1 — 63%	Level 3 — 16% Level 2 — 46% Level 1 — 38%	Level 3 — 14% Level 2 — 38% Level 1 — 48%
Content emphasis	Academic — 45% Outside school — 55%	Academic — 100% Outside school — 0%	Academic — 39% Outside school — 61%	Academic — 100% Outside school — 0%

Table 10–2 presents a further breakdown of the reading passages for the four state tests. The table presents data on the number of passages, their length in words, the average number of questions asked, and the like. In addition, it presents the number of passages on each of the various readability levels from grades 4 through 13 and beyond.

From table 10–2, some variations emerge: two tests had passages averaging three hundred or more words and two passages averaging about one hundred words. The number of questions on each passage also varied — from two to

Table 10–2.   Characteristics of State Test Passages

	A-1978	B-1979	C-1978/1979	D-1979
Number of passages containing connected text	15	3	13	15
Average number of questions per passage	2	22	3	7
Average number of words per passage	125	329	137	323
Number of passages at each readability level:				
Grade-4 Level	2	0	0	1
Grade-5 to -6 Level	2	0	2	3
Grade-7 to -8 Level	5	2	5	2
Grade-9 to -10 Level	3	1	2	3
Grade-11 to -12 Level	3	0	3	2
Grade-13 Level and above	0	0	1	4
Average Level	7–8	7–8	9–10	9–10
Level for 75% read	9–10	7–8	9–10	11–12
Percent of questions *not* based on reading passages	43	0	29	0

twenty-two — and the percentage of questions not based on passages varied from 0 to 43%. The breakdown by readability in table 10–2 presents additional data on passage difficulty. Most of the tests contain passages of a wide range of difficulty, from about a fifth- to sixth-grade level to an eleventh- to twelfth-grade level. Only two — the ones that average a grade 9 to 10 level — contain passages at a grade-13 level or above. The readability levels of the passages at three-fourths difficulty are also presented.

Table 10–3 presents the data on the four commercially published tests. The readability levels have a broader range than the state tests — from a grade 5 to 6 to a grade 11 to 12 level. The reading maturity, like that of the state tests, tends to be low on Stage 2 — familar ideas — and Stage 3 — introductory information on a single view. Only one test had passages on a Stage-4 level (7%); this test also was on the highest readability level, grade 11 to 12.

Question complexity was also low, concentrating on a level of facts (Level 1). A minority of the questions required contrast and comparisons (Level 3). The content of the commercially produced tests presents the greatest contrast with the state tests: all four of the puslishers' tests focus on outside school content, whereas half of the state tests were mainly concerned with these topics.

Table 10–4 presents breakdowns by passage characteristics. The passages are generally shorter than for the state tests; they contain fewer questions per passage, and more questions are not based on passages. Table 10–4 includes a breakdown by readability levels of the separate passages and an estimate of the level of the passage at three-fourths difficulty.

The reading-stage levels were also low, reflecting the generally low level of literacy required. The highest stage level of the four tests is 3, characteristic of factual material presented within a single point of view and typical of reading at grades 4 to 8. One of the tests was on a Stage-2 level, characteristic of materials "already known." None of the passages was on Stage 4, which is typical of high school reading and characterized by multiple views.

The question-complexity index found most of the passages to be on levels 1 and 2, calling for recall of facts and use of facts. Three of the tests had some level-3 questions, with the largest percentages (16% and 14%) on the two tests at readability levels of grade 9 to 10. The seventh- to eighth-grade level tests had 0% and 5% level-3 questions.

The emphasis was about equally divided, with two of these state tests predominently "academic" (100% each) and two predominently concerned with "outside school" content (61% and 55%). Thus although the academic tests contained no outside school content, the outside school tests contained appreciable amounts of academic content.

Table 10–3.   Publishers' High School Level Reading Minimum Competency Tests

Tests	I-1976	II-1977	III-1978	IV-1978
Level of Difficulty (Dale-Chall Readability)	5–6	11–12	7–8	7–8
Reading Stages	Not Analyzed	Stage 4 — 7% Stage 3 — 86% Stage 2 — 7%	Stage 4 — 0% Stage 3 — 100% Stage 2 — 0%	Stage 4 — 0% Stage 3 — 60% Stage 2 — 40%
Question Complexity	Level 3 — 0% Level 2 — 55% Level 1 — 45%	Level 3 — 10% Level 2 — 46% Level 1 — 44%	Level 3 — 5% Level 2 — 43% Level 1 — 52%	Level 3 — 6% Level 2 — 34% Level 1 — 60%
Content emphasis	Academic — 0% Outside school — 100%	Academic — 10% Outside school — 90%	Academic — 0% Outside school — 100%	Academic — 10% Outside school — 90%

Table 10–4. Characteristics of Passages on Publishers' Tests

	I-1976	II-1977	III-1978	IV-1978
Number of passages containing connected text	3	16	12	10
Average number of questions per passage	1	2	6	4
Average number of words per passage	72	121	107	130
Number of passages at each readability level:				
Grade-4 Level and below	1	1	0	2
Grade-5 to -6 Level	1	0	3	1
Grade-7 to -8 Level	1	1	3	4
Grade-9 to -10 Level	0	5	6	1
Grade-11 to -12 Level	0	5	0	0
Grade-13 Level and above	0	4	0	2
Average Level	5–6	11–12	7–8	7–8
Level for 75% read	5–6	11–12	9–10	9–10
Percent of questions not based on reading passages	92	42	0	67

Summary of Findings

Our analyses of eight MCTs reveal considerable differences in how minimum competency is defined for eleventh-grade high school students. If we take these eight tests as representative of such tests, and if we used the mean passage difficulty as an index of competency, it would seem that a student would be considered competent if he or she could read on a fifth- to sixth-grade level on one of these tests; on a seventh- to eighth-grade level on four of the tests; on a ninth- to tenth-grade level on two; and on an eleventh- to twelfth-grade level on one. If we use the 75% cutoff instead of the 50%, then most of the tests would be judged more difficult, averaging grade 9 to 10 readability level. Which estimate is the true or better one is difficult to determine, for the passing level is usually determined by the student results. Because we do not know which is the more realistic estimate of readability, we present both.

The content of the tests — whether real life or academic — varies by developer. The commercial publishers prefer real life content, whereas the states are divided, half preferring academic content and half real life.

The indexes of reading maturity (reading-stage level) and question complexity indicated that generally a low level of cognitive complexity is required on these tests. Most passages and questions were classified as being on a factual, single viewpoint level that is more characteristic of the upper elementary grades than of high school reading.

How Can It Be Determined that Schools Have Taught for Minimum Competency?

It would seem that evidence of a match between the tests and the instruction over an eleven-year period would be one way of approaching this question. Comparisons of readability, reading maturity, question complexity, and content emphasis can be obtained for samples of the curriculum and particularly for the required textbooks.

Something to this effect was done in our study on the relation of textbooks to declining SAT scores (Chall et al. 1977) for the Advisory Panel on the Scholastic Aptitude Test Score Decline (1977). We compared various estimates of difficulty of the most widely used textbooks used in grades 1, 6, and 11 by various cohorts for reading, literature, grammar and composition, and social studies with the reading passages on the SAT taken by each of several cohorts. Among our findings was the seeming mismatch between the textbooks and the SAT. The SAT passages proved to be more difficult than any of the materials analyzed, including the textbooks for the 11th grade. Two of the SAT verbal tests were on the level of grades 13 to 15 and four were on the level of grades 11 to 12. The history, literature, and grammar and composition textbooks for the eleventh grade had an average readability level of grades 9 to 10.

One can question, then, whether the students were being adequately prepared by the curriculum for the SAT in that it required reading on a level higher than that they were exposed to. A further finding — that the cohorts exposed to the more difficult textbooks made the higher SAT scores — suggests also that the factor of optimum difficulty may be a central one in reading development.

The optimal matching of difficulty of textbooks to competency tests as well as to students' ability seems to be a significant factor in teaching and in testing. During the past thirty to fifty years, there has been a trend among publishers and schools toward the lowering of the levels of readability at the elementary, high school, and college levels. For students who have lagged behind in reading over many years, additional questions must be raised to determine whether the school has taught what is required for minimum competency. The main concern here is not with those students officially classified as having a learning disability (LD). Many states excuse such students from taking the reading competency tests as well as from receiving a regular diploma. At issue here are larger numbers of students who are not LD, but who are many years behind in reading, even though most have average or higher mental ability. These students usually start off at a low level of performance and are promoted from year to year, receiving instruction at their so-called appropriate level, which is at an ever-growing gap with national norms for their grade level. Many of these students test as low as fourth to fifth grade, equivalent on standardized norm-referenced tests when they are in the twelfth grade. Would the school be justified in saying that proper instruction was given to fulfill competency requirements? Can the student claim at eleventh grade that the school did not fulfill its obligations to instruct for competency because instruction never reached the average level of the MCT? Can the school then claim that the student was instructed on the level matching his or her ability?

Conclusion

The reading difficulty of these eight minimum competency reading tests — if we use the mean passage difficulty as a criterion — ranged from a fifth- to sixth-grade readability level to an eleventh- to twelfth-grade level; the mean was a seventh- to eighth-grade level. The reading passages were further characterized by factual material presented within a single viewpoint. The questions asked also required factual recall responses. Six of the tests contained real life content; only two were predominently academic. The content emphasis did not seem to be related to difficulty, reading maturity, or response types.

The purpose in presenting these analyses was to suggest ways of defining and assessing minimum competency for reading. These same analyses might be used for analyzing textbooks and other instructional materials in specific content areas, thus affording a way to compare the tests to the curriculum materials.

What should minimum competency in reading be for eleventh to twelfth graders of normal cognitive abilities? Although we should guard against denying a competency classification and a diploma because of past negligences and biases of schools and society — or even as a result of ignorance — of what ultimate good is it for the student to be awarded a high school diploma when he or she has elementary school reading ability? Would it not make more sense to make up the deficiencies by providing the student with the proper diagnostic and remedial service — as is now done in community colleges — in order to reach the proficiency he or she is capable of? This level of literacy — a high school reading level — would then enable the student to compete for jobs in industries that offer a future rather than for those lower-level jobs. Matching competency tests to the school curriculum can be risky. The process may become circular, and it is possible that both standards may be wrong. Yet it seems worthwhile to try to effect more workable guidelines for matching texts and other curriculum materials with realistic competency standards (Chall 1979).

Notes

1. Chall, Jeanne S., *Reading Stages* 1977, 1979, 1982, forthcoming. Each reading passage was read in its entirety and the Reading Stage Level assigned was the highest level of processing required for understanding what was read.

Stage 0 — Prereading, "pseudo reading."

Stage 1 — Reading that is still mainly associating written-to-spoken words (decoding).

Stage 2 — Reading that confirms what is already known. Reading "the familiar" for practice in developing fluency. Energy is still concentrated on words; therefore vocabulary is within meaning vocabulary, although this is not always recognition vocabulary.

Stage 3 — Reading for new knowledge from one viewpoint: facts, concepts, and how to do things. The vocabulary goes beyond the elemental, common experiences, including words that are unfamiliar and those that are learned from books and school.

Stage 4 — Reading from multiple viewpoints; involving greater depth of treatment, dealing with more than one set of facts, theories, or viewpoints.

Stage 5 — Reading from a qualitative, relativistic point of view to construct and reconstruct new knowledge.

2. Response on Question Complexity Levels, from Chall, J.S., Conard, S., and Harris, S. (1977).

Level 1 — Questions requiring recall and reiteration of facts, asking what, where, who, when, and requiring listing and defining.

Level 2 — Questions requiring recall and use of facts, asking how, why, and requiring description.

Level 3 — Questions requiring the acknowledgment of more than one point of view and requiring asking, comparing, and contrasting.

Level 4 — Questions incorporating the first three levels, requiring the reader to justify and support.

References

Bloom, B.S. Editor (and others) *Taxonomy of Educational Objectives Handbook I: Cognitive Domain*. New York: David McKay Co., Inc. 1956, pp. 201–204.

Carroll, J.B., and Chall, J.S., eds., *Toward A Literate Society*. New York: McGraw-Hill, 1975.

Chall, J.S., Conard, S., and Harris, S. *An Analysis of Textbooks in Relation to Declining S.A.T. Scores*. Prepared for the Advisory Panel on the Scholastic Aptitude Test Score Decline, jointly sponsored by the College Board and Educational Testing Service, June, 1977. Princeton, N.J.: College Entrance Examination Board, 1977.

Chall, J.S. "Minimum Competency in Reading: An Informal Survey of the States." *Phi Delta Kappa* 60, No. 5, (January 1979).

Chall, J.S. "The Great Debate: Ten Years Later, with a Modest Proposal for Reading Stages," in *Theory and Practice of Early Reading*. Lauren B. Resnick and Phyllis A. Weaver eds., Hillsdale, New Jersey: Lawrence Erlbaum, 1979.

Chall, J.S. "Textbook Difficulty, Reading Achievement, and Knowledge Acquisition." A Proposal Submitted to the Spencer Foundation, May 1979.

Chall, J.S. *Stages of Reading Development*. New York: McGraw-Hill, forthcoming.

Davis, F.B. "Research in Comprehension in Reading." *Reading Research Quarterly,* 1968, 4, pp. 499–545.

Ruddell, R.B. *Reading-Language Instruction: Innovative Practices*. Englewood Cliffs, New Jersey: Prentice-Hall, Inc., 1974.

Wirtz, W., Chairman. *On Further Examination. Report of the Advisory Panel on the Scholastic Aptitude Test Score Decline*. New York: College Board, 1977.

11 THE SEARCH FOR CONTENT VALIDITY THROUGH WORLD KNOWLEDGE

Roger W. Shuy

The basic questions to be asked of any test are quite simple. Does the test question measure what it intends to measure? Does if confuse one kind of skill or knowledge with another? Does the test question require the test taker to violate conventions of ordinary behavior, knowledge, or language use in order to answer correctly? Does the test question assess that which is most important to measure or what is really needed? What knowledge or abilities do students who do poorly have that are not measured? Does the test question embody a standard that is fair to all test takers? Are the knowledge and skills tested the right ones by which to judge the thing assumed to be judged by the test questions?

Testing is conventionally viewed as the relationship of the information about what could be tested to what is actually tested. This chapter argues that such a relationship is myopic and that it does not take into consideration the crucial contexts of available real knowledge — the knowledge of the test constructor and the knowledge of the test taker. A test must be seen as not just a piece of paper but, rather, as a social event in which communicative competence plays an extremely important role. This chapter will address both the issues of context and information being tested, particularly in the setting of minimal competency testing (MCT).

Some Dimensions of Validity

In order to get at the meaning of terms or constructs such as *content validity, instructional validity,* and/or *curricular validity,* we first need to consider the larger concept of validity, especially as it is examined in the education of children. A model from communication theory can be instructive in this regard. One of the simplest models of communication specifies that a communication event is made up of a Sender of a Message, a Message, and the Receiver of the message. The event itself occurs in a cultural or social context but either the sender or the receiver of the message may also operate in different cultures, subcultures, or social environments that cause them to color their sending or receiving in terms of that culture, subculture, or social environment. Validity, then, must be examined in relationship to all three components: Sender, Message, and Receiver, as well as in relationship to the cultures, subcultures, or social contexts (hereafter, referred to only as social context) in which the communication takes place.

As obvious as this simple model may seem, it has significance at all levels of education, including testing, and it is frequently overlooked at all levels. Validity can be considered a global issue, but by examining its component parts we can find areas of potential or real breakdown of validity that are masked in the overall perspective. Taking the model given, for example, we find the following three areas of validity assessment of any communication:

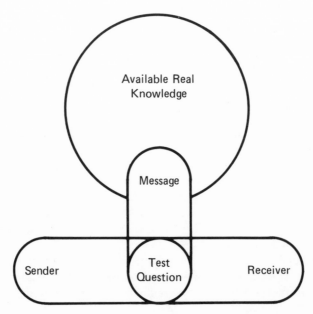

Figure 11-1. Intersection of Sender, Message and Receiver to Available Real Knowledge to the Test Question

1.   Sender to Message.
2.   Message to Receiver.
3.   Message to available world knowledge.

These three areas of validity assessment can be diagrammed as shown in figure 11–1. That is, validity can be assessed along the dimension of the sender and the message, the receiver and the message, and the stock of available real knowledge and the message. Translated into the context of testing, this means that validity can be assessed on the dimension of test writer to test question (Sender to Message), test taker to test question (Receiver to Message), and test question to available knowledge from which the test question was drawn (Knowledge to Message). To assume that validity can be defined by any part of this matrix without the others is to be, by definition, incomplete and potentially erroneous.

The reasons why validity might be challenged in any of these dimensions are many. The following are only suggestive:

1.   The Sender may *distort* the message in his or her sending of it by inaccuracy, unclarity, or incompleteness.
2.   The Receiver may *distort* the message in his or her receiving of it by inaccuracy, unclarity, or incompleteness.
3.   The Message itself may be distorted in its attempted representation of what is known and available by inaccuracy, unclarity, or incompleteness.
4.   The social contexts of the Sender or Receiver may *distort* the intention of the other.

To be valid, then, all dimensions of validity must be accounted for. Next, the term *distortion* must be explained. The exact language of any text works systematically to present the communicative intent of the writer. As Freeman et al. point out (1981), ''the language forms and organization of a written passage can be viewed as a system of 'clues' which a reader must use (consciously or not) to reconstruct meaning.'' The evaluation of any test must include an evaluation of the language content, structure, and organization in the test questions and the instructions to discover what help they give the test taker and to determine what the test taker needs to know and do to answer the test questions adequately.

World Knowledge

One recently recognized area of potential difficulty in test questions concerns the knowledge that readers need to know about the things referred to in test questions. That is, in addition to the vocabulary used to represent things, the reader needs to know related information about these things and their organization or role in the real world. Spiro (1980) and others have noted that reading is an active process by which the reader reconstructs the writer's intended meaning and integrates this with what he or she already knows about the world. Thus the meaning does not exist solely in the words of the text but includes many kinds of contexts, prior knowledge, attitudes, task context, and other things. Many reading researchers demonstrate that good readers predict meaning through such world knowledge (Goodman and Goodman 1977; Griffin 1977; Morgan 1978; Larkin et al. 1979). This work is supported by psychologists who claim that readers integrate prior knowledge with new data (Kintch and Van Dijk 1978; Freedle and Hale 1979; Rummelhart 1980). Figure 11–2 amends the figure 11–1 representation of the Intersection of Sender, Message, and Receiver with Available Real Knowledge by adding the Receiver's World Knowledge to the equation.

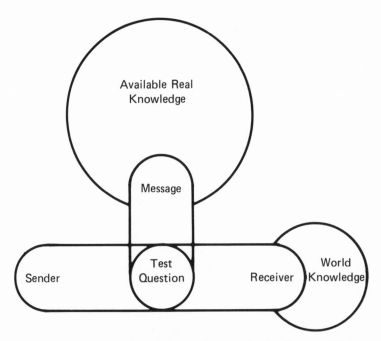

Figure 11–2. Intersection of Test Question Communication Context with Receiver's World Knowledge

The claim of most tests used in MCT is that such prior knowledge is not necessary and that the test taker is assessed only on the basis of what was learned in the curriculum. If this actually happens, the test can achieve instructional validity. (Note that instructional validity is not to be confused with curricular validity, which will be addressed later.) Freeman (1981) notes, for example, that in the New

York State "Degrees of Reading Power Test," in five of the twelve passages released to her for analysis, ". . . the factual background information needed for overall passage comprehension is markedly more abstract and more removed from everyday life than that required for the first half of the test (p. 31)."

World knowledge (or background knowledge) can bias test scores by promoting a good score because one has that knowledge irrespective of the ability to answer the question at hand or, lacking world knowledge, by impeding comprehension of the intention of the test question irrespective of one's ability to answer it. To be fair, world knowledge must be shared by all members of the test-taking community and not be required in order to answer the question appropriately.

The role that world knowledge plays in MCT, as in all other testing, is related to two of the dimensions of figure 11–2: the dimension of Sender to Message and the dimension of Message to Receiver. These two dimensions, if the communication is successful, must be undistorted and lead to the effective communication of Sender–Message–Receiver in which the world knowledge is equal and clear and in which prior knowledge is, indeed, not crucial to the correct answer. That is, the question is dependent only on the student's ability to answer on the basis of the

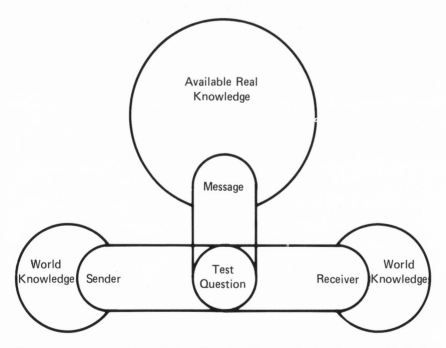

Figure 11–3. Intersection of Test Question Communicative Context with Both Sender and Receiver's World Knowledge

question alone which has been learned through effective instruction. World knowledge is also part of the repertoire of test makers and the same possibilities exist for the test senders as for the test receivers. Figure 11–3 amends the earlier diagrams of this intersection of the communicative context of a test situation. Thus the mismatch of the world knowledge and world knowledge assumptions of the test maker (Sender) with those of the test taker (Receiver) can create problems of validity.

Content Validity

Two kinds of test validity are at stake here: content validity and instructional validity. Content validity has many levels of understanding. Is the content *accurate*? Is the question *representative* of what could have been asked to assess the content completely and accurately? Does the question ask the most *important* aspects of the content being assessed? Does the question ask for the *developmentally relevant* or appropriate aspects of the content? Does the question ask for the information within the *context* appropriate to ascertain it? Content validity, then, rests on these five important characteristics: accuracy, representativeness, importance, developmental relevance, and contextualization.

Accuracy

Problems of accuracy are the easiest to find and are the least likely to be encountered. Occasionally it is determined that an SAT question has been scored inaccurately because the key is in error or because a logical approach to a question could be taken that is quite different from the one expected by the scorer. A much more common problem with accuracy, however, grows out of a contrast in world-knowledge assumptions between the test maker (Sender) and the test taker (Receiver). For example, students who have learned, with some justification, not to believe everything they read, especially in the self-touting style of advertisements, bring to their reading of an advertisement a skepticism that can enable them to discount the claim of the Florida Statewide Assessment grade 11, book 2 question that appears as an advertisement for a restaurant. The claim is made in this question (number 18) that the bread is homemade. Irrespective of the laws on false representation, the public tends to take a cynical view of claims about what is homemade and what is not. The question about this advertisement asks the student to determine which statement is fact as opposed to opinion. What is *really* asked for is which of the following is *claimed* by the advertisement — quite a different matter from what is *fact*. World knowledge about advertisements can, in this case, work against the correct answer. In fact, the question also works against what may well have been the teacher's effort to help students learn to read critically, a skill far more important than the simple matching task required of this question.

A similar situation was pointed out by Asa Hilliard in his testimony in *Debra P.* v. *Turlington*. The world knowledge of inner-city children, Hilliard observed, would cause them to answer incorrectly question number 48 in the same test. Question 48 read: Charlene is looking for a job as a sales clerk; where is she likely to get the least help? Hilliard points out that newspaper ads are, for most black people, the least likely place to get help, even though this answer is the one considered correct by the test.

Accuracy, then, is a critical issue in determining content validity. If the world knowledge of the test maker does not match that of the test taker, the question may not accurately measure what is sought. The two examples just given illustrate different polarities of test takers. Those who have learned to read critically and, therefore, view advertisements with a certain cynicism, may well be judged inaccurately because of their superior ability and sensitivity with the uses of language. Those who have learned from their cultural background the world knowledge that newspaper employment advertisements do not work for the good of the black community may well be judged inaccurately because of this very knowledge, which is apparently unavailable to the test maker. In both cases, a mismatch exists; in both cases, inaccuracy is the issue.

Representativeness

The problem of discrete-point testing is probably the most insolvable issue of all of testing. How can we ever know that the questions we select to represent the totality of knowledge studied are the best ones to represent that knowledge? This question plagues every teacher each time a test is prepared and it is (or should be) central to the concerns of all makers of standardized tests. The crucial question is often addressed in the same way that makers of the Federal Licensing Examination for physicians address it — by having a board of medical authorities select the questions to represent the desired and required knowledge necessary in various areas such as orthopedics, obstetrics, anatomy, pharmacology, et cetera.

In the area of communication skills, one might well want to know how effectively a student can speak, listen, read, or write. Because speaking, writing, and listening are very difficult to test, however, we seldom see much effort at measuring them. Instead, we see tests of reading ability — which we think we know how to measure — used as the entire examination representing in some mysterious way the student's ability to talk, listen, and write. It should be noted here that writing assessment has been making considerable strides forward in recent years, as evidenced by the most recent National Assessment of Writing and by the work of the Southwest Regional Educational Laboratory in their assessment of the writing ability of California schoolchildren.

At issue with the Florida State Assessment Test is this matter of representativeness. All questions that purport to represent "communication skills" are paper-pencil reading questions. In the form of that test cited by Asa Hilliard in his direct testimony, fifty-nine reading questions represent communication skills ability. Those of us who define communication in far broader terms than just reading are aghast at such practice. But there is more.

Even if reading ability *were* the best representation of communicative ability, all aspects of reading must be represented if the test is to be valid. To be sure, the entire reading-testing industry suffers from the same problems that faced the Florida Statewide Assessment people, but this does not diminish the problem. If one defines reading ability as the capability of finding the intended meaning of the printed page and integrating it with one's own knowledge to find meaning in the world, one might take a different approach to assessment than to present over 50% of the questions on finding the details in a reading passage. In the form cited by Hilliard, thirty-two of the fifty-nine questions were instructions to the reader to find a detail or fact in the reading passage given. Only eight questions asked for the main idea or holistic sense of the passage. Eight other questions asked the reader only to match the question with the label of a section of a printed form, and seven questions asked the student to distinguish between fact and opinion in the selected passages. Although it is becoming more and more recognized that the ability to inference from the clues of the printed page is a higher-order ability than mere detail searching or short-term memory ability, only four questions asked for this ability on this particular test.

One wonders how this ratio of questions for the measurement of reading ability was derived. Does short-term memory or the ability to find the details of a passage represent 54% of what a reader needs to know? Does finding the main idea represent 14% of that ability? Or is it only that we do not really know how to ask good questions to get at comprehension? Is it so much easier to test for short-term memory that we ask this kind of question simply because we know how to?

A basic question of content validity concerns whether or not the test samples the domain of knowledge. Discrete-point testing assumes that it does, but along with such an assumption comes the question of construct validity. A normal process of construct validity is to discriminate good from bad test performers in real-life situations. But common practice is to use a test of some sort (or some other measure) to determine whether or not students who had the treatment do better on that test than those who did not have the program. For example, a few years ago, Southwest Regional Research Laboratory writing researchers attempted to measure the writing ability of Los Angeles sixth graders by having them write an essay comparing reading with mathematics. Most children did such a poor job with this assigned topic that the SWRL researchers decided that the task was not a natural event for sixth graders. The next year, the students were asked to write a letter to a friend, persuading him or her to watch a favorite television program. This task proved to be a more natural event for sixth graders to accomplish, and a range of good to poor performance was established. In the earlier comparison test, the writing assignment did not sample the domain of knowledge; in the persuasion assignment, it did. However much reliability the first test could be shown to have, it failed in construct validity because of a content validity failure to sample the domain of knowledge appropriate for the test takers.

The issue of representativeness is a gravely important one in matters such as MCT. The major content of reading is comprehension and inferencing. The minor content is the ability to remember or find the details or match the words of the question with those on the printed forms. Even more significant is the representativeness of reading ability, even if well measured, to be the sole representative of communication skills which include speaking, listening, and writing as well.

Importance

The effort of MCT to find potential or real-life settings in which to assess ability may well be applauded. Despite the criticisms that filling out job and credit card application forms or reading tour guide indexes and restaurant reviews may not be the most relevant focuses of learning, these tasks *do* move testing away from abstract questions about the rules of grammar or decontextualized problems of multiplication or division. To the layperson or businessperson who complains about students not being able to function adequately, these tasks seem sensible and concrete.

I would like to assert, however, that they do not represent what is normally taught and only if one's view of education is entirely vocational should they be taught at all. One great danger of this movement toward the presumably practical is that the test, as is usually the case, will become the tail that wags the dog and will quickly change the curriculum to match the test.

The major difficulty with teaching to the test, however, is far deeper. One can teach children to do almost any task, and most of them have been tried. What learning should be about, however, is generalization. What we need to teach are the *generalizable functions* that can lead a student to *be able* to read a fire manual, a telephone book, or a rental advertisement or to write a request letter, a job application, or a hurricane-warning announcement. These generalizable functions are both linguistic and cognitive. If we teach students to write one kind of business letter by model alone — without a grasp of the language and cognitive underpinnings of that task — we may well produce students who can write that kind of letter, should the occasion ever arise to do so, but they will not be able to compose variations or modifications of that kind of letter. At the heart of this problem is a view of language and cognition that is somewhat as shown in figure 11–4. In contrast with this model of straight task accomplishment from idea to specific writing behavior is one that is mediated by generalizable language strategies that are gradually becoming known as language functions. Language functions are simply the ways people use language to get things done. As obvious as it may seem to teach such functions, they are not often taught. We tend to teach the *forms* of language, not the functions. We teach grammar, spelling, punctuation, and vocabulary. We do *not* teach how to request, deny, clarify, report opinions, evaluate, complain, seek clarification, predict, apologize, offer, et cetera. This is a level of language analysis referred to by a number of names, including speech acts (from philosophy), pragmatics (from linguistics), and communicative competence (from anthropology). The term *language functions* seems less intimidating and more self-explanatory; in this discussion, it is used in contexts outside the academic fields that spawned it. Language-function use is an intermediary and generalizable step between the idea and behavior shown in figure 11–4, as shown in figure 11–5. Functional learning differs from straight task learning in that the focus of teaching is on generalizable skills in using language functions and the various strategies used to reveal these functions, depending on context, participants, topic, et cetera. The teaching should be on how to write, speak, read, and hear these functions that are used in language to get things done. The ultimate test of the learning of these functions — the testing of them — is questionable. What we are testing, until such time as language functions are taught and learned, is merely staight task learning — if the task is taught at all — or guesswork — if the task is not taught directly. If we believe that education is the learning of competence that is generalizable for new contexts, the ability to request information, for example, should be learned and practiced in the schools in a number of contexts. Testers will not learn whether or not the student has learned the *principle* from straight task teaching and testing. We only learn this from the application of general knowledge and competence to new problems, tasks, and settings.

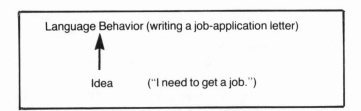

Figure 11–4. Representation of Straight Task Learning

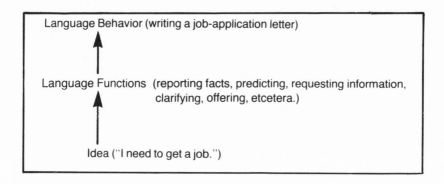

Figure 11–5. Representation of Functional Learning

Generalizability as the major focus of learning — and, consequently, as the major focus of testing — is also easily illustrated in mathematics. By far, the heaviest concentration of mathematics instruction is on computational skills. Most of the first six to eight years of mathematics instruction is on drills related to the four basic mathematics operations. Schools report, however, that children do much more poorly on story-problem versions of computation. The 1980 National Assessment of Educational Progress reports, in fact, that of the seventeen-year-olds in their sample, 90% performed adequately in straight computation whereas only 45% performed adequately on problems that were couched in words and sentences. A study by Firsching (1981) of a Pennsylvania school system's mathematics program supports this report of the story-problem issue. In the schools he studied, computation was taught as a single-step operation and was measured well when the operations were kept separate. Story problems, however, required multiple-step operations (that is, addition plus multiplication plus division plus subtraction) which empirical evidence demonstrates were not taught in the classroom. Not only were the combination of operations not taught, but the sequencing of multiple operations was also omitted.

The generalizability issue thus is not only an *important* aspect of validity; it is also a *context* aspect. Figure 11–6 sets the communicative skills and computational skills components of testing in the framework of generalization.

This leads us back to the information represented in Figure 11–3. Just as the presuppositions about world knowledge may differ between test maker (Sender) and test taker (Receiver) leading to content invalidity, so may content invalidity be found in minimal competency tests between Available Real Knowledge and the Message (in this case, the test). The question now becomes, ''Is the competence in

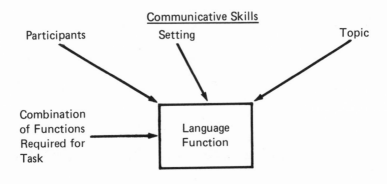

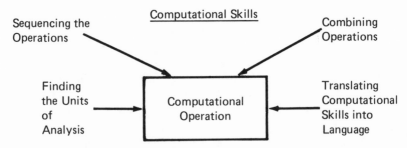

Figure 11–6. Communicative Skills and Computational Skills Set in a Framework of
Generalization

communication discoverable through questions which *may* reflect the curriculum
(if the students are taught how to fill out job applications or analyze fire manuals)
when the curriculum does not teach generalizable principles upon which this
ability rests?'' This issue becomes one of instructional validity. If the curriculum
does not provide the necessary principles and generalizability for effective application of learning, what right do we have to test that learning? This argument is not
necessarily an attack on the minimal competency test which attempts to assess
communicative ability; it is more an attack on the curriculum which does not teach
that which is thought to be necessary to measure. In this case, content validity is
affected by curriculum invalidity. That is, the content of language functions is
available to the schools to be taught but they choose not to do so, for whatever
reasons, yielding, therefore, curriculum invalidity. This is not a matter of the lack
of available content. It is an issue of curricular choice.

Developmental Relevance

Issues related to the development of learning have been obscured by a number of factors, including the inadequacies of our knowledge base about developmental norms in areas such as reading, writing, and speaking as well as by the national mania for basics that, though ill-defined, usually seems to refer to the later competence in the subject. For example, it has become recognized that decoding skills in reading instruction are useful to learn — primarily as a starting strategy in literacy but certainly not as an end in themselves nor as a skill of any interest to teachers once the child has learned the essential comprehension skills. In other words, the assessment of decoding skills in mature readers would be a waste of time and energy, however useful such measurement might be as an indication of very early decoding-skills ability.

In the same way, the measurement of writing ability suffers an even greater handicap. There is no known, acceptable theory of writing development, making it extremely difficult to know how to measure it — to say nothing of how to teach it (Shuy 1978, 1981). One of the major problems of assessing either written or spoken language production is that meaningful language production occurs in *natural* contexts and not in decontextualized settings such as those required by standardized tests. To measure anything other than these natural contexts, such as actual, meaningful written or spoken language use, is to measure something other than writing or speaking. To attempt to do so is to admit that the assessment is not getting at writing or speaking but, rather, is measuring something else and pretending that it is the same thing.

What one might examine — if one were to assess the spoken or written production of students, which is probably by far the most important aspect of communication skills — is what sociolinguists refer to as communicative competence (Hymes 1964, 1972). The forms of language use, the pronunciation, vocabulary, and grammar of oral language and the spelling, punctuation, grammar, and vocabulary of written language are only part of the picture. Of even greater interest to those who are interested in assessing spoken or written language ability are the ways students use language to get things done (identified earlier as the use of appropriate strategies for revealing language functions such as promising, complaining, giving directives, denying, reporting facts and opinions, requesting, et cetera. Along with these propositional functions, educators concerned with measurement should be interested in assessing the use of sequencing functions such as opening, closing, maintaining, referencing, and, when appropriate, interacting. Also, we should be concerned about assessing the writer's or speaker's ability to accomplish style or register shifting in relationship to shifting topics, participants, and settings. This combination of form and function is at the heart of communicative skill assessment. To judge writing or speech on the basis of form alone is equivalent to measuring the reading ability of good readers by asking them questions about the initial decoding skills that they learned only to get started in reading and soon learned to ignore in favor of processing larger and larger language units.

Any attempt to achieve content validity, then, must assess the ability in question in relationship to the appropriate developmental stage that is offered by the knowledge base of the field. Unless that knowledge base is clear and sound, however, any effort to assess this ability is subject to error. In the case of communication skills, several crucial problems obtain. As noted earlier, communication is productive (that is, speaking and writing) as well as receptive (that is, reading and listening). To assess only one of these four components, such as reading, is *not* to assess communication skills at all — but *only one* receptive skill. One could easily argue that it would be far more useful to measure a productive rather than a receptive communication skill as one measures communication skills. But in order to assess communicative skills of both a productive and receptive type, one needs to have first outlined clear and agreed-upon levels of development that are appropriate for measurement. There is as much danger in assessing early skills of mature learners as there is in measuring later skills of beginning learners. Neither approach tells you very much that is worth knowing. Perhaps most significant of all, however, is that what is *most* worth measuring — the student's ability to use language to get things done — is seldom measured at all, partly because it is often not in the curriculum (that is, curriculum invalidity) and partly because it requires a context and approach that is difficult to assess. Real communication is self-generated, interactive, and functional (Staton 1981); that is, it has the same characteristics as good oral language. Writers or speakers have something to say that they want to say, they say or write it to a known audience, and they accomplish what they want to get done by saying or writing it; this is at the heart of communication skills. To do anything less does not yield content validity. Then all of this must be set in the context of what is developmentally appropriate to the students being assessed.

Contextualization

Much of what has been considered cultural bias is actually part of a much larger aspect of the mismatch of the assumptions and presuppositions of the Sender and the Receiver, the test maker and the test taker. This is not to say the cultural bias does not exist. Rather, there are many kinds of subcultures besides blacks, bilingual groups, or other minorities. There are differences in presupposition and assumption based on regional differences, socioeconomic differences, age differences, sex differences, urban-rural differences, religious differences, and even, as noted earlier, on developmental differences. If one were to ask students why they answered test questions the way they did, one would find that the students often have the right answers for the wrong reasons or the wrong answers even though they knew what the right answer was (Bauman 1981). What causes this mismatch often stems from the decontextualizing of the test situation. The social context of testing is worthy of considerable attention as an ethnographic phenomenon.

All tests assume the student's comprehension of the instructions, and the test questions themselves depend on linguistic comprehension (Wolfram and Fasold 1974). The interpretation of the task requires matching the interpretation of the test maker by the test taker. This involves comprehension of the sentence meanings, including the assumptions, implications, and presuppositions of each set of in-structions and each question. The test situation itself requires the student to enter a setting that is decontextualized from real-life situations. The more abstract the context, the further from what linguists call "natural events" we get. If the goals of MCT are to represent real-life situations, such as reading instruction manuals, it would seem reasonable that the same desirable intention would be extended even further to still more natural contexts, particularly those that call on writing and speaking tasks — not just on reading. Only six of the fifty-nine questions in the Florida statewide test cited by Hilliard are even marginally concerned with writing, and not one concerns speaking. Such a ratio makes the claim of measuring "communication skills" totally inadequate. Even the six questions that involve presumed productive competence are basically reading questions, asking the students to match and select the correct item from among four possible answers to insert on a replica of a personal check. No actual writing is done by the student. Thus the setting for measuring communication skills is not only the decontextual-ized *physical* situation of a paper-pencil, special-time, nonrealistic life event, but the test is also decontextualized *academically* from the aspects of communication that it purports to represent.

It has been said that the best way to assess the abilities of firefighters, carpen-ters, teachers, or physicians is to observe their effectiveness as they do their work. With language-related tasks such as reading, listening, speaking, or writing, decontextualization of task is distortion of task to the extent that the task is no longer language. There is no way that language — oral and written — can be assessed, measured, or diagnosed optimally and accurately outside of the natural contexts in which it occurs. That is, to assess writing ability, one has to get the test taker to write. To assess speaking, one has to get the test taker to speak. To assess reading or listening, one has to get the test taker to read or listen. No academic decontextualization will measure language. It will measure something else such as conscious knowledge and memory of presumed subskills or rules. More com-monly, it will measure memory of the forms of language but not the ability to use the forms to accomplish language functions. Even if it does these things, however, it will capture the student's language as though it were categorical rather than variable (Labov 1974; Wolfram 1969), decontextualizing it from all the sociolinguistic richness that makes language effective and appropriate. The importance of testing language skills in context cannot be underestimated.

What Can Be Done?

This chapter has argued that MCTs have, in theory at least, one strong asset: they attempt to assess skills in settings that represent real-life usefulness. This idea has theoretical merit but a number of procedural weaknesses. Part of these weaknesses come from curricular validity — the failure of the curriculum to guide teachers in teaching the generalizable skills and even the available knowledge base. Also, part of these weaknesses stem from test construction content invalidity. Although reading ability is part of communication skills, it is generally regarded as a receptive skill and cannot represent the other communication skills of writing, listening, and speaking. Other defects — accuracy, representativeness, importance, developmental relevance, and contextualization — are combined weaknesses of test-development theory and curricular invalidity, both of which lead to content invalidity. A last problem grows out of failures in construct validity to sample the domain of knowledge in real-life contexts, which lead to still more content invalidity.

In essence, we are testing for minimal competency before the curriculum, the art of test development, and, in some cases, where the knowledge base is not yet sound enough to provide guidelines of what to expect (this is true of writing, in particular). It would seem reasonable to remediate these weaknesses before we attempt any further testing of this type. Otherwise, we will continue to get results that are meaningless to interpret.

What steps can we take to overcome these weaknesses in the system? We certainly need more research knowledge about the development of writing and speaking ability. We need to match what we already know about the development of reading ability to the tests that attempt to assess it, clarifying developmental skills, such as decoding, from real reading (comprehending). In the reading area, we also need to develop a knowledge-based theory of the relative importance of different comprehension skills to each other in a developmental framework determining, in the process, what types of comprehension (main idea, inferencing, detail memory, matching skills, vocabulary, et cetera) are appropriate measures of high school, elementary school, and beginning-level proficiency. Perhaps most significant of all, we need to begin teaching the generalizable skills of language functions that can be more critical assessments of communicative ability — productive and receptive — than any of the language forms usually tested along with more honest measures of what a student can do to use language to get things done. The things that get done may well be reading or writing fire instruction manuals, advertisements, business reports, or rental advertisements, but the crucial intermediary steps of learning various strategies for realizing the language functions necessary to read or write them are grossly overlooked. In short, we go to the product without first passing through the generalizable process. We teach and test items, not principles.

The real test of competency is found in the real-life situations in which our graduates find themselves. Employers complain that our students cannot read, write, speak, or listen well enough in the tasks they have to perform. Surely this is the key to our problem. To test for minimal competency in reading, writing, speaking, and listening, the best task is one that closely emulates these real-life tasks as naturally as possible (McClelland 1973). The testing industry says we cannot do this, largely because it would take too long, cost too much, or because we do not really know how to do it. This seems to be a poor response to the problem. Perhaps we should either learn to test properly or stop pretending to know what we are doing.

As a short-term solution, the following four suggestions are offered:

1. Take the suggestion of Mehan (1980) and Bauman (1981) seriously. Individually field-test the questions on children of many cultures in a systematic way. That is, walk the students through the questions one by one, asking them how they arrived at the answers that they give. As those of us who have tried this simple approach have learned, we often discover differences in world knowledge between test maker and test taker that we had never dreamed of. Students often get the wrong answers even with the right thinking; they also often get the right answers with the wrong thinking. Careful monitoring of such information can provide valuable clues about cultural differences of the sort that Hilliard's testimony in *Debra P*. v. *Turlington* exposed. It is true that test makers field-test their examinations, but not at this crucial level of analysis. Discrimination in scores is not adequate unless we know *why* that discrimination is present. It is not surprising that black children performed much worse than white children in the Florida Statewide Assessment. As Hilliard's testimony clearly points out, the world knowledge of the test taker did not match that of the test maker.

2. Contextualize the language of communicative skills questions. As noted earlier, language ability does not decontextualize well. Test reading ability with reading questions, but do not claim that reading ability represents speaking ability, writing ability, or listening ability. Test writing ability by giving a writing task that is functional, developmentally appropriate, meaningful, and doable. The only way to know whether or not a student can write is

to have him or her write. The same must be said of speaking and listening ability. Such testing is not amenable to large group testing or machine-graded scoring. It is expensive and time-consuming but if the experience of the National Assessment of Educational Progress and that of SWRL's Writing Division are any indication, it can be done for writing at least. Speaking tests require individualization, which is even more expensive and time-consuming because it requires tape recordings of individuals talking. Early efforts at such testing carried out in a Los Angeles school indicate that, at present, it takes approximately one-half hour per student to analyze such data. Listening skills are more amenable to group testing with a standard tape-recorded stimulus.

3. Organize reading comprehension skills into a hierarchy. If research cannot yet tell us whether main ideas, memory for details, inferencing, vocabulary, or study skills are the most critical for the age level we want to test, we should use common sense to estimate what we think is most important. Surely the memory for details category should not be represented by 54% of the questions, as the Florida Statewide Assessment has indicated. Common sense would tell us that understanding the main ideas and inferencing are of a higher order even though they are harder to construct as test questions.

4. Test for generalizable functions and skills, not for individual forms. This is an issue of function over form. Perhaps the general public is not yet ready for this, but accomplishing things with language — the cognitive goal of language use — is more important than the social goal of correctness. If we were to assess the language ability of, say, a Puerto Rican teenager in New York who could distinguish in pronunciation between *shoes* and *choose* but who could not request clarification effectively and another New York Puerto Rican teenager who confused *shoes* and *choose* but *could* request clarification effectively, we would have to conclude that the second person was more ready to function successfully in life. This is *not* to say that the "sh-ch" contrast is not socially important. It is only to say that the functional-cognitive use of language outranks the doctrine of social correctness.

The generalizable functions of language — both productive (that is, writing and speaking) and receptive (that is, reading and listening) — include such things as reporting facts, predicting, evaluating, requesting information, clarifying, denying, offering, apologizing, reporting opinions, promising, requesting clarification, et cetera. These language functions should be taught and could be tested in such a way that, when combined, offer evidence of a student's ability to speak or write effectively. By testing for generalizable skills and functions, we can avoid the dangers of straight task learning and testing outlined earlier. Such a procedure also guards against the ultimate eventuality toward which MCT is now headed: toward the teaching of the test, or the tail wagging the dog.

Perhaps the most useful product of all this interest in MCT is the effect that such thinking should offer to research. By getting into such a muddle, we have revealed many areas in which our knowledge base is weak, our curriculum is outmoded, and our goals are trivial. The issue should have a profound effect on directing research toward addressing the five characteristics of content validity outlined earlier: accuracy, representativeness, importance, developmental relevance and contextualization. If it does not, we will not make much progress.

References

Bauman, J. *Linguistic Structure as a Factor Influencing the Validity of Standardized Reading Comprehension Tests*. Final Report to National Institute of Education (Project No. G-80-0149). Washington, D.C.: The Center For Applied Linguistics, 1981.

Firsching, J. "Speaker Expectations and Mathematics Word Problems," Paper presented at Southwest Conference on Linguistics, Georgetown University, 1981. Mimeographed.

Freedle, R., and Hale, G. "Acquisition of New Comprehension Schemata for Expository Prose by Transfer of a Narrative Schema," in R. Freedle, ed., *New Directions in Discourse Processing, Vol. II: Advances in Discourse Processes*. Norwood, N.J.: Ablex Publishing Corp., 1979.

Freeman, C., Tucker G.R., and Zwicky, A. *A Study of the Degrees of Reading Power Test*. Final Report to the Ford Foundation. Washington, D.C.: The Center for Applied Linguistics, 1981.

Goodman, K., and Goodman, Y. "Learning about Psycholinguistic Processes by Analyzing Oral Reading." *Harvard Educational Review* 47, No. 3 (1977).

Griffin, P. "Reading and Pragmatics: Symbiosis," in R. Shuy, ed., *Linguistic Theory: What Can It Say About Reading?* Newark, Del.: International Reading Association, 1977.

Hilliard, A. Testimony presented in the case of *Debra P. v. Turlington*.

Hymes, D. Introduction. In J. Gumperz and D. Hymes, eds., *The Ethnography of Communication*. Special issue of *American Anthropology* 6, No. 2 (1964).

Hymes, D. "Models of the Interaction of Language and Social Life," in J. Gumperz and D. Hymes, eds., *New Directions in Sociolinguistics*. New York: Holt, Rinehart & Winston, 1972.

Kintch, W., and Van Dijk, T. "Toward a Model of Text Comprehension and Production." *Psychological Review* 85, No. 5 (1978).

Labov, W. *Socialinguistic Patterns*. Philadelphia, Pa.: University of Pennsylvanie Press, 1972.

Larkin, D., Dieterich, T., Freeman, C., and Yanofsky, N. *Theoretical Considerations in the Revision and Extension of Miscue Analysis*. Rockville, Md.: Montgomery County Public Schools, 1979.

McClelland, D. "Do Intelligence Tests Tap Abilities that Are Responsible for Job Success?" *American Psychologist* (January 1973) pp. 3–14.

Mehan, H. *Learning Lessons: Social Organization in the Classroom*. Cambridge, Mass.: Harvard University Press, 1980.

Morgan, J. "Toward a Rational Model of Discourse Comprehension," in *Theoretical Issues in Natural Language Processing*. 2. Urbana-Champaign, Ill.: University of Illinois, 1978.

National Assessment of Educational Progress. "Writing Achievement, 1969–1979: Results from the Third National Writing Assessment." Denver, Colo.: National Assessment of Educational Progress, 1980.

Rummelhart, D. "Schemata: The Building Blocks of Cognition," in Spiro, Bruce, and Brewer, eds., *Theoretical Issues in Reading Comprehension*. Hillsdale, N.J.: Lawrence Erlbaum Associates, 1980.

Shuy, W. "Toward a Developmental Theory of Writing," in C. Fredericksen and J. Dominic, eds., *Writing: Process, Development, and Communication*. Hillsdale, N.J.: Lawrence Erlbaum Associates, 1981.

———— "Relating Research on Oral Language Functions to Research on Written Discourse." Paper presented at American Educational Research Association, annual meeting 1981.

Staton, J. "It's Just Not Gonna Come Down in One Little Sentence: A Study of Discourse in Dialogue Journal Writing." Paper presented at AERA annual meeting, Center for Applied Linguistics, 1981.

Wolfram, W. *A Sociolinguistic Description of Detroit Negro Speech*. Washington, D.C.: Center for Applied Linguistics, 1969.

Wolfram, W. and Fasold, R.W. *The Study of Social Dialects in American English*. Englewood Cliffs, N.J.: Prentice-Hall, 1974.

APPENDIX A

Debra P. v. *Turlington,* United States District Court,
M.D. Florida, Tampa Division, July 12, 1979.
As Amended August 7 and 8, 1979

DEBRA P., a minor, by Irene P., her mother and next friend, Wanda W., a minor, by Ruby W., her mother and next friend, Luwanda K., a minor, by Willa K., her mother and next friend, Terry W., a minor, by Doris W., his mother and next friend, Brenda T., a minor by Willie T., her father and next friend, Vanessa S., a minor, by Mamie S., her mother and next friend, Thomas J. H., Jr., a minor by Thomas J. H., Sr., his father and next friend, Gary L. B., a minor, by Ezell B., his father and next friend, Valisa W., a minor, by Charles W., her father and next friend, Huey J., a minor, by Melvin G., his guardian and next friend, on behalf of themselves and all other persons similarly situated, Plaintiffs,

v.

Ralph D. TURLINGTON, Individually and as Commissioner of Education, Florida State Board of Education, Governor Bob Graham, Individually and as Chairman thereof, Secretary of State George Firestone, Attorney General Jim Smith, Comptroller Gerald A. "Jerry" Lewis, Treasurer William Gunter, Commissioner of Agriculture Doyle Conner, Commissioner of Education Ralph D. Turlington, all Individually and as members thereof, Florida Department of Education, School Board of Hillsborough County, Florida, a Corporate Body Public, Roland H. Lewis, Individually and as Chairman thereof, Cecile W. Essrig, Carl Carpenter, Jr., Ben H. Hill, Jr., A. Leon Lowery, Sam Rampello, and Marion Rodgers, all Individually and as members thereof, and, Raymond O. Shelton, Individually and as Superintendent of Schools of Hillsborough County, Defendants.

No. 78–892 Civ. T–C.

United States District Court,
M. D. Florida,
Tampa Division.

July 12, 1979.

As Amended Aug. 7 and 8, 1979.

Plaintiffs brought action challenging constitutional and statutory validity of Florida state student assessment test, a functional literacy examination. The District Court, Carr, J., held that: (1) in view of history of segregation in Florida public schools, test unlawfully discriminated against black children in violation of equal protection clause; (2) test had adequate content and construct validity and bore rational relation to valid state interest; (3) plaintiffs failed to establish that test was racially or ethnically biased; (4) failure to apply test to private school was not unconstitutional; (5) inadequacy of notice provided prior to indication of diploma sanction, objectives, and test was a violation of due process clause; (6) use of test to classify students for remediation was constitutionally permissible, and (7) state would be enjoined from requiring passage of test as requirement for graduation for period of four years.

Ordered accordingly.

1. Civil Rights ⊕9
Constitutional Law ⊕220(3)

Where de jure segregation existed in Florida public schools from 1885 to 1967, where racial discrimination existed from 1967 through 1971, where, by commencement of school term 1971–1972, actual physical integration of schools was generally completed but remediation with specifically delineated objectives and programs did not commence until 1977, where there existed intent to discriminate through 1971 and, although proof of present intent to discriminate was insufficient, past purposeful discrimination affecting black pupils was perpetuated by Florida state student assessment test, a functional literacy test, use of test as a requirement for receipt of high school diploma violated equal protection clause and federal statutes, U.S.C.A.Const. Amend. 14; Civil Rights Act of 1964, § 601, 42 U.S.C.A. § 2000d; 20 U.S.C.A. § 1703.

2. Constitutional Law ⊕215

Disproportionate impact is not sole touchstone of invidious racial discrimination forbidden by Constitution, but it is a relevant factor to be considered. U.S.C.A. Const. Amend. 14.

3. Schools ⚖️163

Florida state student assessment test, a functional literacy test, was a valid and reasonable measure for dividing students into classifications for purpose of high school graduation and reasonably evaluated objectives established by Florida State Board of Education, as test has both adequate content validity and adequate construct validity. U.S.C.A.Const. Amend. 14; West's F.S.A. § 229.57 et seq.

4. Constitutional Law ⚖️220(3)

Florida state student assessment test, a functional literacy test, was not unconstitutionally racially or ethnically biased against black students. West's F.S.A. § 229.57 et seq.; U.S.C.A.Const. Amend. 14.

5. Constitutional Law ⚖️220(3)

Strict scrutiny test did not apply in determining constitutionality of Florida's failure to require private school students to pass functional literacy examination as a condition of receiving high school diplomas, where ability to attend private schools was clearly affected by student's or his parents' financial resources, even though blacks were, as a class, without substantial financial resources. U.S.C.A.Const. Amend. 14.

6. Constitutional Law ⚖️209

Fact that decisions of legislative or administrative bodies affect certain groups disproportionally does not signal strict scrutiny analysis in determining whether decisions violated equal protection clause of Fourteenth Amendment. U.S.C.A.Const. Amend. 14.

7. Schools ⚖️163

Florida's legislative decision to apply state student assessment test, a functional literacy examination, only to public schools, over which state had significant curricular, instructional, and financial control, was both reasonable and constitutional, as state was not required to correct all problems of education in one clean sweep but could attack problems in a logical fashion. West's

F.S.A. § 229.57 et seq.; U.S.C.A.Const. Amend. 14.

8. Constitutional Law ⚖️278.5(5)
Schools ⚖️178

Notice given by state of Florida prior to and since implementation of functional literacy testing program, as well as adequacy of time to prepare for examination after objectives were first established, was constitutionally inadequate and violated due process rights, where passage of examination was condition to receiving a diploma, as high school students had property right in graduation from high school with a standard diploma if they had fulfilled requirements for graduation other than passage of examination and students also had liberty interest in being free of adverse stigma associated with receiving certificate of completion which was given to students who failed examination but otherwise satisfied requirements for graduation. U.S.C.A. Const. Amend. 14; West's F.S.A. § 229.57 et seq.

9. Constitutional Law ⚖️251.1

Due process is a flexible standard dependent upon facts and circumstances of each individual case. U.S.C.A.Const. Amend. 14.

10. Civil Rights ⚖️9

Utilization of Florida state student assessment test, a functional literacy examination, to classify and group students for remediation pursuant to Florida Compensatory Education Act of 1977 did not unlawfully discriminate against black students even though compensatory education program for those students who failed examination was disproportionately composed of black children because more black children failed examination than white children, where purpose of compensatory education program was to assist students and not to resegregate them, where legislature had given program ample financial support, where pupil alignment in programs was not static, and where program constituted only at most two classes or hours per day. West's F.S.A. § 236.088; U.S.C.A.Const. Amend. 14; Civil Rights Act of 1964, § 601, 42 U.S.C.A. § 2000d; 20 U.S.C.A. § 1703.

11. Schools ⟐ 13(20)

Where Florida statute requiring passage of functional literacy examination as a condition to receiving high school diploma unconstitutionally discriminated against black students due to history of past discrimination in Florida public schools, state would be enjoined from requiring passage of examination as a requirement for graduation for period of four years but would be allowed to utilize examination as a requirement for graduation in the school term 1982–1983; in the interim, the examination could be administered and directed by state to assist in the identification and remediation of examination's skill objectives and scores could be retained in a fashion consistent with manner in which state retained other achievement test scores. West's F.S.A. § 232.246(1)(a–c).

Morris W. Milton, St. Petersburg, Fla., Stephen F. Hanlon, Robert J. Shapiro, Bay Area Legal Services, Tampa, Fla., Diana Pullin, Roger L. Rice, Richard Jefferson, Center for Law and Education, Cambridge, Mass., Terry L. DeMeo, Legal Services for Greater Miami, Miami Fla., for plaintiffs.

James D. Little and Judith A. Brechner, State Board of Education, Tallahassee, Fla., W. Crosby Few, Tampa, Fla., for Hillsborough County defendants.

MEMORANDUM OPINION

CARR, District Judge.

I

THE CLAIMS AND CLASSES

The Plaintiffs in the instant action present a broad based constitutional and statutory challenge to the Florida Functional Literacy Examination (i. e. State Student

1. The preceding named individual Defendants are the members of the Florida State Board of Education (i. e. the Governor and Florida Cabinet).

2. The preceding named individual Defendants through Mr. Lewis are the members of the Hillsborough County School Board.

Assessment Test, Part II; hereinafter referred to either as the SSAT II or the functional literacy examination). Fla.Stat. § 229.57, et seq. Plaintiffs contend in a complaint filed October 16, 1978, that the SSAT II violates their Fourteenth Amendment due process and equal protection rights and also violates their rights pursuant to 42 U.S.C. § 2000d and 20 U.S.C. § 1703.

The Court on March 21, 1979, certified three classes of Plaintiffs:

Class A are all present and future twelfth grade public school students in the State of Florida who have failed or who hereafter fail the SSAT II.

Class B are all present and future twelfth grade black public school students in the State of Florida who have failed or who hereafter fail the SSAT II.

Class C are all present and future twelfth grade black public school students in Hillsborough County, Florida who have failed or who hereafter fail the SSAT II.

The Defendants in the case are Commissioner of Education, Ralph D. Turlington, the Florida Board of Education, Governor Bob Graham, Secretary of State George Firestone, Attorney General Jim Smith, Comptroller Gerald A. Lewis, Treasurer William Gunter, Commissioner of Agriculture Doyle Conner,[1] the Florida Department of Education [hereinafter referred to as the DOE], the School Board of Hillsborough County, Florida, Roland H. Lewis, Cecile W. Essrig, Carl Carpenter, Jr., Ben H. Hill, Jr., A. Leon Lowery, Sam Rampello, Marion Rodgers,[2] and Superintendent of Schools of Hillsborough County, Raymond O. Shelton.

A brief summary of the Plaintiffs' claims in conjunction with the certified classes will facilitate an understanding of the Court's opinion.[3] The first claim asserts that the

3. A more extensive and analytical review of the Plaintiffs' claims is presented in Parts IV, V and VI.

Defendants have either designed or implemented a test or testing program (i. e., SSAT II) which is racially biased and/or which violates the equal protection clause of the Fourteenth Amendment, 42 U.S.C. § 2000d, and 20 U.S.C. § 1703. The first claim relates to Classes A, B and C.

The second claim contends that Defendants have instituted a program of awarding diplomas without providing the Plaintiffs with adequate notice of the requirements (i. e., passage of the SSAT II) or adequate time to prepare for the required examination in violation of the Fourteenth Amendment. The second claim, like the first, relates to Classes A, B and C.

The third claim asserts that the Defendants have used the SSAT II in conjunction with Fla.Stat. § 236.088 as a mechanism for resegregating the Florida public schools through the use of remedial classes for those students failing the examination in violation of the Fourteenth Amendment, 42 U.S.C. § 2000d, and 20 U.S.C. § 1703. The third claim relates to Classes B and C.

The Plaintiffs' prayer for relief seeks a declaratory judgment finding that the requirement for passage of the SSAT II as a prerequisite for a normal graduation diploma is a violation of the due process and equal protection clauses of the Fourteenth Amendment, 42 U.S.C. § 2000d and 20 U.S.C. § 1703. The Plaintiffs additionally request an injunction restraining the Defendants from requiring SSAT II passage as a prerequisite to receiving a high school diploma. Finally, Plaintiffs seek an injunction to both purge their scholastic records of any acknowledgement of the SSAT II failure and to issue an Order prohibiting the utilization of the SSAT II results as a means of structuring classes in remediation.

II

JURISDICTION

The Court has jurisdiction to consider the Plaintiffs' claims pursuant to 28 U.S.C. § 1343(3) and (4) and 28 U.S.C. §§ 2201, 2202.

III

HISTORICAL AND LEGISLATIVE BACKGROUND

A. THE TEST

In 1976, the Florida Legislature enacted a comprehensive piece of legislation known as the "Educational Accountability Act of 1976." *Laws of Florida 1976*, Vol. 1, Chapter 76–223, pp. 489–508. Part of the stated intent of the legislature was:

(a) [to p]rovide a system of accountability for education in Florida which guarantees that each student is afforded similar opportunities for educational advancement without regard to geographic differences and varying local factors . . . (d) [to g]uarantee to each student in the Florida system of public education that the system provides instructional programs which meet minimum performance standards compatible with the state's plan for education . . . (f) [to p]rovide information to the public about the performance of the Florida system of public education in meeting established goals and providing effective, meaningful and relevant educational experiences designed to give students at least the minimum skills necessary to function and survive in today's society. Fla.Stat. § 229.-55(2)(a), (d), (f).

In a subsection of the Act entitled "Pupil Progression" the legislature established three standards for graduation from Florida public high schools. Fla.Stat. §§ 232.-245(3) (1977); 232.246(1)–(3). The first requirement mandated that the students complete the minimum number of credits for graduation promulgated by their school board. The second requirement made compulsory the mastery of basic skills and the third required "[s]atisfactory performance in functional literacy as determined by the State Board of Education . . .." Fla. Stat. § 232.245(3) (1977). The pupil progression subsection also provided that each school district must develop procedures for remediation of students who were unable to meet the required standards. The legislation also provided for a comprehensive testing program to evaluate basic skill development at periodic intervals. Fla.Stat. § 229.-

57.[4] In 1978, the Act was amended by the Florida Legislature to require passage of a functional literacy examination prior to receipt of a state graduation diploma. Those students who completed the minimum number of required high school credits but failed the functional literacy examination would receive a certificate of completion. Fla.Stat. § 232.246.[5]

At the time of trial the SSAT II had been administered on three separate occasions: Fall, 1977; Fall, 1978; Spring, 1979. A review of the results of the three administrations will be discussed in the following section.

B. THE TEST RESULTS

A review of the results of the October, 1977, administration of the SSAT II indicates that there were substantial numbers of students who failed the test. Of the 115,901 students taking both sections of the test, approximately 41,724 or 36% failed one or both sections. A breakdown of the results on a racial basis shows that 78% of the black students failed one or both sections as compared to 25% of the white students. On the communications section of the SSAT II, 26% of the black students failed as compared to 3% of the white students.

The second administration results followed a similar pattern. Of the 4,480 black students taking the test for a second time, 3,315 or 74% failed one or both sections. The percentage of failure among white students retaking both sections was 25% or 1,675 students. Of the 13,345 black stu-

---

4. Fla.Stat. § 229.57 provides:

(1) Statewide Testing.—The primary purpose of the statewide testing program is to provide information needed for state-level decisions. The program shall be designed to:

(a) Assist in the identification of educational needs at the state, district, and school levels.

(b) Assess how well districts and schools are meeting state goals and minimum performance standards.

(c) Provide information to aid in the development of policy issues and concerns.

(d) Provide a basis for comparisons among districts and between districts, the state, and the nation, when appropriate.

(e) Produce data which can be used to aid in the identification of exceptional educational programs or processes.

(2) The Statewide Assessment Program.— The Commissioner is directed to implement a program of statewide assessment testing which shall provide for the improvement of the operation and management of the public schools. The statewide program shall be timed, as far as possible, so as not to conflict with on going district assessment programs. As part of the program the commissioner shall:

(a) Establish, with the approval of the state board, minimum performance standards related to the goals for education contained in the state's plan, including, but not limited, to basic skills in reading, writing and mathematics. The minimum performance standards shall be approved by April 1 in each year and they are established, for a period of no less than three, nor more than five, years.

(b) Develop and administer in the public schools a uniform, statewide program of assessment to determine, periodically, educational status and progress and the degrees of achievement of approved minimum perform-

ance standards. The uniform statewide program shall consist of testing in grades 3, 5, 8, and 11 and may include the testing of additional grades and skill areas as specified by the Commissioner.

5. Fla.Stat. § 232.246 provides: General requirements for high school graduation.—

(1) Beginning with the 1978-1979 school year, each district school board shall establish standards for graduation from its schools which shall include as a minimum:

(a) Mastery of the minimum performance standards in reading, writing and mathematics for the 11th grade, established pursuant to ss. 229.565 and 229.57, determined in the manner prescribed by rules of the state board; and

(b) Demonstrated ability to successfully apply basic skills to everyday life situations as measured by a functional literacy examination developed and administered pursuant to rules of the state board; and

(c) Completion of a minimum number of academic credits, and all other applicable requirements prescribed by the district school board pursuant to s. 232.245

. . . .

(3) A student who meets all requirements prescribed in subsection (1) shall be awarded a standard diploma in a form prescribed by the state board; provided that a school board may, in lieu of the standard diploma, award differentiated diplomas to those exceeding the prescribed minimums. A student who completes the minimum number of credits and other requirements prescribed by paragraph (1)(c), but is unable to meet the standards of paragraph (1)(a) or paragraph (1)(b), shall be awarded a certificate of completion in a form prescribed by the state board.

dents being reexamined on the mathematics section 46% or 6,139 failed.

The results of the third administration of the SSAT II which were released during the trial illustrate the same disparity in the failure rates among white and black students. Sixty percent (60%) of the black students retaking the mathematics section of the test for a third time failed as compared to 36% of the white students. Between October, 1977, and May, 1979, the number of students who were in Florida public high schools first as juniors and then as seniors had been reduced to 91,000 students. Of the approximately 91,000 high school seniors, 3,466 or 20.049% of the black students had not passed the test compared to 1,342 of 1.9% of the white students. The failure rate among black students was approximately 10 times that among white students. In all, approximately 5,300 students or 5.8% had failed to pass the SSAT II by the time of the end of their senior year in high school.

C. THE EFFECTS

Rather than following a specific item by item format for the findings of fact, the Court will utilize a narrative approach. The Court notes that in resolving conflicts in the testimony it relied upon its evaluation of the witnesses and their demeanor while testifying.

The denial of a standard diploma based on the failure of the SSAT II triggers a number of economic and academic deprivations. The State of Florida Career Service Department, for instance, employs only 10% of its labor force from those people who do not have high school diplomas. The jobs found in this 10% "no diploma" category have been described as both "menial" and "dead end" positions. The State of Florida

requires only a high school diploma for another 10% of its work force. The remaining 80% of the jobs in state government require a high school diploma and experience or some higher academic degree. A certificate of completion will not be considered a diploma for purposes of employment with the State of Florida.

Similarly, admission to one of the nine universities in Florida is predicated upon receipt of a high school diploma. A certificate of completion will not be considered an adequate substitute for the diploma. The denial of a diploma has a disproportionate effect on the college attendance of black students.[6]

The stigma which results from the failure of the SSAT II is a very serious problem. Students who have failed the test are often branded with the label "functionally illiterate."

D. ADMITTED FACTS AND JUDICIAL NOTICE

Prior to the commencement of the trial, the parties agreed that certain facts need not be proved. A list of those facts is contained in the parties' pretrial stipulation filed April 23, 1979. Those facts pertain primarily to the statutory duties and responsibilities of the Florida State Board of Education and the Florida Department of Education. There is agreement as to the existence of a dual school system in Florida, although the agreement is without temporal boundaries, and as to the fact that historically black children have not fared well on standardized tests in Florida schools.[7]

The Court on the first day of trial took judicial notice of certain relevant facts, statutes, and judicial decisions. The majority of the matters which Plaintiffs request-

---

6. The evidence provided by Dr. Eckland clearly illustrates that large numbers of black students who graduate in the lowest two deciles of their high school classes go on to participate in higher education if they have a diploma. The black students in the lowest two deciles roughly correlates to those black students who failed the SSAT II. Dr. Eckland's review of the National Longitudinal Study showed that the denial of a diploma to the black students in Florida who

failed the SSAT II upon the second administration would result in a 20% decline in black students college attendance.

7. Numerous other facts have been admitted which if relevant, will be discussed in the Section IV, V and VI of this Memorandum Opinion. Further recitation of those facts in this section is unnecessary.

ed that the Court judicially notice were previously admitted by the Defendants.[8] The Court has specifically taken judicial notice both of the de jure segregation of Florida schools in the period 1885 to 1967 and that as a result of attending segregated schools prior to the implementation of unitary school systems many members of Classes B and C received an unequal education to that received by white students during those years. *Brown v. Board of Education*, 347 U.S. 483, 74 S.Ct. 686, 98 L.Ed. 873 (1954).

E. RACIAL DISCRIMINATION AND FLORIDA PUBLIC EDUCATION (1885–1967)

Although the Court's principal focus concerning racial discrimination in Florida public education revolves around the period 1967–1979, and more specifically 1967–1971, it is helpful to provide a historical over-view of the conditions existing prior to 1967.[9] From 1890 to 1967 Florida public education operated a dual school system; dual in the sense that there were two complete and separate school systems for black and white Florida public school children. *See Green v. County School Board of New Kent County*, 391 U.S. 430, 88 S.Ct. 1689, 20 L.Ed.2d 716 (1968); *Singleton v. Jackson Municipal Separate School District*, 419 F.2d 1211 (5th Cir. 1969). Likewise, there was absolute segregation of school faculty on a racial basis. Black and white teachers even maintained separate professional associations and unions. The physical facilities, the size and scope of the curricula, the libraries, the duration of the school day and year, the

supplies, and the texts in black schools were inferior to those in white schools. Black schools during this period were obviously inferior.[10] The dual school system and its inherent inequality was perpetuated not only by the policies and practices of local school boards, but also by the Florida Constitution and statutes.[11] Although the Supreme Court's holding of separate but equal was the law of the land during the bulk of this period, the corresponding component of equality was constantly overlooked and never enforced in relation to black Florida public schools. *Plessy v. Ferguson*, 163 U.S. 537, 168 S.Ct. 1138, 41 L.Ed. 256 (1896).

IV

FIRST CLAIM

A. INTRODUCTION

[1] The Plaintiffs' first claim is a multi-pronged equal protection, Title VI and Equal Educational Opportunities Act challenge to the SSAT II. The essence of the claim is the Plaintiffs' contention that SSAT II perpetuates and reemphasizes the effects of past purposeful discrimination. Beyond this core allegation, Plaintiffs contend (1) that the test is unreliable, invalid and not correlated to the public school curriculum, (2) that the test instrument is racially biased, and finally (3) that passage of the test was not required for graduation in Florida private schools. Plaintiffs further contend that the higher percentage of black twelfth grade failures was the probable and foreseeable consequence of enactment and

---

8. The Court's colloquy on the record with counsel as to those matters is clear as to which facts were admitted and which were judicially noticed. *See also* Parties' Pretrial Stipulation.

9. The Court at the commencement of trial specifically limited the focus of the inquiry into discrimination to the period 1967 to present, but permitted Plaintiffs to present expert opinion evidence regarding an overview of the history of discrimination in the Florida public schools.

10. On this issue, the Court cannot help but refer to Judge Heebe's statement in a case involving similar issues:

It becomes readily apparent to anyone familiar with the nature of white and black schools in the South that children going to the white school would be provided with better facilities, faculties, educational materials than their counterparts in the black schools. *Moses v. Washington Parish School Board*, 330 F.Supp. 1340, 1345 (E.D.La.1971).

11. *See* Paragraphs 9 to 16 in Plaintiffs' Proposed Request for Judicial Notice. These matters were admitted by the Defendants.

implementation of the statutory scheme by the Defendants.

B. RACIAL DISCRIMINATION AND FLORIDA PUBLIC EDUCATION (1967–1971)

All three classes of Plaintiffs embarked upon their public school educations in the school term 1967–1968. The testimony has clearly indicated that almost all of the Plaintiffs attended segregated public schools which were part of the dual school alignment of the earlier period. While the expert witness testimony on this issue confirms the existence of segregated schools in Florida on a broad geographic scale, the Plaintiffs have placed special emphasis on Hillsborough County, Florida. A review of the appendix to Judge Krentzman's Opinion in *Mannings v. The Board of Public Instruction of Hillsborough County, Florida*, No. 3554 Civ. T–K (unpublished opinion, May 11, 1971) [12] illustrates the attendance during 1967–1971 by race at selected Hillsborough County public schools. The evidence is clear and convincing that Hillsborough County schools in the period 1967–1971 were uniformly racially segregated and that a unitary school system did not exist during that period. This finding is applicable to the state as a whole during the same period.

In *Brown v. Board of Education*, the Supreme Court held:

We conclude that in the field of public education the doctrine of 'separate but equal' has no place. Separate educational facilities are inherently unequal. Therefore, we hold that the Plaintiffs and other similarly situated for whom the actions have been brought are, by reason of the segregation complained of, deprived of equal protection of the laws guaranteed by the Fourteenth Amendment. *Brown, supra*, 347 U.S. at 495, 74 S.Ct. at 692.

Thus, it is clear that the separate facilities in Florida public schools for white and black children during the period 1967–1971 violated Plaintiffs' equal protection rights under the Fourteenth Amendment. The *Brown* finding that separate facilities were inherently unequal is manifestly applicable. [13]

Beyond the question of inherent inequality due to segregation is the question of the inferiority of black schools during the same period. While Plaintiffs contend that a *Brown* showing which has been made is sufficient to shift the burden to Defendants, the Plaintiffs produced vast amounts of evidence of the inferiority in fact of black schools during the period 1967–1971. The evidence clearly indicates that black public schools in Florida were inferior in their physical facilities, course offerings, instructional materials, and equipment. There is little doubt but that the pervasive racial isolation condemned in *Brown* [14] in conjunction with the inferiority of black schools created an atmosphere which was not as conducive to learning as that found in white schools. [15] Further, this education-

---

12. Although Judge Krentzman's Opinion in *Mannings* has been often cited as a model decision in the area, it was never published. In *Mannings v. Board of Public Instruction of Hillsborough County, Florida*, 427 F.2d 874 (5th Cir. 1970), the Fifth Circuit reversed Judge Lieb's desegregation order and held:

We proceed to a determination of the status with respect to each of the six essential elements which go to disestablish a dual school system. Tested in this frame of reference, we find the Hillsborough system deficient in student assignments to certain schools, and to a degree in faculty and staff assignment throughout the system. *Mannings, supra* at 876.

The Fifth Circuits finding above was made on May 11, 1970, exactly one year before Judge Krentzman's final desegregation Order was entered. *See also Mannings v. Board of Public*

Instruction of Hillsborough County, Florida, 277 F.2d 370 (5th Cir. 1960).

13. *See* Plaintiff's "Request for Court to take Judicial Notice of Facts," No. 23, filed April 20, 1979. The Court at the commencement of trial in light of *Brown* and with the substitution of the word "unequal" for the word "inferior" took judicial notice of Request No. 23. While *Brown* made an inherent inequality finding, Judge Krentzman in *Mannings* found factual inequality in Hillsborough County Schools.

14. *Brown, supra* note 11, at 494, 74 S.Ct. 686.

15. The Defendants at trial attempted to illustrate that at least one white school was older, or more in need of repair, than a black school. The inequality of only one school vis-a-vis only one other school is not the issue in this case.

al environment constituted a serious impairment to Class B and C Plaintiffs' ability to learn, especially in the early grades which most educators view as a formative stage in intellectual development.[16]

C. THE TRANSITION PHASE (1971–1979)

By the commencement of the school term 1971–1972, the actual physical integration of Florida public schools was generally completed. With integration came a host of human problems. Although children of all races suffered in the initial years of integration, black children suffered to a greater degree. The most significant burden which accompanied black children into the integrated schools was the existence of years of inferior education. Plaintiffs in Classes B and C had attended segregated schools which were inferior for the first four years of their education. Other problems presented to black children were disparate busing schedules, lingering racial stereotypes, disproportionate terminations of black principals and administrators, and a high incidence of suspensions. While the problems enumerated above do not constitute the denial of an equal educational opportunity during this period, they do attest to the difficulty in making significant academic gains. Additionally, the state during part of this period did not offer the leadership or the funding to mount a wide-scale attack on the educational deficits created during segregation. Remediation with specifically delineated objectives and programs did not commence until 1977.

Black children in the period after segregation ended were presented with numerous problems. Not only did the Class B and C Plaintiffs have to adjust to social, cultur-

al and linguistic differences of the integrated schools, but they had to do so without an adequate educational foundation. The vestiges of the inferior elementary education they received still are present and affect their performance. Although remediation is now underway in a meaningful sense, the effects of past purposeful segregation have not been erased or overcome.

D. THE INTENT TO DISCRIMINATE

[2] While *Washington v. Davis*, 426 U.S. 229, 96 S.Ct. 2040, 48 L.Ed.2d 597 (1977), is instructive that disproportionate impact is "not the sole touchstone of invidious racial discrimination forbidden by the Constitution", it is a relevant factor to be considered. *Id.* at 242, 96 S.Ct. at 2049. The disproportionate impact of the diploma sanction on black school children imposed by failure of the SSAT II is clear. *See Castaneda v. Partida*, 430 U.S. 482, 97 S.Ct. 1272, 51 L.Ed.2d 498 (1977). The results of the first administration of the SSAT II in October, 1977, indicated that 77% of the black students taking the mathematics section failed that portion of the test compared to only 24% of the white students. While numerically less students failed the communication section of SSAT II, the percentage of failure among black students was eight times that of white students (i. e. 26% black failures compared to 3% white failures).

The results of the second administration of SSAT II in October, 1978, followed a similar pattern. The percentage of failure among black students was greatly disproportionate to white students. The third and final SSAT II administration results indicated that three times as many black students failed as white students. Since black students comprise approximately one-

---

The class action proportion of the instant suit has forced the Court to view the relative quality of the black and white schools from a very broad perspective.

16. *See* Fla.Stat. § 230.2311:

(1) The Legislature recognizes that the early years of a pupil's education are crucial to his future and that mastery of the basic skills of communication and computation is essential to the future educational and personal success of

an individual. . . . Early childhood and basic skills development programs shall be made available by the school districts to all school age children, especially those enrolled in kindergarten and grades one through three, and shall provide effective, meaningful, and relevant educational experiences designed to give students at least the minimum skills necessary to function and survive in today's society.

fifth of Florida public schools, the ratio of black to white failures based on the percentage of population is 10 to 1. Approximately 20% of black students who have taken the test three times have not passed as compared to 1.9% of the twelfth grade white students.

As discussed previously, the policies and practices of local school boards together with the Florida Constitution and statutes attest to the intentional creation and maintenance of a dual school system in Florida. Until the school term 1971–1972, the condition of segregated schools persisted throughout the state. The intent to discriminate in the period 1967–1971 has clearly been identified.

In addition to the evidence of past intent, the Plaintiffs presented evidence relative to present intent. Numerous witnesses who were Florida Department of Education employees testified that they anticipated a high percentage of black failure on the SSAT II. The Defendant, Ralph Turlington, the Florida Commissioner of Education, acknowledged that he also anticipated a high black failure rate with regard to the implementation of the SSAT II testing program. Defendant Turlington additionally admitted that a certain portion of the black failure must be attributed to the inferior education the Plaintiffs in Classes B and C received during the dual school period.

With *Washington v. Davis, supra,* the Supreme Court commenced the redefinition of intent in discrimination cases.[17] Instead of relying solely on disproportionate racial impact, the Court focused on whether an identifiable discriminatory purpose was present. Noting that the Plaintiffs had not asserted a claim for intentional discrimination or purposeful discrimination, the Supreme Court reversed the lower courts' finding of a constitutional violation. In a concurring Opinion Justice Stevens addressed the type of proof necessary to establish discriminatory purpose.

Frequently the most probative evidence of intent will be objective evidence of what actually happened rather than evidence describing the subjective state of mind of the actor. For normally the actor is presumed to have intended the natural consequences of his deeds. *Id.* 426 U.S at 253, 96 S.Ct. at 2054.

In *United States v. Texas Education Agency,* 564 F.2d 162 (1977), *rehearing denied,* 579 F.2d 910 (5th Cir. 1978), *cert. denied,* ⸺ U.S. ⸺, 99 S.Ct. 3106, 61 L.Ed.2d 879 (1979) Judge Wisdom addressed the standard for intent after *Dayton Board of Education v. Brinkman,* 433 U.S. 406, 97 S.Ct. 2766, 53 L.Ed.2d 851 (1977), *Village of Arlington Heights v. Metropolitan Housing Development Corp.,* 429 U.S. 252, 97 S.Ct. 555, 50 L.Ed.2d 450 (1977), and *Washington v. Davis, supra.* Applying the "objective standard" found in *Monroe v. Pape,* 365 U.S. 167, 187, 81 S.Ct. 473, 5 L.Ed.2d 492 (1961), Judge Wisdom held that "official decisionmakers would be held to have intended the reasonably foreseeable consequences of their decisions". *Texas Educa-*

---

17. The Court in this section and Section V has reviewed a number of law review articles which have been of considerable assistance. Baldwin and Nagan, *Board of Regents v. Bakke: The All-American Dilemma Revisited,* 30 U.Fla.L.Rev. 843 (1978); Brest, *The Supreme Court, 1975 Term-Forward: "In Defense of the Antidiscrimination Principle,"* 90 Harv.L. Rev. 1 (1976); Lewis, *Certifying Functional Literacy: Competency Testing and Implications for Due Process and Equal Educational Opportunity,* 8 J.L. and Educ. 145 (1979); McClung, *Competency Testing Programs: Legal and Educational Issues,* 47 Fordham L.Rev. 651 (1979); Perry, *The Disproportionate Impact Theory of Racial Discrimination,* 125 U.Pa.L.Rev. 540 (1977); Tribe, *Perspectives on Bakke: Equal Protection, Procedural Fairness or Structural Justice,* 92 Harv.L.Rev. 864 (1979); Vernon, *Due Process Flexibility in Academic Dismissals: Horowitz and Beyond,* 8 J.L. and Educ. 45 (1979); Yudof, *Equal Educational Opportunity and the Courts,* 51 Texas L.Rev. 411 (1973); *Developments in the Law—Equal Protection,* 82 Harv.L.Rev. 1065 (1969); Note, *Reading the Mind of the School Board: Segregative Intent and the De Facto/De Jure Distinction,* 86 Yale L.J. 317 (1976); Note, *Proof of Racially Discriminatory Purpose Under the Equal Protection Clause; Washington v. Davis, Arlington Heights, Mt. Healthy, and Williamsburg,* 12 Harv.C.R.C.L.L.Rev. 725 (1977); Note, *Proving Discriminatory Intent from a Facially Neutral Decision with a Disproportionate Impact,* 36 Wash. & Lee L.Rev. 109 (1979).

tion Agency, supra at 167. In the instant case, it is clear that the most significant official decision maker, the Commissioner of Education, Ralph Turlington, foresaw that the effect of the implementation of the SSAT II would result in greatly disproportionate numbers of black failures. Even in the face of actual statistics regarding the number of black failures on the field tests and the early administrations, the Commissioner persisted in his opinion that the diploma sanction should be implemented in the 1978–1979 school term. This opinion was maintained even after the Report of the Task Force on Educational Assessment Program, also known as the McCrary Report.

The Supreme Court in a recent decision, *Personnel Administrator of Massachusetts v. Feeney*, —— U.S. ——, 99 S.Ct. 2282, 60 L.Ed.2d 870 (1979), discussed the standard for proof of discriminatory intent in a case challenging a veterans preference statute on equal protection grounds. In rejecting a strict foreseeability test, the Court held

"Discriminatory purpose," however, implies more than intent as volition or intent as awareness of consequences. *See United Jewish Organizations v. Carey*, 430 U.S. 144, 179, 97 S.Ct. 996, 1016, 51 L.Ed.2d 229 (concurring opinion). It implies that the decisionmaker, in this case, a state legislature, selected or reaffirmed a particular course of action at least in part "because of," not merely "in spite of," its adverse effects upon an identifiable group. *Id.* at ——, 99 S.Ct. at 2296.

In a footnote, however, the Court conceded that inevitability or foreseeability of a consequence has a bearing on the discriminatory intent. *Id.* note 25, at ——, 99 S.Ct. 2282. While foreseeability was by no means dispositive or the touchstone, it was possible to draw inferences from the action where the adverse consequences were clear and obvious. Whether those inferences, if found, could be dispelled by other legitimate interests was critical to the Court's final determination.

Plaintiffs have not asserted that the Florida legislature in creating the Educational Accountability Act was motivated by racial animus. Plaintiffs, though, have contended that the Commissioner of Education and certain members of the DOE had first hand knowledge of the effects of the test on black school children and the obvious linkage of their performance to the inferior education received during segregation. This information was forwarded to the State Board of Education. The adverse consequences were clear to the State Board of Education at the critical stages of the development and implementation of the SSAT II.

The legitimate interest in implementing a test to evaluate the established state-wide objectives is obvious. The minimal objectives established could be continually upgraded and the test could be utilized not only to gauge achievement, but also to identify deficiencies for the purpose of remediation. The legitimate interests in the test program are substantial, but the timing of the program must be questioned to some extent because it sacrifices through the diploma sanction a large percentage of black twelfth grade students in the rush to implement the legislative mandate. While state Defendants have demonstrated a disregard of the reasons for the disproportionate black failure (i. e. the inferior education received during segregation and the dearth of interim remediation), the Court has not been presented with sufficient proof that the motivation for implementing the program was in *Feeney* terms "because of" the large black failure statistics. [The *Feeney* decision was announced after the trial in this case was completed and neither party addressed the issue of intent beyond that posed in *United States v. Texas Education Agency, supra, Washington v. Davis, supra*, and *Arlington Heights, supra*. The analysis of the instant decision is not affected by *Feeney* beyond the question of intent because the Supreme Court has held that neutral mechanisms (i. e. tests) with discriminatory effects are to be analyzed in the same vein as overtly discriminatory mechanisms (i. e. veterans preferences). *Feeney, supra*, —— U.S. at ——, 99 S.Ct. 2282.] Although the proof of present intent to discriminate is insufficient, the Court is of the opinion that past purposeful discrimination affecting Plaintiffs in Classes B and C is perpetuated by the test and the diploma sanction regardless of its neutrality.

The Supreme Court on numerous occasions has invalidated facially neutral programs which perpetuate past racial discrimination. *Louisiana v. U. S.*, 380 U.S. 145, 85 S.Ct. 817, 13 L.Ed.2d 709 (1965); *Guinn v. U. S.*, 238 U.S. 347, 35 S.Ct. 926, 59 L.Ed. 1340 (1915). In *Gaston County v. United States*, 395 U.S. 285, 89 S.Ct. 1720, 23 L.Ed.2d 309 (1969), the Supreme Court held that the use of a literacy test as a method of qualifying voters in North Carolina perpetuated the past denial of equal educational opportunities. Although the decision was premised on the interpretation of the Voting Rights Act of 1965, the Court addressed a number of issues similar to those presented in the instant case. The Supreme Court focused particularly on the history of educational discrimination in North Carolina finding the "historic maintenance of a dual school system, but [also] . . . substantial evidence that the County deprived its black residents of equal educational opportunit[y]". *Id.* at 291, 89 S.Ct. at 1723. In finding "it is only reasonable to infer that among black children compelled to endure a segregated and inferior education, fewer will achieve any given degree of literacy than will their better-educated white contemporaries", the Court held "[I]mpartial administration of the literacy test today would serve only to perpetuate the inequities in a different form". *Id.* at 295, 297, 89 S.Ct. at 1725, 1726. The Fifth Circuit has followed the guidance of the Supreme Court in the perpetuation area. *Kirksey v. Board of Supervisors of Hinds County*, 528 F.2d 536 (5th Cir. 1976), *rev'd en banc*, 554 F.2d 139 (5th Cir. 1977); *Meredith v. Fair*, 298 F.2d 696 (5th Cir. 1962). Several of the recent Fifth Circuit decisions are worthy of close consideration. In *McNeal v. Tate*, 508

F.2d 1017 (5th Cir. 1975), and in *United States v. Gadsden County School District*, 572 F.2d 1049 (5th Cir. 1978), the Fifth Circuit considered the constitutionality *vel non* of ability groupings in public schools.[18] In both cases, the ability groupings, which were derived by teacher evaluation and standardized testing, resulted in a high concentration of white students in the upper division or advanced classes and a high concentration of black students in the lower divisions. The *McNeal* Court focused particularly on the nexus between the inferior education in the dual system and the present ability categorization. Regardless of the fact that the ability groupings fostered segregation, the Court in *McNeal* proceeded with an analysis which, if proved, would legitimize the segregation. The Court stated:

If it does cause segregation, whether in classrooms or in schools, ability grouping may nevertheless be permitted in an otherwise unitary system if the . . . method is not based on the present results of past segregation or will remedy such results through better educational opportunities. *McNeal, supra* at 1020.
. . . The testing rationale of both *Singleton*[19] and *Lemon*[20] would bar the use of this method of assignment until the district has operated as a unitary [school] system without such assignments for a sufficient period of time to assure that the underachievement of the slower groups is not due to yesterday's educational disparities. Such a bar period may be lifted when the district can show that steps taken to bring disadvantaged students to peer status have ended the educational disadvantages caused by prior segregation. *McNeal, supra* at 1020–21.

Florida public schools in the main have been physically unitary since 1971. Although the human problems recounted in a previous section have limited the full appre-

---

18. The Court will address the application of *McNeal* and *Gadsden County* again in Section VI(B) of this Memorandum Opinion relative to the Plaintiffs' allegation that the results of the SSAT II were being used for purposes of resegregation.

19. *Singleton v. Jackson Municipal Separate School District*, 419 F.2d 1211 (5th Cir. 1969).

20. *Lemon v. Bossier Parish School Board*, 444 F.2d 1400 (5th Cir. 1971).

ciation of the benefits of a unitary education, the conditions were not such that the system cannot be called unitary. The Defendants have failed to rebut the fact that the disproportionate failure of Class B and C Plaintiffs on the SSAT II resulted from the inferior education they received during the dual school system portion of their education. Defendants have stressed the third component of *McNeal* and contend the SSAT II, the diploma sanction, and the remediation program will remedy the past effects of discrimination through better educational opportunities. The Defendants emphasized the increase in the percentage of Plaintiffs in Class B and C who have passed the test since its first administration. While the increased passing rate is impressive and Florida teachers and students are to be commended for their achievement, the Court has serious reservations about attaching a constitutional imprimatur to a program which penalizes students who have been denied equal educational opportunity. Certainly the Court wishes that every student could and would pass the SSAT II, but it is not so naive as to assume that there will not be failure regardless of the nature of the test or its takers. Yet failure premised on equal educational opportunities, unaffected by the dual school system of the past is of a completely different genre than that presented in the instant case.

In *Green v. County School Board of New Kent County*, 391 U.S. 430, 88 S.Ct. 1689, 20 L.Ed.2d 716 (1968), the Supreme Court reflected upon the import of *Brown* I and II.

It was such a dual systems that 14 years ago *Brown* I held unconstitutional and a year later *Brown* II held must be abolished; school boards operating [under] such school systems were *required* by *Brown* II "to effectuate a transition to a racially nondiscriminatory school system". *Green* at 435, 88 S.Ct. at 1693.

Brown II was a call for the dismantling of well-entrenched dual systems tempered by an awareness that complex and multifaceted problems would arise which would require time and flexibility for a successful resolution. School boards such

as the respondent then operating state-compelled dual systems were nevertheless clearly charged with the affirmative duty to take whatever steps might be necessary to convert a unitary system in which racial discrimination would be eliminated root and branch. *Green, supra* at 437–438, 88 S.Ct. at 1694.

After *Green* not only was it necessary to eliminate physical segregation of public schools, but it was also necessary to eliminate the effects of such purposeful discrimination. *Swann v. Charlotte-Mecklenburg Board of Education*, 402 U.S. 1, 91 S.Ct. 1267, 28 L.Ed.2d 554 (1971). The Supreme Court's decisions in *Columbus Board of Education v. Penick*, —— U.S. ——, 99 S.Ct. 2941, 61 L.Ed.2d 666 (1979) and *Dayton Board of Education v. Brinkman*, —— U.S. ——, 99 S.Ct. 2971, 61 L.Ed.2d 720 (1979) confirm the Court's analysis in this regard. The Supreme Court in *Dayton* and *Columbus* focused on past purposeful segregation in public schools and the effects of such action. The reiteration by the Supreme Court of the affirmative duty to remedy the effects of segregative policies and practices announced in *Brown* II and followed in *Green, Swann, Columbus* and *Dayton* is of particular significance. In the instant case, the principal effect of the dual school system was the inferior education given black school children. The evidence indicates that black school children, in the language of *McNeal* "still wear [the] badge of their old deprivation—underachievement". *McNeal, supra* at 1019. The effects of racial isolation and the deprivation of equal educational opportunities are again and again cited by Florida school districts in applications for federal funds for educational remediation. While there has been a substantial, but recent effort to eradicate the learning deficits created during the dual school period, the goals of such programs have not been achieved. The results on three administrations of the SSAT II evidence this fact.

The evidence and the ratios of passage of the SSAT II, both numerically and proportionately, indicate that race more than any other factor, including socio-economic status, is a predictor of success on the test. The fact that 20% of the black students failed the SSAT II compared to only 1.9% of the white students indicates that peer status has not been achieved. In the Court's opinion, punishing the victims of past discrimination for deficits created by an inferior educational environment neither constitutes a remedy nor creates better educational opportunities. When students regardless of race are permitted to commence and pursue their education in a unitary school system without the taint of the dual school system, then a graduation requirement based on a neutral test will be permitted. The Court must conclude that utilization of the SSAT II in the present context as a requirement for the receipt of a high school diploma is a violation of the equal protection clause of the Fourteenth Amendment, 42 U.S.C. § 2000d, and 20 U.S.C. § 1703. The Court will discuss in a subsequent section the nature and duration of the injunctive relief to be extended to the Plaintiffs in Classes B and C.

E. THE DEVELOPMENT AND VALIDITY OF THE TEST INSTRUMENT

1. *Introduction*

In this section the Court will consider the manner in which the test was developed and its validity from both a constitutional and professional testing perspective. The Court is considering the claims in this section as they relate to Classes A, B, and C. The Court will additionally address the effects of the public perceptions of the test as opposed to the state's definition and perceptions of the test. Certain related issues, such as curricular validity and whether the tests were equated, will be discussed in Section V.

2. *Test Development*

When the Educational Accountability Act became effective on July 1, 1976, it included a provision which required satisfactory performance on an examination of functional literacy for high school graduation in the school year 1978–1979. Fla.Stat. § 232.-245(3) (1977). Although the State Board of Education (i. e. the Governor and Florida Cabinet) was statutorily authorized to approve of the design of the test, the task of formulating a test of functional literacy fell upon the Florida Department of Education.

At the time of the passage of the legislation, the DOE was presented with a formidable task, that of designing a test to meet the scanty legislative language within the strict time limitations established. While the DOE had been working for some time on state-wide objectives for basic skills, it had not been oriented toward designing a functional literacy test. In fact, the Director of the Student Assessment Section of DOE, Dr. Thomas Fisher, summed up the problem in a letter to Senator Donnell C. Childers:

> It is also apparent that most educators have not thought in terms of functional (i. e. practical or applied) skills for high school students, therefore the Department of Education does not have a preexistent set of functional objectives which may be assessed.

> This creates a situation in which we must either create such objectives and then construct matching tests or purchase an existing test thus simultaneously adopting the matching objectives. In other words, in the first case, we define what Florida students should learn and measure it. In the second case, a commercial company tells us what Florida students should learn and this is then measured. Exhibit CT–396.

Soon after this letter, the DOE decided upon objectives for the functional literacy test. Basically, the objectives enumerated in December, 1976, were the practical applications of eleven reading and writing eleventh grade basic skills and thirteen mathematics eleventh grade basic skills. At the same time the objectives were decided upon, the DOE contracted with the Educational Testing Service to draft specific items or questions to match the objectives.

During the period from June, 1976, to February, 1977, the DOE staff was continuing to debate on exactly what "functional literacy" meant. A final definition was promulgated by the DOE on February 18, 1977.

For purposes of compliance with the Accountability Act of 1976, functional literacy is the satisfactory application of basic skills in reading, writing and arithmetic, to problems and tasks of a practical nature as encountered in everyday life. Exhibit CT–332.

A slight modification of this definition appeared subsequently in both the State Board of Education Rules and the 1978 amendments to the Educational Accountability Act. *Rules and Regulations of the State of Florida*, Chapter 6A–1.942(2)(a) (1978); Fla.Stat. § 232.246(1)(b) (1978 Supp.).

In March, 1977, the Educational Testing Service provided the DOE with sample items. The DOE at the same time leased several items from another commercial testing company. A field test was conducted in the latter part of March, 1977, in five Florida counties. After the field test, the DOE entered into a contract with the Educational Testing Service to write item specifications from the items or questions previously drafted. An item specification is essentially a blueprint for a particular question which permits an item writer to design numerous questions using the same assessment criteria but with different factual contexts.

The functional literacy examination which was administered in October, 1977, contained 117 questions covering the twenty-four skill objectives. The test is a criterion-referenced examination; that is, one designed to assess whether the taker has a mastery or competence in the particular skills tested. The functional literacy examination was not designed to rank students vis-a-vis other students, although it obviously sorts out passers and failers by use of a cut-score. The test was created to evaluate achievement in those skills which the DOE and the State Board of Education deemed necessary to meet the legislative mandate of functional literacy.

After the initial administration of the functional literacy test, the DOE contracted with National Evaluation Systems to design additional test items. Utilizing the item specifications created by the Educational Testing Center, National Education Systems produced 240 additional test questions in January, 1978. Those items were field tested in the Spring of 1978.

The test and the item specifications are secure documents. The DOE has labored continuously since the creation of the test to make certain that no test is either stolen or reproduced. Although there have been several breaches of the security precautions, the test has remained, except to eleventh and twelfth grade public school students, a well kept secret.

Before discussing the validity issues, the Court must refer to a matter which is at the crux of the controversy between the litigants. The test as legislatively created was to be one of functional literacy. Functional literacy has not been defined in a way which is acceptable to either all educational academicians or the public. The testimony, in fact, indicates that there are at least eleven known definitions of functional literacy. What is functional literacy to one person may not be functional literacy to another person, but it is clear that the term "functional illiterate" has a universally negative inference and connotation. While "*illiteracy*" is itself a negative and impact ladened word, "*functional illiteracy*" further compounds these implications by focusing on the individual's inability to operate effectively in society. The categorizing of an individual without reference to a specific standard can be both detrimental and debilitating without justification. As one of the Plaintiffs' experts commented, students who fail the functional literacy test perceive of themselves as "global failures". Another of the Plaintiffs' experts testified that the biggest flaw in the Florida program was its name alone. The Court is in complete agreement. Beyond the economic and academic implications of failure on the test, the stigma associated with the term functional illiteracy is the most substantial harm presented.

While the Court recognizes this, problem, it cannot be oblivious to the definition of functional literacy provided by the DOE, ratified by the State Board of Education, and legislatively approved. While the meaning of functional literacy is clear to the reader of the amended statute or the Rules of the State Board of Education, it is not to the Florida public. In an attempt to escape the impact of the terminology utilized in the original statute, the State Board of Education adopted a new name for the functional literacy test: the State Student Assessment Test II (SSAT II). Still the test remains the Florida functional literacy examination in the mind of the public and the name change has not dispelled the implications of the original denomination. Regardless of how the public perceives the test, the Court must analyze it from the definition [21] provided by the state in conjunction with the twenty-four objectives.[22] The Court must not permit public perceptions to be the guide for statutory interpretation.

Prior to analyzing the evidence presented concerning the validity of the test, it is critical to understand the applicable legal

21. See Exhibit CT-332, quoted at page 258 supra.

22. Rules and Regulations of the State of Florida, Chapter 6A-1.942(2)(a) (1978) provides:
(2) State Student Assessment Test—Part II
(a) . . . The test shall be:
1. Designed to measure the student's ability to successfully apply basic skills to everyday life situations.
2. Composed of two (2) standards, one (1) comprising functional communication skills and one (1) comprising functional mathematics skills, as follows:
(a) Communications.
The student will, in a real world situation, determine the main idea inferred from a selection.
The student will, in a real world situation, find who, what, where, which, and how information in a selection.
The student will, in a real world situation, determine the inferred cause and effect of an action.
The student will, in a real world situation, distinguish between facts and opinions.
The student will, in a real world situation, identify an unstated opinion.
The student will, in a real world situation, identify the appropriate source to obtain information on a topic.
The student will, in a real world situation, use an index to identify the location of information requiring the use of cross-references.
The student will use highway and city maps.
The student will include the necessary information when writing letters to supply or request information.
The student will complete a check and its stub accurately.
The student will accurately complete forms used to apply for a driver's license, employment, entrance to a school or training program, insurance, and credit.
b. Mathematics

The student will determine the elapsed time between two (2) events stated in seconds, minutes, hours, days, weeks, months, or years.
The student will determine equivalent amounts of up to one hundred dollars ($100.00) using coins and paper currency.
The student will determine the solution to real world problems involving one (1) or two (2) distinct whole number operations.
The student will determine the solution to real world problems involving decimal fractions or percents and one (1) or two (2) distinct operations.
The student will determine the solution to real world problems involving comparison shopping.
The student will determine the solution to real world problems involving rate of interest and the estimation of the amount of simple interest.
The student will determine the solution to real world problems involving purchases and a rate of sales tax.
The student will determine the solution to real world problems involving purchases and a rate of discount given in fraction or percent form.
The student will solve a problem related to length, width, or height using metric or customary units up to kilometers and miles, conversion within the system.
The student will solve a problem involving the area of a rectangular region using metric or customary units.
The student will solve a problem involving capacity using units given in a table (milliliters, liters, teaspoons, cups, pints, quarts, gallons), conversion within the system.
The student will solve a problem involving weight using units given in a table (milligrams, grams, kilograms, metric tons, ounces, pounds, tons), conversion within the system.
The student will read and determine relationships described by line graphs, circle graphs, and tables.

standards. The Plaintiffs contend that the test is violative of both the due process clause and equal protection clause of the Fourteenth Amendment. Under the Plaintiffs' due process analysis, if the test were shown to be arbitrary and unreasonable, then the Court would be compelled to invalidate it. *Thompson v. Gallagher*, 489 F.2d 443 (5th Cir. 1973). Similarly, if the test by dividing students into two categories, passers and failers, did so without a rational relation to the purpose for which it was designed, then the Court would be compelled to find the test unconstitutional. *Reed v. Reed*, 404 U.S. 71, 92 S.Ct. 251, 30 L.Ed.2d 225 (1971); *Lindsley v. Natural Carbonic Gas Co.* 220 U.S. 61, 31 S.Ct. 337, 55 L.Ed. 369 (1911). While the Court can find no decision which is directly on point, several recent decisions involving the utilization of tests for employment purposes warrant consideration. In *Griggs v. Duke Power Co.*, 401 U.S. 424, 91 S.Ct. 849, 28 L.Ed.2d 158 (1971), the Supreme Court focused on the statutory language in Title VII of the Civil Rights Act to prohibit the utilization of required tests for purposes of employment which have a discriminatory impact if they are unrelated to job qualification or performance. In a case decided solely on constitutional grounds, the Fifth Circuit in *Armstead v. Starkville Municipal Separate School District*, 461 F.2d 276 (5th Cir. 1972) decided that the use of the Graduate Record Examination (GRE) for hiring and retention of high school teachers was unconstitutional. Finding that the GRE scores created an absolute classification of teachers into two categories, those qualified and those unqualified, the Court then proceeded to determine whether the test was a valid and reliable mechanism for making such a decision. In finding that it was not reasonably related to its purpose, the Court held:

> We agree with the lower Court's finding that GRE score requirement was not a reliable or valid measure for choosing good teachers. It was undisputed that the GRE was not designed to and could not measure the competency of a teacher or even indicate future teacher effective-

ness. However, it was established that the cut-off score would eliminate some good teachers. Consequently we find that it has no reasonable function in the teacher selection process. *Armstead, supra* at 280.

[3] In the instant case, the Court must determine whether the test utilized was a valid and reasonable measure for dividing students into classifications for the purpose of high school graduation. While the Courts in *Griggs* and *Armstead* concerned themselves with the job relatedness facet of the test, the Court in this case can only be concerned with whether the test reasonably or arbitrarily evaluates the skill objectives established by the State Board of Education. Thus, the Court must not focus on the title of the test or the public perceptions of functional literacy, but rather must analyze the test from the perspective of its objectives and the definition provided by its designers.

Both parties agree that the functional literacy test should have content validity, but they disagree as to whether the test does, in fact, have content validity.

Evidence of content validity is required when the test user wishes to estimate how an individual performs in the universe of situations the test is intended to represent. Content validity is most commonly evaluated for tests of skill or knowledge; . . .

To demonstrate the content validity of a set of test scores, one must show that the behaviors demonstrated in testing constitute a representative sample of behaviors to be exhibited in a desired performance domain. American Psychological Association, *Standards for Educational and Psychological Tests*, 28 (1974).

The Plaintiffs have persistently contended that the Florida test domain or the boundary for the designated skills or knowledge does not match any definition of functional literacy. While the Court would agree that the domain of the Florida test does not equate with every definition of functional literacy or for that matter with many definitions, it does match the one given by the

DOE and the State Board of Education. It would also appear that the Florida legislature is satisfied with the manner in which the State Board of Education has fulfilled its mandate. The Court is satisfied that the skill objectives of the Florida test are adequately evaluated by the test items and that the test has adequate content validity.

Whether the functional literacy test has or needs to have construct validity is another disputed issue. The Plaintiffs contend that the test must have construct validity and it does not. The Defendants contend that construct validity is not essential for the test, but it has it anyway. A construct is a "theoretical idea developed to explain and organize some aspects of existing knowledge". *Id.* at 29. Certainly "functional literacy" is, in the abstract, like "anxiety" or "clerical ability" a construct. Functional literacy in the instant case, however, is a construct about which only limited hypotheses can be made. The definition of functional literacy provided by the state does not attempt to address and resolve all the many hypotheses which can be made about functional literacy. In the Court's evaluation it need not. Particularly instructive of this fact is a statement found in the construct validity section of the American Psychological Association's Standards covering testing.

> It is important to note in this that the investigation of construct validity refers to a specific test and not necessarily to any other test given the same label. *Id.* at 30.

Thus while other states may design tests of functional literacy, they need not all conceive of functional literacy in the same fashion for their tests to have construct validity. A construct is always capable of definition and the measure of a test's construct validity is whether the hypotheses made about the defined construct will predict behavior. In the instant case, the Court is satisfied that the Florida test has adequate construct validity.

The Court has also considered the other alleged flaws [23] in the test development and instrument and find them to be without constitutional merit. The educational experts presented by the Plaintiffs have given the Court an education in "state of the art" educational measurement and testing. But the "state of the art" is not to be equated with the constitutional standards for Fourteenth Amendment due process and equal protection review. The Court is of the opinion the functional literacy test bears a rational relation to a valid state interest and thus is constitutional.

F. TEST ITEMS BIAS

[4] The Plaintiffs contend that the functional literacy test consists of racially biased test questions or items which are less likely to be correctly answered by black students than by white students.

The evidence indicates that the professional testing companies which wrote the items for the functional literacy test reviewed the items for possible racial or ethnic bias. Additionally the DOE staff with the assistance of groups of teachers analyzed the test questions for possible racial bias. The DOE also commissioned a scatter plot analysis of the test to determine the possibility of item bias. While some of the questions do seem to have factual settings unfamiliar to certain racial groups, the

---

23. The Plaintiffs mounted a frontal assault upon a number of practices and procedures utilized by the DOE in the design and implementation of the test. Among the flaws asserted and considered were: the failure of DOE to solicit public input into the design of the test and its definition; the drafting of item specifications after the writing of items; the continual use by DOE of definitions of functional literacy extraneous and inconsistent with the official definition; the inadequacy of the research prior to the selection of a cut-score; the questionable research methodology of the Defendants' construct validity study; the failure to follow the APA standards for the design and implementation of tests which affect the lives of the takers in a significant fashion; the failure of DOE to adequately publicize what the test is and its inherent limitations; the inadequacy of the form notice sent to parents and students regarding the interpretations of scores on the test; the reliability of the test. While some of the above mentioned flaws were indeed errors of considerable magnitude, they do not cross either individually or collectively the line between inadequacy and constitutional infirmity.

Court is of the opinion that this distraction is minimal and unpervasive. The Court is not convinced by the Plaintiffs' evidence that the test or any item should be invalidated for racial or ethnic bias.

G. THE APPLICATION OF THE SSAT II TO PRIVATE SCHOOLS

1. Introduction

The Plaintiffs contend that the application of the SSAT II testing program to only public schools is a violation of the equal protection and due process clauses of the Fourteenth Amendment. The Plaintiffs have set forth several arguments in this regard. Plaintiffs in Classes B and C first contend that the application of the test to only public schools creates a racial classification. Because of black students' financial inability to attend private schools, they are unable to escape the effect of the test as readily as many white students. Plaintiffs in all classes contend that the application of the test to only public schools does not bear a rational relationship to the alleged purpose of the legislation. Plaintiffs on this ground assert that the state has an interest in assuring that *all* of its students, not just public school students, receive instruction in basic practical application skills.

2. Private Schools in Florida

Private schools in Florida today educate approximately 10% of the school age students. Prior to desegregation, 8% of the school age children attended private schools. This relative increase in attendance at private schools has outpaced the growth of the state population. In 1960, black students composed 4% of the students attending private schools. By 1970, the percentage of black students in private schools had increased to 5%. Thus at present, approximately 95% of the students attending private schools are white. The racial composition of Florida public schools is 20% black students and 80% white students.

3. The State Regulation of Florida Private Schools

Florida private schools are regulated only to a minimal degree. The principal form of regulation is found in Fla.Stat. § 229.808 which requires annual registration. The entire registration process consists of filing a form with only four questions: "the name and address of the institution, names of administrative officers, enrollment, and number of teachers." *Id.* at § 229.808(1). The exemptions to the registration act essentially void its limited effectiveness. *Id.* at § 229.808(2). Besides registration, private schools' only other state imposed regulation is that they keep attendance records. Fla.Stat. §§ 232.02, 232.021.

The State of Florida does not regulate any substantive matter affecting education in private schools. There are no regulations regarding instruction in basic skills or in any way mandating a curriculum. The State of Florida does not accredit private schools and does not require them to be accredited by any professional accrediting association. Instruction in Florida private schools need not be in English, in fact, at least ten schools in Dade County which grant diplomas give instruction in Spanish. Additionally, one school in West Florida teaches its students in Urdu (a Pakistani language). A graduation diploma from any Florida private school meets the state's employment criteria for jobs requiring a diploma. Likewise, a diploma from a Florida private school will meet the initial requirement for admission to one of Florida's state universities.

4. Constitutionality

[5] The Plaintiffs in Classes B and C have attempted to align race with the financial inability (i. e. lack of wealth) to attend private schools. From this alignment, the Plaintiffs would urge application of strict scrutiny to the legislative decision not to apply the SSAT II to private schools. Such an analysis is constitutionally without merit.

[6] The Supreme Court in *San Antonio Independent School District v. Rodriguez,* 411 U.S. 1, 93 S.Ct. 1278, 36 L.Ed.2d 16 (1978) held that classifications based on

wealth were not constitutionally suspect, thus not requiring strict scrutiny. The ability to attend private schools is clearly affected by the student's or his parents' financial resources. While it is also clear that blacks in America, as a class, are without substantial financial resources, these two categories, wealth and race, do not merge in this instance into one suspect classification. Quite often decisions of legislative or administrative bodies affect certain groups disproportionately. This alone does not signal strict scrutiny. *New York City Transit Authority v. Beazer,* 440 U.S. 568, 99 S.Ct. 1355, 59 L.Ed.2d 587 (1979).

[7] The legislative decision to apply the SSAT II only to public schools also passes constitutional muster under the rational relation analysis. As the Supreme Court stated in *Ambach v. Norwick,* 441 U.S. 68, 99 S.Ct. 1589, 60 L.Ed.2d 49 (1979), "[t]he State has a stronger interest in ensuring that the schools it most directly controls, and for which it bears the cost, are as effective as possible . . . ." *Id.* note 8, 99 S.Ct. at 1595. The state need not correct all the problems of education in one clean sweep, but can attack the problems it identifies in a logical fashion. The decision made in the instant case to apply the SSAT II only to public schools over which the state already had significant curricular, instructional, and financial control was both reasonable and constitutional.

Whether the state could require the taking and passage of the SSAT II for a diploma in private schools and subsidize the cost is not the question presented herein. The Supreme Court will address this issue in its next term. *Committee for Public Education and Religious Liberty v. Levitt,* 461 F.Supp. 1123 (S.D.N.Y.1978) *cert. granted,* 440 U.S. 978, 99 S.Ct. 1785, 60 L.Ed.2d 238 (1979).

V

SECOND CLAIM

A. INTRODUCTION

[8] In this section, the Court will consider the allegations of the Plaintiffs in all classes in the second count of the complaint concerning the adequacy of the notice prior to and since the implementation of the functional literacy testing program. The Court will also consider the adequacy of the time to prepare for the examination after the objectives were first established. The Plaintiffs' allegations in this claim state that the schedule imposed by the Defendants violated their Fourteenth Amendment due process rights.

While the Court in Section IV has discussed the development of the test instrument itself, the Court in this section will review the development of the test in relation to the testing objectives, the implementation schedule and the state-wide, in-school instruction. The Court will also consider in this section whether the test instruments were equated.

B. THE TESTING SCHEDULE

In April, 1977, the State Board of Education formally approved the DOE draft of the Minimum Student Performance Standards. The Standards established objectives for instruction in mathematics and communication skills for grades 3, 5, 8 and 11. The functional literacy objectives were derived from eleventh grade basic skills objectives. While there had been considerable in-put from public school teachers during the development of the basic skills objectives, the DOE staff designed all the functional literacy objectives without external assistance. Basically, the DOE staff redesigned twenty-four of the basic skill objectives so that they would present the objectives in practical application contexts. During the summer of 1977, the DOE distributed to all Florida public schools the basic skill and functional literacy objectives. It thus appears that public school teachers were aware of the objectives of the functional literacy examination four months in advance of the first administration of the test, but only two months were available for instruction in the application of the skills. The results of the first administration reflect the obvious inadequacy of the prior instruction in the stated objectives.

From December, 1977, the date the results of the first administration were released, until April, 1979, the date the third and last administration was held, only thirteen months of instructional time intervened. During this period remediation classes for those students who failed were held in almost every Florida county. The DOE had designed instructional materials to assist in the remediation programs, but those materials were not immediately available. During the Spring of 1978, the remediation programs with the assistance of state funds were working effectively. The programs for remediation in most counties are presently on-going and have received additional state funding.

C. INSTRUCTION IN FLORIDA PUBLIC SCHOOLS

Aside from the questions of the sufficiency of the instruction since the announcement of the functional literacy objectives and the adequacy of the time to prepare for the objectives, the Court must inquire into the instruction of the objectives prior to the implementation of the act. Historically, Florida public education has been administered solely by sixty-seven autonomous county school boards. Each school board controlled the design of the curriculum, the selection of the required textbooks and the establishment of graduation requirements. With local school boards in a controlling position, the interests of the county and their particular region of the state would dictate educational emphasis. The nuances of instruction and objectives would differ greatly between the various counties. The texts used in Florida counties varied a great deal. There was no uniformity as to the selection of instructional materials until very recently. Even now when the DOE approves several texts for use for individual courses in the schools, no one text contains all of the functional literacy objectives. In fact, a review of several texts is necessary for complete instruction in the mathematics or communications functional literacy objectives. After the adoption of the 1968 Florida Constitution, the legislature and the DOE began to play a more centralized role

in the education of Florida public school children. The DOE began to plan for basic skill objectives in 1972–1973 and implemented testing programs to evaluate the success of such instruction, but throughout the period of the Plaintiffs' education, the individual counties remained the single most important entities for the design and implementation of instructional programs and the selection of textbooks.

This problem is indicative of a much larger issue. Although there is evidence that certain skills were not taught in Florida public schools, let us assume *arguendo* that all the skills were taught. The atmosphere of the instruction prior to the implementation of the basic skills and functional literacy objectives was neutral and devoid of the present objectives. While all instruction is important, there are obvious methods of motivating students and emphasizing certain skills. The principal problem with the instant program is that the instruction in previous years took place in an atmosphere without the specific objectives now present and without the diploma sanction. Instruction of the skills necessary to successfully complete the functional literacy test is a cumulative and time consuming process. Knowledge of how to successfully perform the functional literacy skills is not taught in any specific grade, in any specific class, or from any specific type of teacher. It is critical that at the time of instruction of a functional literacy skill, the student knows that the individual skill he is being taught must be learned prior to his graduation from a Florida public school. Instruction in the specific skills is critical, but likewise so is identification of whether the skills have been learned. Teaching and learning are not always coterminous. Fla.Stat. § 236.-088. Until recently, there was no statewide testing program to evaluate learning and to direct remediation.

The Plaintiffs' expert witnesses testified that the principal problem with the testing program was not the diploma sanction or the announcement of state-wide objectives but the implementation schedule. The Court is in agreement that the present program of instruction in specific basic skill and functional applications with periodic testing to identify both mastery and deficiencies is a step forward. It sets objectives, defines goals, evaluates achievement and, if necessary, remediates deficiencies. The program acclimates students to standardized testing and will relieve some of the immense pressure when it comes time to take the functional literacy examination. The benefits of the overall program inure differentially to those students who have been in the system for longer periods of time. But as asserted by one of the Plaintiffs' witnesses, "the functional literacy program was a test looking for a plan of instruction".

The Report of Task Force on Educational Assessment Programs, which was appointed by the State Board of Education, summarized the timing problems in the following fashion:

> The problems created by the abrupt schedule for implementing the Functional Literacy Test were most severe for the members of Florida high school graduation class of 1979. At the eleventh hour and with virtually no warning, these students were told that the requirements for graduation had been changed. They were suddenly required to pass a test constructed under the pressure of time and covering content that was presumed to be elementary but that their schools may or may not have taught them recently, well, or perhaps at all.
>
> In retrospect, the Task Force believes that the schedule for implementing statewide high school graduation standards was too severe. We feel that most of the problems that are identified in later sections of this report are the result of trying to do too much in too little time. Consequently, we believe that the problems can and will be solved over time. Task Force on Educational Assessment Programs, *Competency Testing in Florida Report to the Florida Cabinet (Part 1)* 4 (1979).

While the problems identified by the Court and the Task Force are major issues, they are compounded by requiring passage of the functional literacy examination for graduation. If the functional literacy testing program were designed to evaluate skills to aid in remediation alone, then the Court would not find the program suspect in any fashion not already identified. While the Defendants contend the diploma sanction is an essential facet of the program which increases the stimulus to learn and the motivation to achieve, the Plaintiffs contend that the diploma sanction is a punitive measure which is excessive and not the least restrictive manner in which to achieve the goals identified by the state. In *Mahavongsanan v. Hall*, 529 F.2d 448 (5th Cir. 1976), the Fifth Circuit considered the application of due process standards to the denial of an academic degree. In that case the Plaintiff, who was pursuing a graduate degree in education, objected on constitutional and contractual grounds to the university's decision to require a comprehensive examination for receipt of the degree after the commencement of her studies. While the Fifth Circuit reversed the District Court's grant of injunctive relief, it did so on the basis of an analysis of the facts. The Court, in doing so, implicitly acknowledged that termination for academic reasons created a due process right to timely notice.

The Supreme Court in *Board of Curators of the University of Missouri v. Horowitz*, 435 U.S. 78, 98 S.Ct. 948, 55 L.Ed.2d 124 (1978), decided last term that Charlotte Horowitz, the Plaintiff, who had been terminated from medical school for academic reasons, had been afforded ample due process and refused to require a pre-termination hearing. In support of the constitutional ruling, the Court singled out the manifest problems with the intervention of the judiciary into the realm of academic evaluation. Although the Court in a footnote cited with approval the statement that " '[t]here is a clear dichotomy between the student's due process rights in disciplinary dismissals and academic dismissals' ", the distinction between what the rights of the two classes of individuals are is not clearly and unequivocally drawn.

In *Horowitz* the Plaintiff had been evaluated in her clinical rotations by a number of physicians in addition to having her work supervised and critiqued by her chief docent. The Plaintiff received repeated warnings of her substandard performance and was placed on academic probation by the Council of Evaluation, a group of physicians and medical students who reviewed academic performance. After further review and recommendations the Council of Evaluation decided that the Plaintiff should not be permitted to graduate. This decision was approved by the Coordinating Committee and the Dean of the Medical School and was also sustained by the University's Provost for Health Services. Considering the practical problems with judicial reevaluation of academic performance and the facts relative to Ms. Horowitz's particular case, the Court decided that the Plaintiff had received adequate due process and a pretermination hearing was not necessary.

The practical problems in *Horowitz* were manifest. Sifting through an individual student's past clinical record, rehashing physician evaluations, and litigating bedside manner were problems foreign to judicial expertise. The factual context in the instant case is very different. The Court is not asked to evaluate an individual student's performance, but to resolve a dispute involving the legislative decision to implement a test which determines graduation from high school with the standard credential, a diploma. While the factual inquiry is considerably different so are the parties. The Plaintiff in *Horowitz* was pursuing graduate education in advanced studies. The Plaintiffs in all classes in the instant case were participating in secondary education required by the state compulsory education law. Fla.Stat. § 232.01 *et seq.* Although some of the Plaintiffs are beyond the sixteen year age limitation in the Florida Statute, the majority of the time they have spent in the Florida public schools was required.

The Court is convinced that the Plaintiffs in Classes A, B, and C have a property right in graduation from high school with a standard diploma if they have fulfilled the present requirements for graduation exclusive of the SSAT II requirement (i. e. successful performance on the SSAT I and completion of the necessary number of credits). *Goss v. Lopez*, 419 U.S. 565, 95 S.Ct. 729, 42 L.Ed.2d 725 (1975). The Supreme Court in *Goss* recognized that even the suspension of a student for one day infringed upon the students' property right in attending school. Students in Florida are required to attend school pursuant to the state's compulsory attendance statute. Fla.Stat. § 232.01 *et seq.* Graduation is the logical extension of successful attendance. While the state has redefined in a sense what successful attendance for purposes of a diploma should be, the Court is of the opinion that the SSAT II requirement should be excluded for the same reasons that the notice of the test has been shown to be inadequate. The Court is also of the opinion that the Plaintiffs have a liberty interest in being free of the adverse stigma associated with the certificate of completion. *Wisconsin v. Constantineau*, 400 U.S. 433, 91 S.Ct. 507, 27 L.Ed.2d 515 (1971). This stigma is very real and will affect the economic and psychological development of the individual. Although public disclosure of the different graduation credentials did not occur this year, the only reason for this was a settlement between the parties so as to avoid the necessity of the Court hearing preliminary injunction motions during the middle of the trial.

[9] Due process has and always will be a flexible standard dependent upon the facts and circumstances of each individual case. *Cafeteria & Restaurant Workers Union v. McElroy*, 367 U.S. 886, 81 S.Ct. 1743, 6 L.Ed.2d 1230 (1961).

" '[D]ue process,' unlike some legal rules is not a technical conception with a fixed content unrelated to time, place and circumstances." It is "compounded of history, reason, the past course of decisions." *Id.* at 895, 81 S.Ct. at 1748 (quoting *Joint Anti-Fascist Refugee Committee v. McGrath*, 341 U.S. 123, 162, 71 S.Ct. 624, 643–644, 95 L.Ed. 817 (1951)).

The Court finds the facts in the instant case compelling. The Plaintiffs, after spending ten years in schools where their attendance was compelled, were informed of a requirement concerning skills which, if taught, should have been taught in grades they had long since completed. While it is impossible to determine if all the skills were taught to all the students, it is obvious that the instruction given was not presented in an educational atmosphere directed by the existence of specific objectives and stimulated throughout the period of instruction by a diploma sanction. These are the two ingredients which the Defendants assert are essential to the program at the present time. The Court is of the opinion that the inadequacy of the notice provided prior to the invocation of the diploma sanction, the objectives, and the test is a violation of the due process clause.

Since the time of the release of the results of the first test, remediation classes have been attempting to teach the skills. The effectiveness of the remediation programs is somewhat in doubt at the present time because of the failure of the state defendants to carry out equating studies. These studies would have shown the relative degree of difficulty among the three administrations of the functional literacy test. Based on the present evidence it is impossible to determine whether the tests are becoming easier or whether the remediation program is accomplishing its goal. In either event, large numbers of students have not passed the functional literacy test. The evidence indicates that the instruction of functional literacy skills to older students is more difficult, particularly because the unidentified deficiencies of earlier years have become ingrained. The expert testimony upon which the Court has relied indicates that four to six years should intervene between the announcement of the objectives and the implementation of the diploma sanction. While the Court is loathe to interfere in the operations of the Florida public schools, it is compelled to act because of its constitutional obligation. The Defendants had other constitutionally acceptable alternatives such as phased introduction of the objectives in all grades without the diploma sanction and longer term remediation. The Court cannot help but focus on the fact that the present Plaintiffs in all classes have been the victims of segregation, social promotion and various other educational ills but have persisted and remained in school and should not now, at this late date, be denied the diplomas they have earned by mastery of the basic skills and completion of the minimum number of academic credits.

The Defendants are concerned that the momentum, interest, credibility, and support of Florida public education now present will be undermined if the Court finds the test or the implementation schedule invalid. The Defendants are further concerned that they will be without a sanction or deterrent if the Court voids the linkage of the functional literacy test to the diploma. While the denial of the diploma has a certain deterrent value, its application in the instant case would be analogous to asserting that the immediate and indefinite incarceration without a trial of an individual upon the suspicion of the commission of a crime would have a deterrent effect on other potential offenders. No doubt it would. But in our country, the Constitution, including the due process clause, stands between the arbitrary government action and the innocent individual. *St. Ann v. Palisi*, 495 F.2d 423 (5th Cir. 1974). The implementation schedule in effect relative to the functional literacy testing program with the diploma sanction is fundamentally unfair. The Court in Section VIII will discuss the nature and extent of injunctive relief to be extended to all Plaintiffs.

VI

THIRD CLAIM

A. INTRODUCTION

[10] The Plaintiffs in Classes B and C contend in their third claim that the utilization of the SSAT II to classify and group students for remediation pursuant to the Compensatory Education Act of 1977, Fla.

Stat. § 236.088, perpetuates the effects of past purposeful discrimination and resegregates them in violation of the Fourteenth Amendment, 42 U.S.C. § 2000d and 20 U.S.C. § 1703. The Plaintiffs in these classes further assert that the Defendants foresaw that a substantial number of black twelfth grade students would fail the SSAT II and thus would be placed in compensatory education classes with high proportions of black children and low proportions of white children.

B. RESEGREGATION

The evidence indicates that the compensatory education program for those students who have failed the SSAT II is disproportionately composed of black children. This is attributable to the fact that more black children have failed the SSAT II than white children. The reason for this has been fully explained elsewhere in this Opinion. Although the Court has found in a previous section that the test is valid and reliable, at least for the purpose of identifying certain skill deficiencies, it has also found that the test perpetuates the effects of past purposeful discrimination. The final question, one posed in *McNeal, supra*, and *Gadsden County, supra*, is whether the testing program along with the compensatory education classes, although they cause resegregation of certain classrooms, will remedy the present effects of past discrimination through better educational opportunities.

In addressing this question, the Court must reflect upon the evidence produced upon this issue. While the compensatory education classification results in disproportionate numbers of black children being placed in the classes, the evidence indicates that the pupil alignment in the compensatory education programs is not static. The progression of students out of the compensatory education program seems to be fluid and the increase in the passage percentages evidence the efficacy of the program. Additionally, the compensatory education program constitutes only at most two classes or hours per day. The remainder of the school

day is spent in regular classes which do not contain this disproportionate racial composition. The defendants must be constantly wary that the utilization of the SSAT I and II and the compensatory education program do not isolate and stigmatize any children for longer than is necessary to compensate for the identified deficits. Thus far the record is clear that the purpose of the compensatory education program is to assist students and not to resegregate them. The state's obligation to instruct and remediate all students relative to the SSAT II skills has been commenced. The results of the program are encouraging although serious questions concerning equating are still unresolved. The legislature has given the program ample financial support and hopefully it will do so in the future. By the end of the Court's injunction, all students should be ready and able to compete on an equal footing. Thus while the diploma sanction punishes those who suffered under segregation, the compensatory education program assists him. The *McNeal* rationale for permitting the program to exist, regardless of its disproportionate racial composition has been satisfied as to the compensatory education facet, but not by the diploma sanction. Accordingly, the Court finds that there has been neither a constitutional nor a statutory violation because of the utilization of the results of SSAT II as a mechanism for remediation even if the compensatory education classrooms are disproportionately black.

VII

CONCLUSION

In 1954 the Supreme Court recognized the essential role of public education in our society.

Today, education is perhaps the most important function of state and local governments. Compulsory school attendance laws and the great expenditures for education both demonstrate our recognition of the importance of education to our democratic society. It is required in the performance of our most basic public responsibilities, even service in the armed forces. It is the very foundation of good citizenship. Today it is a principal instrument in awakening the child to cultural values, in preparing him for later professional training, and in helping him to adjust normally to his environment. *Brown v. Board of Education,* 347 U.S. 483, 493, 74 S.Ct. 686, 691, 98 L.Ed. 873 (1954).

Because of this seminal role, it is critical to *provide* and *administer* education in a manner which comports with our historical and constitutional notions of fairness and equality. Any deviation from this course would seriously affect not only the individual student but our society as a whole. The Court has herein noted several breaches of this fundamental responsibility of government and has been compelled to act. The injunctive relief granted will be of a limited duration, only that time necessary to purge the taint of past segregation and inadequate notice. At the end of the injunctive period, the state will be permitted to pursue its educational policies and goals free of intervention.

VIII

DECLARATORY AND INJUNCTIVE RELIEF

[11] Pursuant to the findings in Sections IV D. and V, the Court is of the opinion that declaratory and injunctive relief are both appropriate and proper in the present instance. In a separate Order the Court will declare that Fla.Stat. § 232.-246(1)(b) (1978 Supp.) is, as applied, in the present context a violation of the equal protection and due process clauses of the Fourteenth Amendment. 42 U.S.C. § 2000d, and 20 U.S.C. § 1703. The two remaining requirements for graduation found in Fla.Stat. § 232.246(1)(a) and (c) (1978 Supp.) remain in full force and effect.

In light of the evidence relating to the necessary period of time to orient the students and teachers to the new functional literacy objectives, to insure instruction in the objectives, and to eliminate the taint on educational development which accompanied segregation, the Court is of the opinion that the state should be enjoined from requiring passage of the SSAT II as a requirement for graduation for a period of four (4) years. In the school term 1982–1983, the state will be permitted to utilize the SSAT II as a requirement for graduation. In the interim the SSAT II can be administered as directed by the State DOE to assist in the identification and remediation of the SSAT II skill objectives. The state Defendants will be permitted to retain the SSAT II scores in a fashion consistent with the manner in which the state retains other achievement test scores.

The Court is of the opinion that the present remediation program is not constitutionally or statutorily invalid. The progress of students out of the program and the limited duration of the daily instruction comports with applicable standards.

DONE AND ORDERED in Chambers in Jacksonville, Florida this 12th day of July, 1979.

APPENDIX B

Debra P. v. *Turlington,* United States Court of Appeals, Fifth Circuit, Unit B, May 4, 1981

statutory validity of Florida State Student Assessment Test, Part II, which is designed to measure functional literacy and passage of which is condition to receipt of high school diploma. The United States District Court for the Middle District of Florida, George G. Carr, J., 474 F.Supp. 244, found the diploma aspect unconstitutional, and appeal and cross appeal were taken. The Court of Appeals, Fay, Circuit Judge, held that: (1) students' expectation of a diploma if they satisfied attendance requirements and passed required courses was an implied property interest for constitutional purposes; (2) if test covered materials not taught it was unfair and violated equal protection and due process; (3) there was no due process or equal protection violation because test was given only in public schools; (4) immediate use of diploma sanction violated equal protection as punishing black students for vestiges of prior dual school system; and (5) there was neither a constitutional nor statutory violation in using test results as a mechanism for remediation only.

Affirmed in part, vacated in part and remanded.

1. Federal Courts ☞942

Since state of Florida did not make any effort to make certain whether functional literacy test required for high school diploma covered material actually studied in the classroom and since record was insufficient in proof on that issue, constitutional challenge to such requirement was remanded for further finding. West's F.S.A. § 232.-246(1)(b), (4); U.S.C.A.Const. Amend. 14.

2. States ☞4.6

State's plenary powers over education come from the powers reserved to the states through the Tenth Amendment. U.S.C.A.Const. Amend. 10.

3. States ☞4.6

As long as it does so in a manner consistent with the mandates of the Federal Constitution, a state may determine the length, manner and content of any education it provides. U.S.C.A.Const. Amends. 10, 14.

DEBRA P., a minor by Irene P., her mother and next friend et al., Plaintiffs-Appellees, Cross-Appellants,

v.

Ralph D. TURLINGTON, individually and as Commissioner of Education et al., Defendants-Appellants, Cross-Appellees.

No. 79–3074.

United States Court of Appeals,
Fifth Circuit.
Unit B

May 4, 1981.

Rehearing En Banc Denied
Sept. 4, 1981.

Florida high school students brought class action challenging constitutional and

4. Federal Courts ⟐172

Federal courts interfere with state educational directives only when necessary to protect freedoms and privileges guaranteed by the United States Constitution. U.S.C. A.Const. Amends. 10, 14.

5. Civil Rights ⟐9

If a state provides an educational system, it must do so in a nondiscriminatory fashion. West's F.S.A.Const. Art. 9, §§ 1–5; U.S.C.A.Const. Amends. 10, 14.

6. Constitutional Law ⟐277(1)

In establishing a system of free public education and in making school attendants mandatory, the state of Florida has created an expectation in students that if they attend during the required years and take and pass required courses they will receive a diploma, and such expectation constitutes "property interest" as that term is used constitutionally; although state constitutionally might not be obligated to establish and maintain a school system, its action in doing so, requiring attendance and creating a mutual expectation that a student who is successful will graduate with a diploma gives rise to an implied property right. West's F.S.A. Const. Art. 9, §§ 1–5; U.S.C. A.Const. Amend. 14.

See publication Words and Phrases for other judicial constructions and definitions.

7. Constitutional Law ⟐242.2(5), 278.5(5)

Requirement for Florida high school diploma that a student pass a functional literary test would violate equal protection and due process clauses of Federal Constitution if the test covered material not taught the students. West's F.S.A. § 232.246(1)(b), (4); U.S.C.A.Const. Amend. 14.

8. Constitutional Law ⟐213.1(1)

When the state encroaches on the concepts of justice lying at the basis of our civil and political institutions, it is obligated to avoid action which is arbitrary and capricious, does not achieve or even frustrate the legitimate state interests, or is fundamentally unfair. U.S.C.A.Const. Amends. 5, 14.

9. Schools ⟐178

A state may condition the receipt of a public school diploma on the passing of a test so long as it is a fair test of that which was taught. West's F.S.A. § 232.246(1)(b), (4); U.S.C.A.Const. Amends. 10, 14.

10. Constitutional Law ⟐242.2(5)
   Schools ⟐178

Having a functional literacy examination as a requirement for a public high school diploma bars a rational relation to a valid state interest in public education; however, such a test must be a fair test of that which was in fact taught and if it is not fair, i. e., covers matter that was not taught in the classroom, it cannot be said to be rationally related to a state interest and its use violates equal protection. West's F.S.A. § 232.246(1)(b), (4); U.S.C.A.Const. Amend. 14.

11. Constitutional Law ⟐242.2(5), 278.-5(5)

Florida's state student assessment test, i. e., functional literacy test required to secure public high school diploma, does not violate due process or equal protection because it is given only in public schools; not only does a state need not correct all problems of education in one fell swoop but it has a stronger interest in those for which it pays the cost and the state presently exercises very limited control over private schools. West's F.S.A. §§ 232.021, 232.-246(1)(b), (4); U.S.C.A.Const. Amend. 14.

12. Constitutional Law ⟐242.2(5)

In considering equal protection attack on Florida requirement that students pass a functional literacy test to receive a high school diploma trial court was to consider impact of legislative action on the community, historical background and sequence of events leading up to such requirement, including fact that until 1967 Florida operated a dual school system and that from 1967 to 1971 segregation persisted and predominantly black schools remained inferior and that greater failure rate of blacks on the test could be attributed to unequal education they received during the "dual schools" period. West's F.S.A. § 232.246(1)(b), (4); U.S.C.A.Const. Amend. 14.

13. Constitutional Law ⟷220(3)

Absent failure to demonstrate either that disproportionate failure of black students on functional literacy test required for Florida public high school diploma was not due to present effects of past intentional segregation or, that as presently used, the diploma sanction was necessary to remedy those effects, immediate use of the diploma sanction was impermissible as punishing black students for deficiency created by prior dual school system. West's F.S.A. § 232.246(1)(b), (4); U.S.C.A.Const. Amend. 14.

14. Civil Rights ⟷9.5

If Florida state student assessment test, which was designed to measure functional literacy, was a fair test of what was taught in the public schools, its use as a graduation requirement, i. e., condition for diploma, would not violate Title VI of Civil Rights Act, i. e., prohibition against exclusion from participation in or discrimination under federally assisted programs on ground of race, etc. West's F.S.A. § 232.-246(1)(b), (4); Civil Rights Act of 1964, § 601, 42 U.S.C.A. § 2000d.

15. Schools ⟷178

Since Florida state student assessment test, which was designed to measure functional literacy and passage of which was prerequisite to receipt of high school diploma, perpetuated past racial discrimination as to black students the diploma sanction violated Equal Educational Opportunities Act which requires an educational agency to take affirmative steps to remove the "vestiges" of dual school systems. West's F.S.A. § 232.246(1)(b), (4); Equal Educational Opportunities Act of 1974, § 204, 20 U.S.C.A. § 1703.

16. Civil Rights ⟷9

Constitutional Law ⟷242.2(5), 278.-5(5)

Using results of Florida state student assessment test, which is designed to measure functional literacy, a mechanism for remediation only, as opposed to diploma de-

nial for failure to pass, violates neither federal constitutional guarantees of due process and equal protection or Title VI of Civil Rights Act of 1964 or Equal Educational Opportunities Act. West's F.S.A. § 232.-246(1)(b), (4); Civil Rights Act of 1964, § 601, 42 U.S.C.A. § 2000d; Equal Educational Opportunities Act of 1974, § 204, 20 U.S.C.A. § 1703; U.S.C.A.Const. Amend. 14.

———

W. Crosby Few, Tampa, Fla., James D. Little, Gen. Counsel, Judith A. Brechner, Deputy General Counsel, State Board of Education, Tallahassee, Fla., for defendants-appellants cross-appellees.

Irving Gornstein, Washington, D. C., amicus curiae, U. S. A.

Stephen F. Hanlon, Robert J. Shapiro, Bay Area Legal Services, Inc., Tampa, Fla., Diana Pullin, Cambridge, Mass., Roger L. Rice, Richard Jefferson, Center for Law and Ed., Peter M. Siegel, Miami, Fla., for plaintiffs-appellees, cross-appellants.

David Rubin, Stephen J. Pollak, Richard M. Sharp, Washington, D. C., amicus curiae.

Appeal from the United States District Court for the Middle District of Florida.

Before FAY and VANCE, Circuit Judges and ALLGOOD *, District Judge.

FAY, Circuit Judge:

The State of Florida, concerned about the quality of its public educational system, enacted statutory provisions leading to the giving of a competency examination covering certain basic skills. Many students

---

* District Judge of the Northern District of Alabama sitting by designation.

1. The requirements are set out in Fla.Stat.Ann. § 232.246 (West Supp.1980) to which we will frequently refer:

232.246 General requirements for high school graduation

(1) Beginning with the 1978–1979 school year, each district school board shall establish standards for graduation from its schools which shall include as a minimum:

(a) Mastery of the minimum performance standards in reading, writing, and mathematics for the 11th grade, established pursuant

passed the examination but a significant number failed. The failing group included a disparate number of blacks. This class action, brought on their behalf, challenges the right of the state to impose the passing of the examination as a condition precedent to the receipt of a high school diploma. The overriding legal issue of this appeal is whether the State of Florida can constitutionally deprive public school students of their high school diplomas on the basis of an examination which *may* cover matters not taught through the curriculum. We hold that the State may not constitutionally so deprive its students unless it has submitted proof of the curricular validity of the test. Accordingly, we vacate the judgment of the district court and remand for further findings of fact.

I.

In 1976, the Florida Legislature enacted the Educational Accountability Act of 1976. Laws of Florida 1976, Vol. 1, Ch. 76–223, pp. 489–508. The intent of the legislature was to provide a system of accountability for education in the state and to ensure that each student was afforded similar educational opportunity regardless of geographic location. Fla.Stat.Ann. § 229.55(2)(a) (West 1977). The legislature established three standards for graduation from Florida public schools. First, the students were required to complete a minimum number of credits for graduation. Second, they were required to master certain basic skills. Third, they were required to perform satisfactorily in functional literacy as determined by the State Board of Education.[1]

to ss. 229.565 and 229.57, determined in the manner prescribed after a public hearing and consideration by the state board;

(b) Demonstrated ability to successfully apply basic skills to everyday life situations as measured by a functional literacy examination developed and administered in a manner prescribed after a public hearing and consideration by the state board; and

(c) Completion of a minimum number of academic credits, and all other applicable requirements prescribed by the district school board pursuant to s. 232.245.

(2) The standards required in subsection (1), and any subsequent modifications there-

Each school district was directed to develop procedures for remediation, and a statewide testing program was outlined. Fla.Stat. Ann. § 229.57 (West 1977 & Supp.1980). In 1978, the Act was amended to require passage of a functional literacy examination prior to receipt of a state high school diploma.

At the time of the trial of this lawsuit, the examination, the SSAT II, had been administered three times. The failure statistics showed a greater impact on black students than on white students. In the Fall, 1977 administration, 78% of the black students taking the exam failed one or more sections of the test as compared with 25% of the white students. Of the 4,480 black students taking the test for the second time in Fall, 1978, 74% failed one or both sections. Twenty-five percent of the whites retaking the test failed. On the mathematics section alone, 46% of the blacks retaking the test failed. The results of the third administration in Spring, 1978, which were released during trial, indicated that 60% of the blacks taking the mathematics exam for the third time failed as compared with 36% of the whites. In May, 1979, of the approximately 91,000 high school seniors in Florida public schools, 3,466, or 20.049% of the black students had

to, shall be printed in the Florida Administrative Code even though said standards are not defined as rules.

(3) The state board shall, after a public hearing and consideration, make provision for appropriate modification of testing instruments and procedures for students with identified handicaps or disabilities in order to ensure that the results of the testing represent the student's achievement, rather than reflecting the student's impaired sensory, manual, speaking, or psychological process skills, except when such skills are the factors the test purports to measure.

(4) A student who meets all requirements prescribed in subsection (1) shall be awarded a standard diploma in a form prescribed by the state board; provided that a school board may, in lieu of the standard diploma, award differentiated diplomas to those exceeding the prescribed minimums. A student who completes the minimum number of credits and other requirements prescribed by paragraph (1)(c), but who is unable to meet the standards of paragraph (1)(a) or paragraph (1)(b), shall be awarded a certificate of com-

not passed the test as compared with 1,342, or 1.9% of the white students.[2]

Plaintiffs-appellees, Florida high school students, filed this class action in the United States District Court for the Middle District of Florida, challenging the constitutionality of the Florida State Student Assessment Test, Part II (SSAT II) under the due process and equal protection clauses of the Fourteenth Amendment. They also challenged the test under Title VI of the Civil Rights Act of 1964, 42 U.S.C. § 2000d (1976) and the Equal Educational Opportunities Act, 20 U.S.C. § 1703 (1976). Plaintiffs were certified in three classes:

Class A—all present and future twelfth grade public school students in the State of Florida who have failed or hereafter fail the SSAT II

Class B—all present and future twelfth grade black public school students in the State of Florida who have failed or who hereafter fail the SSAT II

Class C—all present and future twelfth grade black public school students in Hillsborough County, Florida, who have failed or hereafter fail the SSAT II

Class A, B, and C claimed that appellants[3] designed and implemented a testing

program which is racially biased and violates the Equal Protection Clause of the Fourteenth Amendment. These three classes also claimed that appellants violated the Fourteenth Amendment in instituting a program denying diplomas without sufficient notice or time to prepare for the exam.

Classes B and C, the black students, claimed that the SSAT II is a device for resegregating the Florida public schools in violation of the Fourteenth Amendment, 42 U.S.C. § 2000d, and 20 U.S.C. § 1703 because those failing the test are placed in remedial classes which tend to contain more blacks than whites. Plaintiffs sought declaratory and injunctive relief.

The District Court, *Debra P. v. Turlington*, 474 F.Supp. 244 (M.D.Fla.1979) found that Fla.Stat.Ann. § 232.246(1)(b)[4] as applied in the present context, violated the equal protection clause of the United States Constitution, Title VI of the Civil Rights Act of 1964, and the Equal Educational Opportunities Act as to plaintiffs in classes B and C. It held that section 232.246(1)(b) (West Supp.1981) violated the due process clause of the United States Constitution as to plaintiffs in classes A, B, and C. Defendants-appellants were enjoined from the use of the test as a requirement for receipt of diplomas until the 1982–1983 school year. The court found that the use of the examination for remediation violated neither the Constitution nor statutes.

On appeal, the appellants contend that the court erred in finding that the use of the test violates due process because there

pletion in a form prescribed by the state board. However, any student who is otherwise entitled to a certificate of completion may, in the alternative, elect to remain in the secondary school on either a full-time or a part-time basis for up to 1 additional year and receive special instruction designed to remedy his identified deficiencies. This special instruction shall be funded from the district's state compensatory education funds.

(5) The public hearing and consideration required in paragraphs (a) and (b) of subsection (1) and in subsection (3) shall not be construed to amend or nullify the requirements of security relating to the contents of examinations or assessment instruments and related materials or data as prescribed in s. 232.248.

2. *Debra P. v. Turlington*, 474 F.Supp. 244, 248–249 (M.D.Fla.1979).

3. Named defendants-appellants are: Commissioner of Education Ralph D. Turlington; the Florida State Board of Education: Governor Bob Graham, Secretary of State George Fire-

stone, Attorney General Jim Smith, Comptroller General Gerald A. Lewis, Treasurer William Gunter, Commissioner of Agriculture Doyle Conner; the Florida Department of Education (DOE); the School Board of Hillsborough County, Florida: Roland H. Lewis, Cecile W. Essrig, Carl Carpenter, Jr., Ben H. Hill, Jr., A. Leon Lowrey; and Superintendent of Schools of Hillsborough County, Raymond O. Shelton. Defendants were sued in their individual as well as official positions.

4. *See* note 1 *supra.*

5. As of March, 1978, 33 states had taken some type of action to mandate minimum competency standards, and movements were under way

was adequate notice and no property right was involved. They contend that the graduation requirement is not a punishment, does not deprive students of a "liberty" interest and does not violate the equal protection clause. Appellants contend that the court erred in finding 20 U.S.C. § 1701 and 42 U.S.C. § 2000d to be applicable. In their cross-appeal, plaintiffs-appellees contend that the district court erred in limiting the period of the injunction to four years and in upholding the validity of the examination.

[1] We find, based upon stipulated facts, that because the state had not made any effort to make certain whether the test covered material actually studied in the classrooms of the state and because the record is insufficient in proof on that issue, the case must be remanded for further findings. If the test covers material not taught the students, it is unfair and violates the Equal Protection and Due Process clauses of the United States Constitution.

II.

[2, 3] At the outset, we wish to stress that neither the district court nor we are in a position to determine educational policy in the State of Florida. The state has determined that minimum standards must be met and that the quality of education must be improved. We have nothing but praise for these efforts.[5] The state's plenary powers over education come from the powers reserved to the states through the Tenth Amendment, and usually they are defined in the state constitution.[6] As long as it

in three more. See C. Pipho, Minimum Competency Testing in 1978: A Look at State Standards, 59 *Phi Delta Kappan* 585 (1978); M. S. McClung, Competency Testing Programs: Legal and Educational Issues, 47 *Fordham L.Rev.* 651 (1959).

6. Florida's original grant of educational authority appeared in the Constitution of 1868, Art. VIII, § 2. The section stated that the "legislature shall provide a uniform system of common schools, and a university," and further provided that they would be free. Present authorization is found in the Florida Constitution of 1968, Art. IX, §§ 1–5.

does so in a manner consistent with the mandates of the United States Constitution, a state may determine the length, manner, and content of any education it provides.

[4] The United States courts have interfered with state educational directives only when necessary to protect freedoms and privileges guaranteed by the United States Constitution. In 1899, for example, in the case of *Cumming v. Board of Education*, 175 U.S. 528, 20 S.Ct. 197, 44 L.Ed. 262, the Court upheld the decision of a local board to close a black school while keeping a white school open. Finding that the decision was based on economic reasons, the Court said:

[T]he education of the people in schools maintained by state taxation is a matter belonging to the respective States, and any interference on the part of Federal authority with the management of such schools cannot be justified except in the case of a clear and unmistakable disregard of the rights secured by the supreme law of the land.

175 U.S. at 545, 20 S.Ct. at 201, 44 L.Ed. at 266. While the outcome of the *Cumming* case might be questioned in this post *Brown* era, it must be remembered that it was not until just before the First World War that compulsory school attendance laws were in force in all states.[7] Public education was virtually unknown at the time of the adoption of the Constitution. In 1647 Colonial Massachusetts directed its towns to establish schools, and in 1749, Franklin proposed the Philadelphia academy. Until after the turn of the century, education was primarily private and usually sectarian. *Lemon v. Kurtzman*, 403 U.S. 602, 645–47, 91 S.Ct. 2105, 2127–28, 29 L.Ed.2d 745, 774–75 (1976). Once part of the government, however, education became a significant governmental responsibility. As the Court noted in *Brown v. Board of Education*, 347 U.S. 483, 493, 74 S.Ct. 686, 691, 98 L.Ed. 873, 880 (1954):

Today, education is perhaps the most important function of State and local

7. *Brown v. Board of Education*, 347 U.S. 483, 489–90 n.4, 74 S.Ct. 686, 691, n.4, 98 L.Ed. 873, 878 n.4 (1954).

governments. Compulsory school attendance laws and the great expenditures for education both demonstrate our recognition of the importance of education to our democratic society.

Stating that the provision of education ranks at the apex of the functions of a state, the Court in *Wisconsin v. Yoder*, 406 U.S. 205, 92 S.Ct. 1526, 32 L.Ed.2d 15 (1971) was required to balance the state's need for its citizens to be educated against the citizens' hallowed right to free exercise of religion. "There is no doubt," the Court said, "as to the power of a state, having a high responsibility for education of its citizens, to impose reasonable regulations for the control and duration of basic education." 406 U.S. at 213, 92 S.Ct. at 1532, 32 L.Ed.2d at 24.

[5] Though the state has plenary power, it cannot exercise that power without reason and without regard to the United States Constitution. Although the Court has never labeled education as a "fundamental right" automatically triggering strict scrutiny of state actions, *see San Antonio School District v. Rodriguez*, 411 U.S. 1, 93 S.Ct. 1278, 36 L.Ed.2d 16 (1972), it is clear that if the state does provide an educational system, it must do so in a non-discriminatory fashion. "Among other things, the State is constrained to recognize a student's legitimate entitlement to a public education as a property interest which may be protected by the Due Process Clause . . ." *Goss v. Lopez*, 419 U.S. 565, 574, 95 S.Ct. 729, 736, 42 L.Ed.2d 725, 734 (1975).

III.

[6] It is in the light of the foregoing discussion of the relationship between the state and federal governments that we must analyze the plaintiffs' claims that SSAT II violates the equal protection and due process clauses of the Fourteenth Amendment. It is clear that in establishing a system of free public education and in

making school attendance mandatory,[8] the state has created an expectation in the students. From the students' point of view, the expectation is that if a student attends school during those required years, and indeed more, and if he takes and passes the required courses, he will receive a diploma. This is a property interest as that term is used constitutionally. *See Goss v. Lopez*, 419 U.S. 565, 579, 95 S.Ct. 729, 738, 42 L.Ed.2d 725, 737 (1975). Although the state of Florida constitutionally may not be obligated to establish and maintain a school system, it has done so, required attendance and created a mutual expectation that the student who is successful will graduate with a diploma. This expectation can be viewed as a state-created "understanding" that secures certain benefits and that supports claims of entitlement to those benefits. *Board of Regents v. Roth*, 408 U.S. 564, 577, 92 S.Ct. 2701, 2709, 33 L.Ed.2d 548 (1972). As the trial court noted, "graduation is the logical extension of successful attendance." 474 F.Supp. at 266; and as appellees note in brief, before SSAT II, a student completing the necessary number of credits would graduate with a diploma. (Brief of Appellees at 52).

[7] Based upon this implied property right, we find that the trial court was correct in holding that the implementation schedule for the test violated due process of law. In its finding, the court quoted from the report of the state's own task force:

> The problems created by the abrupt schedule for implementing the Functional Literacy Test were most severe for the members of Florida high school graduation class of 1979. At the eleventh hour and with virtually no warning, these stu-

8. Fla.Stat.Ann. § 232.01 (West Supp.1981) mandates that children between the ages of 6 and 16 attend school.

9. In St. Ann, two students were indefinitely suspended because of their mother's behavior. The court considered this punishment without personal guilt to be a violation of a fundamental concept of liberty. Although the *St. Ann* case is factually dissimilar to the one we here consider, it is clear that in neither case can the state arbitrarily interfere. The case of *Maha-*

dents were told that the requirements for graduation had been changed. They were suddenly required to pass a test constructed under the pressure of time and covering content that was presumed to be elementary but that their schools may or may not have taught them recently, well, or perhaps at all.

In retrospect, the Task Force believes that the schedule for implementing state-wide high school graduation standards was too severe. We feel that most of the problems that are identified in later sections of this report are the result of trying to do too much in too little time. Consequently, we believe that the problems can and will be solved over time. Task Force on Educational Assessment Programs, *Competency Testing in Florida Report to the Florida Cabinet (Part 1)* 4 (1979).

474 F.Supp. at 265.

[8] The due process violation potentially goes deeper than deprivation of property rights without adequate notice. When it encroaches upon concepts of justice lying at the basis of our civil and political institutions, the state is obligated to avoid action which is arbitrary and capricious, does not achieve or even frustrates a legitimate state interest, or is fundamentally unfair. *See St. Ann v. Palisi,* 495 F.2d 423, 425 n.5 (5th Cir. 1974).[9] We believe that the state administered a test that was, at least on the record before us, fundamentally unfair in that it *may* have covered matters not taught in the schools of the state.

Testimony at trial by experts for both plaintiffs and defendants indicated that several types of studies were done before and after the administration of the test.

vongsanan v. Hall, 529 F.2d 448 (5th Cir. 1976) is distinguishable in that in that case the plaintiff sought to require the state to give her a college diploma despite her failure to take a comprehensive examination. The court found that there was no denial of procedural or substantive due process because plaintiff had refused the university's efforts to tailor a special program to her needs. The expectations of college and high school students would certainly be different.

The experts agreed that of the several types of validity studies,[10] a content validity study would be most important for a competency examination such as SSAT II. The trial court apparently found that the test had adequate content validity, 474 F.Supp. at 261, but we find that holding upon the record before us to be clearly erroneous. In the field of competency testing, an important component of content validity is curricular validity, defined by defendants' expert Dr. Foster, as "things that are currently taught." (Tr.2845)[11] This record is simply insufficient in proof that the test administered measures what was actually taught in the schools of Florida.

During the course of pre-trial litigation, defendant-appellants stipulated as follows:

No effort was made by the Florida Department of Education to ascertain whether or not all the minimum student performance standards were in fact being taught in Florida public schools. (Stipulation 114)

The Florida Department of Education did not conduct any formal studies which

10. Basic types of validity as defined by the American Psychological Association, *Standards for Educational and Psychological Tests* (1974) are as follows:

Criterion—related validity—measurements of how well the test items predict the future performance of the test takers and how well the test results correlate with other criteria which might provide the same type of information.

content validity—measurements of how well a test measures a representative sample of behaviors in the universe of situations the test is intended to represent.

construct validity—how well the test measures the construct (defined as the theoretical idea developed to explain and organize some aspects of existing knowledge) for which it was designed.

For an excellent discussion of the APA Standards as they relate to competency testing, *see* M.S. McClung, Competency Testing Programs: Legal and Educational Issues, 47 *Fordham L. Rev.* 651, 683 (1979).

11. There is evidence in the record that care was taken in constructing a test which would match the objectives of the schools. The trial court's discussion of the development 474 F.Supp. at 257–259, indicates that the test was probably a good test of what the students *should* know but

showed whether or not the skills measured on the test were in fact taught in the public schools in the State of Florida. (Stipulation 117)

On oral argument before this Court, counsel for the appellants stated that the stipulations meant only that the state did no *formal* studies of the correspondence between what was tested and what was taught. She assured this Court that the state could prove that the test covered things actually taught in the classrooms. That may be the case, but this record does not establish such proof.

Dr. Thomas H. Fisher, Administrator of the Student Assessment Section, Department of Education, testified that the DOE merely assumed that things were being taught. (Tr.2844) Dr. John E. Hills, professor of Educational Research at Florida State University, testified that the test reliably and validly assessed applications of basic communications and math skills to everyday situations (Tr.2945), but he agreed that everything on the test might not have been taught.[12] Appellants placed into evi-

not necessarily of what they had an opportunity to learn.

12. A portion of Dr. Hill's testimony appears below:

Q You're saying then that an item which might include an element that had not been taught in school might cause some problems in this regard?

A Well, an item which is not part of the objectives of what we're trying to teach in school. I don't think you can probably comfortably say that every single thing that a person might have to do on a practical application problem has to be specifically taught. I would feel uncomfortable with that, because I don't think schools can teach every single thing.

But the objective may be. They can apply the problem, the techniques to a tin roof. Did we teach about tin roofs in school? Well, I don't know that we do.

But you sort of assume that that's available to most people.

Q We have no way of knowing though whether something that is included in an objective is in fact included in all of the classrooms in the State of Florida. We have already had that testimony from Dr. Fisher. So it would be possible that a test item might impact more severely on a particular minority group because those children simply did not have as

dence some math books and communications teaching materials, but at least one teacher, Mr. Crihfield, testified that he did not cover the whole book in class. (Tr. 3055).

We acknowledge that in composing items for a test, the writer is dealing with applications of knowledge, and therefore the form of the test question would not necessarily be the same as the form of the information taught in class. We think, however, that fundamental fairness requires that the state be put to test on the issue of whether the students were tested on material they were or were not taught.

[9] We note that in requiring the state to prove on remand that the material was covered in class, we are not substituting our judgment for that of the state legislature on a matter of state policy. *See Ferguson v. Skrupa,* 372 U.S. 726, 731, 83 S.Ct. 1028, 1031, 10 L.Ed.2d 93, 98 (1963); *Memphis Light, Gas and Water Division v. Craft,* 436 U.S. 1, 9, 98 S.Ct. 1554, 1560, 56 L.Ed.2d 30, 39 (1978). We do not question the right of the state to condition the receipt of a diploma upon the passing of a test so long as it is a fair test of that which was taught. Nor do we seek to dictate what subjects are to be taught or in what manner. We do not share appellants' fear that our decision would prevent new items from being added to the curriculum. Those decisions would properly be left with the school authorities. As the United States Supreme Court said in *San Antonio School District v. Rodriguez,* 411 U.S. 1, 43, 93 S.Ct. 1278, 1302, 36 L.Ed.2d 16, 49 (1972):

The ultimate wisdom as to these and related problems of education is not likely to be divined for all time even by the scholars who now so earnestly debate the issues. In such circumstances, the judiciary is well advised to refrain from imposing on the States inflexible constitutional

part of their educational experience attention to that particular matter?

A Well, if they have not been taught the basics that it seems are part of the schools' essential material, then I'd say you're right. You know, there's—let's turn now to construct validity.

restraints that could circumscribe or handicap the continued research and experimentation so vital to finding even partial solutions to educational problems and to keeping abreast of ever-changing conditions.

Just as a teacher in a particular class gives the final exam on what he or she has taught, so should the state give its final exam on what has been taught in its classrooms.

[10] It follows that if the test is found to be invalid for the reason that it tests matters outside the curriculum, its continued use would violate the Equal Protection Clause. In analyzing the constitutionality of the examination under the Equal Protection Clause, the trial court stated, "[i]f the test by dividing students into two categories, passers and failers, did so without a rational relation to the purpose for which it was designed, then the Court would be compelled to find the test unconstitutional." 474 F.Supp. at 260. Analyzing the test from the viewpoint of its objectives, the court found that it does have adequate construct validity, that is, it does test functional literacy as defined by the Board.[13] We accept this finding and affirm that part of the trial court's opinion holding that having a functional literacy examination bears a rational relation to a valid state interest. That finding is, however, subject to a further finding on remand that the test is a fair test of that which was taught. If the test is not fair, it cannot be said to be rationally related to a state interest.

[11] We affirm the trial court's finding that the test items were not biased and that the test does not violate due process or equal protection by the fact that it is given only in public schools. As the court pointed out, the state need not correct all the problems of education in one fell swoop and it

13. Functional literacy is defined as "the ability to apply basic skills in reading, writing, and arithmetic to problems and tasks of a practical nature as encountered in everyday life." Exhibit CT 26 at 23 (Task Force Report).

has a stronger interest in those for which it pays the cost. *See Ambach v. Norwick*, 441 U.S. 68, 77, 99 S.Ct. 1589, 1595 n.8, 60 L.Ed.2d 49, 57 (1979). At present, the State of Florida exercises very limited control over private schools.[14]

IV.

[12] In considering appellees' equal protection claim, the trial court was required to consider the impact of the legislative action upon the community, the historical background, and the sequence of events leading up to the legislative action. *Village of Arlington Heights v. Metropolitan Housing Development Corp.*, 429 U.S. 252, 266–268, 97 S.Ct. 555, 563–65, 50 L.Ed.2d 450, 4d6566 (1977). The trial judge found that until 1967, Florida operated a dual school system intentionally segregating on the basis of race. The court found that the period from 1967 to 1971, segregation persisted and predominantly black schools remained inferior in physical facilities, course offerings, instructional materials, and equipment.[15] Appellant Turlington admitted that in part the failures of the black students taking the SSAT II could be attributed to the unequal education they received during the "dual schools" period. The record clearly indicates that appellants were aware of the possibility that more blacks than whites would fail the test.

14. *See* Fla.Stat.Ann. §§ 232.021, 229.821 (West 1977).

15. In making this finding, the trial court relied on "vast amounts of evidence" and upon judicial notice as well as expert testimony. The plaintiffs had originally asked the court to take judicial notice that as a result of attending segregated schools prior to the implementation of unitary school systems, many of the members of Classes B and C received an education inferior to that received by white students during the period. Based upon *Brown v. Board of Education*, 347 U.S. 483, 495, 74 S.Ct. 686, 692, 98 L.Ed. 873, 881 (1954) and upon *Mannings v. Board of Public Instruction of Hillsborough County, Florida*, 427 F.2d 874 (5th Cir. 1970), the trial court took judicial notice that the education received by the blacks was unequal. Tr. 36; 474 F.Supp. at 251, n.13.

16. The trial court took judicial notice that many of the students in classes B and C attended segregated schools prior to the implementa-

[13] Finding insufficient evidence to support a holding that there was *present* intent to discriminate as defined by the Court in *Personnel Administrator v. Feeney*, 442 U.S. 256, 99 S.Ct. 2282, 60 L.Ed.2d 870 (1979) (that the law was enacted in spite of or because of the foreseen racial impact), the trial court held that the past purposeful discrimination affecting appellees in classes B and C is perpetuated by the test and diploma sanction. In attempting to justify the use of an examination having such a disproportionate impact upon one race, the appellants failed to demonstrate either that the disproportionate failure of blacks was not due to the present effects of past intentional segregation or, that as presently used, the diploma sanction was necessary to remedy those effects. *See McNeal v. Tate County School District*, 508 F.2d 1017 (5th Cir. 1975). The trial judge was, therefore, correct in holding that the immediate use of the diploma sanction would punish black students for deficiencies created by the dual school system.[16]

[14] With respect to the question whether administration of the test violates Title VI, 42 U.S.C. § 2000d (1976),[17] counsel for the United States conceded on oral argument before this court that if the test was found to be a fair test of what was taught in the schools, its use as a gradua-

tion of the unitary school system. As stated by the trial court, the remedy was as follows:

> In light of the evidence relating to the necessary period of time to orient the students and teachers to the new functional literacy objectives, to insure instruction in the objectives, and to eliminate the taint on educational development which accompanied segregation, the Court is of the opinion that the state should be enjoined from requiring passage of the SSAT II as a requirement for graduation for a period of four (4) years.

474 F.Supp. at 269.

17. Appellees argue that further studies of the "differential validity" of the test should be done to determine whether the SSAT II tests blacks as blacks. We decline to disturb the trial court's finding that the test was valid in this respect. *See* 474 F.Supp. at 261 n.23.

tion requirement would not violate Title VI.[18] We agree with this conclusion.

[15, 16] Because the test perpetuates past discrimination as to classes B and C, the diploma sanction violates the EEOA, 20 U.S.C. § 1703 (1976) which requires an educational agency to take affirmative steps to remove the "vestiges" of dual school systems.[19] We affirm the holding that there is neither constitutional nor statutory violation in using the results of SSAT II as a mechanism for remediation only. 474 F.Supp. at 268.

CONCLUSION

We recognize that the interests of the State of Florida in both the remediation and diploma denial aspects of the basic competency program are substantial. The trial court noted an impressively increasing passing rate for which Florida teachers and students are to be commended. We hold, however, that the State may not deprive its high school seniors of the economic and educational benefits of a high school diploma until it has demonstrated that the SSAT II is a fair test of that which is taught in its classrooms and that the racially discriminatory impact is not due to the educational deprivation in the "dual school" years.

AFFIRMED IN PART, VACATED AND REMANDED IN PART.

APPENDIX C

Debra P. v. *Turlington,* United States Court of
Appeals, Fifth Circuit, September 4, 1981.
On petition for Rehearing and
Petition for Rehearing En Banc.

DEBRA P., a minor by Irene P., her mother and next friend et al., Plaintiffs-Appellees, Cross-Appellants,

v.

Ralph D. TURLINGTON, Individually and as Commissioner of Education et al., Defendants-Appellants, Cross-Appellees.

No. 79-3074.

United States Court of Appeals, Fifth Circuit.

Sept. 4, 1981.

Appeals from the United States District Court for the Middle District of Florida; George C. Carr, District Judge.

ON PETITION FOR REHEARING AND PETITION FOR REHEARING EN BANC

(5 Cir., 1981, 644 F.2d 397).

Before FAY and VANCE, Circuit Judges and ALLGOOD *, District Judge.

PER CURIAM:

A member of the Court in active service having requested a poll on the reconsideration of this cause en banc, and a majority of the judges in active service not having voted in favor of it, rehearing en banc is DENIED.

In dissenting statements from the court's refusal to consider this case *en banc,* two of our brothers have expressed concern about the ramifications of the panel opinion. With great respect for their views but shocked at their misinterpretations, we file this statement in hope of assisting others involved.

* District Judge of the Northern District of Alabama, sitting by designation.

Specifically, the panel assigned this matter did *not* :

a. Forbid a state from providing quality education.

b. Decree that the aim of public education is to confer a diploma and not to educate.

c. Find that black children were not ready for quality education.

d. Order any educational requirements (high or low) for a state school system.

e. Inject itself in any way in the curriculum of the state school system.

f. Suggest that black students be treated differently from white students.

To suggest that the panel opinion has somehow found a constitutional right to a diploma in the *absence of an education* is to play word games which we feel are both inappropriate and unfounded. Apparently our dissenting brothers would approve of "social promotions" coupled with a denial of a diploma as complying with the legal requirements of equal educational opportunities within a unitary school system. Even more distressing is the assumption inherent in the language of the dissents that the black students involved here had not attended class and satisfactorily passed all examinations given in those courses prescribed as necessary for the receipt of a diploma.

What the record in this case clearly establishes and what the panel of this court did hold includes:

a. That a diploma has a unique value in the market place.

b. That the State of Florida requires attendance in school between certain ages.

c. That the State of Florida has established a public school system.

d. That if certain attendance requirements are met and if specified courses of study are satisfactorily completed (passed)—a diploma will be awarded.

e. That mutual expectations are thus created between the state and the students.

f. That *if* a student complies with the established requirements and *if* he or she has satisfactorily passed these required courses of study, there is a property right in the expectation of a diploma.

g. That if a state is going to impose as a condition for receipt of a diploma a functional literacy test over and above whatever tests, examinations or grading requirements exist for specific single classes (world history, business mathematics, etc.), that test must be a fair test of material presented within those required courses of study.

h. That the State of Florida is to be commended for its concern over the quality of the *education* being furnished by its public school system.

i. That the State of Florida may utilize a functional literacy examination for both remedial purposes and as a condition for the awarding of a diploma.

To suggest that the State of Florida has allowed, or that the panel approved, the awarding of a diploma to any child who had received no learning is to misread both the record and the court's opinion.

Before GODBOLD, Chief Judge, and RONEY, TJOFLAT, HILL, FAY, VANCE, KRAVITCH, FRANK M.

JOHNSON, Jr., HENDERSON, HATCHETT, ANDERSON, and THOMAS A. CLARK, Circuit Judges.

RONEY, Circuit Judge, specially concurring:

It has been two years since the district court decided this case. Both parties appealed from that decision. Neither party has suggested the case be heard by the en banc court. This is sufficient reason for this Court to decline to consider the case en banc, even without considering the record, the issues and all of the matters discussed by my dissenting colleagues, which have neither been briefed nor argued to nonpanel members, and whether or not the dissents have correctly or incorrectly read the panel decision. In this kind of litigation, the parties' decision as to where they next want to attempt to resolve these complex problems is entitled to great deference without the interference of unrequested, judicially forced, prolonged and expensive en banc procedures which could delay any decision from this Court by at least a year. This Court exists to decide cases, to serve the litigants. We do well when we remember that simple fact. The denial of en banc consideration is justified, whatever the merits of the particular matters argued in the dissents and for whatever reasons an individual judge may have voted.

TJOFLAT, Circuit Judge, dissenting:

A panel of this court has held that public high school students have a *constitutionally* protected property interest in receipt of a high school diploma, and that the state may not withhold that diploma, despite a student's inability to pass a functional literacy exam, unless the state can prove that it has taught, and perhaps taught *well, Debra P. v. Turlington,* 644 F.2d 397 (5th Cir. 1981), the material covered on the exam. Thus, this federal court has told the State of Florida that it is *constitutionally* required to award diplomas to students who are functionally illiterate.

Moreover, the panel has held it *constitutionally* impermissible for the State of Florida to presently require the same level of functional literacy from black and white high school students. This constitutional prohibition is to continue until the state demonstrates that racially disproportionate student illiteracy cannot be attributed to the educational deprivations of past racial segregation in the schools. The panel has provided no guidance concerning how the state is to go about proving this negative proposition.

These holdings are obviously of great moment; they will have far-reaching effect throughout the six states of the Fifth Circuit and will signal to all other states the futility of attempting to improve educational systems in the face of federal interventionism. In one blow our circuit has created a mighty disincentive for the pursuit of excellence in education. This case undoubtedly is en banc worthy, and I vigorously dissent from the court's refusal to rehear it.

The panel opinion states the facts of this case clearly. *Debra P.,* at 400. My concern is not with the panel's interpretation of those facts, but rather with both the substantive character and the practical ramifications of the law the panel creates and applies to those facts.

To focus this dissent I will restate briefly the two holdings of the panel that are, in my mind, most problematic. The first holding concerns due process. The panel finds that Florida has created a property interest in the expectation of receiving a high school diploma, and that this property interest is protected by the due process clause. Moreover, despite finding that Florida's functional literacy exam accurately tests basic functional literacy skills, *Debra P.,* at 406, the panel holds that refusing diplomas to students failing the exam will violate the students' due process rights if the exam test matters not covered in the classroom. According to the panel, an exam covering such matters is fundamentally unfair. I believe this holding is contrary to established Fifth Circuit precedent and that it flies in the face of the spirit of the Supreme Court caselaw on students' educational rights.

The second panel holding that poses great difficulty for me concerns the equal protection clause. The record below indicates that the functional literacy test has a disproportionate impact on black students. The panel views the higher incidence of black failure on the exam as linked directly to the unequal education blacks received during the years of racial segregation. Thus, the argument goes, denying a diploma for failure of the literacy exam perpetuates past racial discrimination. Because the state has failed to demonstrate that denying a diploma is necessary to remedy the continuing effects of past discrimination, the state scheme must fall as violative of the fourteenth amendment. I believe this panel holding is a grievous affront to the fundamental principles underlying the landmark case of *Brown v. Board of Education,* 347 U.S. 483, 74 S.Ct. 686, 98 L.Ed. 873 (1954).

The Due Process Analysis

I believe the panel is incorrect in identifying receipt of a diploma as a property interest protected by the due process clause. The panel relies upon *Goss v. Lopez*, 419 U.S. 565, 95 S.Ct. 729, 42 L.Ed.2d 725 (1975), to support its discovery of this protected interest, *Debra P.*, at 403, yet *Goss* should not be read to encompass purely academic matters; in *Board of Curators of the University of Missouri v. Horowitz*, 435 U.S. 78, 98 S.Ct. 948, 55 L.Ed.2d 124 (1978), the Supreme Court indicated that the minimum due process requirement of *Goss* is limited to disciplinary determinations that inhibit a student's access to education. *Horowitz* at 87–91, 98 S.Ct. 954–56. The Court, therefore, has distinguished the role a court may play when called upon to interfere with state disciplinary proceedings and its role in reviewing academic decisionmaking in an educational system. Id. Thus, denying *access* to education triggers rigorous due process analysis: denying academic certification does not. Other courts have recognized this distinction, *see Gaspar v. Bruton*, 513 F.2d 843, 850 (10th Cir. 1975), and indeed, I believe it to be the basis of controlling caselaw in this circuit.

In *Mahavongsanan v. Hall*, 529 F.2d 448 (5th Cir. 1976), this circuit held that a university's decision to require students to pass a comprehensive examination as a prerequisite to receiving an M.A. degree was a reasonable *academic* regulation. In so holding, this court stressed that educational institutions have "wide latitude and discretion . . . in framing their academic degree requirements." *Id.* at 450. Indeed, the court went on to emphasize that a state educational institution is entitled to modify its rules and regulations "so as to properly exercise its educational responsibility." *Id.* This was so despite the district court's determination, *Mahavongsanan v. Hall*, 401 F.Supp. 381, 383 (N.D.Ga.1975) *rev'd*, 529 F.2d 448 (5th Cir. 1976), unrefuted in the

Court of Appeals, that the exam in question tested "abilities and materials which may not necessarily be instructed within the student's program of study." A contrary holding, this court emphasized, could only be explained by confusing "the court's power to review *disciplinary* actions by educational institutions on the one hand, and *academic* decisions on the other hand." *Mahavongsanan*, 529 F.2d at 449. Despite this exhortation, the panel in *Debra P.* has done just that, converting this confused perspective into law. Thus, I am at a loss in attempting to square *Debra P.* with the prior, controlling authority of *Mahavongsanan*.

It follows directly from *Horowitz, Bruton* and *Mahavongsanan* that *education*, not receipt of a diploma, is a property interest deserving of rigorous due process protection. To confuse the two is entirely inappropriate, as education is quite distinct from receipt of a diploma. A diploma supposedly signifies attainment of a certain level of academic proficiency. Thus, ideally, a diploma indicates that the state has performed fully its self-assumed duty to provide a student with an education and that the student has been successful in participating in that education. Therefore, as the panel stresses, at 403, a diploma illustrates *successful* progress through one's education. Academic success is not a property right—the relevant right is to a full and fair opportunity for an education.

By positing a rigorously safe-guarded property interest in receipt of a diploma, the panel has triggered a due process analysis that fails to correspond to the true constitutional character of the student expectation in question. A student's expectation is protectable only insofar as that expectation comports with the reasonable demands of the relevant educational institution. One simply should not be said to have a due process property interest in a diploma absent performance equaling established academic standards, for a student has only a conditional right to a diploma. *Horowitz.* The panel has turned this reasoning on its head, providing rigorous protection for the diploma interest *before* student compliance with purely academic requirements.

Even more troublesome than the identification of the diploma property right, however, is the panel's inquiry into the fundamental fairness of Florida's functional literacy exam. No one contests that the Florida's Legislature instituted the functional literacy exam as a diploma prerequisite out of a concern for "the quality of its public educational system." *Debra P.,* at 400. Moreover, as noted earlier, the district court has found and the panel accepts that the examination tests validly the everyday, practical application of the basic functional literacy skills of reading, writing and arithmetic. *Id.* at 406. For example, the exam tests a student's ability to complete an employment application, to "determine the inferred cause and effect of an action," to comparison-shop, to solve problems "involving purchases and a rate of discount," and other skills of undoubted everyday utility. *Debra P. v. Turlington,* 474 F.Supp. 244, 259 n.22 (M.D.Fla.1979). We must recognize, therefore, that Florida is testing fundamental, indeed minimal, intellectual maturation; the test inquires not into abstract academic matters but rather into the ability to apply basic skills in the context of real-life performance situations. We also must recognize that the decision to impose this exam requirement is a clear articulation of state policy: the Florida Legislature has decided that successful completion of a public high school education necessarily entails

achievement of a minimum level of practical literacy. It would be difficult to formulate a more reasonable or more skeletal policy of public education.

With these considerations in mind, I find very disquieting the panel's determination that the exam must be labeled unfair and constitutionally impermissible if Florida fails to demonstrate that it tested material actually taught in each of its classrooms. This holding places a very onerous burden on the state, for it must prove that each and every student sitting for the functional literacy test was taught, and perhaps taught well, *Debra P.,* at 404, each bit of knowledge that plays a role in the examination. One can only hypothesize what threshold of proof the district court, in the absence of adequate direction from this court, will require of the state. Several difficulties are clear, however. First, the state will have to prove that the material covered on the functional literacy exam was taught, and, by definition, taught adequately, while simultaneously justifying an inevitable amount of underachievement on the exam. In effect, the state will have to show that a student's failure to achieve functional literacy after twelve years of public education is not attributable to ineffective instruction. Surely one cannot assert that adequate teaching always produces true learning, yet it is much less self-evident that this disharmony is subject to proof in a court of law.

Second, this imposing theoretical difficulty of proof will be compounded, for the state must carry this burden for every complaining student in the context of each course that student attended. There is great potential for litigation concerning the effectiveness of individual teachers. Will a student be entitled to a diploma simply because one of his teachers "did not cover the whole book in class," *Debra P.*, at 406? How will Florida be able to test students who transfer into the Florida educational system? The potential for litigation is almost endless; the state's burden is oppressive at best.

Third, the nature of the matter tested, functional literacy, belies the reasonableness of the state's burden. As I have stated, to test functional literacy is to test whether a student has absorbed basic skills and, during the process of growth, learned to convert those skills into the attributes of minimum intellectual maturity. One can, with an acceptable degree of error, attempt to measure the teaching of basic skills, but trying to measure the teaching of the process of maturation derived from acquiring those skills is extremely difficult. Under *Debra P.* the state certainly will have to prove the link between teaching and maturation, and will have to validate the methods employed, (potentially in each classroom), to convey the fruits of that linkage to the student.

These few reflections illustrate clearly the signal *Debra P.* conveys to the states. That message is that the federal judiciary will create significant disincentives for state efforts to improve the quality of education. To my mind, the barriers the panel places between the State of Florida and achievement of its educational goals can only be characterized as constitutionally unjustifiable. Furthermore, those barriers portend subsequent federal intrusions inhibiting state educational policy. For example, will *Debra P.*'s federally-imposed curricular validity requirement lead to a federally-dictated basic curriculum, or federally-mandated textbook uniformity, thus eliminating the flexibility the states must have in implementing their education programs?

The panel's approach simply paves the way for extremely vexatious litigation, while demonstrating the very intrusiveness into state educational concerns that the Supreme Court has so clearly denounced.

The Supreme Court has recently noted that " 'Judicial interposition in the operation of the public school system of the Nation raises problems requiring care and restraint. . . . By and large, public education in our Nation is committed to the control of state and local authorities.' " *Horowitz*, 435 U.S. at 91, 98 S.Ct. at 955, quoting *Epperson v. Arkansas*, 393 U.S. 97, 104, 89 S.Ct. 266, 270, 21 L.Ed.2d 228 (1968). The Court expresses similar sentiment in the landmark case of *San Antonio School District v. Rodriguez*: "[T]he judiciary is well advised to refrain from imposing on the states inflexible constitutional restraints that could circumscribe or handicap the continued research and experimentation so vital to finding even partial solutions to educational problems . . . ." *Rodriguez*, 411 U.S. 1, 43, 93 S.Ct. 1278, 1302, 36 L.Ed.2d 16 (1972). Even the panel acknowledges that

"[T]he education of the people in schools maintained by state taxation is a matter belonging to the respective States, and any interference on the part of Federal authority with the management of such schools cannot be justified except in the case of a clear and unmistakable disregard of the rights secured by the supreme law of the land."

Debra P., at 403 quoting *Cumming v. Board of Education*, 175 U.S. 528, 545, 20 S.Ct. 197, 201, 44 L.Ed. 262 (1899). In the face of this authority the panel nevertheless insists upon placing itself between the state of Florida and its high school students.

In sum, the panel has misidentified a property interest and consequently has applied an entirely inappropriate, because both incongruent and excessively intrusive, constitutional analysis to the facts of this case. The decision frustrates an admirable state policy decision to require that public school students be literate before they are certified as academically proficient. One need not be proficient to understand that this frustration will be more than temporary. This circuit has given the state a choice between escaping expensive, time-consuming and demoralizing litigation and fighting an expensive two-front war; attempting to improve education while looking over its shoulder to assure that everything possible is being done to prepare for the inevitable onslaught of due process actions founded upon the most arcane of alleged educational deficiencies. *See, e. g., Debra P.* at 406 (evidence in record that "at least one teacher" did not cover an entire textbook in one of his courses). It is not our place to put state idealism to such a test.

In one step the panel has removed the state incentive to provide quality education, for each state attempt to demand academic proficiency will be subject to the same eviscerating analysis used to reject Florida's attempt to demand functional literacy from its public school graduates. We have only ourselves to blame if Florida abandons its present policy and reverts to the old, admittedly deficient system of social promotion, graduation and certification. Moreover, we should not be surprised if other states in this circuit heed the panel's signal and avoid even attempting a reformation of their educational policies. The transitory impact of the state gesture will simply not be worth the subsequent sting of federal interventionism.

The Equal Protection Analysis

The state of Florida has decided that it will demand equal performance from both black and white students on its functional literacy exam. The panel, in the most paternalistic fashion, has found this race-neutral approach violative of the equal protection clause. Its holding, stated simply, is that the *constitution* prohibits the State of Florida from treating black and white students equally. Besides the inevitable impact this decision will have on black pride and white hubris, it is, in the most fundamental sense, a perversion of the principle of equality enunciated by the high Court in *Brown v. Board of Education*, 347 U.S. 483, 74 S.Ct. 686, 98 L.Ed. 873 (1954).

If *Brown* stands for anything, it is that in the educational arena a state must treat black and white students equally. Any inherently unequal educational treatment of the races is unconstitutional racial discrimination of the most nefarious sort. That discrimination is iniquitous because it is the prerequisite for successful state imposition of unequal status—to sanction racially unequal educational achievement is to cripple and stigmatize, it is forcibly to lock a race of people into a deprived class with cruelly limited horizons and illusory hopes. For me, therefore, it is inexcusably iniquitous to compel the state to certify as academically proficient an avowedly functionally illiterate minority student based on the institutionalized assumption that he cannot be expected to achieve on the same level as white students. Quite simply, it is to celebrate and perpetuate the hollow certification that accompanied black graduation pre-*Brown*.

The record in *Debra P.* demonstrates that the functional literacy exam has a disproportionate impact on blacks. There also is evidence in the record indicating that the higher incidence of black failure may be attributable in significant part to the legacy of the inherently unequal education provided by Florida's previously segregated educational system. When these facts are joined with the construct validity of the literacy exam, they speak volumes. Yet, their message may be put succinctly: at least partly because of racial segregation, black students in Florida are ending their high school years as functional illiterates. The panel has held that the state must give these illiterate students a diploma certifying successful completion of twelve years of public education. This poses a most incongruous resolution of the dilemma. Black students have a right to an equal education. The state has failed to provide that equal education, and thus a significant number of minority students are functionally illiterate. To correct this, Florida established the prerequisite of the literacy exam, coupled with a statutory authorization that "special instruction designed to remedy . . . identified deficiencies," *Debra P.*, at 401 n. 1 quoting Fla.Stat.Ann. § 232.246 (West Supp.1980), be provided to those who demonstrate an inability to pass the examination. Moreover, Florida has decided to hold back a high school diploma until a student does demonstrate literacy, thus providing an added incentive for pursuit of essential skills. To this the panel responds by asserting that Florida has violated the Constitution.

To be in compliance with the fourteenth amendment, the panel asserts, Florida must give illiterate black students a diploma. I can think of no more otiose, worthless equality than this distribution of paper credentials. To deny a student a diploma is, at worst, a regretable necessity. Under *McNeal v. Tate County School District*, 508 F.2d 1017,

1020 (5th Cir. 1975), I believe the denial of a diploma is a necessary and entirely reasonable means to remedy the evil, indeed, the badge of slavery, which is black functional illiteracy. In the long run, this state decision seems the wise approach, and it is not for us to second-guess the state. Functionally illiterate graduates possessing a diploma may have less trouble than non-diploma holders in initial employment opportunities, but their futures are bleak. Inadequate performance at work, severely limited opportunities for social mobility, every ill that afflicts the illiterate minority individual will be theirs. It is no remedy for these students, disadvantaged at the hands of the state, to be meaninglessly certified. The wrong has been suffered and now it must be corrected. It is no answer to cover the fundamental hurt with an empty equality of form that ignores the underlying substance. Indeed, if anything, this empty equality is the most wicked perpetuation of the legacy of segregation.

Certainly any resolution of this case would be difficult. It will never be easy to try to correct the manifold evils created by generations of racial discrimination. We must however, never lose sight of the fundamental goal of equality. Our duty is to further attempts to eliminate the vestiges of inequality, not to intrude paternally on good-faith state attempts to ensure real educational equality.

To conclude, I simply cannot believe that the fourteenth amendment requires us to force a state to abandon a rational scheme designed to correct the palpable heritage of segregated, inherently unequal education in favor of mandatory state certification of illiterate students. The panel rules that the state must continue to sanction this meaningless graduation until it can demonstrate that disproportionate black student functional illiteracy is "not due to the educational deprivation [of] the 'dual school' years." *Debra P.*, at 408. The state disincentive here is remarkable: how long will it take before the heritage of educational segregation is eradicated? Furthermore, how much litigation will it take before the federal courts determine that *each* school district in the Fifth Circuit, with its unique, district history and demography, has outlasted the effects of segregation? We have lived too long with the legacy of racial inequality to believe that the effects of history are of short duration. Indeed, they are all-pervasive, and we do a great deal to extend these all-pervasive effects by requiring Florida to give diplomas signifying educational proficiency to black functional illiterates. We perpetuate the cycle; instead of racial hatred generating racially separate and inherently unequal systems, the spirit of federal paternalism has intervened to impose racially unequal standards of educational proficiency within a single school system. Now the inequality is to be imposed under a single roof, yet the affront to basic racial equality is not lessened. And this racial affront is all the more demeaning because it acts as a great deterrent to black student achievement—why strive to achieve if the rubber stamp of academic certification is available to all?

In my mind, these disincentives are real; they will shape the conduct of both

educators and pupils to the detriment of society. When it is appropriate for a federal court to exercise jurisdiction, it should strive to further the spirit of equality. Today, we have done just the opposite. The state should be allowed to correct the deficiencies of the segregated years *immediately* by requiring of black students the equality of performance that is the *only* demonstration of equal respect, and by providing the means for these students to attain the necessary level of performance, as Florida has done here. *Debra P.*, at 400–01 n. 1. It will be in the dignity of certification for *equal* achievement that the proof of social equality is revealed. To mandate anything short of this is to consign the teachings of *Brown* to the realm of mere idealism.

I respectfully dissent.*

HILL, Circuit Judge, dissenting from Court's denial of Petition for Rehearing En Banc.

A majority of the active judges in Administrative Unit B of the court, acting under our rules for the entire court, has voted against rehearing and reconsidering this case *en banc.* I dissent from this action of our court.

This case finds it constitutionally sound —indeed, mandated—that a state continue the pre-*Brown*[1] practice of handing

---

* This dissent was written and circulated among the judges before the panel entered its order denying rehearing en banc. In entering its order, the panel has chosen to comment on this dissent, and that of my Brother Hill, to the denial of en banc rehearing. This commentary takes the form of an attempted explanation of *Debra P.*, and purportedly is issued "in hope of assisting others" in interpreting the decision. This commentary, however, has no legal implications for the interpretation and application of *Debra P.*; that decision must stand on its own.

The commentary of the panel judges has no precedential significance despite its appearance as well-intentioned judicial gloss. It does, however, cast further doubt upon the wisdom of the denial of en banc consideration—if *Debra P.*, as originally drafted, requires such a thorough-going attempted explanation, further consideration of the case, if only to clarify *with the force of law* its holding, seems appropriate.

1. *Brown v. Board of Education*, 347 U.S. 483, 74 S.Ct. 686, 98 L.Ed. 873 (1954).

out meaningless high school diplomas to black boys and girls who have not been required to achieve even a minimal education. Our court's refusal to reconsider this case en banc can only be premised upon a conclusion, unstated though it be, that those who labored so long and hard to strike down segregated education were not working to achieve quality education for minority race children but sought to deny it to all children.

Specifically, our court has held [2] that:

(1) The Constitution forbids a state from providing quality education to, and requiring a modicum of learning by, the children in its public school system.

(2) The aim of public education must, under law, be to confer a diploma and must not be to provide an education.

(3) By operating a public school system, a constitutionally protected expectation is created in the attendee that he or she will receive a diploma, not an education.

(4) That, at the time of the Supreme Court's decision in *Brown v. Board of Education*, 347 U.S. 483, 74 S.Ct. 686, 98 L.Ed. 873 (1954), the black

children of this land were not ready for non-segregated education in schools providing a quality education and requiring some minimal level of attainment for graduation.

(5) *Because black children are a part of the student body*, educational requirements of a state school system must be kept at a low level!

None of the teachings of decided cases supports this assault by our court upon the aspirations of the people of Florida for quality education for their children. The goal of the civil rights movement, that minority race children be provided quality education, are frustrated by this holding. The vestiges of segregated education, which handed out public school diplomas to minority race children but did not provide them quality education, are perpetuated. Before this holding became the law of the Fifth Circuit Court of Appeals, careful and full *en banc* reconsideration should have been indulged.

My expression of concern ought not be taken as a whimsical disregard for the serious attention given this case by our court's panel and by Hon. George C. Carr, the district judge whose opinion, *Debra P. v. Turlington*, 474 F.Supp. 244 (M.D. Fla.1979), evidences great care and pains-

2. Since the preparation of this dissent, the panel has entered its order denying rehearing. Further, there is added to that order a statement by two judges of this court and a senior district judge a writing in the nature of a response to this dissent and to the dissent of Judge Tjoflat. The response undertakes to interpret the panel's opinion.

Assuming without deciding that the panel opinion needs interpretation, its holding for our court does not. Subject to the limited remand discussed in footnote 4 hereafter, the panel opinion affirms the district court's judgment. It is abundantly clear that the district court enjoins the State of Florida from requiring passage of the functional literacy test as a condition for the awarding of a diploma during the

next four years. The panel affirms this injunction forbidding the State from using that test. The interpretation of the panel opinion proffered by two of our judges who were on the panel says that the panel held "That the State of Florida may utilize a functional literacy examination ... as a condition for the awarding of a diploma." Rehearing en banc being denied, such a reversal of the district court's injunction cannot be accomplished without rehearing and reconsideration by the panel. If the use of this test be not enjoined in this litigation, my concerns are largely put to rest. What I write is upon the assumption that the district court's injunction has been, on appeal, affirmed.

taking consideration. Rather, I seek to express my conviction that the judgment is contrary to law and that its premise is the wrong premise.

The premise accepted by the court, from which the entire syllogistic exercise is derived, is that, in education, the diploma is the thing. The child's expectation that he or she will receive a diploma without having achieved even a minimum degree of education is held to be a constitutionally protected property right. Yet, before *Brown*, the evil that existed was largely that *diplomas* were being awarded to minority race children even though, in "inherently unequal" systems, they were not being afforded *education* equal to that being administered to others. Nowhere does the court consider the real value of an educational system to the pupil—learning. The Supreme Court was not misled by the free and easy award of diplomas. It emphasized the real value of the educational system to the pupil by observing:

> Today, education is perhaps the most important function of state and local governments. Compulsory school attendance laws and the great expenditures for education both demonstrate our recognition of the importance of education to our democratic society. It is required in the performance of our most basic public responsibilities, even service in the armed forces. It is the very foundation of good citizenship. Today it is a principal instrument in awakening the child to cultural values, in preparing him for later professional training, and in helping him to adjust

normally to his environment. In these days, it is doubtful that any child may reasonably be expected to succeed in life if he is denied the opportunity of an education.

347 U.S. at 493, 74 S.Ct. at 691.

It is undoubtedly true that the appearance of having been educated may be accomplished by the conferring of a diploma. Nevertheless, if the child has received no learning, even the most emphatic judgment and order of the most diligent court cannot supply it.

The panel's holding makes Mr. Bumble correct.[3] Happily the panel's holding is not the law.

The panel pays lip service to the law: "Neither the district court nor we are in a position to determine educational policy in the State of Florida." At 402. Nonetheless, they conclude that the expectation of receiving a diploma is a property interest protected by the Fourteenth Amendment. This holding enables the panel (and will require all bound by our opinion) to analyze the diploma requirements established by the State of Florida. Specifically, the panel, in affirming the district court, embraces the view that use of the State's functional literacy test even though validated as to content[4] *see* 474 F.Supp. at 261, and not infected with cultural bias towards minority students, *see* 407 n. 17, may not be a requirement for graduation under the Constitution of the United States. Today, the court finds a functional literacy test wanting. Tomorrow, the court may find the state's math requirements are unfair. And the

---

3. "If the law supposes that," said Mr. Bumble ... "the law is a ass, a idiot." C. Dickens, *Oliver Twist*, Ch. 51 (1838).

4. Of course, the panel held that the test "*may* have covered matters not taught in the schools

of the state." At 404 (emphasis in original). One would suppose that on remand this ambiguity in the record could be quickly resolved in favor of the State by testimony from one familiar with the State's high school curriculum.

next day, the court may find that history is unnecessary to the high school curriculum or that, its teacher being less than adequate, a history test or examination is unconstitutional. I hope this never comes to pass. The fact remains, however, that the panel has established a constitutional basis for the judiciary to assume the role of state educators.

The panel cites *Goss v. Lopez*, 419 U.S. 565, 95 S.Ct. 729, 42 L.Ed.2d 725 (1975) as authority for its intrusion into the State's educational system. *Goss v. Lopez* provides no such authority. Rather, *Goss v. Lopez* simply required "effective notice and [an] informal hearing permitting the student to give his version of the events" before the student could be suspended for ten days and thus denied participation in the learning process for *disciplinary reasons*. *Id.* at 583, 95 S.Ct. at 740 (emphasis added). Nowhere in its opinion does the Court approve of judicial review of state academic policy. Furthermore, four members of the Court dissented from the limited holding of *Goss v. Lopez* reasoning that "[t]he decision unnecessarily opens avenues for judicial intervention in the operation of our public schools that may affect adversely the quality of education." *Id.* at 585, 95 S.Ct. at 741.

In *Board of Curators, Univ. of Mo. v. Horowitz*, 435 U.S. 78, 98 S.Ct. 948, 55 L.Ed.2d 124 (1977) the court vigorously refused to sanction judicial intervention into academic decisions.

Academic evaluations of a student, in contrast to disciplinary determinations bear little resemblance to the judicial and administrative factfinding proceedings to which we have traditionally attached a full-hearing requirement. In *Goss*, the school's decision to suspend the students rested on factual conclusions that the individual students had participated in demonstrations that had disrupted classes, attacked a police officer, or caused physical damage to school property. The requirement of a hearing, where the student could present his side of the factual issue, could under such circumstances "provide a meaningful hedge against erroneous action." *Ibid.* The decision to dismiss respondent, by comparison, rested on the academic judgment of school officials that she did not have the necessary clinical ability to perform adequately as a medical doctor and was making insufficient progress toward that goal. Such a judgment is by its nature more subjective and evaluative than the typical factual questions presented in the average disciplinary decision. Like the decision of an individual professor as to the proper grade for a student in his course, the determination whether to dismiss a student for academic reasons requires an expert evaluation of cumulative information and is not readily adapted to the procedural tools of judicial or administrative decisionmaking.

Id. at 89–90, 98 S.Ct. at 954–955. The same logic prohibits a court from reviewing the graduation requirements established by a State. Indeed, our circuit has long been of the view that academic decisions should be left to the states and the appropriate educational bodies. *Mahavongsanan v. Hill*, 529 F.2d 448 (5th Cir. 1976). In sum, there is a bright line of demarcation between extending minimal due process safeguards to protect a student's access to learning, *see Goss v. Lopez* and using the Due Process Clause to make decisions regarding the quality of education for the State of Florida. *See Horowitz.*

The district court had presented only the difficulties encountered by minority race students said to result from their having attended the first three grades of elementary education in a segregated system. Thus, on this record, the district court merely postponed a quality education for three years. *See* 474 F.Supp. at 269. Of course, a pupil's achievement in an educational system may be affected by home and other social environment outside the classroom. Upon the principle laid down by this case, may we not expect the assertion that it is unconstitutional to provide and require quality education and achievement as long as the environment outside the classroom is affected by previous segregation in society and in education. In short, this case at least suggests that minority race children shall not be subjected to and afforded quality education until history has been repealed and the fact that there was segregation be no longer a fact. We may hand down judgment after judgment, but we will not alter historical fact.

It has been said that public education has been in decline in recent years. If it is so, it is deplorable. If it is so, it is not difficult to find at least a cause. There is a limit to the time, effort, funds and other resources that state officials and taxpayers can devote to education and related matters. One has but to review litigation in this court during recent decades to obtain an idea of the amount of those limited resources that have been diverted from the process of educating to devious, clever efforts to thwart the teachings of *Brown*. There is evidence in the record in this case that at least one state has now resolved to turn from such untenable frustrations and return to the restoration of quality to its educational system. I submit that the judges of this court, charged in brief after brief and argument upon argument with the destruction of public education, should, judiciously (and personally for what that's worth), rejoice at such a development.

Instead, we endorse the charge levelled against the courts and solemnly find that the Constitution and the law mandate that quality education, since *Brown*, be forbidden.

Subject to the counseling I might have received from the lawyers on rehearing, I am convinced that this is wrong.

Index

283

List of Contributors and Conference Participants

Robert Calfee, School of Education, Stanford University, Stanford, California 94305

Jeanne S. Chall, Reading Laboratory, Graduate School of Education, Harvard University, Cambridge, Massachusetts 02138

Robert E. Floden, College of Education, Michigan State University, East Lansing, Michigan 48824

Ann Freeman, Graduate School of Education, Harvard University, Cambridge, Massachusetts 02138

Donald J. Freeman, College of Education, Michigan State University, East Lansing, Michigan 48824

Walt Haney, Huron Institute, Cambridge, Massachusetts 02138

Gaea Leinhardt, Learning Research & Development Center, University of Pittsburgh, Pittsburgh, Pennsylvania 15260

Benjamin Levy, Graduate School of Education, Harvard University, Cambridge, Massachusetts 02138

Robert L. Linn, Department of Educational Psychology, University of Illinois, Champaign, Illinois 61820

George F. Madaus, The Center for the Study of Testing, Evaluation and Educational Policy, Boston College, Chestnut Hill, Massachusetts 02167

Andrew C. Porter, College of Education, Michigan State University, East Lansing, Michigan 48824

Diana Pullin, Center for Law and Education, Inc., Washington, D.C. 20002

William H. Schmidt, College of Education, Michigan State University, East Lansing, Michigan 48824

George F. Madaus, The Center for the Study of Testing, Evaluation and Educational Policy, Boston College, Chestnut Hill, MA 02167

John R. Schwille, College of Education, Michigan State University, East Lansing, Michigan 48824

Roger W. Shuy, Georgetown University and The Center for Applied Linguistics, Washington, D.C. 20007

Richard L. Venezky, Department of Educational Studies, University of Delaware, Newark, Delaware 19711

Decker F. Walker, School of Education, Stanford University, Stanford, California 94305

Participants at the Conference on the Courts and the Content Validity of Minimum Competency Tests, BOSTON COLLEGE, CHESTNUT HILL, MA 02167, OCTOBER 13 and 14, 1981

Peter W. Airasian, School of Education, Boston College, Chestnut Hill, MA 02167

Gerald W. Bracey, Director of Research, Evaluation and Testing, State Department of Education, Richmond, Virginia 23216

James P. Breeden, Office of Planning & Policy, Boston Public Schools, Boston, MA 02108

Robert Calfee, School of Education, Stanford University, Stanford, California 94305

Jeanne Chall, Director, Reading Laboratory, Graduate School of Education, Harvard University, Cambridge, MA 02138

Christiane Citron, Esq., Law and Education Center, Education Commission of the States, Denver, Colorado 80295

Stephen Cotton, Esq., Center for Law and Education, Inc., Cambridge, MA 02138

Douglas Glasnapp, University of Kansas, Lawrence, Kansas 66045

Walter Haney, Huron Institute, Cambridge, MA 02138

Alan Hartman, Massachusetts Department of Education, Boston, MA 02116

Stephen Ivens, The College Board, New York, New York 10106

Richard Jefferson, Esq., Center for Law and Education, Inc., Gutman Library, Cambridge, MA 02138

Gaea Leinhardt, Learning Research & Development Center, University of Pittsburgh, Pittsburgh, Pennsylvania 15260

Roger T. Lennon, Briarcliff Manor, New York 10510

Robert Linn, Department of Educational Psychology, University of Illinois, Champaign, Illinois 61820

Byron Marlowe, Research Specialist, Florida Teaching Profession/National Education Association, Tallahassee, Florida 32301

Marjorie Martus, Project Director, Public Education Division, Ford Foundation, New York, New York 10022

Jason Millman, Department of Education, Cornell University, Ithaca, New York 14853

Frederic A. Mosher, Program Officer, Carnegie Corporation of New York, New York, New York 10022

Melvin R. Novick, College of Education, University of Iowa, Iowa City, Iowa 52242

Joseph J. Pedulla, The Center for the Study of Testing, Evaluation and Educational Policy, Boston College, Chestnut Hill, MA 02167

John Poggio, Department of Education, University of Kansas, Lawrence, Kansas 66044

Robert Pressman, Esq., Center for Law and Education, Inc., Gutman Library, Cambridge, MA 02138

Diana Pullin, Esq., Center for Law and Education, Inc., Washington, D.C. 20002

Roger Rice, Esq.. Center for Law and Education, Inc., Cambridge, Massachusetts 02138

William Schmidt, College of Education, Michigan State University, East Lansing, Michigan 48824

Roger Shuy, Center for Applied Linguistics, Washington, D.C. 20007

Daniel Stufflebeam, The Evaluation Center, Western Michigan University, Kalamazoo, Michigan 49008

Paul Tractenberg, Professor of Law, Rutgers School of Law, State University of New Jersey, Newark, New Jersey 07102

Ralph Tyler, Director Emeritus, The Center for Advanced Study of Behavorial Sciences, Chicago, Illinois 60610

Richard Venezky, Department of Educational Studies, University of Delaware, Newark, Delaware 19711

Decker Walker, School of Education, Stanford University, Stanford, California 94305

John J. Walsh, School of Education, Boston College

Paul Weckstein, Esq., Center for Law and Education, Inc., Cambridge, MA 02138

LaMonte G. Wyche, Sr., School of Psychology, Department of Psychoeducational Studies, Howard University, Washington, D.C. 20059